BELIEF IN THE WORD

Francis J. Moloney, S.D.B.

BELIEF
IN THE WORD

FORTRESS PRESS
MINNEAPOLIS

Cover image: Detail of the face of Christ from stained-glass window (ca. 1950s), Notre-Dame-de-Toute-Grâce, Assy, France, by Georges Rouault. Used with permission of Yale Institute of Sacred Music, Worship & the Arts.
Cover design: Patricia Boman
Interior book design: The HK Scriptorium, Inc.

Library of Congress Cataloging-in-Publication Data

Moloney, Francis J.
  Belief in the Word : reading the fourth Gospel, John 1-4 / Francis
J. Moloney.
    p.   cm.
  Includes bibliographical references and index.
  ISBN 978-0-8006-2584-9
    1. Bible. N.T. John I–IV – Criticism, Narrative. 2. Narration in
the Bible. I. Title.
  BS2615.2.M57 1993
  226.5′06 – dc20   92-21757
                                                       CIP

The paper used in this publication meets the minimum requirements of American National Standard for Information Sciences – Permanence of Paper for Printed Library Materials, ANSI Z329.48-1984. ∞™

Manufactured in the U.S.A.   AF 1-2584

*For the Catholic Community
in Melbourne*

Contents

Preface

WE HAVE THE FOUR Gospel stories because Christians have been influenced by these narratives of the life and teaching, death and resurrection of Jesus of Nazareth. There is something *in the narratives themselves* that has spoken to the Christian experience over the centuries. Behind the narratives stands the perennial challenge of the life and person of Jesus, but the Gospel stories make their own impact. This happens not only because they tell the story of Jesus but also because each Gospel narrative tells that story in a certain way.

Critical scholarship has long devoted its attention to a detailed analysis of the world that formed the Gospels; but questions have been raised over the last decade concerning the relevance of this historical-critical method.[1] Biblical scholars have rightly used the historical-critical method as a tool to ensure that the world *behind the text* is not forgotten in the appropriation of the world *in the text*. Perhaps more attention now needs to be devoted to the world *in front of* the text. Biblical scholarship is developing new methods which concentrate on the reader of the text.[2]

[1] See, e.g., A. L. Nations, "Historical Criticism and the Current Methodological Crisis," *SJT* 36 (1983) 59-71; E. Schüssler Fiorenza, "The Ethics of Interpretation: De-Centering Biblical Scholarship," *JBL* 107 (1988) 3-17.

[2] For a good overview of the history of biblical interpretation, see R. Morgan and J. Barton, *Biblical Interpretation* (The Oxford Bible Series; Oxford: Oxford University Press, 1988).

R. Alan Culpepper has recently asked: "How does this text guide the reader in the construction of its meaning, and what responses does it elicit from the reader?"[3] Culpepper has given us the program. We must search out the elements within the Johannine narrative that guide us to its meaning and the reader's response to that meaning. I am consciously reading the Fourth Gospel within the context of the rich results of some 150 years of critical scholarship to which I am the privileged heir. Yet I am also attempting a reading of the Fourth Gospel along lines suggested by the rise of narrative criticism in contemporary biblical scholarship. Following the principles of this approach, I am paying particular attention to the way in which an implied reader evolves from the temporal flow of a narrative. The members of the Johannine community, the evangelist's intended reader, must have found that this story of Jesus spoke to their experience, as they accepted it as their story and passed it on to subsequent generations. The real reader of today shares that response as the Fourth Gospel continues to be relevant for the Christian story.[4]

After an introduction to some aspects of the theory of a narrative reading of the Fourth Gospel (chapter 1), I will read the first four chapters of the Fourth Gospel: 1:1-18 (chapter 2), 1:19-51 (chapter 3), 2:1-12 (chapter 4), 2:13–3:36 (chapter 5), 4:1-42 (chapter 6), and 4:43-54 (chapter 7). Each of these exegetical chapters begins with a section entitled "The Shape of the Narrative," which surveys the *spatial aspect* of the passage. All stories have a form and shape, and narrative criteria are used to uncover this aspect in each case. More detailed attention, however, is given to the second section, which follows the *temporal flow* of the process of reading: "Reading the Narrative." It is in these sections that I trace the implied reader, a heuristic device particularly helpful in understanding the temporal aspect of the reading process. The work closes with a summary of the reading suggested by John 1-4 (chapter 8). A narrative study must follow the spatial and temporal flow of the text from the beginning. The present work attempts to initiate such a reading of the Fourth Gospel. I plan to continue my approach into two further volumes (John 5-12 and 13-20).

There is a contemporary tendency to understand a text only in terms of the meaning the reader finds there.[5] In this study the *text itself* is at the

---

Developments beyond the traditional historical-critical methods are well surveyed on pp. 133–296.

[3] R. Alan Culpepper, "The Johannine *hypodeigma*: A Reading of John 13:1-38." *Semeia* 53 (1991) 133. Culpepper has developed his understanding of this program in "Commentary on Biblical Narratives," *Forum* 5,3 (1989) 87-102.

[4] My first chapter will explain the theory of narrative that lies behind this terminology.

[5] For a good introduction to this theory, see J. P. Tompkins, ed., *Reader-Response Criticism:*

center of my analysis. I consistently direct my reading of John 1–4 toward a discovery of the emerging implied reader, created as the text unfolds.[6] This heuristic device can only be traced through close attention to the text. It must not simply reflect the experience of a contemporary reader.

This study has been researched and written with the support of two centers of learning: the Bodleian Library at the University of Oxford, where the project began in 1989, and the library of the Ecole Biblique et Archéologique Française, where I was the Catholic Biblical Association of America Visiting Lecturer for 1989–1990. The Senate of Catholic Theological College granted me a sabbatical year in 1990 and provided some initial funding to make travel possible. Without my appointment to Jerusalem as the CBA's Visiting Professor to the Ecole Biblique, this work would never have been written. As I researched and wrote this study I was often tempted to return to waters that I had already successfully navigated. In a special way Mark Coleridge urged me on. I have been further assisted by the interest of Justin Taylor, S.M., Benedict T. Viviano, O.P., Marie-Emile Boismard, O.P., and Jerome Murphy-O'Connor, O.P., who read whole or part of the manuscript during my stay in Jerusalem. As I prepared the script for publication, Nerina M. Zanardo, F.S.P., read it twice. I am particularly grateful to her.

I am dedicating this work to the Catholic Community of Melbourne. The Johannine community had to tell and retell the story of Jesus to make sense of the story of its life. May the Catholic Community of Melbourne continue this age-old practice.

From Formalism to Post-Structuralism (Baltimore: Johns Hopkins University Press, 1980); see also J. Culler, *On Deconstruction: Theory and Criticism after Structuralism* (London: Routledge & Kegan Paul, 1983) 64–83.

[6] I will sometimes refer to the author of the Gospel of John (and also the implied author and narrator) as "he" in recognition of the male gender used in those places where he appears (see 13:23; 13:25; 19:35; 21:24) and of the traditional name "John." Because it is a literary construct, the implied reader is without gender; however, because the implied reader is credited with both affective and cognitive experiences, a more personal pronoun is sometimes demanded. This is difficult. Given the present state of the English language, I may often repeat the noun "reader" more than is necessary, or sometimes revert to the passive, to avoid a male or female pronoun. I will occasionally write "he or she." I am aware that this overloads the text somewhat, but I am loath to use the neologism s/he.

Abbreviations

AB   Anchor Bible
ACR   *Australasian Catholic Record*
AnBib   Analecta Biblica
AnGreg   Analecta Gregoriana
ANRW   W. Haase and H. Temporini, eds. *Aufstieg und Nieder-gang der römischen Welt: Teil II: Principat—Religion.* Berlin: Walter de Gruyter, 1979–84.
AusBR   *Australian Biblical Review*
BAGD   W. Bauer, W. F. Arndt, and F. W. Gingrich. *A Greek-English Lexicon of the New Testament and Other Early Christian Literature.* 2d ed. Rev. and augmented by F. W. Gingrich and F. W. Danker. Chicago: University of Chicago Press, 1979.
BBB   Bonner Biblische Beiträge
BBET   Beiträge zur biblischen Exegese und Theologie
BDF   F. Blass and A. Debrunner. *A Greek Grammar of the New Testament and Other Early Christian Literature.* Rev. and trans. R. W. Funk. Chicago: University of Chicago Press, 1961.
BETL   Bibliotheca Ephemeridum Theologicae Lovaniensis
BEvT   Beiträge zur evangelischen Theologie

BGBE	Beiträge zur Geschichte der biblischen Exegese
Bib	*Biblica*
BibOr	*Bibbia e Oriente*
BibT	*The Bible Today*
BJ	Bible de Jérusalem
BLE	*Bulletin de la littérature ecclésiastique*
BLS	Bible and Literature Series
BN	*Biblische Notizen*
BNTC	Black's New Testament Commentaries
BTB	*Biblical Theology Bulletin*
BTS	Biblische theologische Studien
BU	Biblische Untersuchungen
BVC	*Bible et Vie Chrétienne*
BZ	Biblische Zeitschrift
CahEv	Cahiers Evangile
CahRB	Cahiers de la Revue Biblique
CBAA	Catholic Biblical Association of America
CBQ	*Catholic Biblical Quarterly*
CCSL	Corpus Christianorum Series Latina. Turnhout: Brepols.
DRev	*Downside Review*
Ebib	Etudes bibliques
EKKNT	Evangelisch-Katholischer Kommentar zum Neuen Testament
ETL	*Ephemerides Theologicae Lovanienses*
ETR	*Etudes théologiques et religieuses*
EvQu	*Evangelical Quarterly*
EvTh	*Evangelische Theologie*
ExpT	*Expository Times*
FB	Forschung zur Bibel
FRLANT	Forschungen zur Religion und Literatur des Alten und Neuen Testaments
FThSt	Frankfurter theologische Studien
GBS.NT	Guides to Biblical Scholarship. New Testament Series
HeyJ	*The Heythrop Journal*
HKNT	Handkommentar zum Neuen Testament
HTCNT	Herder's Theological Commentary on the New Testament
HTKNT	Herders Theologische Kommentar zum Neuen Testament

HTR	*Harvard Theological Review*
HZNT	Handbuch zum Neuen Testament
ILBS	Indiana Literary Biblical Series
ICC	International Critical Commentary
Int	*Interpretation*
ITQ	*Irish Theological Quarterly*
JAAR	*Journal of the American Academy of Religion*
JB	Jerusalem Bible
JBL	*Journal of Biblical Literature*
JNES	*Journal of Near Eastern Studies*
JSNT	*Journal for the Study of the New Testament*
JSNTSup	Journal for the Study of the New Testament Supplement Series
JSOTSup	Journal for the Study of the Old Testament Supplement Series
JTS	*Journal of Theological Studies*
ktl.	Greek: *kai ta loipa=et cetera*
LAS	Libreria Ateneo Salesiano
LCL	Loeb Classical Library
LD	Lectio Divina
LSJ	H. Liddell, R. Scott, and H. S. Jones, *A Greek-English Lexicon.* Oxford: Clarendon, 1968.
LumVie	Lumière et Vie
LXX	The Septuagint
MeyerK	Meyer Kommentar
NAB	New American Bible
NCB	New Century Bible
NEB	New English Bible
NEchtB	Die neue Echter Bibel
N.F.	Neue Folge
NJB	New Jerusalem Bible
NJBC	*The New Jerome Biblical Commentary,* ed. R. E. Brown, J. A. Fitzmyer, and R. E. Murphy. Englewood Cliffs, N.J.: Prentice Hall, 1989.
NovT	*Novum Testamentum*
NovTSup	Supplements to Novum Testamentum
NRT	*Nouvelle Revue Théologique*
NTAbh	Neutestamentliche Abhandlungen
NTS	*New Testament Studies*
NVB	Nuovissima Versione della Bibbia

OBO   Orbis Biblicus et Orientalis
ÖTK   Ökumenischer Taschenbuchkommentar zum Neuen
       Testament
PG   *Patrologiae cursus completus, series graeca*, ed. J. P.
       Migne.
PIBA   *Proceedings of the Irish Biblical Association*
PL   *Patrologiae cursus completus, series latina*, ed. J. P. Migne.
RB   *Revue Biblique*
RechBib   Recherches Bibliques
RevExp   *Review and Expositor*
RevScRel   *Revue des Sciences Religieuses*
RevThom   *Revue Thomiste*
RivBib   *Rivista Biblica*
RSR   *Recherche de science religieuse*
RSV   Revised Standard Version
SBB   Stuttgarter biblische Beiträge
SBLDS   Society of Biblical Literature Dissertation Series
SBLMS   Society of Biblical Literature Monograph Series
SBS   Stuttgarter Bibelstudien
SBT   Studies in Biblical Theology
ScEccl   *Sciences Ecclésiastiques*
ScEs   *Science et Esprit*
ScrB   *Scripture Bulletin*
SDB   *Dictionnaire de la Bible Supplement*, ed. L. Pirot, A.
       Robert, H. Cazelles, and A. Feuillet. Paris: Letouzey,
       1928–.
SJLA   Studies in Judaism and Late Antiquity
SJT   *Scottish Journal of Theology*
SNTSMS   Society for New Testament Studies Monograph Series
Str-B   H. Strack and P. Billerbeck. *Kommentar zum Neuen
         Testament aus Talmud und Midrasch.* 6 vols. Munich:
         C. H. Beck, 1922–61.
SuppRivB   Supplementi alla Rivista Biblica
s.v.   sub voce
TDNT   G. Kittel and G. Friedrich, eds., *Theological Dictionary
        of the New Testament.* 10 vols. Grand Rapids: Eerdmans,
        1964–76.
ThD   Theologische Dissertationen
TLZ   *Theologische Literaturzeitung*
TOB   Traduction Oecuménique de la Bible

TR	*Theologische Rundschau*
TS	*Theological Studies*
TuW	Theologie und Wirklichkeit
TV	*Theologische Versuche*
UBSGNT	*The Greek New Testament*. United Bible Societies.
VC	*Vigiliae Christianae*
VD	*Verbum Domini*
VT	*Vetus Testamentum*
WBC	Word Biblical Commentary
WMANT	Wissenschaftliche Monographien zum Alten und Neuen Testament
WUNT	Wissenschaftliche Untersuchungen zum Neuen Testament
ZAW	*Zeitschrift für die Alttestamentliche Wissenschaft*
ZBG	M. Zerwick. *Biblical Greek Illustrated by Examples*. Rome: Biblical Institute Press, 1963.
ZNW	*Zeitschrift für die Neutestamentliche Wissenschaft*
ZTK	*Zeitschrift für Theologie und Kirche*

Chapter One

Preparing to Read the Fourth Gospel

A GROWING INTEREST in the Bible as literature[1] and an awareness of the narrative nature of much biblical material[2] are producing studies that focus their attention on the impact of the biblical text on the reader.[3] C. H. Talbert has already produced two volumes that "read" a text, and R. C. Tannehill has completed a similar approach to the Lukan corpus.[4] J.-N. Aletti has written an elegant narrative study of Luke, and

---

[1] See, e.g., N. Frye, _The Great Code: The Bible and Literature_ (New York: Harcourt Brace Jovanovich, 1982); and S. Prickett, _Words and The Word: Language, Poetics and Biblical Interpretation_ (Cambridge: Cambridge University Press, 1986); see also R. Alter and F. Kermode, eds., _The Literary Guide to the Bible_ (London: Collins, 1987).

[2] See especially R. Alter, _The Art of Biblical Narrative_ (New York: Basic Books, 1981); A. Berlin, _Poetics and Interpretation of Biblical Narrative_ (Sheffield: Almond Press, 1983); M. Sternberg, _The Poetics of Biblical Narrative: Ideological Literature and the Drama of Reading_ (ILBS; Bloomington: Indiana University Press, 1985); S. Bar-Efrat, _Narrative Art in the Bible_ (JSOTSup 70, BLS 17; Sheffield: Almond Press, 1989). For a survey, see M. Gerhart, "The Restoration of Biblical Narrative," _Semeia_ 46 (1989) 13-29. For some initial suggestions for New Testament narratives, see N. R. Petersen, _Literary Criticism for New Testament Critics_ (GBS.NT; Philadelphia: Fortress Press, 1978).

[3] For surveys, see E. V. McKnight, _The Bible and the Reader: An Introduction to Literary Criticism_ (Philadelphia: Fortress Press, 1985); idem, _Post-Modern Use of the Bible: The Emergence of Reader-Oriented Criticism_ (Nashville: Abingdon, 1988). See especially S. D. Moore, _Literary Criticism and the Gospels: The Theoretical Challenge_ (New Haven: Yale University Press, 1989); and R. M. Fowler, "Postmodern Biblical Criticism," _Forum_ 5,3 (1989) 3-30.

[4] C. H. Talbert, _Reading Luke: A Literary and Theological Commentary on the Third Gospel_ (New

a Dutch reading of the Gospel of Mark by B. van Iersel has appeared in English.[5]

One of the pioneering studies in this area was the work of R. Alan Culpepper on the literary design of the Fourth Gospel,[6] but this work is not a systematic reading of the text itself. After a section devoted to narrative theory, Culpepper tests the text of the Fourth Gospel as narrative in the light of the major elements of such theory (narrator, point of view, time, plot, characters, implicit commentary, implied reader). The present study will attempt to "read" the Johannine Gospel as a unified narrative.[7] The Gospel text meant something for a real author who passed on the storytelling of the Johannine community.[8] The author selected from the many Jesus-traditions that would have been present in the Johannine community and arranged them as the narrative of a Gospel. Does this Gospel mean anything to us, as we both listen to its story and pass it on to another generation?

SYNCHRONIC OR DIACHRONIC?

The present study of the Fourth Gospel attempts to make sense of the Gospel as we have received it. Such a reading is sometimes called *synchronic*. The text is read from verse to verse, from chapter to chapter, allowing the Gospel *as it now stands* to force the interpreter to understand it in its own right. The epoch-making commentaries on the Fourth Gospel produced in this century, especially those of J. H. Bernard (1928), W. Bauer (1933), and R. Bultmann (1941), did not follow this method.[9] They were

---

York: Crossroad, 1982); idem, *Reading Corinthians: A Literary and Theological Commentary on 1 and 2 Corinthians* (New York: Crossroad, 1987); R. C. Tannehill, *The Narrative Unity of Luke-Acts: A Literary Interpretation* (2 vols.; Philadelphia/Minneapolis: Fortress Press, 1986, 1990).

[5] J.-N. Aletti, *L'art de raconter Jésus Christ* (Paris: Seuil, 1989); B. van Iersel, *Reading Mark* (Edinburgh: T. & T. Clark, 1989).

[6] R. A. Culpepper, *Anatomy of the Fourth Gospel: A Study in Literary Design* (Philadelphia: Fortress Press, 1983).

[7] I am sensitive to the important distinction made by R. M. Fowler ("Who is 'the Reader' in Reader-Response Criticism?" *Semeia* 31 [1985] 5-10) between the reader and the critic. I share his agenda: "To be a critical reader means for me: (1) to affirm the enduring power of the Bible in my culture and in my own life; (2) and yet to remain open enough to ask any question and to risk any judgment, even if it should mean repudiating (1)" (p. 10).

[8] By "text" I mean the words as they are recorded in the 26th edition of Nestle-Aland, *Novum Testamentum Graece* (Stuttgart: Deutsche Bibelstiftung, 1979). The Nestle-Aland text is not accepted uncritically.

[9] J. H. Bernard, *A Critical and Exegetical Commentary on the Gospel according to St John* (2 vols.;

marked by a *diachronic* approach to the text, in which it is not the text itself that dictates terms to the interpreter (synchronic) but the history of what happened *in the formation of the text* that determines the issue (diachronic). This is not the place for a full-scale history of Johannine scholarship.[10] The diachronic approach has had a lasting effect on Johannine scholarship. Most feel free to rearrange certain texts which create difficulties in the canonical order. From some quarters there is still a lively interest in the question of sources,[11] and the gnostic background to the Gospel is often taken for granted.[12] Decades of assiduous scholarship have thrown increasing and helpful light on the history of the community.[13] Yet whoever may have been responsible for the final shape of the Gospel consciously took stories from the recorded memory of the community and laid them side by side to form the Gospel. This process may have been repeated many times until our Gospel was eventually produced. Because of this process, the final product, even though it sometimes has untidy seams, is thoroughly Johannine in all its parts.[14]

ICC; Edinburgh: T. & T. Clark, 1928); W. Bauer, *Das Johannesevangelium erklärt* (HKNT 6; Tübingen: J. C. B. Mohr [Paul Siebeck], 1933); R. Bultmann, *Das Evangelium des Johannes* (MeyerK; Göttingen: Vandenhoeck & Ruprecht, 1941; Eng. trans. *The Gospel of John: A Commentary* [Oxford: Blackwell, 1971]).

[10] For a summary, see R. Kysar, *The Fourth Evangelist and His Gospel* (Minneapolis: Augsburg, 1975); and more recently idem, "The Fourth Gospel: A Report on Recent Research," *ANRW* 2.25.3, pp. 2389–2480.

[11] Particularly important are the two volumes of R. T. Fortna, *The Gospel of Signs: A Reconstruction of the Narrative Source Underlying the Fourth Gospel* (SNTSMS 11; Cambridge: Cambridge University Press, 1970); idem, *The Fourth Gospel and its Predecessor: From Narrative Source to Present Gospel* (Studies in the NT and its World; Edinburgh: T. & T. Clark, 1989). See also J. Becker, *Das Evangelium des Johannes* (2 vols.; ÖTK 4/1-2; Gütersloh: Gerd Mohn; Würzburg: Echter-Verlag, 1979, 1981) 1:112–20; and U. C. von Wahlde, *The Earliest Version of John's Gospel: Recovering the Gospel of Signs* (Wilmington, Del.: Michael Glazier, 1989). For a survey, see Kysar, *Fourth Evangelist and His Gospel*, 225–30; idem, "Fourth Gospel," 2398–2402.

[12] See, e.g., K. Rudolph, *Gnosis: The Nature and History of an Ancient Religion* (Edinburgh: T. & T. Clark, 1983) 159–60, 305–6; L. Schottroff, *Die Glaubende und die feindliche Welt: Beobachtungen zum gnostischer Dualismus und seiner Bedeutung für Paulus und das Johannesevangelium* (WMANT 37; Neukirchen-Vluyn: Neukirchener Verlag, 1970). On this, see T. Onuki, *Gemeinde und Welt im Johannesevangelium: Ein Beitrag zur Frage nach der theologischen und pragmatischen Funktion des johanneischen "Dualismus"* (WMANT 56; Neukirchen-Vluyn: Neukirchener Verlag, 1984) 38-54.

[13] The recent commentaries of E. Haenchen (*John 1-2* [2 vols.; Hermeneia; Philadelphia: Fortress Press, 1984]), J. Gnilka (*Johannesevangelium* [NEchtB; Würzburg: Echter-Verlag, 1989]), and Becker (*Johannes*) continue this method. Becker's work is particularly reminiscent of Bultmann.

[14] One of the difficulties in separating the "strata" of the Fourth Gospel lies in the fact that the Gospel *as a whole* has a very unified style and language. See the syntheses of C. K. Barrett, *The Gospel according to St John* (London: SPCK, 1978) 5-15; and G. Segalla, *Giovanni* (NVB 36; Rome: Edizioni Paoline, 1976) 74-85.

The practice of telling stories, handing them down from generation to generation, is not unique to the Johannine community. However, the repeated telling of the stories of other people eventually leads to their becoming the storyteller's own. It is thus important to understand the Gospel of John as a single utterance. C. H. Dodd once wrote that we must respect the text as it is and not try to improve on it, as it "was devised by somebody—even if he were only a scribe doing his best."[15] A synchronic approach to the text of the Fourth Gospel is an attempt to uncover the literary skills and the theological vision of Dodd's "scribe doing his best."[16]

Such an interpretation of an ancient text, however, is immediately open to the criticism of subjectivism. Diachronic approaches attempt to discover factors *outside* the text itself that can render our interpretations more objective. The history of modern exegesis shows that such objectivity has never really been achieved,[17] but the accusation can still be made: if the only authority is the text itself, then interpretation will be largely the result of personal reaction to the text.

Narrative texts were written for readers. A real author writes a narrative to communicate a point of view to the intended reader through an implied author who tells a story to an emerging implied reader, often through the agency of a narrator speaking to a narratee.[18] Once a narrative text has a life and a history of its own, the reader *in* the text and the many possible readers *of* the text must play a determining role in the interpretation of that text and in its lasting value.

Even in a synchronic reading of a narrative, where so much attention is devoted to the impact a text makes on a reader, there are objective controls that guide the interpreter. The real author tells the story by following certain literary conventions. The use of time, the arrangement of scenes to form a plot, the use of space and the delineation of both character and setting, all part of the narrator's craft, come into play. One of the features

[15] C. H. Dodd, *The Interpretation of the Fourth Gospel* (Cambridge: Cambridge University Press, 1953) 309.

[16] Von Wahlde allows that this is an important principle, but still claims that it is methodologically unsound (*Earliest Version of John's Gospel*, 23–24 n. 16).

[17] See R. Morgan and J. Barton, *Biblical Interpretation* (The Oxford Bible Series; Oxford: Oxford University Press, 1988) 286.

[18] For a brief description of the principles of narrative that I have just sketched, see S. Chatman, *Story and Discourse: Narrative Structure in Fiction and Film* (Ithaca, N.Y.: Cornell University Press, 1978) 146–51. He has a useful, simple diagram on p. 151. See also Culpepper, *Anatomy*, 3–11. There is a further helpful diagram, based on a more complex one from Chatman (*Story and Discourse*, 267), on p. 7. For a simple presentation of narrative criticism, see T. J. Keegan, *Interpreting the Bible: A Popular Introduction to Biblical Hermeneutics* (New York: Paulist Press, 1985) 92–109.

of contemporary literary readings of the Gospels has been the increased attention given to these characteristics of the storyteller's trade.

A real author must make important choices in assembling a narrative. This is the case for any narrative, and the redaction critics have devoted a great deal of attention to the discovery of the conscious choices that each of the evangelists made in composing a particular version of the Jesus story. We know from the story of Jesus as it has been told in the Synoptic Gospels that there were many traditions about the life and teaching of Jesus available to the early church. Even though he may have overstated his case, Werner Kelber has shown the importance of the paradigm shift that took place when oral tradition became written Gospel in Mark, and the Pauline diatribe became the Pauline letters.[19] A similar shift from a storytelling tradition into a fixed (some would say static), written tradition must have taken place in the formation of the Gospel of John.

The Fourth Evangelist shaped a text according to his particular criteria; he decided to include some narratives that came to him from his storytelling tradition and to exclude others; the elements he chose to include have been ordered and framed within the narrative as he wishes to tell it. At times the Johannine text has been accused of dislocation, marked by clumsy seams. The interpreter, however, must also admit the possibility that such seams are deliberately intended and attempt to read the narrative in the light of this possibility.[20] Written over forty years ago, Sir Edwin Hoskyns's words retain their significance: "We must not rest from exegesis until the apparent gaps have been filled up so completely that each discourse moves step by step as an ordered, a theologically ordered, whole."[21]

What the real author of the Fourth Gospel desired to communicate can be rediscovered only through a careful investigation of the story as

---

[19] W. H. Kelber, *The Oral and Written Gospel: The Hermeneutics of Speaking and Writing in the Synoptic Tradition, Mark, Paul, and Q* (Philadelphia: Fortress Press, 1983). See the discussion around this book in L. H. Silberman, ed., *Orality, Aurality and Biblical Narrative* (*Semeia* 39; Decatur, Ga.: Scholars Press, 1987). For a more positive appreciation of the process from orality to textuality, see P. Ricoeur, "The hermeneutical function of distanciation," in *Paul Ricoeur: Hermeneutics and the Human Sciences: Essays on language, action and interpretation*, ed. J. B. Thompson (Cambridge: Cambridge University Press, 1981) 131-44.

[20] One is faced with a choice. Either the author has lost control of the sources and the interpreter has the duty to make sense out of the resulting confusion, or the author deliberately created passages that we find difficult and the interpreter must seek the author's reason for doing so. For some telling points on this problem, see G. Genette, *Narrative Discourse: An Essay in Method* (Ithaca, N.Y.: Cornell University Press, 1980) 143-55; see also W. Kelber, "Narrative as Interpretation and Interpretation of Narrative: Hermeneutical Reflections on the Gospels," *Semeia* 39 (1987) 107-33.

[21] E. C. Hoskyns, *The Fourth Gospel*, ed. F. N. Davey (London: Faber & Faber, 1947) 201.

a finished and carefully constructed whole. Thus attention must be given to the particular shape of each narrative unit within the Fourth Gospel and to an explanation of that unit, both in terms of its own internal message and in terms of the shape and message of the Fourth Gospel as a whole.

The identification of narrative units and an understanding of their relationship to one another in the Gospel as a whole must also be determined by devoting attention to the rhetoric used by the author: relationships between incidents, inclusions, the use of key words, direct and indirect speech, foreshadowing and retrospection, double-meaning words, the deliberate use of misunderstanding and irony. Similar attention must be paid to the details of time, scenes, space, and character. But even when this has been done with care, one must humbly accept that no definitive interpretation of any text can be established, by whatever method.[22] All interpreters must face the fact that no single interpretation can claim to have said the last word on the passage. One of the attractions of the historical-critical method was the hope that we would have greater control over the objective meaning of the biblical text. This has not happened; nor will it happen in the use of the more synchronic, reader-oriented methods. Contemporary literary criticism is teaching us that "we read by the only light we possess, 'our own,' a light not really distinguishable from the surrounding 'green night'; and it teaches 'a fusky alphabet.'"[23] No single interpretation of any narrative—let alone the enigmatic narrative of the Fourth Gospel—should ever claim to have produced the final word. As Edgar V. McKnight has said, "The meaning of a text is inexhaustible because no context can provide all the keys to all of its possibilities."[24]

The hermeneutical questions that any narrative text poses to an interpreter arise from a possible clash of worlds. The Fourth Gospel is the product of a world that is behind the text. The text can be approached as a window through which one looks in an attempt to catch sight of that world behind the text. Such has been the task of traditional historical-critical scholarship. There is a further world created by the narrative itself. This

---

[22] It has been said that modern literary approaches are not producing anything new in biblical interpretation. See especially S. D. Moore, "Doing Gospel Criticism as/with a 'Reader,'" *BTB* 19 (1989) 85-93. Moore hints that there is a need to join the present movement to a "non-foundational" philosophy. See also idem, "Narrative Commentaries on the Bible: Context, Roots, and Prospects," *Forum* 3,3 (1987) 53: "Disclosure of the metaphysical underbelly of our critical systems might be the difficult but worthwhile goal of a narrative commentary in the destructive mode."

[23] E. Freund, *The Return of the Reader: Reader-Response Criticism* (New Accents; London: Methuen, 1987) 19.

[24] McKnight, *Post-Modern Use of the Bible*, 241.

is the world of the narrative: its characters, its time line, the geographical background, the cultural and religious values embodied there, to mention but a few of the elements that form that world. The text can be approached as a portrait, presenting its own world. The interpreter, however, belongs to the world in front of the text which may or may not be reflected or called into question by a text that can be viewed as a mirror. The interplay of these worlds cannot be ignored in a critical account of the act of reading.[25]

One must attempt to build a bridge between these worlds, to find the horizon where they merge. But the tensions and even conflicts that might exist between the worlds behind the text, in the text, and in front of the text can often result in "a fusky alphabet."[26]

> We live neither within closed horizons, nor within one unique horizon. Insofar as the fusion of horizons excludes the idea of a total and unique knowledge, this concept implies a tension between what is one's own and what is alien, between the near and the far; and hence the play of difference is included in the process of convergence.[27]

WHICH AUTHOR?

There were probably many authors of the traditions behind the Fourth Gospel. These various traditions, mostly oral, were forged into the literary unit we call the Gospel of John, by a real author. This historical person is traditionally called John or the Fourth Evangelist.

But the narrative is held together by the point of view of an omniscient

---

[25] This terminology has been used by M. Krieger, *A Window to Criticism* (Princeton, N.J.: Princeton University Press, 1964) 3–70; and further discussed by Petersen, *Literary Criticism*, 24–48.

[26] See especially P. Ricoeur, "The task of hermeneutics," in *Paul Ricoeur: Hermeneutics and the Human Sciences*, ed. Thompson, 43–62; idem, "Hermeneutics and the critique of ideology," ibid., pp. 63–100. It is important to insist that no interpretation can have the "final word," but we do have a traditional text to interpret. Radical reader-response criticism would seem to deny this. See the programmatic collection of essays written from 1970 to 1980 by S. Fish, *Is There a Text in This Class? The Authority of Interpretive Communities* (Cambridge, Mass.: Harvard University Press, 1980). For a description of these recent directions, see P. J. Rabinowitz, "Whirl without End: Audience-Oriented Criticism," in *Contemporary Literary Theory*, ed. G. D. Atkins and L. Morrow (London: Macmillan, 1989) 94. See also Moore, *Literary Criticism*, 108–30.

[27] Ricoeur, "The task of hermeneutics," 62; see also idem, "Hermeneutics and the critique of ideology," 75–78. See also E. Schüssler Fiorenza, "Toward a Critical-Theological Self-Understanding of Biblical Scholarship," in *Bread not Stone: The Challenge of Feminist Biblical Interpretation* (Boston: Beacon Press, 1984) 128–36.

and omnipresent implied author who is part of the narrative itself. Wayne Booth describes this phenomenon as "the intuitive apprehension of a completed artistic whole; the chief value to which *this* implied author is committed, regardless of what party his creator belongs to in real life, is that which is expressed by the total form."[28] The "person" of the real author cannot be found within the narrative, but the "persona" of the real author is all-pervading in the implied author.

The implied author speaks through a narrator, who can be hidden in the narrative (a covert narrator) or an obvious presence (an overt narrator).[29] In some modern narratives the narrator may be unreliable and may temporarily lead the reader down wrong paths. This is not the case with any biblical narrator and certainly not the case with the narrator in the Fourth Gospel. It can be said that the Fourth Evangelist, the implied author, and the narrator (largely covert, except for interventions in 19:35 and 20:31) act as one.[30] The reader can be sure that the real author, the implied author, and the narrator are at one in their attempt to tell the story of God's action in the world in the person of Jesus of Nazareth.[31]

Culpepper has written: "Although the implied author and the real author may be distinguished from the narrator in theory, in John the narrator is the voice of the author and the vocal expression of the choices and perspectives of the implied author."[32] The author uses the choices and perspectives of the implied author to direct the point of view, or the several points of view, expressed throughout the work. Through the voice of the implied author created within the text itself by the real author that point of view is made clear: "Discovering the point of view of the implied author . . . is the first step in discovering the meaning and purpose of the story."[33]

---

[28] W. Booth, *The Rhetoric of Fiction* (2nd ed.; Chicago: University of Chicago Press, 1983) 73-74; see pp. 70-77 on the implied author and pp. 160-63 on omniscience.

[29] On this, see Chatman, *Story and Discourse*, 196-262; G. Prince, *Narratology: The Form and Functioning of Narrative* (Janua Linguarum Series Maior 108; Berlin/New York/Amsterdam: Mouton, 1982) 7-16; Bar-Efrat, *Narrative Art in the Bible*, 13-45; J. L. Staley, *The Print's First Kiss: A Rhetorical Investigation of the Implied Reader in the Fourth Gospel* (SBLDS 82; Atlanta: Scholars Press, 1988) 27-30, 37-41.

[30] Wayne Booth's term "undramatised narrator" applies well to the narrator in the Fourth Gospel (*Rhetoric of Fiction*, 151-52).

[31] Sternberg argues that such is the case for all biblical narrative (*Poetics of Biblical Narrative*, 53-83).

[32] Culpepper, *Anatomy*, 232; but see Staley, *Print's First Kiss*, 11-13.

[33] Berlin, *Poetics and Interpretation*, 82; see pp. 43-82 on the whole question of point of view in biblical narratives. See also M. H. Abrams, *A Glossary of Literary Terms* (5th ed.; New York:

To identify the point of view of the real author and the implied author may presuppose too much. It is here that traditional redaction criticism fails to appreciate fully the complexities of the way narrative works. For several decades we have perhaps spoken and written too confidently of the *theologische Leistung* of the various evangelists. We can never finally discover the point of view of the real author. The Gospels are comparatively simple narratives, not given to the modern sophistications of unreliable relationships between author, narrator, and reader. Therefore, the desires of the real author are reflected in the point of view of the implied author, yet the former lies outside our scientific control. We can only work with the text itself, and that limits us to the rediscovery of the point of view of the implied author,[34] even though, in the case of the Fourth Gospel, one senses that the real author's intention is not far distant.

WHICH READER?

The Fourth Evangelist did not compose the final version of the Gospel with a modern reader in mind. Similarly, while the Evangelist wrote a Gospel narrative for the members of a given community at the end of the first century, he had no control over how they would respond to the narrative. *Within the text itself* we can sense the presence of yet another reader who emerges as the tale is told. The reader is twice addressed as "you" (see 19:35; 20:31).[35] There is a reader implied by the narrative who is an *intratextual* phenomenon.[36]

The implied reader knows what has already been read: the words, sentences, paragraphs, and pages. The reader waits for the next word, sentence, paragraph, and page to discover what the narrator has to tell.[37]

Holt, Rinehart & Winston, 1988) 144. For a somewhat different view, see S. Rimmon-Kenan, *Narrative Fiction: Contemporary Poetics* (New Accents; London: Methuen, 1983) 71–85.

[34] See Genette, *Narrative Discourse*, 26–29; idem, *Nouveau discours du récit* (Collection Poétique; Paris: Seuil, 1983) 93–107.

[35] The narrator addresses the implied reader in the plural in 19:35 and 20:31. Prince uses the presence of "you" in texts as the sign of the narratee (*Narratology*, 16–26). Narratee and implied reader must often be distinguished in modern narratives, but the two coalesce in the Fourth Gospel.

[36] Because the implied reader is a textual effect, "it" is not a person, a "he" or a "she." Yet the author composes a narrative in such a way that the implied reader emerges from the narrative, *as if this reader were personal*. For a good summary of the implied reader in contemporary literary theory, see W. S. Vorster, "The Reader in the Text: Narrative Material," *Semeia* 48 (1989) 22–27; for the application of this literary theory to New Testament narratives, see pp. 28–36.

[37] See Fish, *Is There a Text*, 26–27, 43.

The implied reader, therefore, is not a person but a heuristic device used to trace the temporal flow of the narrative. The reader emerges as a forward-looking textual effect who also knows and recalls what has happened and has been revealed in the story so far.[38]

The unexplained reference to the resurrection in 2:22 and the author's statement of intention in 20:30-31 show that the implied reader is credited with some knowledge of Jesus' story.[39] But the implied reader has no knowledge of the *Johannine version* of the life, death, and resurrection of Jesus. Statements about "the hour" of Jesus (2:4; 7:30; 8:20; 12:23; 13:1; 17:1; 19:27), his being "lifted up" (3:14; 8:28; 12:32), and his glorification (7:39; 12:16) can only puzzle the implied reader. The reader's knowledge and understanding of the Johannine story evolve as the narrative unfolds.

The implied reader is part of the spatial gaps and temporal flow of the narrative itself.[40] Yet the eventual response of intended and real readers results from the relationship that is established between them and the narrative's implied reader. Indeed, the Christian tradition of reading, and the community of readers through the ages which the Bible presupposes, would be rendered impossible if such were not the case. The relationship may sometimes be uncomfortable. The text may produce pleasure, pain, ambiguity, and even hostility, but some form of relationship must exist. If it does not, the text will disappear in the dust on the shelves.[41]

---

[38] Out of respect for the terminology used by literary critics, I will continue to refer to the implied reader, but several readers are implied by the Johannine narrative (see 19:35; 20:31). The mutuality of the love command (see, e.g., 13:34-35) also implies more than one person. One could more properly speak of the implied readers of the Fourth Gospel.

[39] See Culpepper, *Anatomy,* 222-23. There is a well-known textual difficulty associated with the tense of the verb *pisteuein* in 20:31, whose solution I have presupposed in this affirmation. I am accepting the present subjunctive as the better reading and thus maintaining that the author leads a believing implied reader through a narrative that summons to greater belief. On the textual problem, see R. E. Brown, *The Gospel According to John* (2 vols.; AB 29, 29A; Garden City, N.Y.: Doubleday, 1966, 1970) 1056; and R. Schnackenburg, *The Gospel according to St John* (3 vols.; HTCNT 4/1-3; London: Burns & Oates; New York: Crossroad, 1968-82) 3:338. Both of these scholars opt for the present subjunctive, and Schnackenburg claims that even if the text is aorist it would not be "ingressive." It would indicate "a new impulse in their faith."

[40] Following, among many, the indications of Fowler, "Who is 'the Reader,'" 10-15. See also B. C. Lategan, "Coming to Grips with the Reader in Biblical Literature," *Semeia* 48 (1989) 3-17. Moore points out that the "reader" may best be described as a "listener" (*Literary Criticism,* 84-95). My presentation of a virginal experience of the narrative applies equally well to a listener, as Moore (pp. 87-88) acknowledges. He exaggerates the "Gutenberg galaxy" theory (see p. 95). The great patristic commentaries were pre-Gutenberg but belong more to the modern galaxy than the aural-oral one imagined by Moore. See G. Steiner, *Real Presences: Is there anything in what we say?* (London: Faber & Faber, 1989) 30-31.

[41] On this relationship, see Booth, *Rhetoric of Fiction,* 137-44, 294-95. From now on all

This reference to the Bible leads to a further reservation. The narrative that we are about to read is a Gospel. The structures and terminology detected and defined in recent times in literary circles come from scholars who are working with narrative *fiction*.[42] The Gospel of John is not a narrative fiction in any ordinary sense. Whatever the historical value of the narrative of the Fourth Gospel, it was not creatively invented in the same way that a novelist or a storyteller composes narratives.[43] The text of the Fourth Gospel had a long history before it came to be presented in its final form. This history had its beginnings in the event of the person of Jesus of Nazareth – however imaginatively the subsequent tradition handled that event.

Thus, although my work is an attempt to read the Gospel of John received and transmitted to a further generation as a narrative text, it is not simply that. The diachronic and synchronic go hand in hand in a reading of the Fourth Gospel because of its witness to Jesus Christ. Adela Yarbro Collins rightly insists that we

> give more weight to the original historical context of the text. This context cannot and should not totally determine all subsequent meaning and use of the text. But if, as I am convinced, all meaning is context bound, the original context and meaning have a certain normative character. I suggest that Biblical theologians are not only mediators between genres. They are also mediators between historical periods. . . . Whatever tension there may be between literary- and historical-critical methods, the two approaches are complementary.[44]

My tracing of the implied reader can justifiably be a search for a construct produced by a long storytelling tradition (synchronic) which had its beginnings in Jesus (diachronic).[45]

---

reference to "the reader" indicates "the implied reader." Intended or real readers will be named as such.

[42] See, e.g., the clear description of the project by W. Iser, *The Act of Reading: A Theory of Aesthetic Response* (London: Routledge & Kegan Paul, 1978) 3–19.

[43] For the classical statement on the uniqueness of biblical narrative, see E. Auerbach, *Mimesis: The Representation of Reality in Western Literature* (Princeton, N.J.: Princeton University Press, 1953) 3–23. See also W. Kelber, "Biblical Hermeneutics and the Ancient Art of Communication: A Response," *Semeia* 39 (1987) 100–101. A deconstructionist approach would regard all writing and all figures as fiction. For a survey, see H. N. Schneidau, "The Word against the Word: Derrida on Textuality," *Semeia* 23 (1982) 23–24.

[44] A. Yarbro Collins, "Narrative, History and Gospel," *Semeia* 43 (1988) 150, 153; see also J. Barton, "Reading the Bible as Literature: Two Questions for Biblical Critics," *Literature and Theology* 1 (1987) 135–53.

[45] See, however, the deconstructionist critique of Schneidau, "The Word against the Word," 17.

Paul Ricoeur has insisted that both fiction and history are narrative.[46] While it is tempting to distinguish between empirical narrative, which refers to controllable data, and fictional narrative, which does not, Ricoeur points out that both forms of narrative make referential claims and are not to be distinguished on this basis.[47] "Every day we are subjects of a narrative, if not heroes of a novel."[48]

The shape of the narrative of the Fourth Gospel gives a broad hint that the author has composed it for a reader. The Gospel opens with a key to the mystery of God and Jesus which stands behind the narrative of the Gospel story (1:1-18).[49] Thus instructed, the reader begins to read a narrative. The author has given the reader the full facts about Jesus Christ's original union with God and his revealing role in coming from such origins into the human story (see 1:9-11, 14, 18).

The narrative that follows, however, is full of characters who have not read the prologue. Indeed, many of them "misunderstand" Jesus when he utters his great revelations (see, e.g., 1:38; 2:19-20; 3:3-4; 4:10-11; 6:32-34; 18:37-38). The author is not telling these stories to inform the reader about past events or characters from the life of Jesus. The author is not *primarily* interested in the disciples, Nicodemus, the Samaritan woman, "the Jews," or Pilate. He is interested in the reader's being called to decision in the light of what has been told in the prologue. Indifference is out of the question. The reader stands either on the side of Jesus, by accepting all that he has come to make known in terms of his being the one who tells God's story (1:1-18), or on the side of those who regard such revelation as incredible or as nonsense.

Throughout the Gospel the narrator makes important comments on the narrative which are directed toward the reader (see, e.g., 2:21-22, 23-25; 3:31-36; 4:43-45; 5:1, 9b; 6:4; 7:2; 10:22). The use of this commentary by an author to speak directly to the reader is one of the clearest indications of the author's "point of view."[50] While some modern and contemporary

---

[46] P. Ricoeur, "The narrative function," in *Paul Ricoeur: Hermeneutics and the Human Sciences*, ed. Thompson, 274–96.

[47] Ibid., 288–96. A forceful defense of the unity between fiction and history in the biblical narratives is found in Sternberg, *Poetics of Biblical Narrative*, 23–35. Sternberg, however, argues through the whole of his book for the uniqueness of biblical narrative, because of the central place of God in the story and in the telling of the story.

[48] G. Genette, *Narrative Discourse*, 230.

[49] R. H. Lightfoot, *St. John's Gospel*, ed. C. F. Evans (Oxford: Oxford University Press, 1956) 78. See also M. D. Hooker, "The Johannine Prologue and the Messianic Secret," *NTS* 21 (1974–75) 40–58; C. K. Barrett, "The Prologue of St John's Gospel," in *New Testament Essays* (London: SPCK, 1972) 27–48. From a rhetorical point of view, see Staley, *Print's First Kiss*, 47.

[50] See the indications of such commentary in M. C. Tenney, "The Footnotes of John's Gospel,"

narratives may use the technique to lead the reader astray temporarily, this never happens in the Gospel of John. What the narrator communicates directly to the reader through commentary is a reliable representation of the overall point of view of the omniscient author.[51]

This author, finally, informs the reader that he is bearing personal and authentic witness to the blood and water flowing from the side of the pierced Jesus "that you also may believe" (19:35). The same call to faith comes even more solemnly at the end of the narrative. The book has been written to call the reader, who already knows the story of Jesus, into deeper faith: "These things are written that *you may go on believing* that Jesus is the Christ, the Son of God, and that believing you may have life in his name" (20:31). The "you" in this statement refers to the implied reader, not to the characters in the story . . . nor the Johannine community nor the real reader, in the first instance.

The implied reader in a narrative is always communicating with the real reader of the narrative, *as the narrative unfolds.* A message is transmitted, but the real reader may not always receive the transmission equally well. When we misread what is being transmitted, there is no communication. Sometimes we only receive the communication partially as a result of our careless or distracted reading. Nevertheless, there are times when we receive the transmission exactly. This happens when we are reading in tandem with the implied reader, caught up in the flow of the narrative. In these situations we sometimes may not like what the implied reader transmits to us, so we change stations or switch off. But often we are attracted by the transmission, and thus go on receiving. Two thousand years of reading indicate that the church has been attuned to the transmission of the Johannine implied reader and has thus gone on receiving.

Contemporary literary studies have taught us sensitivity to the reader who gradually emerges as the narrative unfolds, but Gospel criticism must not abandon the pursuits of historical-critical scholarship, which has devoted great attention to the rediscovery of the experience of the Johannine community. The interpreter's role, as Adela Yarbro Collins said, is to "mediate between historical periods." The *historical* intended reader was addressed by a *historical* real author through a narrative. The modern

---

Bibliotheca Sacra 117 (1960) 350-64; Culpepper, *Anatomy,* 17-18; and G. C. Nicholson, *Death as Departure: The Johannine Descent-Ascent Schema* (SBLDS 63; Chico, Calif.: Scholars Press, 1983) 32-33.

[51] My chief objection to the brief study of J. L. Staley, *The Print's First Kiss,* is his oversubtle introduction of an implied author who plays tricks with the implied reader. On the reliability of the Johannine narrator, see Culpepper, *Anatomy,* 32-33.

interpreter of the narrative is also conditioned by his or her *historical* context. A neglect of history leads to the danger of a new fundamentalism.

THE INTENDED READER:
THE JOHANNINE CHRISTIANS

Historically, the encounter between a real author and the Johannine Christians bore fruit. We have the Fourth Gospel in the Bible because this was the case. Although the real author *of the narrative* is beyond our scientific control, the intentions of the real author are reflected in the implied author *in the narrative*. The same can be said for the implied reader *in the narrative* and the intended reader *of the narrative*.

Recent diachronic scholarship has made considerable progress in the rediscovery of the experience of the Johannine Community.[52] Inasmuch as we are dealing with a Christian community, we can take it for granted that classical messianic terminology would have been applied to Jesus of Nazareth at a very early stage. There would have been a gradual refinement and a deeper understanding of this terminology with the passing of time. But the use of such language within the Johannine community to speak of Jesus would have created early tensions between the Christian group and the local representatives of Israel.

There are, however, numerous indications in the Gospel that the Johannine Christians took further initiatives creating even more tensions, which prepared the way for the final breakdown between themselves and their original heritage found within Judaism. The concentration on the mission to the Samaritans in chap. 4 is a strong indication that the community had begun to develop an understanding of Jesus that transcended Judaism and its Temple (see especially the implications of 4:20-24). The Samaritan villagers eventually come to confess: "We have heard for ourselves, and we know that this is indeed the Savior of the world" (4:42).

The introduction of non-Jewish elements certainly caused a great deal of the theological development of the early church. One need only think of the problems behind the writings of Paul and Matthew. The introduction of Samaritans and Hellenists into the Johannine group would have caused its members to look again at their understanding and their

---

[52] What follows is a summary statement of my understanding of the history of the community behind the finished Gospel. For an earlier survey, see F. J. Moloney, "Revisiting John," *ScrB* 11 (1980) 9–15.

preaching of the person of Jesus of Nazareth. A shift in meaning of the term from the Jewish messianic use of "son of God" to a more personal understanding of "Son of God" expressing Jesus' unique union with a God whom he called "my Father" (see especially 5:17) would have been unacceptable to a Jewish audience, and the similar use of the "I am" expression to refer to Jesus (see 4:26; 6:20; 8:24, 28, 58; 13:19; 18:5) would have met similar opposition.

The mounting tension between the Johannine community and postwar synagogue Israel seems to have led eventually to a complete expulsion from the synagogue. The evidence for this final rift is most clearly recovered from the description of the experience of the man born blind in chap. 9. A growing faith in Jesus is shown through the progression of the formerly blind man's understanding of Jesus. In 9:11 he describes Jesus as "the man called Jesus." In v. 17 he goes further, claiming that "he is a prophet." After further interrogation and abuse, he states, in v. 33: "If this man were not from God." Having reached the important Johannine moment of wondering about Jesus' "origins" (from God), he is "cast out" (v. 34: *exebalon auton exō*). Jesus enters the story once again and calls the man, now formally "cast out" of the synagogue, to express his faith in Jesus, the one whom he sees and hears, as the Son of Man. The man falls on his knees and confesses: "Lord, I believe" (vv. 35-38).

The background for this expulsion from the synagogue has already been provided for the reader in "the Jews' " interrogation of the blind man's parents. They refuse to speak for their son because "they feared the Jews, for the Jews had already agreed that if one should confess him to be the Christ, he was to be put out of the synagogue" (v. 22). The expression "to be put out of the synagogue" (*aposynagōgos genētai*) is found only in the Fourth Gospel (see also 12:42; 16:2).

The final rift between the Johannine community and official post-70 A.D. Judaism is reflected in the story of the man born blind. It is also to be found in the other places where the process of putting Christians out of the synagogue is mentioned (12:42; 16:2). This breakdown between a Christian community and the synagogue would have been experienced throughout the communities of the early church; however, the Gospel of John records its own experience by making direct reference to it. The final rift did not come until sometime after 85 A.D., when the synagogue at Yavneh, set up after the disastrous war of 65-70 to restore a shattered Israel, had to deal with the presence of those who believed that the Messiah had already come in the person of Jesus of Nazareth. Under the leadership of Rabbi Gamaliel II, it was decided to exclude all those who believed that

Jesus was the Christ.[53] The expulsion from the traditional synagogue practices of Israel, experienced by the Johannine community, has been
dramatically described in the story of the man born blind.[54]

Once the Johannine community had been forcibly cut away from its
Jewish roots, then even further modifications of the Johannine Gospel seem
to have taken place. An originally Jewish-Christian community now had
to continue its life within the context of a developing hostility with official
Judaism. This is the reason for the apparently negative use of the term
"the Jews" throughout the Gospel.[55] As followers of Jesus Christ, they had
to find their way, living and preaching a Christian message in a strange
new world. They had either to develop an approach and an openness to
this world or close in on themselves and live as a Jewish sect. A decision
to be missionary would have led to contact with the syncretistic Hellenistic
religions. Some early form of what would eventually become Gnosticism
was part of this world.

There are exaggerations on both sides of the debate about John's contact with Hellenistic religions, and especially early Gnosticism. The Fourth
Gospel transcends all these categories in a profound retelling of the Christian story. Bultmann would claim that the discourses in the Fourth Gospel

[53] On this decision, see W. D. Davies, *The Setting of the Sermon on the Mount* (Cambridge:
Cambridge University Press, 1966) 256–315. See, however, J. A. T. Robinson, *The Priority of
John* (London: SCM Press, 1985) 67–93. For the position adopted above, see the analysis of
the rabbinic material in F. Manns, *John and Jamnia: How the Break Occurred between Jews and
Christians c. 80–100 A.D.* (Jerusalem: Franciscan Printing Press, 1988); and K. Wengst, *Bedrängte
Gemeinde und verherrlichter Christus: Der historische Ort des Johannesevangeliums als Schlüssel
zu seiner Interpretation* (2nd ed.; BTS 3; Neukirchen-Vluyn: Neukirchener Verlag, 1983) 45–73.
See also Kysar, "Fourth Gospel," 2426–28; Onuki, *Gemeinde und Welt*, 29–37; and D. M. Smith,
"Judaism and the Gospel of John," in *Jews and Christians: Exploring the Past, Present, and Future*,
ed. J. H. Charlesworth (Shared Ground among Jews and Christians 1; New York: Crossroad,
1990) 83–88. As D. Rensberger has remarked, 9:22, 12:42, and 16:2 are clear (*Johannine Faith
and the Liberating Community* [Philadelphia: Westminster Press, 1988] 26–27). Even if it was
only a local problem, members of the Johannine community were being expelled from the
synagogue.

[54] See the now-classic study of J. L. Martyn, *History and Theology in the Fourth Gospel* (2nd
ed.; Nashville: Abingdon, 1979) 3–41.

[55] The Johannine use of the expression "the Jews" (*hoi Ioudaioi*) says nothing about Israel
as a nation or Judaism as a way to God. The term arises from the concrete experience of
a given Christian community that is experiencing opposition and pain from a group of people
who have literally "shut the door" on them as a sign of their total rejection of the claims
the Johannine story makes for Jesus. Throughout the Gospel the opposition between Jesus
and "the Jews" arises from his claims to have a remarkable oneness with God. The Johannine Jesus and "the Jews" are two sides in a christological debate. The implied reader is asked
to be committed to the side of Jesus, a position that the real author also wished the intended
reader to adopt.

come from a christianized gnostic source, whereas E. Käsemann would argue that John was a naïve docetist gradually leading the Christian story toward Gnosticism.[56] Neither is correct. The community itself is making a journey from an old world into a new world, and John must tell the old story in a new way. Although there are many indications of contact with Hellenistic religions and an early form of Gnosticism, the essential story of the saving revelation of God in Jesus through his life, teaching, death, and resurrection remains firm.[57]

The experience of the Johannine Christians was not only one of receiving a new way of telling the old story. Action was demanded of them. They saw clearly that Christians could not possibly remain in the synagogue (see 12:43-44). Gradually they developed an independent understanding of the primacy of love, rather than of authority. For this reason there is a consistent "upstaging" of Peter by the Beloved Disciple in the narrative (see especially 13:21-26; 20:2-10). The community became more aggressive in its gradual development of a new and higher Christology. Jesus is presented as the Logos, the Son of God "sent" by the Father from "above" to "below" in a way quite unknown to the Synoptic Gospels. There is a development of a special Paraclete pneumatology, an ethic based on love, without the restrictions of a final judgment of one's behavior at the end of time. One has life "now" in the acceptance or refusal of the gift offered by God in the revelation brought by his Son, Jesus (see, e.g., 5:19-30). The Fourth Gospel is marked by a realized eschatology, although the traditional end-time eschatology has not been entirely abandoned (see especially 5:27-29; 6:38-40, 54).

The finished narrative of the Fourth Gospel, addressed to the implied reader, demands a commitment to faith in Jesus as the Christ, the Son of God (20:30-31). Did the implied reader, who emerges as the text unfolds, resonate with the Johannine community, the intended reader, whose troubled history in the early church can now be traced with reasonable confidence? The survival of this Gospel narrative is a positive indication that it did.

---

[56] See R. Bultmann, "Die Bedeutung der neueschlossenen mandäischen und manichäischen Quellen für das Verständnis des Johannesevangeliums," ZNW 24 (1925) 100–146; idem, John, passim. E. Käsemann, The Testament of Jesus according to John 17 (London: SCM Press, 1966) 4–26. For a summary of this discussion, considering both its presuppositions and its consequences, see K. W. Tröger, "Ja oder Nein zur Welt: War der Evangelist Johannes Christ oder Gnostiker?" TV 7 (1976) 64–66.

[57] See Tröger, "Ja oder Nein," 61–80; see the reflections of G. W. MacRae, "The Fourth Gospel and Religionsgeschichte," CBQ 32 (1970) 13–24.

THE COMMUNITY'S JOURNEY
AND THE REAL READER

The real author summons the intended readership into a deeper appreciation of Jesus as the Christ, the Son of God (20:30-31). In writing a Gospel the Fourth Evangelist used the stories about Jesus told and retold in the Johannine community throughout its long life, from its earliest Jewish-Christian days, down to its expulsion from the synagogue into its mission in a new world. Behind this storytelling stands the figure of the Beloved Disciple (whether or not he was John the son of Zebedee need not be decided here).[58] His appreciation of Jesus of Nazareth stands at the beginnings of the Johannine tradition. His ability to reread, retell, and reteach that tradition, without betraying the fundamental elements of the Christian message is one of the main features of the developing christological faith within the community. He challenged his community in his own time. After his death (see 21:21-23), these Christians were prepared to go on facing their new situation, rereading, retelling, and reteaching the heritage left them by the Beloved Disciple. This is what the author of 1 John means, reminding a community of "that which was from the beginning, which we heard" (1 John 1:1) and "this is the message which you have heard from the beginning" (3:11).[59]

The Gospel of John has been written in an attempt to preserve and instruct by making the older traditions understandable to a new Christian generation. The real author tells an old story in a new way.[60] It was inevitable that many of the experiences of the community where the real author had heard the story told, and had also told it, would shape the way in which the final product would emerge. The "story of Jesus" as we now have it

---

[58] In a recent study, J. Kügler, using narrative techniques, has argued that the Beloved Disciple is an "inner-text" reality and cannot be identified with any figure outside the text (*Der Jünger der Jesus Liebte: Literarische, theologische und historische Untersuchungen zu einer Schlüsselgestalt Johanneischer Theologie und Geschichte. Mit einem Excurs über die Brotrede in Joh 6* [SBB 16; Stuttgart: Katholisches Bibelwerk, 1988] 456-88). In narrative terms, the Beloved Disciple is the intratextual narrator in the text. But this does not render the historical question irrelevant. See the recent study of K. Quast, *Peter and the Beloved Disciple: Figures for a Community in Crisis* (JSNTSup 32; Sheffield: JSOT Press, 1989).

[59] On this, see R. E. Brown, *The Epistles of John* (AB 30; New York: Doubleday, 1982) 97-100; and I. de la Potterie, "La notion de 'commencement' dans les écrits johanniques," in *Die Kirche des Anfangs: Festschrift für Heinz Schürmann zum 65. Geburtstag*, ed. R. Schnackenburg et al. (Leipzig: St. Benno-Verlag, 1977) 379-403.

[60] See the overview of possible sources for the "ideolect" of the Fourth Gospel in Onuki, *Gemeinde und Welt*, 19-28; see also Rimmon-Kenan, *Narrative Fiction*, 86-89.

told in the Fourth Gospel is the result of the journey of faith of a particular Christian community in the second half of the first century. The experience of the Johannine community and the rich theological vision it has produced have been caught in a narrative directed to an implied reader via an implied author and a narrator. However slight our knowledge of the real author might be, an author wrote a narrative for intended readers so that they might face "the problem of relating the givenness of the past with the exhilarating experience of the present."[61]

Such reflections are important for our approaching the Fourth Gospel as "real readers." This text has come down to us in its present form because it was received and handed on by the intended reader, the Johannine community. The narrative of the Fourth Gospel is still read in the late twentieth century. The test of its relevance lies in its ability to speak to the faith experience of its real readers. As Seymour Chatman describes it: "When I enter the fictional contract I add another self: I become an implied reader."[62] Does the record of Jesus Christ which we receive from the past in the narrative of the Fourth Gospel have anything to say to the exhilarating and sometimes frightening experience of our own time? Do we "enter the fictional contract" of this particular story of Jesus? How close are our journey and our faith experience to the journey and faith experience of the implied reader in the narrative of the Fourth Gospel? These are the questions that will determine the ongoing relevance of the story told in this Gospel. They can be answered only by a reading of the text during which a relationship between the implied reader and the experience of intended readers and the real reader is established.[63]

The reader of the Fourth Gospel cannot be limited to the implied reader, the Johannine community as the original intended readers of the text, or to the real reader with the text in hand today. As R. M. Fowler has summarized: "The reader has an individual persona (mine), a communal persona (the abstracted total experience of my critical community), and a textual persona (the reader implied in the text)."[64] All must play their part in an ongoing reading of the Fourth Gospel within the Christian community.

The relevance of this text today arises from the relationship established between the implied reader and the real reader. Rightly W. Iser claims that

---

[61] M. D. Hooker, "In His Own Image," in *What about the New Testament: Studies in Honour of C. Evans*, ed. C. Hickling and M. D. Hooker (London: SCM Press, 1975) 41.

[62] Chatman, *Story and Discourse*, 150.

[63] See Steiner, *Real Presences*, 210.

[64] Fowler, "Who is 'the Reader,'" 21.

"the meaning of a literary text is not a definable entity but, if anything, a dynamic happening."[65] The evolving and emerging textual effect of the implied reader from the text initiates such mutuality, not the knowledge, the doctrines, the wisdom, the faith, nor the experience of the real reader.[66]

A series of encounters links the origins of the Johannine story with today's reader. The Jesus-event gave birth to the Johannine community. At a given moment the real author decided to shape a narrative to meet certain needs within the community. In this way an implied author, a narrator, and an implied reader, the fruit of the author's choices and decisions, were created. These choices and decisions, however, were determined by a vision of the needs of the community for which the narrative was shaped. The implied reader, that heuristic device which enables us to sense the temporal flow of the narrative, is therefore shaped by, but not identical with, the intended reader. It represents not so much what the intended reader *was*, but what the real author *wanted the intended reader to become*. Thus arises the intimacy between the real author, the implied author, and the narrator. The implied reader reflects the real author-implied author-narrator's deepest *desires* for a historical Christian community.

Once the narrative existed, the Johannine community entered into a dialogue with the implied reader as it began to read or listen to the text. In doing this the intended reader came into contact with the *desire* of the narrator. This dialogue was fruitful, and the narrative transaction proved significant enough to exceed the bounds of its own time and place. Eventually the narrative came to form part of the Christian New Testament. In this way later readers entered into dialogue with the implied reader, and they in turn came into contact with the narrator's desire. And so the process has continued for almost two thousand years.

The experience of reading a classical text through the centuries indicates that a hard and fast definition of "the reader" is impossible.[67] A classic narrative is still read today by real readers. We continue to enter into dialogue with the implied reader and we find value in it. Insofar as we continue to enter the narrative transaction and find value in it, we also enter into communion with the intended reader. The intended reader both *is* and *is not* the implied reader. The real reader both *is* and *is not* the implied reader. Also, the real reader both *is* and *is not* the intended reader. At the

---

[65] Iser, *Act of Reading*, 22.

[66] A deconstructionist approach to narrative is beyond the scope of my study but could be introduced at this stage.

[67] For a critical survey, see Moore, *Literary Criticism*, 97–107.

point of "*is*" the construct of "the reader" is born.[68] Yet as the liberation and feminist theologians are showing, some contemporary real readers of biblical texts are unhappy with the *desire* of the real author, communicated through the centuries by means of the fictional contract. There is an increasing number of contemporary real readers who cannot identify with many biblical implied readers. Nevertheless, even here the narrative may continue to be relevant because of the antipathy and ambiguity it creates. Relationships between the implied reader and the real reader need not always be favorable, but a relationship there must be.[69]

CONCLUSION

"If . . . all meaning is context-bound, the original context and meaning have a certain normative character. . . . Biblical theologians are not only mediators between genres. They are also mediators between historical periods."[70] A reading of the Fourth Gospel should attempt such a mediation by allowing the mirror of the narrative world of the text to reflect a point of view to the world in front of the text. Throughout, however, one must maintain contact with the world behind the Gospel, which can be seen through the window of the text. Paradoxically, the text is both mirror and window.

In many ways the implied reader has privileges that the real reader cannot share. The implied reader is integral to the journey which is told through the narrative; the real reader may have a different experience. When the narrator speaks, without explanation, of Jewish traditions, feasts, and liturgies, the implied reader is aware of all that is suggested; many real readers are not. The implied reader is assumed to know Greek and to understand double-meaning words, which many real readers do not.[71] The implied reader has some knowledge of Jesus' death and resurrection

---

[68] These four paragraphs arose from discussions with Mark Coleridge. See, for some parallel reflections, Lategan, "Coming to Grips with the Reader," 9–13.

[69] This hermeneutical principle has been highlighted by the liberation and feminist readings of the New Testament. Biblical narratives often produce implied authors, narrators, narratees, and implied readers which reflect an oppressive ideology or androcentrism unacceptable to some contemporary readers. This problem has led to the development of a specifically liberationist or feminist hermeneutic which challenges the myth of the value-free objectivity of the academy into an "advocacy stance."

[70] Yarbro Collins, "Narrative, History, and Gospel," 150.

[71] See Culpepper, *Anatomy*, 212–23; Rimmon-Kenan, *Narrative Fiction*, 117–19.

(see 2:21-22; 20:30-31), but not of the Johannine version of it. The implied reader is hearing this for the first time in the narrative of the Fourth Gospel.

We real readers may find that our response, in dialogue with the experience of almost two thousand years of Christian life, often resonates with that which results from the unfolding relationship between the implied author and the implied reader in the Johannine Gospel.[72] As Honoré de Balzac's narrator informs the implied reader at the beginning of *Père Goriot:* "You may be certain that this drama is neither fiction nor romance. *All is true,* so true that everyone can recognise the elements of the tragedy in his own household, in his own heart perhaps."[73] On the other hand, we may find (and no doubt many do find) that such a response is fatuous in our world of money, muscle, and machinery. But that is not the only thing that might happen. Sometimes we may have a further response which is independent of the implied reader, and thus outside the control of the author. It is unavoidable that our response, either of empathy or antipathy, will be the result of our privileged position as the recipients of almost two thousand years of the Christian practice of reading the Fourth Gospel.[74]

[72] A. M. Solomon, "Story upon Story," *Semeia* 46 (1989) 3.

[73] H. de Balzac, *Old Goriot* (Penguin Classics; Harmondsworth: Penguin Books, 1951) 28.

[74] For further reflections along the lines of this paragraph, see Morgan and Barton, *Biblical Interpretation,* 167-202. See also Prickett, *Words and the Word,* 33-36. Unacceptable is the judgment of Steiner: "The Torah is indeterminately synchronic with all individual and communal life. The Gospels, Epistles and Acts are not" (*Real Presences,* 40). See pp. 40-45.

Chapter Two

The First Page:
John 1:1-18

¶ NARRATIVES FOLLOW a time line, have a plot, and are marked by characters and settings. But the first page of the Fourth Gospel, the first reading experience created by the author for the implied reader, has little of that. Yet if the text as we have it is the deliberate ordering of material by a real author to communicate a point of view through a narrative, the first page of the Gospel of John must be fundamental to the narrative structure of the Fourth Gospel.

The prologue to the Fourth Gospel may be the last part of the Gospel to receive its definitive shape, after a long development within the Johannine community. Diachronic research into its history and structure has its rightful place,[1] but the traditional text is not a "substitute for what had unfortunately been lost."[2] The positioning of the prologue at the very beginning of the narrative is part of the real author's strategy. The reader comes

---

[1] The research into the prehistory of the Johannine prologue is never-ending. G. Rochais provides an up-to-date scheme presenting the pre-Johannine hymns of thirty-seven authors from 1922 to 1983 ("La Formation du Prologue [Jn 1:1-18]," _ScEs_ 37 [1985] 7–9). See pp. 41–44 for the bibliography. See the excellent survey of M. Theobald, _Die Fleischwerdung des Logos: Studien zum Verhältnis des Johannesprologs zum Corpus des Evangeliums und zu 1 Joh_ (NTAbh N.F. 20; Münster: Aschendorff, 1988) 67–119. For recent bibliography, see G. van Belle, _Johannine Bibliography 1966–1985: A Cumulative Bibliography on the Fourth Gospel_ (BETL 82; Leuven: University Press, 1988) 167–88.

[2] R. Alter and F. Kermode, eds., _The Literary Guide to the Bible_ (London: Collins, 1987) 3.

to the prose narrative section of the Gospel (1:19–20:31) armed with the information provided in the poetic narrative of the prologue. Only the omniscient implied author and the narrator have knowledge of the contents of the prologue. No one else in the narrative knows the secrets the author has told the reader in the prologue.

Rudolf Bultmann has sensed the prologue's importance for a reading of the Gospel: "He [the reader] cannot yet fully understand them [motifs in the prologue], but because they are half comprehensible, half mysterious, they arouse the tension, and awaken the *question* which is essential if he is going to understand what is going to be said."[3] A tension is created. The poetic narrative of the prologue produces an implied reader who has been informed of the who and the what of the Word become flesh. The life story told in the body of the Gospel is about the "how" of God's action in Jesus.[4] The prologue is the "telling" while the narrative is the "showing."[5]

R. Alter has argued that the biblical authors' choice of prose fiction as their major means of communication was a conscious break from the highly structured cultic and epic ritual expressions of polytheism.[6] The movement from cultic poetry to prose fiction "could be utilized to liberate fictional personages from the fixed choreography of timeless events and thus could transform storytelling from ritual rehearsal to the delineation of the wayward paths of human freedom, the quirks and contradictions of men and women seen as moral agents and complex centers of motive and feeling."[7]

Something of this happens in the Fourth Gospel. The prologue cannot be regarded as a "fixed choreography of timeless events," yet the epic qualities of the poetic narrative establish an ordered system of relationships between God, his Word, his creation, and its history. The prose narrative of 1:19–20:31 threatens to unsettle that order. Things will not happen as the reader of the prologue might expect. This is so because the prose narrative is a story of God's self-revelation within the context of "the wayward paths of human freedom."

---

[3] R. Bultmann, *The Gospel of John: A Commentary* (Oxford: Blackwell, 1971) 13 (emphasis Bultmann's); see also Theobald, *Fleischwerdung,* 367–71.

[4] See W. Booth, *The Rhetoric of Fiction* (2nd ed.; Chicago: University of Chicago Press, 1983) 255: "Significant literature arouses suspense not about the 'what' but about the 'how.'"

[5] On this, see Booth, *Rhetoric of Fiction,* 3–20; S. Rimmon-Kenan, *Narrative Fiction: Contemporary Poetics* (New Accents; London: Methuen, 1983) 106–8.

[6] R. Alter, *The Art of Biblical Narrative* (New York: Basic Books, 1981) 23–46.

[7] Ibid., 26; see also W. Carter, "The Prologue and John's Gospel: Function, Symbol and the Definitive Word," *JSNT* 39 (1990) 35–58, esp. 48–50.

THE SHAPE OF THE PROLOGUE

Most modern commentators have structured the prologue as a succession of ideas.[8] Alternatively, following an original suggestion from M.-E. Boismard,[9] recent scholarship has attempted to discover a concentric chiasm behind John 1:1-18.[10] But Robert Lowth's *De sacra poesi Hebraeorum* (1753) taught all subsequent readers of biblical poetry to appreciate the importance of the use of parallelism.[11] These principles have been applied to the Johannine prologue.[12] A concentric chiasm has a structure of a, b, c / d / c¹, b¹, a¹, with "d" as the central statement. Synthetic parallelism flows quite differently, according to a system of a, b, c / a¹, b¹, c¹ / a², b², c², and so on.

Firmly situated in a Jewish tradition, the longest poetic passage in the Gospels may reflect the well-established biblical pattern of parallelism.[13] In addition, the real author of the Fourth Gospel has a habit of stating and restating the same themes, in the attempt to establish a point of view

[8] For examples of a bipartite structure, see B. F. Westcott, *The Gospel According to Saint John* (London: John Murray, 1908) 1-2; and Bultmann, *John*, vii. For the more widespread four-part structure, see M.-J. Lagrange, *Évangile selon saint Jean* (Ebib; Paris: Gabalda, 1936) 2-34; and C. K. Barrett, *The Gospel according to St. John* (London: SPCK, 1978) 149-50.

[9] M.-E. Boismard, *St. John's Prologue* (London: Blackfriars, 1957) 76-81. See the same structure suggested thirty-one years later in M.-E. Boismard, *Moïse ou Jésus: Essai de Christologie Johannique* (BETL 84; Leuven: University Press, 1988) 97-99.

[10] See the summaries of R. A. Culpepper, "The Pivot of John's Prologue," *NTS* 27 (1981) 2-6; and Theobald, *Fleischwerdung,* 132-40.

[11] Barrett, *St John*, 150-51. On Lowth, see S. Prickett, *Words and the Word: Language, Poetics and Biblical Interpretation* (Cambridge: Cambridge University Press, 1986) 105-23. On parallelism in biblical poetry, see R. Alter, *The Art of Biblical Poetry* (New York: Basic Books, 1985) 3-26.

[12] M.-F. Lacan, "Le Prologue de saint Jean: Ses thèmes, sa structure, son mouvement," *LumVie* 33 (1957) 91-110; H. Ridderbos, "The Structure and Scope of the Prologue of the Gospel of John," *NovT* 8 (1966) 180-201; S. Panimolle, *Il dono della Legge e la grazia della verità (Gv 1:17)* (Teologia Oggi 21; Rome: Editrice A.V.E.,̀ 1973) 71-105; I. de la Potterie, "Structure du Prologue du Saint Jean," *NTS* 30 (1984) 354-81; G. Zevini, *Vangelo secondo Giovanni* (2 vols.; Commenti Spirituali del Nuovo Testamento; Rome: Città Nuova, 1984, 1987) 1:43-68. See also J. Zumstein, "L'évangile johannique, une stratégie du croire," *RSR* 77 (1989) 224-25. For a survey, see Theobald, *Fleischwerdung*, 140-41.

[13] X. Léon-Dufour would partially accept this suggestion (*Lecture de l'évangile de Jean* [Parole de Dieu; Paris: Seuil, 1988] 1:43-48). His own division of the prologue is based on blending patterns of Hebrew poetry (as understood by H. Gese, "Der Johannesprolog," in *Zur biblischen Theologie: Alttestamentliche Vorträge* [Munich: Kaiser, 1977] 152-201) and the rules of Greek poetry (according to J. Irigoin, "La composition rythmique du Prologue de Jean [1,1-18]," *RB* 78 [1971] 501-14).

through the reader's experience of repetitions in the narrative.[14] Using the image of flowing water, M.-F. Lacan points to the motion of waves. A wave runs onto the beach, only to fall back to gather more strength and more water so that its next rolling motion will carry it farther. The water contained in each wave is the same each time; however, it returns to the sea to replenish itself so that it may make more impression on its next approach to the shore. Similarly, the author of the prologue makes a point, coming back to it in the next passage, only to develop it further.[15]

There are indications in the text of a threefold division. An obvious section runs from v. 1 to v. 5. The first reference to the Baptist in vv. 6-8 opens a second section which runs down to v. 14. The final section again opens with reference to the Baptist, and runs from v. 15 to v. 18. Thus, the three "waves" of the prologue are:

  I. The Word in God Becomes the Light of the World (vv. 1-5)
 II. The Incarnation of the Word (vv. 6-14)
III. The Revealer: The Only Son Turned toward the Father (vv. 15-18)[16]

The sections state and restate the same message. The author communicates to the reader:[17]

1. The Word is announced and described—the basis of the mystery is stated. This can be traced in the narrator's proclamation of vv. 1-2 (I), in the narrator's description of the Baptist's witness in vv. 6-8 (II), and in the direct speech of the Baptist in v. 15 (III).

2. The revelation brought by the Word is coming into the world—the Word is the light of the world. This message is found in the first two sections in the words of the narrator in vv. 3-4 (I) and in v. 9 (II).[18] After v. 14, there is no place for further teaching on the coming of the light into the world in section III. There the concentration is on our appropriation of the gift of the Word.

3. Humankind responds to the gift it has been given. In v. 5b the first section affirms that the darkness has not overcome the light

---

[14] Some fifty years ago E. C. Hoskyns said it well: "The reader is required to move with the movement of the book. He has to bear carefully in mind what the author has already said" (*The Fourth Gospel*, ed. F. N. Davey [London: Faber & Faber, 1947] 66). He then goes on to speak of the author's "self-contained allusiveness" (p. 67).

[15] Lacan, "Le Prologue de saint Jean," 97.

[16] See de la Potterie, "Structure du Prologue," 357–59.

[17] For a detailed analysis of these divisions and the allotting of material from the prologue into the various sections and subsections, see de la Potterie, "Structure du Prologue," 359–67.

[18] This view comes from my belief that the Word enters the human scene as early as v. 4.

(I), while vv. 10-13 show that one can accept or refuse to accept the Word who comes into the world (II).[19] In v. 16 the reader is told of the greatness of the gift received (III).

4. The object of faith is described – the only Son of the Father. It is too early for such a description in the first section (I). The second section concludes in v. 14 with the proclamation of the Word's becoming flesh, the only Son of the Father among us (II). The prologue closes in vv. 17-18 with a final description of the Word. His name is Jesus Christ, and he replaces the former gift of the Law. No one has ever seen God, but the only Son, gazing toward his Father at all times, tells his story (III).

The author has constructed three parallel passages, deepening and expanding the same essential message with each statement and restatement. In each successive section, the author informs the reader of the Word, his coming as the light of humankind, and the response to the gift who is Jesus Christ, the Son of God.

READING THE PROLOGUE

The textual effect of the reader emerges from the Gospel's very first page, a page that plays an important role in the design of the Fourth Gospel.

I. The Word in God Becomes the Light of the World (vv. 1-5)

The reader is sufficiently familiar with Jewish tradition to be aware of the reference to Gen 1:1 in reading the Gospel's first words: *en archē.*[20] In

---

[19] I disagree with de la Potterie on v. 13. Following an early patristic tradition, he reads the singular *egennēthē,* and takes it is a reference to the virginal conception. See "Structure du Prologue," 370-72. Although this position has the support of some important scholars (e.g., Harnack, Burney, Boismard, Dupont, Grelot, Braun, de la Potterie, Hofrichter, Lacan, Mollat, Thyen, Zevini), I follow the Greek manuscript tradition in reading the plural *egennēthēsan.* In my understanding of the shape of the prologue, it thus belongs to v. 12 as a description of the fruits of accepting the one who has come into the world. See the critical study of the suggestions of Harnack, Grelot, and Hofrichter (upon which others depend) by J. W. Pryor, "Of the Virgin Birth or the Birth of Christians? The Text of John 1:13 once more," *NovT* 27 (1985) 296-318. Recently, Theobald argued that *originally* it was singular and was a commentary on v. 14, affirming the Word's origins in God (*Fleischwerdung,* 238-47). It was changed into the plural, linked with the "children of God" in v. 12, and then added to the prologue.

[20] Contrary to R. A. Culpepper (*Anatomy of the Fourth Gospel: A Study in Literary Design*

the biblical tradition, that moment is the "beginning" of all that was. But *before* that *archē* the Word "was." The deliberate choice of the imperfect form of the verb "to be" places the Word outside time, without any controlled "beginning" of his own. The first use of the imperfect form of the verb "to be" indicates the Word's preexistence. In that timeless situation before there ever was time, the Word *ēn pros ton theon*.

The use of the preposition *pros* followed by the accusative case indicates the dynamism of the relationship.[21] There are two parties involved, both individuated by the use of the definite article: *ho logos* and *ho theos*.[22] These two nouns are joined by another use of the imperfect tense of the verb "to be." Here it is used to speak of the Word's relationship with God. It is not a static "being with" which relates these two parties. There is a mutuality involved in the relationship that is difficult to render in succinct English. While it is legitimate to translate "and the Word was turned toward God," there may also be an intention on the part of the author to hint that there was a corresponding turning of God toward the Word.

The intimacy of the mutuality is immediately indicated by the explanation: *kai theos ēn ho logos*. The reader, credited with an awareness of the subtleties of Greek syntax,[23] finds that the two parties of the relationship are so close that what one is, the other also is. However, by placing the complement of the imperfect tense of the verb "to be" before the verb, and the subject after, the author has told the reader: what God was, the Word also was (NEB). This third use of the imperfect form of the verb "to be" predicates that the Word is divine, as God is.[24] But the author has constructed this sentence carefully to inform the reader that the Word is not to be simply identified with God.[25]

[Philadelphia: Fortress Press, 1983] 219-22), I see the implied reader as very familiar with Jewish thought and practice.

[21] This is often denied, on the basis of the argument that the Koine Greek no longer had this meaning. See, e.g., R. Schnackenburg, *The Gospel according to St. John* (3 vols.; HTCNT 4/1-3; London: Burns & Oates; New York: Crossroad, 1968-82) 1:233-34; Boismard, *Moïse et Jésus*, 93-94; Barrett, *St John*, 155. As well as the possible shift of meaning in *pros*, the intimacy of the context should also guide the interpreter. See E. Delebecque, *Evangile de Jean: Texte Traduit et Annoté* (CahRB 23; Paris: Gabalda, 1987) 143.

[22] Lagrange, *Saint Jean*, 2: "*ēn* revient un seconde fois, avec *pros ton theon*, marquant cette fois l'inhérence, et indirectement la distinction." See also G. Segalla, *Giovanni* (NVB 36; Rome: Edizioni Paoline, 1976) 141-42.

[23] See Culpepper, *Anatomy*, 218-19. The narrator never explains these subtleties; it is presupposed that the reader understands.

[24] Since Chrysostom commentators have pointed out that the three uses of *ēn* in v. 1 are for existence, relationship, and predication.

[25] See W. Loader, *The Christology of the Fourth Gospel: Structure and Issues* (BBET 23; Frankfurt:

The reader is in a world outside time and outside his experience, but the notion of the preexistence of the law and the preexistence of the name of the Messiah was not foreign to the reader.[26] The narrator, however, adds a further specification: "He was in the beginning with God." Who is this "he"? A more literal translation would read: "This man was in the beginning turned toward God." The narrator has added a clarification to what has been said so far through the use of a demonstrative pronoun *houtos*. Does this strong pronoun simply look back to *ho logos* as an antecedent, or does the author have someone else in mind? For the moment a question is left hanging. The reader simply does not have sufficient information from vv. 1-2 to be able to say who "this man" might be.

The author is shaping a reader aware of the relationship that has existed from all time between the Word and God. The narrator's fourfold use of the imperfect tense of the verb "to be" (*ēn*) has dominated the temporal aspect of vv. 1-2. Although the reader is familiar with the notion of the preexistence of the law and the name of the Messiah, something more personal and more intimately related to God is being suggested. Furthermore, two elements present in vv. 1-2 already hint that the preexistent Word will have a human story.

The first of these is the choice of the term "the Word." Discussion of the background of this term goes on apace.[27] The expression itself can be found throughout much of the religious literature of antiquity—from Herodotus to Philo in the Greek-Hellenistic world,[28] in different ways throughout the gnostic systems.[29] There are many parallels between the Johannine Logos and Hellenistic Judaism's *sophia*, and throughout the Old

---

Peter Lang, 1989) 156–61. J. H. Neyrey (*An Ideology of Revolt: John's Christology in Social-Science Perspective* [Philadelphia: Fortress Press, 1988] 25–29) has attractively suggested that the use of *theos* in v. 2 reflects one of God's two names (*theos*=creator; and *kyrios*=the one exercising eschatological authority) evidenced by Philo (see *Quaest. Exod.* 2.68; *Vit. Mos.* 2.99; see also John 5:17-20; 20:28). This would lead directly into v. 3: "all things were made through him."

[26] A long tradition of preexistence within Judaism eventually produced the idea of a preexistent Son of Man in the apocalyptic traditions and preexistent wisdom in the wisdom traditions. On this, see R. G. Hamerton-Kelly, *Pre-Existence, Wisdom and the Son of Man* (SNTSMS 21; Cambridge: Cambridge University Press, 1973) 15–21. The rabbis claimed that seven things existed before creation: Torah, repentance, the Garden of Eden, Gehenna, the Temple, and the name of the Messiah. See especially *b. Pesahim* 54a and *b. Nedarim* 39b.

[27] For a survey of the discussion, see F. J. Moloney, *The Word Became Flesh* (Theology Today Series 14; Dublin/Cork: Mercier Press, 1977) 31–35; see also Schnackenburg, *St John*, 1:481–93; Barrett, *St John*, 152–55.

[28] See C. H. Dodd, *The Interpretation of the Fourth Gospel* (Cambridge: Cambridge University Press, 1953) 263–85; and, most recently, T. H. Tobin, "The Prologue of John and Hellenistic Jewish Speculation," *CBQ* 52 (1990) 252–69.

[29] See Bultmann, *John*, 20–31.

Testament, especially the prophets' speaking the word of YHWH.[30] The rabbinic and targumic literature often avoided the use of the name and the presence of God by replacing it with "the Word" (Aramaic *mēmrā'*).[31] Before the Fourth Gospel, the expression "the Word of God" had been used to speak of the Christian message of salvation (see Luke 8:11; Acts 13:5; 1 Thess 2:13; 2 Tim 2:9; Rev 1:9; etc.). The Fourth Gospel as a whole presents Jesus of Nazareth as the one who makes known the Word of God.[32]

But the choice of the Greek expression *ho logos*, whatever its background, allows the author to hint to the reader that from the intimacy between the Word and God which has been described, "the Word" will be spoken (*legein* or *lalein*). A word is essentially about communication. The modality of that communication has not been indicated, but if there is the Word, then it exists to say something.[33]

The second hint still puzzling the reader is the *houtos* of v. 2. Just who might "this man" be? Does it simply refer back to *ho logos* in v. 1, or does it look forward into a human story? Both are possible grammatically, and thus the emerging reader reads on to discover who "this man" might be. Both the Word to be spoken and "this man," who may have a history, allow the author to shape a reader who suspects that the preexistent intimacy described in vv. 1-2 may not be all there is to tell.[34]

Verses 3-4 bristle with exegetical difficulties. What is meant by the expression *panta* in v. 3a (without a definite article)? Where does the major break come in the statements found in vv. 3-4? Is the meaning of the

---

[30] See Rochais, "La formation du prologue," 173–82; Léon-Dufour, *Lecture*, 53–62. For a good survey of the whole discussion, with a strong defense of the background of the Wisdom myth, see E. Haenchen, *John 1-2*, (2 vols.; Hermeneia; Philadelphia: Fortress Press, 1984) 1:135–40. See especially the suggestions of J. Ashton ("The Transformation of Wisdom: A Study of the Prologue of John's Gospel," *NTS* 32 [1986] 161–86) that the prologue is the result of a Christian development of conflicting wisdom traditions within Judaism.

[31] See D. Muñoz León, *Dios-Palabra: Memra en los Targumim del Pentateuco* (Institución San Jeronimo 4; Granada: Santa Rita, 1974); M. McNamara, *Targum and Testament: Aramaic Paraphrases of the Hebrew Bible: A Light on the New Testament* (Shannon: Irish University Press, 1972) 101–6; and especially C. T. R. Hayward, "The Holy Name of the God of Moses and the Prologue of St John's Gospel," *NTS* 25 (1978-79) 16–32.

[32] See H. van den Bussche, *Jean: Commentaire de l'Évangile Spirituel* (Bruges: Desclée de Brouwer, 1976) 69–76; Hoskyns, *Fourth Gospel*, 141, 154–63.

[33] Hoskyns, *Fourth Gospel*, 137. See also Bultmann, *John*, 35: "From the outset God must be understood as 'the one who speaks,' the God who reveals himself." See also G. R. Beasley-Murray, *John* (WBC 36; Waco: Word Books, 1987) 16–17.

[34] See Bultmann, *John*, 34–36. Commenting on v. 1, Barrett correctly notes: "John intends that the whole of his gospel shall be read in the light of this verse. The deeds and words of Jesus are the deeds and words of God; if this be not true the book is blasphemous" (*St John*, 156).

multipurpose Greek verb *ginōmai* the same in each of its three uses in v. 3? In the light of the reference to Genesis in v. 1, and anticipating the further references to creation in v. 10b, the narrator speaks first of the presence of the Word of God in the creation.[35] Throughout vv. 1-2 the imperfect *ēn* was the only verb used, expressing the timelessness of the relationship between the Word and God. In v. 3ab the double use of the aorist *egeneto* looks back to the creative act of God in the past.[36] The intervention of God in creation, placed in the finished past through the use of the aorist, was an act that already revealed the Word.[37] "The fact that the Word creates means that creation is an act of revelation."[38] The Word that God spoke in creation can already be seen and experienced (see Wis 13:1; Rom 1:19-20).

Having established, through the two aorists, that God's creation took place through the Word and that nothing came into being in that creative action without him, the tense of the verb changes. In v. 3c the perfect tense of *ginōmai* replaces the aorists of v. 3ab. Placing my major break between *egeneto oude hen* and *ho gegonen en autǭ*, I read: "All things came into being through him, and apart from him nothing came into being. What appeared in him was life, and the life was the light of humankind."[39]

The narrator has now moved from the use of the imperfect tense (vv. 1-2) to the aorist tense (v. 3ab) to the perfect tense (v. 3c). Each of these

[35] T. E. Pollard has argued that *panta* does not refer to creation, but that "the Son is the mediator of 'all' things that God does and says" ("Cosmology and the Prologue of the Fourth Gospel," *VC* 12 [1958] 147-53; quotation p. 150). Thus, he would claim that v. 3 is not about creation, which is not important for the Johannine theology, but about God's revealing and redeeming acts in Christ. He has been followed by P. Lamarche, "Le Prologue de Jean," *RSR* 52 (1964) 524-25; I. de la Potterie, *La Verité dans Saint Jean* (2 vols.; AnBib 73-74; Rome: Biblical Institute Press, 1977) 1:159-65; and Ashton, "Transformation of Wisdom," 170-75.

[36] See F. Kermode, "John," in *Literary Guide*, ed. Alter and Kermode, 445.

[37] The reflection of God in creation comes from the Wisdom tradition, where a personified Wisdom is the form of God's creative activity and the personal agent of his creation (see Job 28:12-17; Prov 8:12-36; Wis 7:22-8:1; 9:1-3). This thought was applied by the early church to speak of Jesus' presence in creation from the beginnings of time (see 1 Cor 8:6; Col 1:16-17; Eph 1:9-10; Heb 1:3). Among many, see R. E. Brown, *The Gospel According to John* (AB 29, 29A; Garden City, N.Y.: Doubleday, 1966, 1970) 25-26. In agreement with Pollard, Lamarche, de la Potterie, and Ashton, I do not see a creation Christology at the center of the Johannine theology. Revelation is the central theme. However, the possibility of a creation theme, especially as it is subordinated to revelation as I am suggesting, should not be eliminated. The evidence for the role of the Word in creation in vv. 3 and 10b, especially in the light of v. 1, is too strong. R. Kysar exaggeratedly reads the whole prologue in terms of creation and re-creation (*John's Story of Jesus* [Philadelphia: Fortress Press, 1984] 15-18).

[38] Brown, *John*, 25.

[39] For an up-to-date and detailed study of the text-critical problem, see E. L. Miller, *Salvation-History in the Prologue of John: The Significance of John 1:3-4* (NovTSup 60; Leiden: E. J. Brill, 1989) 17-44; for the translation "appeared," see pp. 79-86.

shifts in temporal reference further shapes the reader. The narrator moves from one aspect of the role of the Word to another.[40] The implied reader is no longer asked to speculate on the unity that existed *beyond all time* between the Word and God (vv. 1-2). Nor is the reader still being told of the role of the Word in the *past intervention* of God in creation (v. 3ab). Now the reader is told that an event took place in the past which has a continuing relevance (vv. 3c-4). This is the meaning of the perfect tense of the verb. For the omniscient author, the Word provided life when it appeared, life that is the light of humankind (vv. 3c-4). The life that is light broke into the human story in an event that happened in the past, but the effects of this event are still part of that story.

In each of the three stages referred to, the Word is central. Roles differ, but one stage leads into another. It is the intimacy which exists outside time that forms the basis for the central role of the Word in God's creation. Creation took place "through him" (*di' autou;* see Rom 11:36; Col 1:16; etc.). But that is only a first moment in the revelation of the Word in history. In a second, and perennially significant moment, the Word appeared in the human story, to be the life that is the light of the world. The life was "in him" (*en autǭ;* see 1 Cor 1:5; 2 Cor 1:20; Col 1:19; etc.).

The reader now knows of a history of salvation which can be plotted from the preexistence of the Word to the life and light brought into history through an identifiable human figure.

1. A preexistent Word with God (*pros ton theon*).
2. God's manifestation *ad extra* (*di' autou*) wherein the Word can already be experienced.
3. The Word in the human story as the life that is the light of humankind (*en autǭ*).

A widespread use of the expression "life" can be found in ancient religious literature. It is found in Hellenistic literature,[41] but it also has its place in traditional Jewish thought.[42] It also forms part of the early Christian tradition (see Mark 4:21-22; Matt 5:14; Luke 17:24). The same can be said for "the light." Some scholars have attempted to show that the idea of "the light" in the Fourth Gospel originates in Greek or other pagan myths.[43] It is now widely held that the terminology comes from biblical

---

[40] Much of what follows depends on Miller, *Salvation History,* 76–97.

[41] For a survey, see Barrett, *St John,* 157–58; see also Schnackenburg, *St John,* 1:242–44.

[42] See Barrett, *St John,* 157; Dodd, *Interpretation,* 144–50.

[43] See, e.g., W. Bauer, *Das Johannesevangelium erklärt* (HKNT 6; Tübingen: J. C. B. Mohr [Paul Siebeck], 1933) 119–21; Bultmann, *John,* 40–45 with notes and 342 n. 5.

and Jewish tradition.[44] The use of this terminology in Qumran literature has added further support to this position.[45] The theme is found also in primitive Christian tradition (see Acts 13:47; Phil 2:15; Col 1:12-13; Eph 5:8; 1 Pet 2:9).

As with the choice of the term *logos* and the notion of preexistence, the narrator uses language that a reader, furnished with a traditional Jewish background, does not find foreign. If the Word communicates the knowledge of God, then this knowledge will provide the life for which humankind yearns, a life that gives sense and direction: light. But the light brings clarity of vision which will eventually enable judgment to take place (see especially the association between light and judgment in 8:12, 24; 9:40-41).[46]

The author can now proceed to the third and final aspect to be treated: the response of humankind to the gift. There is a further change in the tense of the main verb used: "and the light shines (present tense: *phainei*) in the darkness, and the darkness has not overcome (aorist tense: *ou katelaben*) it." The light that appeared in the Word is still present to the reader of the poetic narrative (present tense: *phainei*). There was an event in the past which may have looked, to the uninformed, like a victory for the powers of evil over the presence of the light, but such was not the case (aorist tense: *ou katelaben*).[47]

All of this remains mysterious for the implied reader who is asked to accept, on the reliable word of the narrator, that the light now shines (present tense) in the ambiguity of the human condition. The reader is also informed that there was an event in the past (aorist tense) where light and darkness clashed. The light has not been overcome. It shines still. The reader has been told of a response to the Word—an unsuccessful attempt to overcome the light. Barnabas Lindars has remarked: "To the Christian reader the verse already contains a hint of the Passion and Resurrection

---

[44] See, e.g., H. Preisker, "Jüdische Apocalyptik und hellenistischer Synkretismus im Johannes-Evangelium, dargelegt an dem Begriff 'Licht,'" *TLZ* 77 (1952) 673-78; G. Stemberger, *La symbolique du bien et du mal selon saint Jean* (Paris: Seuil, 1970) 44-49; G. Reim, *Studien zum alttestamentlichen Hintergrund des Johannesevangeliums* (SNTSMS 22; Cambridge: Cambridge University Press, 1974) 164-66 (with special reference to Deutero-Isaiah).

[45] For a summary of the Qumran evidence, see H. Braun, *Qumran und das Neue Testament* (2 vols.; Tübingen: J. C. B. Mohr [Paul Siebeck], 1966) 1:122-24; Brown, *John*, 340.

[46] On the importance of "light" in the Johannine theme of judgment, see Barrett, *St John*, 158. On the use of the symbol "light" as implicit commentary throughout the Gospel, see Culpepper, *Anatomy*, 190-92.

[47] Along with most interpreters, I understand the narrator's use of the verb *katalambanein* as meaning "overcome," not its other possible meaning "to grasp intellectually, to comprehend." See BAGD, 412-13. For a survey of the discussion, see Theobald, *Fleischwerdung*, 212-16.

of Jesus."[48] But the implied reader, reading the Johannine story for the first time, does not yet understand Jesus' death as a clash between light and darkness. The reader encounters here a first description of a negative response to the coming of the Word, and a negative form of the verb *lambanein* is used. Some form of this verb will reappear each time the human response is narrated (see vv. 11-12, 16).[49]

II. *The Incarnation of the Word: Son of the Father (vv. 6-14)*

The speculations of vv. 1-5 come to a halt as the reader is drawn quite rudely into history with the first words of v. 6: *egeneto anthrōpos*, "a man appeared." By returning to the aorist tense of the verb *ginōmai* (as in v. 3ab) the narrator again places the reader in contact with the report of an event that took place in the completed past. A man appeared, but he is no longer among us. His "appearance" (unlike that of the life which is the light in vv. 3c-4, where the perfect tense was used) was limited to a given period of time, which has come to an end. The reader encounters a historical person. He is given a name: "his name was John."

He has been "sent from God" (*apestalmenos para theou*). In the Fourth Gospel, John the Baptist is the only human figure associated with God in this way. Jesus is also "from God" (see 1:14; 6:46; 7:29; 9:16, 33; 16:27; 17:8). John's being a "sent one from God" is framed, by the careful construction of the Greek sentence, between two expressions which locate him as a character from the human story: "*a man appeared, sent from God, whose name was John.*" The reader is introduced to a historical figure who is an "apostle" of God. This is the author's way of establishing, from the first appearance of John the Baptist in the story, the authenticity of the witness that he will give to the Word. The reader, who will next read that John came *eis martyrian* (v. 7), knows from the information provided by v. 6 that John the Baptist is the reliable witness par excellence, sent from God.[50]

---

[48] B. Lindars, *The Gospel of John* (NCB; London: Oliphants, 1972) 87.

[49] My associating the event of life and light and the subsequent rejection of that light by the darkness with the historical coming of the Word is widely debated. For a summary of the discussion, see Brown, *John*, 26–27.

[50] It has often been pointed out that the Johannine insertions into the prologue are clumsy, and all scholars who reconstruct a pre-Johannine hymn omit vv. 6-8 and v. 15. Even some who defend the unity of the hymn omit vv. 6-8 and 15. See, e.g., Lindars, *John*, 82.

Three reasons are given for the Baptist's coming (v. 7) which lead the reader from what has already been learned into what is yet to come. (1) He came for testimony (*eis martyrian*). The reader meets, for the first time, the concept of bearing witness, giving testimony. The Baptist is sent from God as an authentic and trustworthy witness. But to whom or what does he witness? (2) He came to bear witness to the light. The reader knows from vv. 3c-4 that only the Word is the light of humankind. The Baptist points to that light, and in doing so gives a further indication to the reader that the light is not the inner workings of a Word–God relationship, but part of the human story. If not, how could "this man" (v. 7a, *houtos*, as in v. 2) give testimony to him? Although the narrative is ostensibly about John the Baptist as witness, the reader is further introduced, via the witness, to the Word, the life, and the light. (3) The final reason given for his coming is "that all might believe through him." The reader is able to recall that the Word was in God, that it was manifested in creation, and that life and light came only through the Word (vv. 1-4). The more speculative poetic narrative of vv. 1-5 is rendered historical through the coming of the Baptist. The reader is reminded that the light is the means of salvation for all humankind.[51] Life can be had if humankind will believe in the light brought by the Word.

The narrator states firmly what the Baptist was not: he was not the light. This must be clear to the reader. The Baptist is the witness to the light (v. 8), but not the light. It is often suggested that the emphatic negative in v. 8a shows the anti-Baptist nature of the insertion of vv. 6-8.[52] Although there were questions about the right relationship between the Baptist and Jesus in the early church (see especially Acts 19:1-7),[53] whatever its diachronic origins may have been, the primary purposes of this section (vv. 6-8) are the following: (1) To open the central section of the prologue by anchoring it in history. The section is not included simply to tell the reader about the Baptist. It does that, but more importantly, the Baptist

---

[51] Taking the *di' autou* as a reference to the Word, and not to the Baptist. Barrett claims that it must refer to the Baptist, as "men do not believe *through* Jesus but *in* him" (*St John*, 160). The *dia* here is to be linked with the gift of the truth which took place *dia Iēsou Christou* in v. 17. Humankind comes to belief because of (in this sense "through") the revealing event of the Word. On this, see BDF, 119 (§223). They describe this use of *dia* with the genitive as: "the circumstances in which one finds oneself because of something."

[52] See, e.g., Bauer, *Johannesevangelium*, 16–18; Bultmann, *John*, 51–52; Brown, *John*, 28; Schnackenburg, *St John*, 1:252–53.

[53] See J. Murphy-O'Connor, "John the Baptist and Jesus: History and Hypotheses," *NTS* 36 (1990) 359–74; M.-E. Boismard and A. Lamouille, *Les Actes des deux Apôtres* (2 vols.; Ebib; Paris: Gabalda, 1990) 2:306–11.

introduces the Word to history by pointing to him as the one and only light. (2) To instruct the reader through the negative of v. 8a that, great and divinely authorized though the witnessing function of the Baptist may have been, he "was not the light." For the reader, John the Baptist is the only historical figure that has appeared so far. He was the *apestalmenos para theou*. What could be greater than that?

Having announced the Word, the narrator can move to the second theme of this central section: the revelation brought by the Word is coming into the world. The Greek of v. 9 is ambiguous, but having seen the synthetic parallelism found in the repetitions of the same themes in vv. 1-5, 6-14, and 15-18, it must be translated: "The true light was coming into the world."[54] The theme is unequivocally stated by the narrator. Over against the many possible "lights" the Word is described as the *true* light. The use of words such as "true," "truth," and "truly" is very important for the author of the Fourth Gospel.[55] Here we find the word *alēthinos*, which indicates, adjectivally, that which is genuine, having the fullness of the qualities its name indicates (see 4:23; 6:32; 15:1; 17:3). The true light, therefore, means that the Word, who is the subject through the prologue, is the uniquely authentic and perfect revelation of God.[56] The narrator tells the reader that the Word, the life which is the light of humankind, is coming into the world and that only this light enlightens humankind. The reader is not called to speculation but is being told of something that is happening. The present tense of the verb (*phōtizei*) tells the reader that the light goes on enlightening humankind. As in v. 5, it is part of the narrator's experience.[57]

The narrator has first linked the character of the Baptist with the light. He bears witness to the presence of the light in the human story (vv. 7-8). Now the author makes explicit for the reader what was implicit in the witnessing of the Baptist: that the light itself was coming into the world. The tension and suspense of the prologue are maintained. The narrator

[54] The Greek *ēn to phōs to alēthinon, ho phōtizei panta anthrōpon, erchomenon eis ton kosmon* is either "He was the true light which enlightens every man coming into the world" or "The true light, which enlightens every man, was coming into the world." While the former has good rabbinic parallels, I am choosing the latter, taking *ēn . . . erchomenon* as a periphrastic construction. On this, see ZBG, 126; and especially P. Borgen, "Logos was the True Light: Contributions to the Interpretation of the Prologue of John," in *Logos was the True Light and Other Essays on the Gospel of John* (Relieff 9; Trondheim: Tapir, 1983) 95–110.

[55] For an exhaustive study, see de la Potterie, *Vérité*; see also Y. Ibuki, *Die Wahrheit im Johannesevangelium* (BBB 39; Bonn: Peter Hanstein, 1972).

[56] See Ibuki, *Wahrheit*, 186–87.

[57] Not all scholars agree that the coming of the Word into history is involved here. For a survey, see Brown, *John*, 28–30.

is making affirmations about the Word, the life, the light, and about what the Word brings into the human story. The emerging reader asks: How?

The narrator has already announced that the Word was in the world (v. 9). He catches up the expression "world" (*kosmos*) repeating two truths already communicated to the reader and adding a third. "He was in the world" is a repetition of the announcement that the true light was coming into the world (v. 9). "And the world was made through him" (*kai ho kosmos di' autou egeneto*) reaches further back, to remind the reader of what was said in v. 3a: "All things came into being through him" (*panta di' autou egeneto*). The reader is familiar with these two affirmations, as they form part of what has already been learned.

In one terse expression, the narrator introduces the reader to a variety of possible meanings for the expression *ho kosmos*.[58] The reader is told first of the material reality of the created world, which provides the context for the coming of the Word. The Word was in this world (v. 10a).[59] The author next refers to a more theological reality of the world which was made through him (v. 10b). It has its origins and gains its sense and purpose through him.[60] But there is another meaning of *ho kosmos* with which the author climaxes v. 10. Although the reader has already been partially prepared for the theme of the rejection of the Word through the author's first indication of a conflict between light and darkness in v. 5, the affirmation of v. 10c comes as something of a shock: "Yet the world knew him not." The reference to the negative response to the Word in v. 5 is now being further developed. There is a power of evil at large that will not accept the revelation brought by the Word. This power of evil is also called *ho kosmos*.[61]

In affirming that the world "did not know" the Word, the narrator uses the expression *ouk egnō*. Throughout his story of Jesus the negative form of the verb *ginōskō* will indicate a willful refusal on the part of the hostile world to accept the revelation brought by the Word (see 3:10; 8:27, 43, 55;

---

[58] See N. H. Cassem, "A Grammatical and Contextual Inventory of the use of *kosmos* in the Johannine Corpus with some Implications for a Johannine Cosmic Theology," *NTS* 19 (1972-73) 81-91; Barrett, *St John*, 161–62; Brown, *John*, 508–10.

[59] The reader will later meet this meaning in 11:9; 17:5, 24; 21:25.

[60] The reader will later find that there is a world loved by God (3:16) of which Jesus Christ is savior (4:42). Jesus takes away the sins of the world (1:29), and his flesh can be the life of the world (6:51). Indeed, he is the light of the world (8:12; 9:5).

[61] For the first time the reader meets a connotation of "the world" that will return in 7:7; 14:17, 22, 27, 30; 15:18-19; 16:8, 20, 33; 17:6, 9, 14-16. The life story of Jesus Christ will teach that there is a prince of evil at large in this world (12:31; 14:30; 16:11), whom Jesus Christ overcomes (16:33).

10:6, 38; 16:3; 17:23, 25a).[62] Such is the case with "the world" in v. 10c. In v. 11 the dramatic nature of the refusal of the Word is further developed.

Repeating the use of the verb "to come," already found in v. 9, the reader learns that the Word came "to his own home." The periphrastic "was coming" (v. 9) is now an aorist "he came" (v. 11a). The narrator tells the reader of an event in the past: the historical event of the coming of the Word into history. When that took place and how it took place are still mysteries to the reader; however, the narrator makes it clear *that* it took place. The expression *ta idia* ("homeland, true dwelling place") was a favorite expression among the Gnostics to speak of the heavenly spheres into which the redeemed would eventually return.[63] That was the real home of the soul, at present lost in the chaos of creation. True to Christian tradition, the author reverses this. "His own home" is not in the heavenly spheres, but in the human story.[64]

His own people (*hoi idioi*) received him not.[65] The author tells of the negative response of those from the human story who did not accept the revelation brought by the Word by using the negative form of the verb *para-lambanein*. This is the narrator's second use of an action word related to the verb *lambanein* to speak of the response to the revelation of the Word. In v. 5 the reader was told that the darkness did not overcome the light (*katalambanein*). The root verb has the primary sense of taking to oneself in a more intimate way.[66] There is more involved in the response to the Word than intellectual assent. The reader will be led to see that the whole person is involved. As yet this is a vague hint, a gap in the narrative yet to be filled. Up to this time the historical appearance of the Word has met only with refusal (vv. 5 and 11).

But there is the possibility of a positive response, and this is indicated for the reader in vv. 12-13. Again we find the verb *lambanein*. In v. 12 it is used in parallel with the verb *pisteuein*:

---

[62] He also uses the negative form of *oidamen* simply to show that lack of knowledge is the result of human ignorance (see 1:26; 7:28; 8:14, 19; 9:29; 15:21). On this, see I. de la Potterie, "*oida* et *ginōskō*: Les deux modes de la connaissance dans la quatrième évangile," *Bib* 40 (1959) 709-25.

[63] For more detail, see the references in Bultmann, *John*, 56 n. 1.

[64] See J. W. Pryor, "Jesus and Israel in the Fourth Gospel—John 1:11," *NovT* 32 (1990) 201-18.

[65] Related to *ta idia*, in Hellenistic mysticism and Gnosticism *hoi idioi* were "the favoured and elect who have received divine revelation and attained the goal of union with God." See Schnackenburg, *St John*, 1:259-60. The exact opposite is the case with the use of the term in our text.

[66] See BAGD, 464-65. As Theobald puts it: "In-Besitz-Nehmen eines Objekts durch ein Subjekt" (*Fleischwerdung*, 212).

hosoi de **elabon** *auton*	*tois* **pisteusousin** *eis to onoma autou.*
to those **who received him**	to those **who believed in his name.**

The emerging reader was not told in either v. 5 or v. 11 what the correct response to the Word might be, as the response of both the darkness and *hoi idioi* is reported as an attempt to overcome or refuse the light. On both occasions a negative use of a verb having the basic root in *lambanein* was used (v. 5: *ou katelaben;* v. 11: *ou parelabon*). In v. 12 the implied reader finds an answer that raises a further question. In vv. 5 and 11 the reader has been made aware that there is a wrong and a right way of "receiving" the Word through the use of verbs based on *lambanein*. In v. 12 the "receiving" is clarified: to receive (*elabon*) the Word one must believe (*pisteusousin*) in his name.[67]

In whose name must one believe? It must be in the name of the Logos, but as yet the Logos has no name. These questions are related to the "how" of the revelation of the Word. They will not be resolved within the prologue itself. Yet the importance of the how is impressed upon the reader in the narrator's next affirmation. Receiving the Word, believing in his name – whatever that may mean, and whoever the Word in history might be – gave power to become children of God. The narrator reports a past event. Some have already been given that power. The verb (*edōken*) is an aorist. The power given is not a promise, a mere possibility, but an achieved fact in the lives of those who received and believed (see 10:18; 17:2). A Johannine theme has been broached for the first time: realized eschatology. One does not have to wait for the end-time to become a child of God; it can happen already if one receives the Word by believing in his name. But the choice of the aorist infinitive *genesthai* (to become) indicates that Johannine faith and realized eschatology call for a continual commitment. There is a process of growth, through which one becomes a child of God.

In v. 10 *the fact* of the rejection of the world was stated, while in v. 11 the author reported *how* this happened: human arrogance refused to receive the Word. We have seen that v. 12 reports *the fact* that some accept the revelation of the Word. Matching v. 11, but in contrast to it, v. 13 reports *how* this takes place. Whereas in v. 11 the rejection of the Word came from human action and initiative, in v. 13 the reader learns that the believer becomes a child of God through the absolute initiative of God.[68] In the

---

[67] See Schnackenburg, *St John*, 1:261–63.

[68] As already mentioned, I am reading *hoi ouk . . . egennēthēsan* (and not *ho ouk . . . egennēthē*) as an explanation of the divine generation of children of God (see n. 19 above). The parallel between vv. 10-11 (fact of rejection and how it happened) and vv. 12-13 (fact of acceptance

world that produced and first read the Fourth Gospel there were three
possible ways in which one could speak of the production of a newborn
child. There was the purely physiological belief that a woman fell pregnant from the coagulation of the woman's blood as a result of mingling
with the male seed.[69] But children of God are not born "of blood." There
was the frailty of the human flesh, which must express itself sexually and
which consequently produced a child. But children of God are not born
"of the will of the flesh." Finally, and most nobly, there are those situations where human beings act as human beings and decide on the birth
of a child. But children of God are not born "of the will of a human being."[70]
All the possible ways in which childbirth happens have been excluded.
The children of God are not the result of any human initiative. They are
born "of God." The reader learns that the divine filiation results not from
human success but from the gift of God. Affirmations continue to be made
without clarification concerning how these events take place.

Throughout this second section of the prologue, the presence of the
Word *in history* has been announced. The Baptist, a figure within history,
announced and described him (vv. 6-8). The coming of the revelation of
the Word into the world was explicitly stated (v. 9), and the possibility of
the refusal or acceptance of the Word has been announced (vv. 10-13). All
three of these features have already been stated in more speculative terms
in vv. 1-5.[71] The central section of the prologue (vv. 6-14) now closes with
a fourth element which is new: the object of faith is described (v. 14).
Although rightly regarded as the high point of the New Testament's confession of belief in the incarnation of God in the person of Jesus Christ,
in narrative terms it is incorrect to claim that v. 14 is the culmination of
the prologue. The incarnation was already presupposed in vv. 3c-5 and
throughout vv. 6-13. It is explicitly stated in vv. 9-11. The clear statement
of v. 14a is best understood as a synthesis of all that has been said on the
issue so far. As v. 5 closed the first section of the prologue with a reference

---

and how it happens) is a structural reason against the reading of the singular in v. 13, associating
it with v. 14 as a description of the Word.

[69] J. H. Bernard (*A Critical and Exegetical Commentary on the Gospel according to St John* [2 vols.;
ICC; Edinburgh: T. & T. Clark, 1928] 1:18) and others have pointed out that the unusual plural
ouk ex haimatōn is to be understood in the sense of the mixing of the female and the male
"bloods."

[70] I have deliberately repeated the word "but" to catch the adversative *alla* of v. 13d. Note
also the ascending dignity of the human generative process: blood, sexual drive, and human
will. See also Segalla, *Giovanni*, 145-46.

[71] Verses 1-2: the announcement and description of the Word; vv. 3-4: the coming of the
revelation of the Word into the world; v. 5: the response to the Word.

to the conflict between the powers of light and darkness which takes place in the incarnate Word, so also the second section concludes with a similar but even clearer statement for the reader on the incarnation of the Word.

The description of the object of faith in v. 14 is made through five statements. The first of these is the celebrated expression: "And the Word became flesh" (v. 14a). For the first time since vv. 1-2 the expression *ho logos* returns, even though it has been presupposed as the subject throughout. As the Baptist was introduced into the story through the aorist tense of the verb *ginōmai* (see v. 6), so also the historical appearance of the Word is introduced: *kai ho logos sarx egeneto* (v. 14a). In sharp contrast to the use of the imperfect tense of the verb "to be" in v. 1: *ho logos ēn pros ton theon*, the reader is now told that, like the Baptist, the Word "appeared," "happened" on the scene of human events.[72]

There are several uses of the word *sarx* in the Fourth Gospel. What the reader will discover is that the meaning of the expression depends on whether *sarx* refers to the flesh of Jesus or the flesh of others in the story. On six further occasions the "flesh" of Jesus is mentioned, all of them in the eucharistic section of John 6 (see 6:51, 52, 53, 54, 55, 56).[73] This use of the word is closely associated with the revelation of God found in the elevation of the body of Jesus on the cross.[74] Such teaching, which depends on the first reference to the word "flesh" in v. 14a, is yet to come for the reader. For a virginal reader of the Johannine story, *sarx* is read in neither

---

[72] See Schnackenburg, *St John*, 1:266-67.

[73] In other places *sarx* is used to speak of the superficialities of worldly judgment (see 3:6; 6:63; 8:14-15), or simply of humankind (1:13, 17:2). On "flesh" in John, see M. M. Thompson, *The Humanity of Jesus in the Fourth Gospel* (Philadelphia: Fortress Press, 1988) 39-49. J. H. Neyrey (*Ideology,* 142-48 and passim) uses 6:63 as a key text indicating the final stage of the Johannine community's development, following Mary Douglas's location of social units, as "weak group/low grid." At this final stage the community rebels against anything "fleshly," even previously accepted community positions concerning Jesus' death, sacraments, tradition, and leadership. Whatever may have been the diachronic origins of 6:63, such a reading of the passage in its present context (synchrony) appears to me to miss the point entirely. See F. J. Moloney, *The Johannine Son of Man* (2nd ed.; Biblioteca de Scienze Religiose 14; Rome: LAS, 1978) 120-23, although I would nowadays modify my understanding of 6:62. In terms of the final form of the Gospel I disagree with Neyrey's judgment: "The Fourth Gospel *ultimately* put value only in spirit, not flesh, only in being from above, not from below, and only in being not of this world, not in being of this world" (Neyrey, *Ideology,* 209; emphasis mine). Not even in his closing remarks about the limitations of the use of Mary Douglas's schemes in biblical scholarship (pp. 210-12) does he raise the complex issue of the standing of the final utterance (the product of the blending of Neyrey's three stages) which is the Gospel of John.

[74] See Moloney, *Son of Man*, 87-123; idem, "John 6 and the Celebration of the Eucharist," *DRev* 93 (1975) 243-51.

a Pauline nor a gnostic sense. At this stage of the reading experience all
that the implied reader is able to grasp is that the preexistent Word (vv. 1-2),
in becoming flesh, can be the communication and revelation of God in
the human situation, through the enfleshed Logos.[75]

The author's choice of words continues to be significant in the next
statement: "and dwelt among us" (*kai eskēnōsen en hēmin*). The verb used
could mean simply "to dwell" or "to live," and there is certainly a primary
allusion to the dwelling of Wisdom in Israel: "The one who created me
assigned me a place for my tent. And he said 'Make your dwelling
(*kataskēnōson*) in Jacob, and in Israel receive your inheritance'" (Sir 24:8;
see also 24:10: "In the holy tabernacle [*en skēnę̄ hagią*] I ministered to him").[76]
From that same background, Lagrange has suggested (via Judg 8:11) that
the expression has a background in the instability of the life of a nomadic
people.[77] It is also possible that the similar-sounding Hebrew verb *šākan*
may have helped in the choice of the expression. The verb is used of the
dwelling of YHWH in Israel (Exod 25:8; 29:46; Zech 2:14), and a derived
word (*šĕkînâ*) is used in rabbinic Judaism to speak of the resting of the glory
(*kābôd*) of YHWH over the tabernacle (see Exod 24:16; 40:35). If this is the
case, it prepares the reader for the later affirmation: "We have seen his
glory" (v. 14d).

The dwelling of the Word, however, is "among us." The narrator claims
to belong to a community of believers. By bringing the experience of the
Word into the story of a community of believers the author brings the
second section of the prologue, where the incarnate presence of the Word
has been the overarching theme, toward a conclusion. The narrator reports
the experience of a believing community: "and we gazed upon his glory"
(*kai etheasametha tēn doxan autou*). The choice of the aorist tense of the verb
theasthai indicates the experience of a given community of believers who,
during the period in which the Word took up his dwelling (complexive
aorist), gazed upon the glory. It was not just a look or a glance. R. E. Brown,

---

[75] Contrary to Bultmann (*John*, 62–66), who argues that taking on base flesh is the lowest
point in the humiliation of the Logos: "The *offence* of the gospel is brought out as strongly
as possible" (p. 63). See also Barrett, *St John*, 165. Contrary also to E. Käsemann ("Structure
and Purpose of the Prologue to John's Gospel," in *New Testament Questions of Today* [London:
SCM Press, 1969] 156–63; and *The Testament of Jesus according to John 17* [London: SCM Press,
1966] 11–20), for whom Jesus' human appearance was understood by the Fourth Evangelist
as an "epiphany," as the Word changes his place but never really changes himself. For the
position adopted above, see, among the majority of commentators, Schnackenburg, *St John*,
1:268–69; see also Thompson, *Humanity of Jesus*, 33–52.

[76] See Barrett, *St John*, 163–64; Brown, *John*, 33–34; Bultmann, *John*, 67 n. 1.

[77] Lagrange, *Saint Jean*, 20–21.

quoting G. L. Philips approvingly, says of the verb: "It means to look at some dramatic spectacle and in a measure to become a part of it."[78] During the historical existence of the Word, believers saw the *doxa*.

This is the first appearance of another term that will play a large role in the unfolding of the Gospel story. The Old Testament often spoke of the visible manifestation of YHWH to his people in terms of *kābôd*, which was (strangely) rendered in the LXX as *doxa* (see, e.g., Exod 33:22; Deut 5:21; 1 Kgs 8:11; Isa 10:1; Hab 2:14).[79] The implied reader, credited with a good knowledge of Jewish traditions, would have been expected to understand the Old Testament habit of speaking of the visible presence of God as *kābôd/doxa*.[80] The reader is being told that during the earthly appearance of the Word God manifested himself in a visible way. This much could be grasped from the internal argument of the prologue itself. If vv. 1-2 are correct, and the reader must take it to be so on the basis of the reliable witness of the narrator, then v. 14c follows logically from the affirmations of v. 14ab.

The link between v. 14c and vv. 1-2 is immediately made in v. 14d: "glory as of the only Son from the Father" (*doxan hōs monogenous para patros*). In vv. 1-2 a relationship was explained in terms of "the Word" and "God." Now "Son" and "Father" are used, in order better to express a relationship that befits a human story. These are the categories Jesus will use throughout the story to speak of the relationship that exists between himself and God. The glory on which the Christians gaze is only the human appearance of this relationship. Although the preexistent Word (vv. 1-2) has been described as becoming flesh, he has not ceased to be divine. The narrator must use a comparative term "as of" (*hōs*). The glory which the Son had with the Father before all time (see 17:5) is unknown and unknowable to the human situation. But the real author and his community believe that they have gazed upon that glory which God made visible to them in his Son. This is the experience reported by the narrator.

---

[78] Brown, *John*, 502. Brown points out that this may be the case for 1:14, but one should not claim more than that. The insistence of Bultmann (*John*, 66-70) that the "seeing" is not a physical so much as a faith experience needs to be stressed. Many "saw" him, but not all "saw" him in the way described by v. 14d.

[79] See R. H. Strachan, *The Fourth Gospel: Its Significance and Environment* (3rd ed.; London: SCM Press, 1941) 103-6; W. Grossouw, "La glorification du Christ dans le quatrième Evangile," in *L'Evangile de Jean: Etudes et Problèmes* (RechBib 3; Bruges: Desclée de Brouwer, 1958) 131-45.

[80] There is a close link between *kābôd/doxa* and the gift of the law. More will be said of the general background and its link with the Sinai traditions in the following chapter. See below pp. 55-57.

Everything affirmed by the narrator in v. 14abcd could be regarded as a rich summary of a truth already stated somewhere during the prologue: the coming of the Word into the world (especially in vv. 4-5 and 9-11). In v. 14e something new is communicated to the reader. The Word is described as *plērēs charitos kai alētheias*.[81] It is widely accepted that the expression *charis kai alētheias* reflects the description of God's loyalty and faithfulness to the covenant and his covenant community in Exod 34:6 (Hebrew: *ḥesed wĕ'ĕmet*).[82] While there may be an allusion to this background, there is more to it. The Word is described as a fullness. Is there not a danger that we might treat the author as if he were Paul in our traditional translation: "full of grace and truth"? Does *charis* in the Fourth Gospel mean what it meant for Paul? Behind Paul and John stands a Greek word that means, quite simply, an unsolicited gift.[83] The reader, who is not the product of Pauline Christianity, where the notion of *charis* as "grace" could be taken for granted, reads that the Word is the fullness of a gift. What then of the *kai alētheias*? The copulative *kai* need not simply indicate an accumulation of things: gift *and* truth. A second noun, joined to another noun in the same case by *kai* can also be an explanation of the former. This is the epexegetical *kai*, or hendiadys.[84] This use of *kai* is recognized in v. 16.[85] If we are correct in understanding the construction of *plērēs charitos kai alētheias* in this way, we now find that the narrator tells the reader that the Word is "the fullness of a gift which is truth."[86] The emerging implied reader is being drawn further into the act of reading, as gaps in the narrative increase and questions are posed. To what might this gift and this truth refer?[87] The reader will not have long to wait for the beginnings of an answer, as the question is resumed in vv. 16-17.

---

[81] I am linking the indeclinable adjective *plērēs* (only indeclinable when followed by a genitive) with the subject of the sentence *ho logos*, via *autou* and *monogenous*, and not to the closer antecedent *doxan*. See F. J. Moloney, "The Fulness of a Gift which is Truth," *Catholic Theological Review* 1 (1978) 30-33.

[82] See M. D. Hooker, "The Johannine Prologue and the Messianic Secret," *NTS* 21 (1974-75) 52-55; A. T. Hanson, "John 1:14-18 and Exodus XXXIV," *NTS* 23 (1976-77) 90-101; Boismard, *Moïse ou Jésus*, 100-105. See, however, the reservations of Ashton, "Transformation of Wisdom," 183 n. 22.

[83] See LSJ, 1978-79; BAGD, 877-88.

[84] Rightly Bultmann, *John*, 73-74. See ZBG, 155 (§460); BDF, 228 (§442 [9]).

[85] See N. Turner, vol. 3 of J. H. Moulton, *A Grammar of New Testament Greek* (Edinburgh: T. & T. Clark, 1963) 3:335; BDF, 228 (§442 [9]).

[86] For a detailed study of this question, see I. de la Potterie, "*Charis* paulinienne et *charis* johannique," in *Jesus und Paulus: Festschrift für Werner Georg Kümmel zum 70. Geburtstag*, ed. E. E. Ellis and E. Grässer (Göttingen: Vandenhoeck & Ruprecht, 1975) 256-82.

[87] Once again the ambiguity of Johannine language is at hand. The term *alētheia* is widely

The real author creates a poetic narrative introduction to the story of Jesus. An implied author tells an implied reader that the one telling the story and his fellow Christians have gazed upon the visible manifestation of God, the fullness of a gift which is truth. The reader asks the question: How did this happen? The prose narrative of the Gospel which follows attempts to answer this question, but the final section of the prologue (vv. 15-18) both concludes the author's introductory instruction of his reader and leads into the narrative.

III. The Revealer: The Only Son Turned toward the Father (vv. 15-18)

The narrator reintroduces the historical figure of John the Baptist, who bears witness by proclaiming (*kekragen*).[88] The message of vv. 6-8 is recalled as the Baptist insists on the secondary nature of his role, but more important is the positive recalling of the initial description of the Word in vv. 1-2. "Its language is the language of the hymn carried over into the incipient narrative."[89] In terms of the temporal sequence of events that are used to determine the human story, there is one who is coming (the present participle *erchomenos*) after John.[90] But in terms of God's saving story, he existed (*gegonen*, the perfect tense of *ginōmai*) before him. The Baptist himself speaks from his place in time and history to the reader, telling how this is possible: "because he *was* before me" (*hoti prōtos mou ēn*). The repeated use of the imperfect form of the verb "to be" to describe the Word in vv. 1-2 (see also the ongoing use of the verb to refer to the Word in vv. 2-4, 8

---

used in Greek and gnostic religions. For a survey showing the uniqueness of the Johannine use of the term, see de la Potterie, *Verité*, 1:23–36. See also Stemberger, *La symbolique*, 140–45. As so often in the Fourth Gospel, widely used religious terminology is given a specifically Christian content. We have already had occasion to mention this in our brief reflections on *ho logos*, *to phōs*, *hē zōē* and *ta idia*. It will occur again in the prologue with the use of *exēgeomai* in v. 18. As Bultmann rightly comments: "The concepts *zōē*, *phōs*, *doxa* and *alētheia* are the kind of motifs for which the reader brings with him a certain prior understanding; but he still has to learn how to understand them authentically" (*John*, 13).

[88] The perfect tense of the verb *krazō* is used here. The present tense is rare and is replaced by the perfect. See BDF, 52 (§101).

[89] Kermode, "John," 447.

[90] In itself "the coming one" (*ho erchomenos*) can be a messianic title in the New Testament, but this does not appear to be the case here. For an analysis of the material and some criteria for establishing a messianic use of the term, see E. Arens, *The ELTHON Sayings in the Synoptic Tradition: A Historico-Critical Investigation* (OBO 10; Freiburg: Universitätsverlag; Göttingen: Vandenhoeck & Ruprecht, 1976) 288–300.

[negatively], 9, and 10) is deliberately recalled. The final section opens with the explicit witnessing of a man in history who points beyond history to describe the coming of the preexistent Word among men and women.

It is taken for granted that the reader understands that the Word has come into the world (vv. 3-4; v. 9). The narrator thus immediately claims that a gift has been given and it has met a response. Looking back to the "fullness of a gift which is truth" in v. 14e, the narrator reflects the context of a believing Christian community (recalling v. 12, the positive use of the verb *lambanein* reappears [see also vv. 5 and 11, where it is used negatively]) to claim: "And from his fullness we have all received" (v. 16).[91] The response of the believing community has been to accept the gift offered.

The Gnostics, especially Valentinian Gnosticism, also spoke of a "fullness" (*plērōma*) in their hierarchies.[92] However, as with the use of the expression *ta idia* (v. 11), we find that the narrator uses words that would be familiar to a wider readership, but changes their application. The "fullness" of the Word is a gift given to the believer. It is something "received" by the believer. In the later gnostic systems it was that distant and lost reality for which the soul yearned. The author is telling the old story in a new way. There is an emerging implied reader with whom the Johannine community, the intended readers, might identify, as they struggle to live and preach their faith in Jesus Christ in a new world after their exclusion from the old and familiar ways of Judaism.

Scholars have been puzzled by the preposition *anti* used in the description of the fullness received by the community of believers: *charis anti charitos*.[93] Taking it for granted that *charis* is to be understood as "grace," the normal sense of the preposition *anti* creates difficulties. Its fundamental meaning is "instead of, in place of."[94] But it is difficult to understand how, from the Word's fullness, believers have received a grace instead of, or in place of, a grace. Thus recourse is had to less common uses of the

---

[91] Many fathers, and some modern scholars, have claimed that v. 16 is still direct speech of the Baptist. This possibility is created by the difficult use of *hoti*, which opens the statement. Scribes sensed the difficulty, and some manuscripts have *kai*. In defense of this reading, see Theobald, *Fleischwerdung*, 180–81. The words belong to the narrator, and *hoti* can, although clumsily, be read as "and." See the discussion, coming to this conclusion, in Schnackenburg, *St John*, 1:275–76.

[92] See especially G. Filoramo, *A History of Gnosticism* (Oxford: Blackwell, 1990) 54–72. See also G. Delling, "*plērēs ktl*," *TDNT* 6:300-301; K. Rudolph, *Gnosis: The Nature and History of an Ancient Religion* (Edinburgh: T. & T. Clark, 1983) 320–22.

[93] For a summary of the discussion, see Brown, *John*, 15–16; and especially R. B. Edwards, "*Charin anti charitos* (John 1.16): Grace and Law in the Johannine Prologue," *JSNT* 32 (1988) 3-6.

[94] BAGD, 73, s.v. *anti*, para. 1. See also LSJ, 153, s.v. *anti*, para. A, I.

preposition, giving it the sense of "upon."[95] This problem disappears if we allow the expression *charis* to have the meaning that I read in v. 14e: an unsolicited gift.[96] The narrator tells the reader that an unsolicited gift has been given and that there has been a response to that gift in a believing community. The description of the gift that has taken the place of a former gift will provide the reader with the culminating revelation of the prologue: a final description of the gift that will lead directly into the story of Jesus Christ (vv. 17-18). The narrator has already described the nature of the gift at the conclusion of his second section in v. 14e. He now enters into a final description of the free gift. As v. 16 closed, the narrator told the reader that from the Word's fullness the believing community received a gift that replaced a gift. The two gifts are now described.

"For the Law was given through Moses" (v. 17a). There can be no lessening of the importance of the former gift. It was from God and it was fundamental for the people of God. Moses was its mediator; however, it was the former gift.[97] There is now another gift which has taken its place (v. 16). The narrator does not speak of "grace and truth," but of *hē charis kai hē alētheia*. Two nouns in the same case are joined by *kai*. Consistent with his use of *charis* in vv. 14 and 16, and again using the *kai* epexegetically, the narrator tells of the gift which is the truth. The Law of Moses was given in the past, but now there is the gift of the truth. This gift is an event that has *happened*. The narrator uses the aorist tense of the verb *ginomai* (*egeneto*) to point to a given historical moment in the past, when the gift of the truth took place *dia Iēsou Christou*. The naming of the Logos as Jesus Christ is a climactic moment for the reader of the prologue. The Word is identified with Jesus Christ. Once the Word has been described as taking flesh (v. 14a) and has been described as "the only begotten Son of the Father" (v. 14d), the narrator proceeds to give a name to a human being: Jesus Christ.

The emerging reader is now ready to read a life story; however, the

---

[95] BAGD, 73, s.v. *anti*, para. 2. Reference is made to Philo (first century A.D.) and Theognis (sixth century B.C.) for examples of such usage. Edwards shows that neither Philo nor Theognis provides a true parallel for this use of *anti* ("Charis anti charitos," 5-6).

[96] In her excellent article, Edwards continues to translate *charis* as "grace" ("Charin anti charitos"). On p. 7 she insists that we must read John in terms of John, and not through Pauline spectacles. On pp. 7-10 she defends the correct understanding of *anti* but continues to use classical Christian terms to speak of grace and law, rather than allowing the word its basic meaning: an unsolicited gift.

[97] O. Hofius argues, via Prov 8:30 and *Aboth Rabbi Nathan* 31, that v. 18 claims that Jesus is God, one with the Father from all time ("'Der in des Vaters Schoss ist' Joh 1,18," ZNW 80 [1989] 163-71). Verses 17-18 polemically deny both saving value and preexistence to the Law (see pp. 169-71).

reader begins reading the life story armed with the knowledge that all that has been said of the Word can now be said of Jesus Christ. The implied reader has also been informed that the gift of God to Israel through Moses has been replaced by the fullness of the gift of the truth, which has taken place through Jesus Christ. How can this be? How can God surpass the gift of Moses through the gift of the truth which takes place through Jesus Christ?[98] The reader will need to work through the narrative to discover answers to the questions of how that were raised by the prologue. It is one thing to affirm that the Logos is Jesus the Messiah, but how did Jesus live out his messianic role?

The conclusion to the prologue (v. 18) both continues the final description of the gift of the Word in Jesus Christ and introduces the reader to the narrative of the Gospel that follows.[99] It opens with a strong negative affirmation: "No one has ever seen God." It was commonly believed, in certain forms of Jewish piety, that the great saints of Israel (Abraham, Moses, Enoch, Isaiah) had ascended to God to receive knowledge of him. On the basis of that ascension to heaven, and the sight of the heavenly things which they had while there, they were able to reveal what they had seen.[100] The narrator disabuses the reader of any such speculation with vigor. Two emphatic expressions are used, the negative pronoun *oudeis* and the adverb *pōpote* to make it clear to the reader that *no one* has *ever* seen God (v. 18a).[101]

Shifting into a more positive approach, the narrator again uses an emphatic pronoun (*ekeinos*) to claim that there is only one who has made God known (v. 18c). The only Son, described as *ho ōn eis ton kolpon tou patros*, has made the invisible known.[102] The author indicates to the reader

[98] The reader knows of Jesus Christ but has no knowledge of the Johannine version of his story.

[99] On the role of 1:18 as a bridge into the life story of Jesus, see G. R. O'Day, *Revelation in the Fourth Gospel: Narrative Mode and Theological Claim* (Philadelphia: Fortress Press, 1986) 33–35.

[100] For a discussion of the Jewish background to this speculation, with reference to both primary and secondary literature, see Moloney, *Son of Man*, 54–55. See also Carter, "Prologue and John's Gospel," 43–48.

[101] Well caught by the translation of Delebecque, *Saint Jean*, 63: "Dieu, personne n'a eu vue de lui, jamais."

[102] There are good witnesses that read "the only God" instead of "the only Son." For a discussion of this, see Brown, *John*, 17. For defense of the reading *monogenēs theos*, on theological as well as textual grounds, see B. A. Mastin, "A Neglected Feature of the Christology of the Fourth Gospel," *NTS* 22 (1975-76) 32–51; D. A. Fennema, "John 1.18: 'God the only Son,'" *NTS* 31 (1985) 124–35. See B. M. Metzger, *A Textual Commentary on the Greek New Testament* (London/New York: United Bible Society, 1971) 198. The reasons given in the added note on that page by A. Wikgren stand behind my decision to read "the only Son."

that the Son is able to make God known because he is *eis ton kolpon tou patros.* Many scholars rightly see a link between this expression and the *pros ton theon* of v. 1 and subsequently translate it as "in the bosom of the Father." They conclude that this refers to Jesus Christ's return to the Father.[103] This interpretation argues that the prologue begins and ends out of time, in the eternity of the union between the Father and the Son (vv. 1-2 and v. 18).[104] Some have suggested that the use of the present participle *ho ōn* allows the author to speak of Jesus' presence with the Father both in heaven and on earth.[105]

The Greek word traditionally translated by "bosom" (*kolpos*) does not indicate a place of indwelling. It means "chest," the external part of the upper body, in both a man and a woman (see John 13:23).[106] The author concludes the prologue to his Gospel, celebrating the incarnation of the Word, by fixing the reader's attention on the role and person of the only begotten Son, Jesus Christ, in his historical existence.[107] There is certainly a return to the idea of a dynamic relationship which exists between the Word and God (v. 1). The dynamism of the relationship is expressed by means of the preposition *eis*, which captures the same idea of a motion toward the Father as *pros* in v. 1.[108] The narrator, however, is not telling the reader of the life of the Son *in* the Father outside of time. Jesus Christ, the only begotten Son, during the whole of his historical existence, was turned toward the bosom of the Father.

The use of the present participle (*ho ōn*) makes the durative aspect of this oneness clear. As the union of the Word and God was described outside time in v. 1, the same union is further described in v. 18. But we are

---

[103] See, e.g., Neyrey, *Ideology,* 101: "1:18 subsequently locates Jesus back in God's bosom, his true home from which he descended (see 1:1-2)."

[104] Most recently, Hofius, "'Der in des Vaters Schoss ist,'" 163-71.

[105] See Strachan, *Fourth Gospel,* 108-9. R. E. Brown translates the expression: "Ever at the Father's side" (*John,* 17).

[106] For further references, see Hofius, "'Der in des Vaters Schoss ist,'" 165 n. 12.

[107] See already F. J. Moloney, "'In the Bosom of' or 'Turned towards' the Father?" *AusBR* 31 (1983) 63-71. For a more comprehensive study, largely followed here, see de la Potterie, *Verité,* 1:228-39; see also, Theobald, *Fleischwerdung,* 260-62.

[108] The classical distinctions between prepositions of motion (e.g., *pros* and *eis*) and place (e.g., *para* and *en*) had been largely lost in Koine Greek. See BDF, 110-11 (§ 205 on *eis* and *en*), 124-25 (§239 on *pros*). See also Bultmann, *John,* 32 n. 3. But one must allow each author to use the prepositions in his own way. For a comprehensive study of the Johannine use of these prepositions in a dynamic sense, see I. de la Potterie, "L'emploi dynamique de *eis* dans Saint Jean et ses incidences théologiques," *Bib* 43 (1962) 366-87. The article is devoted to *eis* with the accusative, but also considers the use of *pros* with the accusative (pp. 379-87). De la Potterie has recently been supported by R. Robert, "'Celui qui est de retour dans le sein du Père' (Jean 1, 18)," *RevThom* 85 (1985) 457-63.

now at the end of the prologue. Jesus Christ is the only begotten Son of the Father. He makes the Father known to the world through the life he lives in unfailing openness and obedience to him. The narrator tells of an enduring relationship which is not, however, an indwelling. Jesus could be seen on earth through the life which he lived; the Father is not available in the same way. The reader is informed of the oneness between the Father and the Son which highlights the Johannine life story of Jesus. Throughout his life in history, Jesus Christ looks constantly to the Father (see especially 4:34; 5:17-30; 10:30; 17:4). Thus v. 18 describes the enduring intimacy of the union between the Father and the historical Jesus.

The choice of the expression *exēgēsato* (aorist of the verb *exēgeomai*) once again shows the real author's desire to speak to the intended readers, via the implied reader, in a language suited to the world in which they lived their Christianity. Although the verb is found in the Lukan corpus (Luke 24:35; Acts 10:8; 15:12, 14; 21:19), it is widely found in the literature of the Hellenistic religions.[109] The basic meaning of the word is "to tell at length, to relate in full,"[110] "to recount a narrative."[111] In Hellenistic literature it is often associated with the making known of divine secrets, and it is often the gods themselves who do this.

The use of the verb *exēgeomai* without an object as the very last word of the prologue has created considerable difficulty.[112] The last word used by the narrator in the poetic prologue to the prose narrative tells the reader that the Word become flesh (v. 14a), the only Son of the Father (v. 14d), Jesus Christ, the fullness of the gift which is the truth (v. 17) has told the story of God (v. 18). Although syntactically difficult, the verb comes at the end of the sentence and thus at the end of the prologue. It leads the reader directly into the prose narrative of the life of Jesus through the *kai* that opens v. 19. The object of the verb ("him," referring back to "God") must be supplied by the reader from the context.

---

[109] See the indications in BAGD, 275. For a comprehensive review of its usage in Greek religions, see de la Potterie, *Verité,* 1:214–26.

[110] LSJ, 593, s.v. *exēgeomai,* para. III.

[111] Barrett, *St John,* 170.

[112] The difficulties are keenly felt in the translation offered by Delebecque (*Saint Jean,* 63): "Un Dieu, Fils unique, Celui qui est, vers le sein du Père, il explica." For a complete discussion of the possible interpretations, see I. de la Potterie, "'C'est lui qui a ouvert la voie'. La finale du prologue johannique," *Bib* 69 (1988) 345–58. De la Potterie concludes that, used without an object, the verb must mean "être le chef," "aller en tête." In response to de la Potterie's desire to eliminate the meaning of "telling the story" or "making known," because of the lack of an object, see R. Robert, "Le mot final du prologue johannique: A propos d'un article récent," *RevThom* 89 (1989) 279–88.

Jesus Christ is the gift in whom the truth has taken place because he makes God known through his life story.[113] The invisible God can now be seen in the story of Jesus Christ. In his conclusion to the prologue and transition into the narrative of the life story of Jesus (v. 18) the narrator tells the reader that (1) no one in the human story has ever seen God (see also 5:37; 6:46; 1 John 4:12-20); (2) the only Son is turned toward the Father in love and obedience throughout the whole of his *historical* presence among women and men (see especially 4:34 and 17:4); and (3) he has told God's story in the *historical* events of his life and death.[114]

The reader next encounters the word *kai* (v. 19) and is led by the author into a reading of the narrative that will tell of those historical events. The narrative must make sense of the prologue, as the prologue has been written to make sense of the narrative.[115]

CONCLUSION

The reader now begins to read a narrative, closely linked to the prologue through the conjunctive *kai*, informed that the Word exists from all time, turned in loving union toward God (vv. 1-2), announced and described in history by the reliable testimony of John the Baptist (vv. 6-8, 15). The Word comes into the world (vv. 3-4, 9), a gift from God that can either be accepted or refused (vv. 5, 10-13, 16). This gift is the fullness of God's gracious gifts, surpassing even the great gift of the Law through Moses: the fullness of the gift which is the truth, Jesus Christ (vv. 14, 17). The life story of Jesus Christ has made God known (v. 18).

While preexistence and the Messiah as the glory of God are exalted

[113] In 1977 I. de la Potterie argued strongly for an interpretation of *exēgēsetai* which points to Jesus as the unique revelation of God (*Vérité,* 1:226-28). He rightly saw this as an explanation of the *alētheia* which comes through Jesus Christ in v. 17. He thus paraphrased v. 18c as "il fut, lui, la révélation" (p. 228). However, he has most recently responded to R. Robert ("La double intention du mot final du prologue johannique," *RevThom* 87 [1987] 435-41) by suggesting a quite different interpretation. See de la Potterie, "'C'est lui qui a ouvert la voie,'" 340-70. He claims that, parallel to 14:6 and in close internal contact with v. 14 it means "Celui qui a ouvert la voie."

[114] I. de la Potterie states: "On ne peut pas 'narrer' ou 'raconter' Dieu, comme on raconte une belle histoire" ("'C'est lui qui a ouvert la voie,'" 347). Put this way, such an affirmation trivializes the possibility that, for the Fourth Evangelist, the life story of Jesus Christ is the story of God's presence in history (see, e.g., 1:14; 3:34; 5:17; 6:45-46; 8:39-47; 10:30; 14:18-24, 31; 17:4). The story of Jesus tells the story of God.

[115] Rightly C. K. Barrett, "The Prologue of St John's Gospel," in *New Testament Essays* (London: SPCK, 1972) 48.

claims, they are not foreign to the reader, who is credited with a knowledge of Jewish thought. But the reader is being further shaped through the information that the Messiah is Jesus. Can this be true? Is the author being honest with the reader? Is the witness of the author, through the words of the narrator, reliable? Answers to those questions can be found only through a narrative telling of facts that match the theory: a life story of Jesus which shows that he does reveal the glory of God.

The reader is part of the drama of the narrative that is about to begin. The implied reader cannot be indifferent, reading on into the life story of Jesus Christ in the light of the prologue. They may or may not match. That remains to be seen. To be given information – however beautifully and profoundly that communication takes place – is not the end of the questioning. The author has shaped a reader who has been informed that the Word became flesh in the person of Jesus who is the Christ. The reader who emerges at the end of the prologue is aware that the theology of the Word has become the theology of Jesus Christ. What has been claimed for the Word in the statement and restatement of the same themes in vv. 1-5 and vv. 6-14 has now been unequivocally identified with Jesus Christ in the final and further statement of those same themes in vv. 15-18. The reader must ask: How can this be in a human story? How can the preexistent Word be the Christ in the life story of the man called Jesus?[116]

The prologue to the Fourth Gospel begins the shaping of the reader. The author acts as teacher, but the truthfulness and even usefulness of all that has been taught is yet to be tested. The author has created an implied reader with exalted notions about Jesus Christ which are to be tested by the story of his life. The implied reader now begins to read a narrative designed to draw the reader more deeply into the privileged experience of a community of believers which the implied author claims to represent: "We have gazed upon his glory. . . . From his fullness we have all received" (vv. 14 and 16).

---

[116] See also O'Day, *Revelation in the Fourth Gospel,* 35. Against J. L. Staley, who argues for an unreliable relationship between a narrator who has told the reader everything in the prologue but keeps undermining that knowledge (*The Print's First Kiss: A Rhetorical Investigation of the Implied Reader in the Fourth Gospel* (SBLDS 82; Atlanta: Scholars Press, 1988) 50 and passim.

Chapter Three

The First Days of Jesus
John 1:19-51

¶ THE READER has been introduced to the prose narrative of the Fourth Gospel by means of a poetic narrative. Despite its largely poetic form, the prologue is a *story* of the Word who became flesh: Jesus Christ. This poetic narrative introduction stands on its own in terms of its form, its content, and its shape. The opening section of the prose narrative (1:19-51) will also be marked by indications of the real author's careful shaping of the material.[1]

THE SHAPE OF THE NARRATIVE

The passage is marked by a series of days, indicated by the narrator: "the next day" (v. 29: *tē epaurion*), "the next day again" (v. 35: *tē epaurion palin*), "the next day" (v. 43: *tē epaurion*). John 1:19-51 tells a story about a succession of events that took place over a period of four days:

---

[1] The present text had a prehistory. For a survey of three hundred years of scholarly approaches to the historical question, see H.-J. Kuhn, *Christologie und Wunder: Untersuchungen zu Joh 1,35-51* (BU 18; Regensburg: Pustet, 1988) 3-68; L. Schenke, "Die literarische Entstehungsgeschichte von Joh 1,19-51," *BN* 46 (1989) 24-57; J. Becker, *Das Evangelium des Johannes* (2 vols.; ÖTK 4/1-2; Gütersloh: Gerd Mohn; Würzburg: Echter-Verlag, 1979) 1:87-105.

(a) *Verses 19-28: Day One.* The witness of the Baptist, who points away from himself as the expected Messiah or messianic precursor toward another standing among them, whom they do not know.

(b) *Verses 29-34: Day Two.* The Baptist, enlightened by the events of Jesus' baptism, witnesses to Jesus as the Lamb of God, the one who baptizes with the Holy Spirit, the Son of God.

(c) *Verses 35-42: Day Three.* Some disciples of the Baptist "follow" Jesus, a rabbi, the Messiah whom *they have found.* Simon, led to Jesus, is told that he will become "Cephas."

(d) *Verses 43-51: Day Four.* Jesus takes the initiative. He calls Philip. Summoned by Philip, a doubting Nathanael is led to the expected Messiah whom *they have found.* Nathanael's confession leads to a promise from Jesus.

This steady progression of days features both "story time" and "plotted time."[2] "Story time" systematically reports events in their correct temporal sequence as the story unfolds. In 1:19-51 the story time is the succession of events over four successive days. "Plotted time" breaks into the logic of the temporal sequence and points the reader either backward (analepsis) or forward (prolepsis) to some past or future moment relevant to the story but which does not form part of the regular succession of events being reported. The temporal axis will lead the reader toward an initial climax to his reading experience. In addition to the "days" outlined above, the first words of the next scene, the wedding at Cana, are marked by a reference to a "day": "On the third day there was a marriage at Cana in Galilee" (2:1).[3]

---

[2] The basic study of this is G. Genette, *Narrative Discourse: An Essay in Method* (Ithaca, N.Y.: Cornell University Press, 1980) 33–85; see further idem, *Nouveau discours du récit* (Collection Poétique; Paris: Seuil, 1983) 15–27. See also S. Rimmon-Kenan, *Narrative Fiction: Contemporary Poetics* (New Accents; London: Methuen, 1983) 43–58; R. A. Culpepper, *Anatomy of the Fourth Gospel: A Study in Literary Design* (Philadelphia: Fortress Press, 1983) 63–70; and A. Reinhartz, "Jesus as Prophet: Predictive Prolepses in the Fourth Gospel," *JSNT* 36 (1989) 3–16.

[3] This series of "days" has often been noticed by scholars. See, e.g., F. Hahn, "Die Jüngerberufung John 1,35-51," in *Neues Testament und Kirche: Für Rudolf Schnackenburg,* ed. J. Gnilka (Freiburg: Herder, 1974) 172–73. B. Olsson works on the basis of six days (*Structure and Meaning in the Fourth Gospel: A Text-Linguistic Analysis of John 2:1-11 and 4:1-42* [Coniectanea Biblica, NT Series 6; Lund: Gleerup, 1974] 102–4, 276). M.-E. Boismard sees it as a week which begins the ministry of Jesus (*Du baptême à Cana (1,19-2,11)* [LD 18; Paris: Cerf, 1956] 14–15). T. Barosse ("The Seven Days of the New Creation in St. John's Gospel," *CBQ* 23 [1959] 507-16), following Boismard, sees here a theology of a new creation in the church. A. Geyser sees it as a week dedicated to anti-Baptist teaching ("The Semeion at Cana of the Galilee," in *Studies in John: Presented to Professor Dr. J. N. Sevenster on the Occasion of His Seventieth Birthday* [NovTSup 24; Leiden: E. J. Brill, 1970] 15–17). For a survey, see A. M. Serra, *Contributi*

Many have seen these days as forming an initial week,[4] but the events at Cana took place "on the third day" (2:1: *tȩ hȩmerą tȩ tritȩ*). This forms our starting point, as the same expression can be found twice in Exod 19:10-19. YHWH instructs Moses on the preparation of the people for the gift of the Law as "on the third day (LXX: *tȩ hēmerą tȩ tritȩ*) the Lord will come down upon Mount Sinai in the sight of the people" (v. 11). The narrator later reports: "On the third day (LXX: *tȩ hēmerą tȩ tritȩ*) there were thunders and lightning . . ." (v. 16). This is the dramatic setting for the gift of the Law, which follows immediately in the narrative of the book of Exodus (Exod 20:1-17).

The Glory of God

According to the tradition of Israel, in the gift of the Law YHWH manifested his glory (Hebrew *kābôd*; LXX Greek *doxa*) among his people.[5] As the reader receives no instructions on this background, he is credited by the author with knowledge of the Jewish notion of the gift of the Law, the "glory of YHWH" on the third day.[6]

At the heart of the description of the phenomena that mark the setting for the gift of the Law as it is found in the Exodus narrative, *kābôd* appears (19:16: "and behold the glory [*kābēd*] was on the mountain"[7]). When the LXX translators rendered *kābēd* as "a thick cloud," they may have been giving the expression one of its early derived meanings, coming from the original

---

dell'antica letteratura giudaica per l'esegesi di Gv. 2:1-12 e 19:25-27 (Scripta Pontificiae Facultatis 'Marianum' 31; Rome: Herder, 1977) 29–44. Against the use of "days," see, e.g., X. Léon-Dufour, *Lecture de l'évangile selon Jean* (Parole de Dieu; Paris: Seuil, 1988) 150–51 n. 1; B. Lindars and P. Borgen, "The Place of the Old Testament in the Formation of New Testament Theology: Prolegomena and Response," *NTS* 23 (1976–77) 64–65; R. Schnackenburg, *The Gospel according to St John* (3 vols.; HTCNT 4/1–3; London: Burns & Oates; New York: Crossroad, 1968–82) 297, 308, 313.

[4] As well as a doubtful basis in the text (Boismard adds a further day by reading *prō* rather than *prōton* in v. 41 to produce seven days), I am troubled by the use of the creation background here. The main issue appears to be the revelation of God in Jesus and the response of the disciples (and the reader). For a more recent insistence on the theme of creation, see L. P. Trudinger, "The Seven Days of the New Creation in St. John's Gospel: Some Further Reflections," *EvQu* 44 (1972) 154–58.

[5] See G. von Rad and G. Kittel, "*dokeō ktl.*," *TDNT* 2:232–55.

[6] The implied reader's knowledge of the story depends entirely on the medium which expresses that story, the linguistic signifiers. When they are not explained to the reader, then he understands those signifiers. Such must be the case for *doxa*.

[7] This is a literal translation of the Hebrew *wĕ'ānān kābēd 'al-hāhār*. The LXX translates *kābēd* as "a thick cloud," as do most English translations.

sense of "to be heavy, to weigh down," but as G. von Rad has claimed, even this early shift of meaning into "cloud" is a reference to the presence of God.[8] The use of "glory" in Exod 19:16 speaks of the physical, visible presence of YHWH among his chosen people. When Deuteronomy makes reference to Sinai, *kābôd* is again applied to this moment. This reflects the awareness in Israel of the central importance of the event of Sinai as a revelation of "the glory of YHWH": "Behold the Lord our God has shown his glory (*kĕbōdô*) and greatness, and we have heard his voice out of the midst of the fire" (Deut 5:24).

"The glory of YHWH" was tangible proof of a covenant relationship between a God who manifested himself and a people who experienced this manifestation. In Exodus it is used to describe YHWH's saving power against the might of Pharaoh (see 14:4, 17, 18) and it is used to speak of his gift of the manna (16:7). Above all, it is used to speak of the numinous vision of YHWH's presence among his people (see 16:10; 24:16, 17; 33:18, 22; 40:34-35). It is also used to speak of the visible presence of their covenant God in the makeshift sanctuary of the tent and the altar (see 29:43).

We are dealing here with a term that plays a significant role in the narrative of the foundational experience of the exodus. The use of the expression is not limited to the exodus. It is found in critical times and places throughout the whole of the Old Testament to describe the saving presence of YHWH to his people. The various traditions use the expression in different ways, but always within contexts that speak of a God that the people experience.[9] It is never a *notion* about a saving God, but the *experience* of that God. The expression is used to speak of a presence that can be seen, heard, felt, and experienced by the people themselves, or by individuals.[10] The rabbis continued the same tradition, using the word *šĕkînâ* to express (and to extend) the same concept. It is especially among the rabbis that the Book of the Law becomes the *šĕkînâ*, and the experience at Sinai becomes the moment par excellence where Israel experienced the *šĕkînâ*.[11]

The expression *kābôd* appears in the Hebrew Bible's account of Sinai only at 19:16. The targums rewrite the text of Exodus 19 with a strong concentration on the gift of the Law on Sinai as the presence of the "glory

---

[8] G. von Rad, *TDNT* 2:239.

[9] Ibid., 2:238-42.

[10] Ibid., 2:240.

[11] See G. Kittel, *TDNT* 2:246. See also G. Dalman, *The Words of Jesus* (Edinburgh: T. & T. Clark, 1902) 229-31; Olsson, *Structure and Meaning*, 70-73.

of YHWH." The technical expression (Aramaic *yiqrā'*) is found in the *Pseudo-Jonathan Targum* on Exod 19:9, 11, 15, 20. It appears in the *Neophiti Targum* on Exod 19:11, 17, 18, 20.[12] This is an indication of the increasing tendency within Judaism to look back to the events of Sinai as decisive in the revelation of "the glory of YHWH."[13]

The Glory of God in John 1:19–2:12

The expression *doxa* played an important role in the theological synthesis of the prologue (1:14), now known to the reader. Already in the prologue the author told the reader of a link that exists between the sight of the revelation of God in Jesus (1:14) and the former gift of God to Moses at Sinai. The fullness of the gift has come through Jesus Christ (1:17). This link is reinforced in the narrative of the first days of Jesus (1:19–2:12). They lead to a further appearance of the expression. *Doxa* reappears in a comment that the narrator makes to the reader: "This, the first of his signs, Jesus did at Cana in Galilee, and manifested his glory (*tēn doxan autou*); and his disciples believed in him" (2:11). The glory of God, which manifested itself at Sinai in the story of Israel has been seen again in this, the first of the signs in the story of Jesus. The Christology of the prologue is now being acted out in the story of Jesus.

But what of the days of 1:19-51? "The third day" of 2:1 may be a hint of a link with Sinai, but there is a deliberate use of a series of days in 1:19-51 which lead to the manifestation of the glory of Jesus in 2:1-12. Once again, an understanding of the Jewish background to the gift of the Law at Sinai, which the author presupposes of the reader, provides guidance. The preparation for the celebration of the gift of the Law became a formal part of Jewish liturgical life. We have, both in the targums[14] and in the rabbinic literature,[15] especially as evidenced in the *Mekilta on Exodus*,[16] explicit directions to Jews for their preparation for the feast of the gift of the Law

---

[12] For a comparative study of the targums on Exod 19:1-20, see J. Potin, *La fête juive de la Pentecôte* (LD 65; Paris: Cerf, 1971) 1:46-70. For the texts themselves, see 2:7-32. For an Italian translation of the text, see A. M. Serra, "Le tradizioni della teofania sinaitica nel Targum dello Pseudo Jonathan Es. 19.24 e in Giov. 1,19-2,12," *Marianum* 33 (1971) 4-5. The same tendency is found in the targum on Exod 24:12, 13, 15, 16, 17; see Serra, "Tradizioni," 6-7.

[13] Potin calls it "la grande formule liturgique" (*La fête juive*, 66). For the texts and further discussion, see Olsson, *Structure and Meaning*, 70-71; and Serra, "Tradizioni," 1-39.

[14] See Potin, *La fête juive*, 1:314-17; see also Serra, *Contributi dell'antica letteratura giudaica*, 64-75.

[15] See Serra, *Contributi dell'antica letteratura giudaica*, 75-86.

[16] Ibid., 75-77.

(Pentecost). Lengthening the instructions found in the book of Exodus, we now find that there are several days during which the people had to make a more remote preparation for the feast.

The tradition behind John 1:19–2:12 appears to be that preserved in the *Mekilta*.[17] There, enlarging on the data of the biblical text, the commentaries on Exod 19:1-2, 3-8, and 9-10 indicate that there had to be three more general days of preparation, culminating in a fourth day. The fourth day began the final three days, which are based on the original directions of YHWH to Moses.[18] The fourth day of the more general preparations was based on the instructions of Exod 19:10-11 ("Go unto the people and sanctify them today . . . and let them wash their garments . . . and be ready against the third day"). It began the immediate preparation, explicitly described in the *Mekilta*: "This was the fourth day of the week."[19] The instructions culminate in the words from Exodus, "And be ready against the third day." The "third day" of Exodus 19 is interpreted in the *Mekilta*: "That was the sixth day of the week on which the Torah was given" (*Mekilta* 19:10).[20]

Like the Fourth Gospel, the *Mekilta* knows of six days: three days of general preparation, culminating in a fourth day. Day four was the first of the three days which came to Jewish liturgical tradition from Exodus 19. Then, "on the third day" (the sixth day overall, according to the *Mekilta*), the gift of the Law was celebrated. John 1:19–2:12 is a narrative through which the reader is introduced to the life story of Jesus. Three days (1:19-28, 29-34, 25-42) are devoted to the witnessing role of the Baptist and the expectations of the first disciples. The reader, who has read the prologue, follows a series of characters ("the Jews," John the Baptist, and disciples

---

[17] See Potin, *La fête juive*, 314–17; and Serra, *Contributi dell'antica letteratura giudaica*, 91–110. The *Mekilta* is tannaitic, one of the earliest of all the midrashim. On this, see J. Lauterbach, ed. and trans., *Mekilta de Rabbi Ishmael* (3 vols.; Philadelphia: Jewish Publication Society of America, 1961) 1:xviii–xxviii. See also E. Schürer, *The History of the Jewish People in the Age of Jesus Christ (175 B.C.–A.D. 135)* (3 vols.; A New English Version Revised and Edited by Geza Vermes, Fergus Millar, and Matthew Black; Edinburgh: T. & T. Clark, 1973-1987) 1:90–91. Both the targums and the rabbis evidence a tendency to lengthen the days of preparation for the feast of Pentecost. They witness a practice that was older and widespread. It is this practice which stands behind John 1:19-2:12. I am not claiming that the author depended directly on any text. He is working from a well-attested way of preparing for the feast of Pentecost presumed to be familiar to the reader.

[18] For an unpointed Hebrew text and an English translation, see Lauterbach, *Mekilta de Rabbi Ishmael*, 2:192–220.

[19] Ibid., 2:210. For the instructions concerning the days of immediate preparation, see pp. 210–12.

[20] Ibid., 2:212.

of the Baptist), who have not. There is an interplay of the reader and the characters in these days of preparation. Only on the fourth day (vv. 43-51) does Jesus take the initiative: he calls Philip (v. 43) and reveals himself through the promise of the Son of Man (v. 51).

The Role of John 2:1-12 in the First Days

Does this background to the days which lead the reader into the life of Jesus mean that 2:1-12 belongs to 1:19-51 as a narrative unit?[21] We have established that the first days of Jesus lead into the revelation of the glory "on the third day" in 2:1-12. The author tells the reader that the *doxa* once revealed at Sinai is now found in Jesus' miraculous activity. But in 4:43-54 the author will tell of another miracle which takes place at Cana. The author leads the reader through a journey from Cana to Cana during which a series of encounters with Jesus will be reported (2:1–4:54).[22]

How can the Cana miracle of 2:1-12 belong to the first days of Jesus (1:19–2:12) and also to a story of a "journey" from Cana (2:1-12) to Cana (4:46-54)? This is the first example of the real author's use of bridge scenes.[23] Divisions between literary units are not impenetrable brick walls. The first Cana miracle (2:1-12) belongs both to what goes before (1:19-51) and to what follows (2:13–4:54). The first days of Jesus (1:19-51) cannot be fully understood without the revelation of the glory (2:11). The reader, who has read through the prologue, learned in 1:17 that: "The Law was given through Moses; the gift of the truth took place through Jesus Christ." The surpassing of the former gift of the Law to Moses, which looked back to Sinai for its sense, is now being acted out in the life story of Jesus. Against a background of days which prepare for the gift of the glory "on the third day," Jesus will manifest his glory, and disciples will begin their journey of faith (2:11).[24]

---

[21] Thus, e.g., R. H. Lightfoot, *St John's Gospel*, ed. C. F. Evans (Oxford: Oxford University Press, 1956) 90-105; B. Lindars, *The Gospel of John* (NCB; London: Oliphants, 1972) 76-133; J. Painter, "Quest and Rejection Stories in John," *JSNT* 36 (1989) 20-23. Léon-Dufour, *Lecture*, 150-52. See the discussion in Schnackenburg, *St John*, 1:283-84.

[22] See F. J. Moloney, "From Cana to Cana (John 2:1–4:54) and the Fourth Evangelist's Concept of Correct (and Incorrect) Faith," in *Studia Biblica 1978 II: Papers on the Gospels: Sixth International Congress on Biblical Studies, Oxford 3-7 April 1978*, ed. E. A. Livingstone (JSNTSup 2; Sheffield: JSOT Press, 1980) 185-213.

[23] For a summary of this phenomenon in the Johannine narrative structure, see G. Mlakuzhyil, *The Christocentric Literary Structure of the Fourth Gospel* (AnBib 117; Rome: Biblical Institute Press, 1987) 104-6.

[24] For the first time in the narrative, the implied reader finds that "his disciples believed

Yet it is also true that the reader arrives at 1:51, having shared in the story of a variety of responses to Jesus, asking questions. The episode of the marriage at Cana (2:1-12) does not simply conclude the narrative of the first days of Jesus.[25] It does that, but it does more. It acts as a bridge between the first days, which it completes (1:19–2:12), and the journey from Cana to Cana (2:1–4:54), which it begins, and where some of the questions raised by 1:19-51 are answered.

READING THE NARRATIVE

Day One: 1:19-28

The first day opens with an indication of the characters in the story: John the Baptist and emissaries of "the Jews" from Jerusalem (v. 19). The reader has already been introduced to John the Baptist in the prologue (1:6-8, 15). He knows that the Baptist is a reliable witness, sent by God (1:6-8). "The Jews" enter the narrative for the first time. Their role is yet to be discovered.[26] The close link between this first reference to the Baptist in the prose narrative and his appearance in the poetic narrative of the prologue establishes the role he will play in these first days.[27] In 1:6-8 the narrator told the reader that John was sent from God to bear witness to the true light so that all might believe. He himself was not the light. The teaching of the prologue is now enacted in the narrative of the story of Jesus. The reader is reminded of the prologue's description of the role of the Baptist in the introductory words of the narrator: "And this is the witness (*martyria*) of John" (v. 19; see 1:7-8).

The Baptist gives a negative witness. He refuses the messianic expectations of Israel which are directed toward him. He is interrogated by the emissaries of "the Jews" (v. 19) and "the Pharisees" (v. 24): "Who are you?"

---

in him." However, these same disciples still have a long way to go in their appreciation of Jesus (see 14:5, 8; 16:12, 17-18, 25, 29-33). Indeed, the Gospel will end with one of the disciples still doubting (20:26-29). On this, see Schnackenburg, *St John*, 1:337.

[25] As well as the link that exists between 2:1-12 and 4:43-54, there is a change of both characters and place between 1:19-51 and 2:1-12. See the further remarks along these lines from M. Theobald, *Die Fleischwerdung des Logos: Studien zum Verhältnis des Johannesprologs zum Corpus des Evangeliums und zu 1 Joh* (NTAbh N.F. 20; Münster: Aschendorff, 1988) 169-71.

[26] Contrary to J. L. Staley, *The Print's First Kiss: A Rhetorical Investigation of the Implied Reader in the Fourth Gospel* (SBLDS 82; Atlanta: Scholars Press, 1988) 75-77.

[27] See M. D. Hooker, "John the Baptist and the Johannine Prologue," *NTS* 16 (1970) 354-58; see also Theobald, *Fleischwerdung,* 272-82.

The discussion is immediately focused on the Christ. It is the negative but reliable witness of the Baptist that introduces the messianic question into the narrative (v. 20b). He refuses any claim to messiahship. The narrator introduces his refusal of messiahship with a series of important verbs which strike the reader as somewhat exaggerated: "He confessed, he did not deny, but confessed" (v. 20a).

If the Baptist is not the Christ, then he must be one of the expected messianic precursors, either Elijah (see Mal 4:5; Sir 48:10-11) or the prophet who would come to usher in the messianic era (see Deut 18:15, 18).[28] This is also denied. The Baptist responds to such questions with an unequivocal use of the words "I am not" (vv. 20, 21, and 27: *ouk eimi*). The reader is being remotely prepared for the one who alone can claim "I am he" (*egō eimi*).[29] The Baptist's interrogators insist that an answer is needed for the people in Jerusalem (v. 22). Waiting for an answer to this request, the reader learns that the witness sent by God (1:6-8) is the fulfillment of the prophecy of Isaiah: "I am the voice of one crying in the wilderness, 'Make straight the way of the Lord'" (v. 23; see Isa 40:3). By using this prophecy, the author has reached beyond the story time. The reader senses a plotted future time, to which the Baptist bears witness, for the coming of "the Lord."

Having found that the Baptist has denied his connection even with the *expected* messianic precursors,[30] his interrogators ask why he is baptizing. There is little indication of any messianic baptism in the time of Jesus. The background to this question may have links with the baptismal practice of the Qumran sect.[31] Whatever one makes of this question from the Jerusalem authorities, the reader is following a discussion between Judaism and the Baptist which presupposes the context of messianic expectation. The Baptist is refusing to be understood or controlled by such categories: "Why are you baptizing, if you are neither the Christ, nor Elijah, nor the prophet" (v. 25).[32] While the Baptist refuses, the representatives of the Jewish world have not moved from their basic presuppositions: the Baptist must be understood in *their* terms. But the baptism of John is merely a baptism of water; there is one among them whom they do not know,

---

[28] See also 1QS 9:11; 4QFlorilegium.

[29] For this suggestion, see E. C. Hoskyns, *The Fourth Gospel*, ed. F. N. Davey (London: Faber & Faber, 1947) 174; see also E. D. Freed, "*Ego eimi* in John 1:20 and 4:25," *CBQ* 41 (1979) 288–89.

[30] See C. K. Barrett, *The Gospel according to St. John* (London: SPCK, 1978) 173.

[31] See especially 1QS 4:20-22.

[32] Barrett explains it well: "The question rather means, Why do you perform what appears to be an official act if you have no official stature?" (*St John*, 174).

whose sandal the Baptist is not worthy to untie (vv. 26-27). The future tense of the plotted time looks beyond the story time of the narrative as the Baptist explains his role in terms of "he who comes after me" (v. 26).

Throughout this first "day" there have been sustained attempts to explain the Baptist within the cultural expectations of first-century messianic hopes. It was the Baptist himself who introduced the messianic question, scotching any discussions along those lines. He has been interrogated by people strongly representative of Judaism: priests and Levites sent by the Jews from Jerusalem (v. 19), that is, sent by the Pharisees (v. 24).[33] They have suspected that the Baptist must be a part of *their* vision of the messianic times. The reader is familiar with the world of Judaism. These expectations did not contradict what he had already been told by the prologue. If Jesus is the Christ (1:17), then it is possible that the Baptist, a witness sent by God (1:6), was the precursor. The Baptist was described in the prologue as not being the light (see 1:8). The reader has now discovered that he is not even the expected messianic precursor. As long as the search for the Messiah continues within the categories and expectations of "the Jews," then he will be among them, but they will not be able to know him (v. 26).

The first of these days has set the narrative firmly within the context of Jewish discussions about the coming Messiah. The Baptist refuses to accept any of the categories of the Messiah or his precursor which his questioners applied to him.[34] He has warned them that there is one among them whom they do not know. This warning is also directed by the author to the reader, who could associate the Baptist with the messianic expectations of Israel. Is the inability to know the one who stands among them the result of their inability to transcend their own messianic schemes?[35] The narrator is not only telling the *einmalig* of the experience of the Baptist but also shaping the messianic understanding of the reader.

But there is also an indication of the experience of the intended reader, the Johannine community. To see this, we need to recall the seemingly pleonastic words used by the narrator to introduce the Baptist's refusal of Jewish messianic categories in v. 20a: "He confessed (*hōmologēsen*), he did not deny, but confessed (*hōmologēsen*)." The twofold use of the verb

---

[33] The interrogation comes from a widespread representation of Judaism: priests and Levites, "the Jews," Pharisees, "from Jerusalem." See P. Perkins, "The Gospel according to John," *NJBC*, 952.

[34] In this the Fourth Evangelist departs from the Synoptic tradition, as the Baptist distances himself from the image of "precursor." For the Fourth Evangelist, he is "witness," not precursor.

[35] See C. Koester, "Hearing, Seeing and Believing in the Gospel of John," *Bib* 70 (1989) 329.

"to confess" recalls the situation of the Johannine community,[36] whose uncompromising confession of Jesus was leading to the community's exclusion from the synagogue. The only other places in the Fourth Gospel where the verb *hōmologein* appears are 9:22 and 12:42, in which some form of exclusion from the synagogue is at stake.[37] John's "confession" before "the Jews" and "the Pharisees" instructs the intended reader, through the reading experience of the implied reader, on the stance that must be taken by any authentic witness to Jesus.

The narrative closes with a reference to John's baptizing activity in Bethany beyond the Jordan (v. 28).[38] The author takes the reader back to the point of departure: the figure of John exercising a ministry that cannot be understood within the categories of the world and culture to which he seemingly belonged. Jesus himself has not appeared in the narrative so far, but the reader's attention has been systematically directed away from the Baptist to "the one among you whom you do not know."

In v. 28 the reader meets an indication from the narrator that the events and characters of the narrative in vv. 19-28 come to a close. Nowhere else in 1:19-51 is the day so clearly brought to an end as on this first day. The second day, which now follows, does not presuppose any audience except the reader. The characters of the priests and the Levites (v. 19) or the Pharisees (v. 24) have been dismissed (v. 28). They are not part of the narrative that follows. They have listened to the negative witness of the Baptist, and the reader has also been part of that audience. The official Jewish characters in the story will not return until 2:13-22, but the reader is always present.

Day Two: 1:29-34

The second day is also devoted to the witness of the Baptist. Again there is a close link with the prologue as it reproduces the "crying out" of the Baptist (see 1:15).[39] Jesus makes his first remote appearance in the narrative, but says or does nothing. John the Baptist proclaims Jesus as the Lamb of God who takes away the sin of the world (v. 29) and the Son of God

---

[36] See above, pp. 14–17.

[37] See Schnackenburg, *St John*, 288; R. Bultmann, *The Gospel of John: A Commentary* (Oxford: Blackwell, 1971) 87–88.

[38] There are several names given for this location in the ancient manuscripts. "Bethany" is the best reading. See the discussion in Barrett, *St. John*, 175.

[39] See M. D. Hooker, "John the Baptist and the Johannine Prologue," 356.

(v. 34).[40] Repeating the words of the prologue, he explains how this relates to his own role: "After me comes a man who ranks before me, for he was before me" (v. 30). The Baptist twice admits that he, like the rest of Israel (see v. 26) "did not know him" (vv. 31 and 33), but he engaged in his baptizing ministry so that this one who comes after him, but who is greater than he, might be revealed to an unknowing Israel (v. 31).

Apart from the silent presence of Jesus himself (v. 29), only the reader is involved in the narrative. He is informed that the Baptist's mission is that Jesus might be revealed to Israel (v. 31). The use of the passive (*phanerōthē*) reinforces the reader's understanding, originally coming from the prologue, that the Baptist's ministry is from God (see 1:6), but that information is for the reader, not for Israel, who is not represented in any way. The witness of vv. 29-34 is directed to the reader.

In a further use of plotted time, the author, through an analepsis, has the Baptist recall events in which the implied reader has played no part. These events make it clear to the Baptist that Jesus is the Lamb of God (v. 29), the Son of God (v. 34), the one "who baptizes with the Holy Spirit" (v. 33). The descent of the Spirit as a dove (see also Mark 1:10; Matt 3:16; Luke 3:22) confirms a promise made to the Baptist: "He on whom you see the Spirit descend and remain, that is he who baptizes with the Holy Spirit" (v. 33).[41] The reader's attention is no longer with the Baptist. The storyteller is not interested in recounting his experiences. The Baptist renders witness to Jesus in a way that transcends Jewish messianic expectation: Jesus is the Lamb of God, "he who baptizes with the Holy Spirit," the Son of God. None of this can be "contained" within the historical, cultural, or religious expectations of Israel. The reader is challenged to go beyond what he knows and understands. The use of analepsis to speak of Jesus' baptism, places Jesus' entry into the narrative outside the reader's knowledge and experience. The events reported in the story from the past took place; the reader must accept the reliable witness of John the Baptist.

---

[40] The text is uncertain here: part of the manuscript tradition has "the chosen one of God" rather than "the Son of God." While the textual tradition in favor of the latter is stronger, it may reflect the developing Christology of the scribes. Nevertheless, I am adopting the reading "the Son of God," largely on the basis of the discussion in F.-M. Braun, *Jean le Théologien II: Les grandes traditions d'Israel, L'accord des Ecritures d'après le Quatrième Evangile* (Ebib; Paris: Gabalda, 1964) 71-73.

[41] For a study of the possible traditions, background, and meaning of these references to the baptism, see G. M. Burge, *The Anointed Community: The Holy Spirit in the Johannine Tradition* (Grand Rapids: Eerdmans, 1987) 50-62.

The mysterious reference to a baptism that is not part of story time leaves the beginnings of Jesus' story outside the control of the reader (see v. 30).

The significance of the Baptist's revelation of Jesus as "the Lamb of God who takes away the sin of the world" has created difficulties for generations of scholars.[42] In line with Johannine thought, "Lamb *of God*" indicates the Lamb's origins. He comes from God, he is sent by God (an objective genitive). Jesus' role as the one who takes away the sin of the world does not flow from an essential divinity, but rather from his having come from God. It is as the Lamb *of God* that he takes away the sin of the world. In accordance with biblical thought, only God takes away, or forgives sin (the Greek verb *airein* carries both meanings in v. 29).[43] Thus John proclaims Jesus as the Lamb, the one through whom God will take away the sin of the world.

But why does the narrator use the term "the Lamb"? Does it come from the Servant of Isaiah 53, the triumphant Lamb of the Apocalypse (see 7:17; 17:14), a Jewish tradition of a Lamb who would lead the flock of God's people or, as is often suggested, the Passover lamb?[44] Perhaps we need to look further than the Passover lamb to the whole of the ritual practice of Israel, where the lamb was used both for the sacrificial rites of communion and reconciliation after sin.[45] Through the use of the lamb, the people of Israel established and renewed their union with God and among themselves after having sinned. Jesus is now presented as the lamb, but he is not of the same order. Again the reader reaches beyond familiar traditions. Jesus is not a cultic offering.[46] Jesus is "of God." The former way of

---

[42] The Fourth Evangelist is adopting a traditional formula of revelation which comes to him from the Old Testament. See M. de Goedt, "Un schème de révélation dans le Quatrième Evangile," *NTS* 8 (1961–62) 143. For a survey of earlier scholarship with bibliography, see E. May, *Ecce Agnus Dei: A Philological and Exegetical Approach to John 1,29. 36* (Washington: Catholic University, 1947). More recently, see J. T. Forestell, *The Word of the Cross: Salvation as Revelation in the Fourth Gospel* (AnBib 57; Rome: Biblical Institute Press, 1974) 157–66; and Kuhn, *Christologie und Wunder*, 531–38.

[43] See Forestell, *Word of the Cross*, 160–61.

[44] For critical surveys, see R. E. Brown, *The Gospel According to John* (2 vols.; AB 29, 29A; Garden City, N.Y.: Doubleday, 1966, 1970) 58–63; G. Stemberger, *La symbolique du bien et du mal selon saint Jean* (Paris: Seuil, 1970) 172–79; and Léon-Dufour, *Lecture*, 170–74 (for the interpretation that follows, see pp. 174–75).

[45] See R. de Vaux, *Ancient Israel: Its Life and Institutions* (London: Darton, Longman & Todd, 1965) 415–21.

[46] This is my main objection to the popular use of the Passover lamb imagery to explain the Lamb of God. The Passover explanation rightly looks to 19:14. The Passover lamb is part of the broader Jewish use of the lamb in its reconciliation and communion sacrifices.

reconciliation with God was through the ritual of the sacrificed lamb. These rites, so important to the history, faith, and culture of the People of God have been transcended. God now gives the fullness of pardon to Israel and to the whole world through the Lamb of God who takes away the sin of the world. Jesus is not a new cultic victim. Rather, he is the one through whom God enters the human story, offering it perfect reconciliation with him.[47]

The Spirit descended like a dove upon Jesus, "and it remained upon him." This is proof for the Baptist that Jesus is the man who ranks before him. The messianic promise of Isa 11:2 has been fulfilled: "And the Spirit of the Lord shall rest upon him, the spirit of wisdom and understanding, the spirit of counsel and might, the spirit of knowledge and the fear of the Lord."[48] However, this "Messiah" is not the one expected by his contemporaries, nor by the reader. The Baptist has prepared for him through a baptism of water, Jesus will baptize with the Holy Spirit (v. 33).

The Baptist's witness concludes with his confession, based on his experience of the baptism, which the reader must accept on the Baptist's word ("I have seen and have borne witness"), that Jesus is the Son of God. It is often asked whether the full Johannine idea of Jesus as the Son of God is implied here, or whether the Baptist is confessing that Jesus fulfills Israel's expectations of a messianic "son of God."[49] The Johannine narrative demands that the Baptist point to Jesus as the Son of God in the full Johannine sense. The question of how the historical John the Baptist understood Jesus need not concern us. We must follow the narrator who has the reliable witness tell the reader that Jesus is the Son of God. The reader has already been told in the prologue that Jesus is the Son of God (1:14, 18). But the characters in the drama have not been told. The reader is caught between both poles of the narrative structure: a story of Jesus being told in the light of the prologue, and characters in the narrative who have not read the prologue. The reader must decide between the messianic expec-

---

[47] Léon-Dufour, *Lecture*, 174.

[48] See W. J. Bittner, *Jesu Zeichen im Johannesevangelium: Die Messias-Erkenntnis im Johannesevangelium vor ihrem jüdischen Hintergrund* (WUNT 2, Reihe 26; Tübingen: J. C. B. Mohr [Paul Siebeck] 1987) 245–46. Both the Synoptic tradition and the Johannine tradition make reference to the presence of the Spirit in the form of a dove. On this symbolism, see F.-L. Lentzen-Deis, *Die Taufe Jesu nach den Synoptikern: Literarkritische und gattungsgeschichtliche Untersuchungen* (FThSt 4; Frankfurt: Josef Knecht, 1970) 170–83.

[49] Jewish speculation on a messianic "son of God" has its roots in 2 Sam 7:14 and Ps 2:7. See the comprehensive treatment of B. J. Byrne, *'Sons of God — Seed of Abraham': A Study of the Idea of the Sonship of God of All Christians in Paul against the Jewish Background* (AnBib 83; Rome: Biblical Institute Press, 1979) 9–78; see especially pp. 16–18 and pp. 59–62.

tations that have been expressed so far by the hopes of Judaism or the reliable witness of the Baptist that Jesus is the Son of God.

The reader must accept the witness of the Baptist simply as witness. The reader alone reads the Baptist's witness to christological truths which are essential for a correct understanding of Jesus. However, the story has not come to an end with John's proclamation. Indeed, as a day of preparation should, it leads the reader to ask questions. Within the context of Jewish messianic expectations, John the Baptist has presented Jesus in terms that transcend those categories. Hence, the second day of preparation both informs and questions the reader.

Day Three: 1:35-42

A link between 1:29-34 and the "following" of the disciples is made through a repetition of the Baptist's witness to Jesus as "the Lamb of God" (v. 35; see v. 29). When this term was first used in v. 29 the implied reader was not aware that John the Baptist had any disciples. Only the reader was told that Jesus was the Lamb of God. Two further characters are now introduced. The Baptist is "standing" with two of his disciples, looking at Jesus "as he walked." While the expression "behold the Lamb of God" in v. 29 has many of the characteristics of a traditional revelation formula, such is not the case here (v. 35).[50] The Baptist points toward a man as he walks by (vv. 35-36). The result of this interaction between the Baptist, who points away from himself, and his disciples who were standing with him, is that they too begin to walk: "they followed Jesus" (v. 37). There is a movement *away* from the Baptist *toward* Jesus. The description of Jesus' response to these "followers" is equally focused on motion. Jesus "turned," breaking his journey, and "gazed upon those following" (*theasamenos autous akolouthountas*, v. 38). He then asks a question that is also of interest to the reader: "What do you seek?" In the first encounter between Jesus and his "followers," Jesus' initiative offers a hint of an answer to their hopes and questions.

The first disciples' response falls short even of the earlier messianic questions raised of John the Baptist. "The Jews" came to the Baptist asking messianic questions (vv. 19-28), but the ex-disciples of the Baptist address Jesus as a respected teacher, "Rabbi," and ask where he is staying (v. 38). The narrator's parenthetic explanation—"Rabbi (which means

---

[50] Brown, *John*, 76; against de Goedt, "Un schème de révélation," 143–44.

teacher)"– is not merely a note for the non-Jewish reader,[51] nor is it simply an indication of the reliability of the narrator, who wants to correct the relationship with the implied reader.[52] The narrator makes clear to the implied reader that these disciples are approaching Jesus as a teacher, and no more. This is the meaning of "where are you staying." It is often read in a symbolic way,[53] but it is the logical question that follows on the recognition of a newly found teacher. Rabbis do not "wander." They have a home where they sit and teach, gathering students. The disciples have failed to grasp their ex-master's indication that Jesus is the Lamb of God (see v. 36). For them, he is a significant teacher, a rabbi whose school they might attend. The reader has little difficulty in seeing the limitations of such an initial response, especially after the reading experience of vv. 29-34.

Jesus invites them to "come and see" (v. 39).[54] This is a promising invitation. One of the two who followed was Andrew, Simon Peter's brother (v. 40).[55] Finding his brother Simon, Andrew makes a confession of faith: "We have found the Messiah" (which means the Christ) (v. 41). There is a development from "rabbi-teacher" to "Messiah-Christ." Is this the first confession of authentic Johannine faith by a disciple? Several hints indicate otherwise. The most significant of these are Andrew's words: "We have found . . ." (v. 41). The reader has read earlier attempts to confine the Baptist's presence and his witnessing role to messianic terms, but has found that such attempts are not sufficient. Here, for the first time, the reader finds one of the characters saying: "We have found." Jesus does not react to these confessions. He is simply present to these first disciples.

There is a hint that true discipleship is not the result of the initiative of characters who find and follow Jesus. To show the primacy of Jesus' seeking and finding disciples, the initiative comes from Jesus in his recognition of Simon, the son of John, and the promise that he shall be called Cephas (v. 42). The future tense of the verb indicates the author's use of plotted time. This prolepsis, and the fact that Jesus gives Simon a further name,

---

[51] It is often explained in this way; see, e.g., Lindars, *John*, 113; Barrett, *St John*, 181.

[52] As claimed by Staley, *Print's First Kiss*, 38, 81–83.

[53] See, e.g., Bultmann, *John*, 100.

[54] The reference to "the tenth hour" is to be taken at its face value, that is, about 4:00 P.M.; see Lindars, *John*, 114; Schnackenburg, *St John*, 1:309.

[55] We are not told who the other ex-disciple of the Baptist might have been. Many scholars see this silence as a hint of the desire of an ex-disciple of the Baptist to remain anonymous. Schnackenburg objects that this cannot be proved and claims "it could only be Philip" (*St John*, 1:310). It is here that M.-E. Boismard reads *prō* rather than *prōton*, thus creating an extra day in the week (*Moïse ou Jésus: Essai de Christologie Johannique* [BETL 84; Leuven: University Press, 1988] 79–81). For a full discussion, see F. Neirynck, "The Anonymous Disciple in John 1," *ETL* 66 (1990) 5–37.

hints to the reader that more of this will be read later in the story. The verb is also in the passive. Something will happen to Simon. For the moment, it must wait, a chord struck, but left with the reader. To be a disciple of Jesus may be a question not only of finding and following but of accepting what Jesus has to give. The reader in the text needs to wait for the further developments that will take place through the story; the figure of Peter-Cephas forms part of the ecclesial experience of the people in front of the text at the end of the first century (see especially 21:20-23).

For the moment, the disciples may believe they have found Jesus. They believe that in Jesus of Nazareth the expected Jewish messianic figure has arrived. The author has already taught the implied reader that such messianic categories may prove to be insufficient (1:19-28). Although this third and final day of remote preparation has been marked by the disciples' inability to reach beyond their own categories of rabbi and Messiah, Jesus' response to them has been full of promise: "What do you seek? . . . Come and see. . . . You shall be called Cephas." It may *appear* that the disciples are on their way to "finding" Jesus, but the promise to Simon is a first hint that there may be more to it.

Through the first three days of remote preparation for the gift of the "glory" various understandings of who Jesus might be have emerged from the narrative. "The Jews" and the disciples have worked within categories they could understand. They accept Jesus according to their own historical, cultural, and religious expectations. The reader is learning that this cannot be. The Baptist has shown that to approach Jesus in such ways is not to understand him: "among you stands one whom you do not know" (v. 26). The disciples have been called to enter into the story of Jesus, who received and encouraged them throughout their first encounter. Indeed, they have begun the process of "seeing" Jesus which will be so important for this Gospel (v. 39). They recognize him as rabbi and Christ. Is this enough for a disciple of Jesus? At this stage of the narrative there seem to be no negative indications from Jesus. Yet these expectations are not what was revealed in the testimony of the Baptist. A tension has been established.

The author will not allow the reader to settle for what is congenial. Such is not the case for the members of the Johannine community in front of the text. If they wish, they can settle for a Christology based on first-century Jewish messianic hopes. Yet the narrative is marked by a rhetoric of persuasion. The real author constructs a narrative with the hope that the intended readers will refuse to settle for what is congenial.

Day Four: 1:43-51

In terms of the "days" throughout 1:19-51, we are now at the fourth day, the first of the "three days" of preparation for the gift of the glory which has its origins in the command of YHWH (see Exod 19:10-15). The more remote preparation is over. In v. 43 a turning point in the narrative arrives. No longer do disciples find Jesus, but he actively finds and calls Philip.[56] The theme of motion returns, as Jesus decides to go to Galilee (v. 43). It is as someone on a journey that he finds and calls Philip to "follow." For the first time in the narrative a disciple of Jesus is the result of Jesus' initiative.[57] Philip is associated with Bethsaida, Andrew, and Peter (see Mark 1:16-20; Luke 5:1-11). This gathering of disciples journeying to Galilee leads to the call of Nathanael. He is "called" not by Jesus but by the other disciples. The author is saying something to the reader about the mission of the disciple, calling other disciples, as is often claimed. Yet from the earlier confession of faith by Andrew (see v. 40) the reader has been made aware that the very first words of the disciples' expression of faith, spoken by Philip to Nathanael, indicate that they are following Jesus under their own terms: "We have found him . . ." (v. 45).

But there is more than a recalling of v. 40. There is a deliberate repetition of the verb "to find," which leads Philip to tell a lie: "He *found* Philip and said to him, 'Follow me'" (v. 43). "Philip *found* Nathanael, and said to him, "We have *found*" (v. 44). Jesus found Philip (v. 43), but now Philip, in repeating the words of Andrew (see v. 41), tells a lie. Despite Jesus' initiative in finding and calling Philip, the disciples fall back into their own way of understanding Jesus. The reader is aware of the lack of truthfulness in Philip's words to Nathanael. The disciples claim to have found "him of whom Moses in the Law and also the prophets wrote, Jesus of Nazareth, the son of Joseph" (v. 45). The disciples are wrong in their understanding of Jesus. Philip tells Nathanael that they know that Jesus is *of Nazareth,* and that he is the son *of Joseph.* Having read the prologue, the reader knows that Jesus "was turned in loving union toward God" (1:1), and that he is "the Son *of God*" (1:18).[58] However, the disciples have not read the prologue.

---

[56] The text is notoriously troublesome, as the verb "decided to go" has no subject, while the verb "said" has Jesus as its subject. I am supposing that the author intends Jesus to be the subject throughout, as Jesus now has the initiative: he found and he called. See also Schenke, "Die literarische Entstehungsgeschichte," 30.

[57] This is seldom noticed; see, e.g., R. Kysar, *John's Story of Jesus* (Philadelphia: Fortress Press, 1984) 19-20.

[58] See Barrett, *St John,* 184.

The author's presentation of the disciples' response in categories they can understand sets up a conflict between the experience of the reader and the response of disciples. The former has read of different origins for Jesus, yet here the disciples of Jesus say that he is a son of Joseph from Nazareth. Similarly, the claim that Jesus is "him of whom Moses in the Law and also the prophets wrote" (v. 45) falls short of the full truth. The reader knows that Jesus is not simply the fulfillment of the Old Testament promises. He is more. The Johannine narrative is presenting a rather singular point of view. The infant church looked constantly to the Old Testament for its witness to Jesus, but that is not enough for the Fourth Evangelist. It is not denied, but it is not enough. The witness of the disciples is the Johannine way of telling a story of the fragility of disciples which, beginning in Mark, is found throughout the Synoptic tradition. It certainly reflects the situation of Jesus' historical disciples and all subsequent disciples of Jesus. The intended reader and every real reader can in some way identify with these first disciples.

But the author does not allow the implied reader such waywardness. The author draws attention to the encounter between Jesus and Nathanael. It is introduced by a return to the question of origins. Nathanael's first words ask whether an unknown and insignificant northern town could be the home of the one who fulfills the Scriptures: "Can anything good come out of Nazareth?" (v. 46). Nathanael, like the other disciples, is mistaken about his origins "out of Nazareth."[59] Philip, repeating the words that Jesus had said to the original disciples – "Come and see" – invites Nathanael to Jesus. The narrative suggests that Nathanael is a part of the experience of the disciples who have come to Jesus so far. The rhythm of the previous day is repeated. Nathanael does not come to faith by seeing Jesus; Jesus has seen him first. The initiative lies with Jesus. He is greeted as an Israelite without guile. Jesus describes a man who is honest in his frankness (unlike Jacob in Gen 27:35-36), without lies (see Ps 32:2; Isa 53:9), who does not prostitute himself to false gods (Apoc 14:5). Here is a man worthy to recognize all that has been promised in the Scriptures (see v. 45). He is stunned by Jesus' knowledge of him and asks a crucial Johannine question: "From where do you know me" (*pothen me ginōskeis;*). As he was

---

[59] It has often been suggested that this remark may have been a popular proverb, but there is no evidence for it outside John 1:45. On this, see K. Dewey, "*Paroimiai* in the Gospel of John," *Semeia* 17 (1980) 90-91. The purpose of the expression within its present narrative context has been well understood by R. Kieffer, *Le monde symbolique de saint Jean* (LD 137; Paris: Cerf, 1989) 24-25. See also P. D. Duke, *Irony in the Fourth Gospel* (Atlanta: John Knox Press, 1985) 54-55.

mistaken over Jesus' origins "from Nazareth," he now asks the right question about the origins of Jesus' knowledge. He is then further stunned by Jesus' telling him: "Before Philip called you, when you were under the fig tree, I saw you" (v. 48).

Many suggestions have been made concerning why Jesus spoke of the fig tree: the comfort of his home (see 1 Kgs 4:25; Micah 4:4; Zech 3:10), his dedication to the study of the Law, and the fig tree as a symbol of good and evil.[60] But Jesus has told Nathanael details about his immediate past which only some visionary authority could have made possible. Anyone who is able to reveal such private matters must be a wonder-worker. Although Jesus' knowledge of Nathanael's having been called by Philip while he was under the fig tree cannot be called a "miracle" in the full Johannine sense of that term,[61] it is the wonder of Jesus' knowledge of both who he is and what he was doing that moves Nathanael to a confession of faith: "Rabbi, you are the Son of God! You are the King of Israel!" (v. 49).[62]

Here we find a confession of Jesus as the fulfillment of Jewish messianic hopes. Indeed, many scholars see this as the original ending of the chapter and claim that vv. 50-51 have been added (clumsily) to the text.[63] Whatever may have been the prehistory of 1:19-51, it is clear that Nathanael has confessed his faith *only* in terms of Jewish messianic expectation. Addressing Jesus as "Rabbi," recalling the limited understanding of the first disciples in v. 38, he then uses two messianic titles: Son of God and King of Israel. Exalted as these confessions may be, they are still bound by Nathanael's own culture, history, and religion.[64]

---

[60] See the survey of Hahn, "Die Jüngerberufung," 187–88. C. R. Koester makes a good case for the background of Zech 3:10, in close association with 3:8, which is messianic ("Messianic Exegesis and the Call of Nathanael [John 1.45-51]," *JSNT* 39 [1990] 23–34). This links Philip's indication that Jesus is the fulfillment of Scripture in v. 45 and Nathanael's use of messianic categories in v. 49.

[61] On this knowledge as a "sign," see U. C. von Wahlde, *The Earliest Version of John's Gospel: Recovering the Gospel of Signs* (Wilmington, Del.: Michael Glazier, 1989) 71 n. 17. F. Hahn, sensitive to this technical issue, writes of "das wunderbare Wissen Jesu" ("Die Jüngerberufung," 187).

[62] Rightly interpreted in this way by F. Hahn ("Die Jüngerberufung," 187–89).

[63] See, e.g., Brown, *John*, 88; R. T. Fortna, *The Gospel of Signs: A Reconstruction of the Narrative Source Underlying the Fourth Gospel* (SNTSMS 11; Cambridge: Cambridge University Press, 1970) 179–89; Boismard, *Du Baptême à Cana*, 105; Kuhn, *Christologie und Wunder*, 153–59. M. Goguel writes of 1:51 as "un débris d'une tradition plus complexe" (*Jean-Baptiste* [Paris: Payot, 1928] 189). For a survey, see J. H. Neyrey, "The Jacob Allusions in John 1:51," *CBQ* 44 (1982) 586–89.

[64] Against Hahn, "Die Jüngerberufung," 189; Barrett, *St John*, 185–86; Brown, *John*, 88 (with some hesitation); Schackenburg, *St John*, 1:317-19; S. Pancaro, *The Law in the Fourth Gospel: The Torah and the Gospel, Moses and Jesus, Judaism and Christianity According to John* (NovTSup

To believe on the basis of the wonder of his having seen him under the fig tree is not enough: "Because I said to you, I saw you under the fig tree, do you believe? You shall see greater things than these" (v. 50). We have arrived at the dénouement. Instead of a blessing, Nathanael is chided for the limitations of his faith expressed through the confession of Jesus as rabbi, Son of God, and King of Israel (v. 49). Nathanael's faith, limited to what the best of Jewish hopes has produced, is the result of Jesus' supernatural knowledge.[65] The reader has not yet been instructed that Jesus will not be wholly content with a confession of faith articulated by a disciple on the basis of a sign. Yet the author wants the reader to appreciate an incipient faith among these first disciples. Their belief in Jesus, expressed through their limited confession of him in terms which they could understand, is not wrong. The disciples, presented by an omniscient author as somewhere between "the truth and the whole truth,"[66] confess their faith in Jesus. But the reader has also been shown their preparedness to settle for what they have found (see vv. 41 and 45), their ability to report untruthfully (see vv. 43-45), their ready use of Jewish messianic titles (vv. 41 and 45), and their mistaken belief that he is from Nazareth, a son of Joseph (v. 45). This leaves them short of true Johannine belief.

The disciples are promised a greater sight as the narrator again reaches outside story time into plotted time: "You shall see greater things than these" (v. 50). There is a promise of greater sight sometime in the future which will depend on a greater faith. It will not be a faith in something they had found (see vv. 41 and 45), but the reception of the gift of God which is Jesus. Not even Nathanael was able to see this, despite his great virtues (v. 47), the quality of his messianic confession (v. 49) and his incipient belief (v. 50).

But the future tense of the plotted time forces the reader to conclude that the events of the story time—no matter how impressive Nathanael's faith in Jesus may appear to be—need to be transcended. There may be a hint for the reader that faith will in some way be linked with Jesus' word ("Because I *said* to you . . . do you believe?). But the promise of Jesus indicates that the "now" of Nathanael's faith (v. 50) is to be transcended

---

42; Leiden: E. J. Brill, 1975) 288-304, and others, who claim that "Son of God" here has the full Johannine christological meaning.

[65] The implied reader has his first hint of the Johannine criticism of a faith which is based on signs. See especially 2:23-25.

[66] A favorite expression of M. Sternberg, *The Poetics of Biblical Narrative: Ideological Literature and the Drama of Reading* (ILBS; Bloomington: Indiana University Press, 1985) 180-85 and especially 230-63.

by a "not yet" in the experience of all the disciples (v. 51). This is the meaning of the words of Jesus, prolonging the promise of the plotted time in v. 51: "Amen, amen I say to you, you will see heaven opened, and the angels of God ascending and descending upon the Son of Man."[67] The use of the double "amen," found only in the Fourth Gospel,[68] tells the reader that he is about to encounter a significant statement which is intimately linked with what went before.[69] Shifting from his discussion with Nathanael ("you" singular in v. 50 and "him" in v. 51a), Jesus now addresses a wider group of disciples ("you" plural in v. 51bc). In doing this the narrator has Jesus reach out of the immediate situation of the "you" of Nathanael to the various disciples who came to him with their limited expressions of faith, and to the reader. The reader is part of the second person plural. All are promised: "You will see." The "sight" of "the Jews" and the disciples needs to be surpassed. There is need for a greater faith, so that the "greater things" of v. 50 may be seen.

In a cosmology where God was "above," the tearing open of the heavens already promised a communication between God and the earth "below," where men and women live out their history. It has already been used in this sense by Isaiah (see Isa 64:1; see also Isa 24:18; Gen 7:11; Ezek 1:1) and in the Synoptic tradition (see Mark 1:10; Matt 3:16; Luke 3:21). The opening of heaven is also important in the Apocalypse to symbolize God's communication with the human story (see 4:1). The scene is set for a "vision" which is described in terms of Jacob's dream, as told in Genesis:

> And he dreamed that there was a ladder set up on the earth, and the top of it reached to heaven; and behold, the angels of God were ascending and descending on it. . . . Then Jacob awoke from his sleep and said, "Surely the Lord is in this place; and I did not know it." And he was afraid, and said, "How awesome is this place! This is none other than the house of God, and this is the gate of heaven" (Gen 28:12, 16-17).

The words of Jesus, following an interpretation already found in Jewish tradition,[70] shifts the movement away from the ladder. The angels ascend and descend upon the Son of Man. He becomes "this place," "the gate of heaven." In Jesus, the Son of Man, God will be revealed.

---

[67] See my detailed study *The Johannine Son of Man* (2nd ed.; Biblioteca di Scienze Religiose 14; Rome: LAS, 1978) 23-41.

[68] The use of a single "amen" is found regularly in the Synoptic Gospels, especially in Matthew (31 times). The double "amen" appears in the Fourth Gospel 26 times.

[69] See J. H. Bernard, *A Critical and Exegetical Commentary on the Gospel according to St John* (2 vols.; ICC; Edinburgh: T. & T. Clark, 1928) 1:67; B. Lindars, *Behind the Fourth Gospel* (Studies in Creative Criticism 3; London: SPCK, 1971) 52-54.

[70] For full detail, see Moloney, *Son of Man*, 26-30.

Jesus is the Son of Man, not, as understood by Jewish and early Christian apocalyptic, as he who will one day come on the clouds of heaven, but in his earthly presence; for in this earthly presence, in which he enjoys continual communion with the Father, he shows to faith the miracle of his doxa.[71]

The first day of the immediate preparation for the gift of the "glory" concludes the first reports of disciples' belief in Jesus. The author has introduced the implied reader to characters who, ignorant of the prologue, were prepared to accept the new Elijah, the prophet, a rabbi, a teacher, the Christ, the Messiah, the one of whom Moses and the prophets had spoken, Son of God and King of Israel. The vigor of Jesus' final intervention (v. 50) and his use of the plural "you" (v. 51) indicate that the reader will not be allowed to settle for the confession of Nathanael. Jesus now calls the characters in the narrative to reach beyond all categories coming to them from their own religion, history, and culture.[72] The author has told the story in this way to make the same demands of the reader at the end of the fourth day of the Gospel's narrative.

Up to this point the narrative has not witnessed an expression of authentic faith. The Baptist performed his task as a reliable witness, but that was to be expected. The reader knows from the prologue that he was sent by God to perform this task (1:6-8). What the reader is now looking for, after the challenge of the conclusion of 1:45-51, is someone in the story who can show the way in which one should receive the Word become flesh and believe in his name (see 1:12-14). The author used the narrative of the Baptist's encounter with Judaism to draw the implied reader beyond Jewish categories. The Baptist spoke of Jesus as the Lamb of God and the Son of God. In telling of Jesus' encounter with the disciples, the reading experience of the reader is taken one step further. Jesus promises that if the disciples' belief transcends all that they can control, they will see greater things: they will see the revelation of the heavenly in the person of Jesus. In Jesus God will be revealed.[73]

---

[71] Bultmann, *John*, 107. See also my conclusions in *Son of Man*, 33–41. See also J. Calloud and F. Genuyt, *L'Evangile de Jean (I): Lecture sémiotique des chapîtres 1 à 6* (Lyon: Centre pour l'Analyse du Discours Religieux, 1989) 43; C. C. Rowland, "John 1.51, Jewish Apocalyptic and Targumic Tradition," *NTS* 30 (1984) 498–507; G. Segalla, *Giovanni* (NVB; Rome: Edizioni Paoline, 1976) 162. For a quite different approach to the Johannine use of "Son of Man" in general, see W. Loader, *The Christology of the Fourth Gospel* (BBET 23; Frankfurt: Peter Lang, 1989) 208–11 (on 1:51, see pp. 121–23). See also J. H. Neyrey, "The Jacob Allusions in John 1:51," 586–605.

[72] See R. Kieffer, *Le monde symbolique*, 41. M. Theobald has attractively suggested that 1:18 and 1:51 are closely related (*Fleischwerdung*, 286–89).

[73] J. Painter studies 1:35–2:11 from a form-critical perspective as "the quest for the Messiah"

CONCLUSION

The three days of remote preparation led to Jesus' active participation in the narrative. On the day described in vv. 43-51, the first of the three intensive days of preparation for the gift of the glory, which will take place "on the third day" (see 2:1, 11), Jesus makes a promise of what the disciples will see. This sight, however, depends upon a quality of faith. There is an important balance in this narrative. It is not only a question of the gradual revelation of who Jesus is. Through the author's presentation of the experience of the first disciples to the reader, it is, perhaps especially, a serious summons to a deeper response in faith to the coming of Jesus.

The carefully organized narrative just read challenges the reader to go further (vv. 50-51).[74] The omniscient author knows that Jesus cannot be understood in terms of current messianic expectation, but the reader does not. The prologue did not dispel all ideas of Jesus' messianic role. The author has composed a narrative in which both the characters and the reader have much to learn. This is an excellent way to begin the story of Jesus. The omniscient and reliable narrator can tell a story that attempts to instruct both disciples and reader.[75] At each intervention of Jesus throughout these first days, important progress toward the full truth has been made. Although much of the narrative is reported with verbs in the aorist tense, in vv. 35, 39, 43, 47, 49 the narrator reports that Jesus "says." In a narrative from the past, the present tense of the verb *legein* is used. On the final day Jesus has promised the disciples the "greater sight" of the Son of Man (vv. 50-51). The narrator has used the present tense of the verb (*kai legei autǭ*) to report direct speech of Jesus that reaches outside story time into the plotted time of a promised future sight of the Son of Man. The promise is also made to the reader.[76] The implied reader looks forward to "the third day" (2:1).

("Quest and Rejection Stories," 20-23). He claims that the quest is fulfilled by 2:1-11 (see pp. 22-23).

[74] Against, e.g., Hahn, "Die Jüngerberufung," 190: "Die Bedeutung der fünf ersten Jünger ist für ihn [all subsequent disciples] das bleibende Paradigma für Nachfolge, Glauben und Schauen." Thus, R. A. Culpepper also claims too much: "In sharp contrast to the Gospel of Mark, where the disciples struggle to discern who Jesus is, in John they know from the very beginning" (*Anatomy*, 116).

[75] On this process, see Sternberg, *Poetics of Biblical Narrative*, 176-79.

[76] Culpepper, *Anatomy*, 31; see further J. Capel Anderson, "Matthew, Gender and Reading," *Semeia* 28 (1983) 24-26.

Faith in the Word of Jesus at Cana: John 2:1-12

⁋ "ON THE THIRD DAY there was a marriage at Cana in Galilee" (2:1a). The long-standing association of "the third day" with the gift of the Law on Sinai in Jewish tradition (Exod 19:16, the targums, *Mekilta*) raises the expectations of the implied reader. The presence of YHWH was experienced in the *kābôd* over the mountain on the third day (Exod 19:16).[1] After four days of preparation through 1:19-51, based on the Jewish celebration of the gift of the Law at Pentecost, and culminating in Jesus' initiative and promise on the fourth day (1:43-51), the episode of the marriage feast at Cana in Galilee in 2:1-12 is introduced by a traditional formula "on the third day." Given the Sinai background, this indication points the reader toward a dénouement.

THE SHAPE OF THE NARRATIVE

There have been attempts to reconstruct an original pre-Johannine miracle story, and a Dionysiac background is sometimes suggested.[2] Whatever

---

[1] My interpretation of "the third day" as a point of arrival for an implied reader familiar with Jewish Sinai traditions eliminates a reference to the resurrection at this stage of the narrative.

[2] E. Schweizer has shown that the usual signs of Johannine style are absent from John

sources the Evangelist may have used, the present shape of 2:1-12 reveals a real author's careful selection and ordering of the material.[3] The action of the narrative is framed by passages that focus attention on the movement of the characters in the story: Jesus, his mother, and the disciples (vv. 1-2 and v. 12). Jesus' brothers are introduced in v. 12, a first mention of characters who will return later in the narrative (see 7:1-10). When they return, the reader will recall that they were present at the first miracle at Cana.[4] Between that frame, there are two verbal exchanges, one in which the mother of Jesus leads the way (vv. 3-5), and another in which the attendants respond silently to the words of Jesus. The encounter between the mother of Jesus and her son leads to the production of the wine and the reaction of the steward (vv. 6-10). Finally, the narrator comments on the significance of the event (v. 11). I propose that 2:1-12 has the following shape:[5]

(a) *Verses 1-2:* The setting of the account, giving indications of the time ("on the third day"), the occasion ("there was a marriage"), the place ("at Cana in Galilee") and the characters involved (the mother of Jesus, Jesus and his disciples). The characters are "there" (v. 1: *ekei*).[6]

(b) *Verses 3-5:* A verbal exchange is narrated. The mother of Jesus tells her son that the wine is gone (v. 3), but he replies in terms of

---

2:1-12 (*Ego Eimi . . . Die religionsgeschichtliche Herkunft und theologische Bedeutung der johanneischen Bildreden, zugleich ein Beitrag zur Quellenfrage des vierten Evangeliums* [FRLANT 38; Göttingen: Vandenhoeck & Ruprecht, 1939] 100). On the Dionysiac background, see W. Bauer, *Das Johannesevangelium erklärt* (HKNT 6; Tübingen: J. C. B. Mohr [Paul Siebeck], 1933) 47; R. Bultmann, *The Gospel of John: A Commentary* (Oxford: Blackwell, 1971) 118-19 and n. 1 on p. 119. This evidence is summarized and rejected by M.-J. Lagrange (*Évangile selon saint Jean* [Ebib; Paris: Gabalda, 1936] 61-62) and C. K. Barrett (*The Gospel according to St John* [London: SPCK, 1978] 188-89). For reconstructions of an original source, see R. T. Fortna, *The Gospel of Signs: A Reconstruction of the Narrative Source Underlying the Fourth Gospel* (SNTSMS 11; Cambridge: Cambridge University Press, 1970) 29-38; idem, *The Fourth Gospel and its Predecessor: From Narrative Source to Present Gospel* (Studies in the NT and its World; Edinburgh: T. & T. Clark, 1989) 48-58; J. McHugh, *The Mother of Jesus in the New Testament* (London: Darton, Longman & Todd, 1975) 462-66.

[3] Our present text is scarcely "extraneous matter lightly worked over" (Barrett, *St John*, 189) or "etwas wie einen erratischen Block" (Schweizer, *Ego Eimi*, 100).

[4] See R. H. Lightfoot, *St. John's Gospel*, ed. C. F. Evans (Oxford: Oxford University Press, 1956) 129.

[5] See also C. Koester, "Hearing, Seeing and Believing in the Gospel of John," *Bib* 70 (1989) 331.

[6] There is also a sense of Jesus and the disciples' having made a journey to arrive at Cana in the use of the verb *eklēthē*.

his "hour" (v. 4). The mother of Jesus speaks to the attendants
(v. 5). The section is marked by direct speech.[7]

(c) *Verses 6-10:* The main action of the miracle story is narrated. In
response to two commands from Jesus, which open the action,
jars are filled and taken to the steward, who discovers that the
water has become wine. The direct speech of the steward,
addressed to the bridegroom, closes the action. After the scene
is set in v. 6, direct speech both opens (v. 7) and closes (v. 10) this
section of the story.

(d) *Verse 11:* The narrator slows down the action to make a comment
for the reader on the manifestation of the glory and the faith of
the disciples.[8]

(e) *Verse 12:* In a final remark from the narrator much of vv. 1-2
returns, but the characters in the narrative who had made a
journey (*eklēthē*) to be "there" (v. 1: *ekei*) at Cana are again set in
motion (*katebē*) until they come to rest in another location, Capernaum (v. 12: *ekei*).

The narrative is rich in Johannine symbolism and points forward to
many of the themes that will develop throughout the Gospel. The encounter between Jesus, the woman and the mother and the first appearance
of the term "the hour" (vv. 3-5) are intimately linked with the scene at the
cross (19:25-27).[9] The superabundance of water changed into the best of
wines begins a series of "signs" which will mark the first half of the Gospel
(see the use of *sēmeion* in 2:23; 3:2; 6:2, 14, 26, 30; 7:31; 9:16; 10:41; 11:47;
12:18, 37; see then 20:30-31). The theme of water will return in chaps. 3,
4, 5, 7, and 9. The revelation of the *doxa* is also an important theme
throughout the Gospel.[10] Such wine, provided by Jesus within the context of a marriage feast, has links with the promise of the messianic age

[7] The important innovation of brief dialogue in direct speech in New Testament narratives
has been noticed by E. Auerbach, *Mimesis: The Representation of Reality in Western Literature*
(Princeton, N.J.: Princeton University Press, 1953) 45-46.

[8] For a summary of the variations in the "speed" of the Johannine narrative, see R. A.
Culpepper, *Anatomy of the Fourth Gospel: A Study in Literary Design* (Philadelphia: Fortress
Press, 1983) 71-73, where he applies the theory developed by G. Genette (*Narrative Discourse:
An Essay in Method* [Ithaca, N.Y.: Cornell University Press, 1980] 86-112).

[9] See, among many, my own reflections on this in F. J. Moloney, "Mary in the Fourth Gospel:
Woman and Mother," *Salesianum* 51 (1989) 431-39.

[10] See the use of the noun *doxa* in 1:14; 5:41-44; 7:18; 11:4, 40; 12:43; 17:5, 22-24; and the
verb *doxazein* in 8:54; 11:4; 12:23, 28; 13:31-32; 17:1-5.

(Isa 25:6-8; 54:4-8; 62:4-5; see also Matt 22:1-14; 25:1-13; Rev 19:7-9) and thus points the unknowing implied reader toward 20:31.

The water is poured from six stone jars that "were standing there, for the Jewish rites of purification" (2:6). The action of Jesus transforms the rites of Israel. The direct speech of the steward, not knowing the source of such richness (*ouk ēdei pothen estin,* v. 9), addresses the bridegroom as the one responsible for the gift of the wine. He indicates that a long history is now coming to its completion: "You have kept the good wine until now" (v. 10).

READING THE NARRATIVE

The narrative opens with an accumulation of important data for the implied reader (vv. 1-2). After the four days of preparation the reader finds that the narrative is now about to report the events of "the third day." There is an immediate link made with marriage, a traditional symbol of the messianic time and the messianic fullness in Israel (see especially Hos 2:19-20; Isa 25:6-8; Jer 2:2; Song of Songs).[11] The characters are presented: the mother of Jesus, Jesus and his disciples. By naming the mother of Jesus first in the list of characters, the author forewarns the reader of her importance for the following narrative.[12] She is even listed before Jesus; however, she is a new character for the reader.[13] The role of the mother of Jesus is crucial to the logic of the narrative. There have been many symbolic interpretations of the figure of the woman, the mother of Jesus, found both here and at 19:25-27, in close connection with "the hour" of Jesus.[14] However rich these readings have been, the reader knows her as "mother" (vv. 1, 3, 5) and "woman" (v. 4). The reader is not aware of a name for this woman other than "the mother of Jesus," and the term used by Jesus himself to

---

[11] For a Davidic and Solomonic ideal messianic reading of the Song of Songs, see R. Tournay, *Quand Dieu parle aux hommes le langage de l'amour: Etudes sur le Cantique des Cantiques* (CahRB 21; Paris: Gabalda, 1982) 83–89.

[12] Against J. Becker, who describes her as "szenisch ersetzbar" (*Das Evangelium des Johannes* [2 vols.; ÖTK 4/1-2; Gütersloh: Gerd Mohn; Würzburg: Echter-Verlag, 1979, 1981] 108).

[13] Contrary to R. A. Culpepper, who argues that the reader knows everyone who is not introduced (*Anatomy,* 212-16). The virginal reader only knows what is learned from the narrative itself.

[14] For an indication of the widespread interest in 2:1-12 from a Marian point of view, see the surveys of A. Smitmans, *Das Weinwunder von Kana: Die Auslegung von Jo 2,1-11 bei den Vätern und heute* (BGBE 6; Tübingen: J. C. B. Mohr [Paul Siebeck], 1966) 54–63; and R. F. Collins, "Mary in the Fourth Gospel – a decade of Johannine Studies," *Louvain Studies* 3 (1970) 99-142.

address her — "woman." It is on the basis of her experience as a woman and a mother that the early church first spoke of her (Gal 4:4; Mark 3:31-35; 6:3), and it is as a prolongation of that earliest reflection that the Johannine Marian material develops.[15]

After the setting of the scene (vv. 1-2),[16] the narrator reports the dialogue between the mother and Jesus. The mother poses the problem of the lack of wine (v. 3).[17] She does not ask a question of her son; she simply states the facts.[18] She is met by the sharp response from her son: "O woman, what have you to do with me? My hour has not yet come" (v. 4). Whatever one might try to make of Jesus' question to his mother, some form of rebuke is involved.[19] The expression "is abrupt and draws a sharp line between Jesus and his mother."[20] She stands "outside" a mysterious "hour" that is part of the unknowable union between the Father and the Son. The reader has an advantage over the mother, having read the prologue. Although "the hour" was not mentioned there, a unique intimacy between God and

---

[15] On the Johannine presentation of the mother of Jesus as a whole, see F. J. Moloney, *Mary: Woman and Mother* (Homebush: St Paul Publications, 1988) 31-50 (on 2:1-12, see pp. 32-37).

[16] It is sometimes suggested that Jesus and his disciples may have been uninvited, and thus were the cause of the shortage of wine. On this, see J. D. M. Derrett, "Water into Wine," *BZ* 7 (1963) 80-97. There is no indication of this in the text.

[17] I am following the shorter reading of v. 3: "When the wine gave out." For an assessment of the evidence, see B. Olsson, *Structure and Meaning in the Fourth Gospel: A Text-Linguistic Analysis of John 2:1-11 and 4:1-42* (Coniectanea Biblica, New Testament Series 6; Lund: Gleerup, 1974) 33-34.

[18] See B. F. Westcott, *The Gospel According to Saint John* (London: John Murray, 1908) 36: "It is enough to state the want."

[19] The interpretation of *ti emoi kai soi* is notoriously difficult. B. Olsson comments: "Scholars' understanding of this event reflects . . . their total interpretation" (*Structure and Meaning,* 35). It is widely used in the Old Testament (see Lagrange, *Saint Jean,* 56; Olsson, *Structure and Meaning,* 36-37; A. H. Maynard, "TI EMOI KAI SOI," *NTS* 31 [1985] 582-83), and it appears in the Synoptic tradition (see Olsson, ibid., 37-38; Maynard, "TI EMOI KAI SOI," 583-84). Is it a statement or a question? Once that has been decided, what does it mean in this context? A complete survey can be found in J.-P. Michaud, "Le signe de Cana dans son contexte johannique," *Laval Théologique et Philosophique* 18 (1962) 247-53. Recently C. H. Giblin has identified a Johannine narrative technique in this process of Jesus' responding negatively to a request and yet performing the action ("Suggestion, Negative Response, and Positive Action in St John's Gospel (John 2.1-11; 4.46-54; 7:2-14; 11.1-44)," *NTS* 26 [1979-80] 197-211). He correctly interprets the Semitic negative response of 2:4 as an "agreement to disagree, so that the party voicing disagreement expresses a concern . . . not to become 'involved' with the specific concerns of the party addressed" (p. 203). J. L. Staley is oversubtle in claiming that it has one meaning for the implied reader and another for the implied author (*The Print's First Kiss: A Rhetorical Investigation of the Implied Reader in the Fourth Gospel* [SBLDS 82; Atlanta: Scholars Press, 1988] 86.

[20] Barrett, *St John,* 191. Olsson, *Structure and Meaning,* 39: "a protest and a strong objection"; see also Maynard, "TI EMOI KAI SOI," 584-85.

the Word (1:1-2, 14, 18), which would lead to a clash between the light and the darkness (v. 5) and the rejection of the Word by his own (vv. 10-11), forms part of the reader's understanding of Jesus.

This is the first reference to a theme that will grow as the Gospel story unfolds. The "hour" will be the moment of Jesus' violent end (see 7:4, 30; 8:20; 12:27) but, strangely, also the moment of his glorification (see 12:23; 13:31), through which he will return to his Father (see 13:1, 32; 17:5). The implied reader does not know this, but the expression "*my* hour" indicates that "the hour" will be a moment in the human, historical experience of Jesus. Having read the prologue, the reader takes it for granted that this "hour" forms part of the plan of the Father for his Son. For the moment it is "not yet." It is a moment of plotted time unsettling the story time through the words of Jesus, the reliable witness par excellence.[21] Jesus responds that his hour "has not yet come." The omniscient author knows that the first miracle at Cana is not "the hour," which is "not yet" (see 7:4, 30; 8:20).[22] The events of Cana set in motion a tension between the "now" and the "not yet" which marks a public ministry moving toward the coming of "the hour" (see 12:23, 27-28, 31-33).[23] A narrative tension has been established by Jesus' reference to an hour that "has not yet come." The reader, who cannot reach outside story time, has been made aware of a plotted time in the future. The implied reader must read on, waiting for the time gap in the narrative to be filled by the eventual succession of events that will bring the story to a fitting end.

The strange response of Jesus to his mother—*ti emoi kai soi;*—makes the reader aware that "the hour" will be the result of Jesus' response to someone other than his mother. It is not the fruit of the request of Mary.[24] "Jesus first makes a remark which brings home the distance between them,

[21] J. L. Staley claims that the position of the possessive pronoun at the end throws the implied reader off guard, inasmuch as the reader would have understood "the hour" to refer to the wedding (*Print's First Kiss*, 88–89). He is correct in claiming that "the implied reader is forced into the role of a learner" (p. 99), but that this is a result of an unstable relationship between the implied author and the implied reader is unacceptable.

[22] Against the interpretation of this expression as marking the arrival of the hour in the revelation of the *doxa*. See, e.g., M.-E. Boismard, *Du Baptême à Cana (Jean 1,19−2,11)* (LD 18; Paris: Cerf, 1956) 154–59. For a survey, see R. E. Brown, *The Gospel According to John* (2 vols.; AB 29, 29A; Garden City, N.Y.: Doubleday, 1966, 1970) 99. It has been advocated by A. Vanhoye ("Interrogation johannique et l'exégèse de Cana," *Bib* 55 [1974] 157-77) and, along somewhat different lines, by R. F. Collins, "Cana (Jn. 2:1-12)—The first of his signs or the key to his signs?" *ITQ* 47 (1980) 79-95; see especially pp. 85-88.

[23] See G. Segalla, *Giovanni* (NVB 36; Rome: Edizioni Paoline, 1976) 165-66.

[24] See Giblin, "Suggestion, Negative Response, and Positive Action," 203.

and then informs her that the law according to which he works is imposed on him by another."[25] Despite the apparent harshness of his response, which places her "outside" an understanding of the mystery of "the hour," the mother says to the servants: "Do *whatever* he *tells* you" (v. 5). She has communicated her trust in the word of Jesus through this command to the servants, telling them to accept all that his spoken command (*ho ti an legē*) communicates. The mother of Jesus is presented to the implied reader as recognizing that Jesus' word is able to bring the gifts of God. The text does not indicate that he responds to her motherly requests.[26] Her command to the servants – "Do whatever he tells you" – shows her openness and trust in whatever "the word of Jesus" might bring.[27]

We must not trivialize the theological program of the Fourth Gospel. What Jesus does flows from his oneness with the Father (see especially 4:34; 5:36; 10:30; 17:4), but in terms of the narrative so far, the reader has not been provided with a shred of information that would assure the mother of Jesus of the efficacy of the word of her son. Her command to the attendants depends entirely on her yet-to-be-verified belief that such would be the case. Westcott has rightly insisted that the key to the narrative is the nature of the relationship between the mother and Jesus: "As soon as this is grasped, the implied request, the persistence of trust, the triumph of faith, are seen to hang together harmoniously."[28]

The background of a Sinai tradition and the giving of a *doxa* that surpasses the first gift of the Law through Moses (see 1:17) is also found here. There is a link between the words of the mother and the words of the assembled people at the foot of Mount Sinai. On three occasions, as the people of Israel receive the Law from the hands of Moses, they commit themselves as a people of God by crying out: "All that the Lord has spoken we will do" (*hosa eipen ho theos poiēsomen* [LXX Exod 19:8]; *pantas tous logous, hous elalēsen kyrios, poiēsomen* [Exod 24:3; see also v. 7]). Whereas the LXX uses *lalein* on two occasions (Exod 24:3, 7) the Johannine choice of *legein*

---

[25] R. Schnackenburg, *The Gospel according to St John* (3 vols.; HTCNT 4/1-3; London: Burns & Oates; New York: Crossroad, 1968-82) 329.

[26] Despite the many reflections on this text which make such a claim. See E. Haenchen, *John 1-2* (2 vols.; Hermeneia; Philadelphia: Fortress Press, 1984) 1:172: "The narrator reports only what is essential."

[27] Schnackenburg trivializes her response: "Unassumingly she does her best to facilitate her Son" (*St John*, 331). See also Lagrange, *Saint Jean*, 57: "C'est le fait d'une mère qui connait le coeur de son fils."

[28] Westcott, *St John*, 36. Commenting on v. 5, Westcott writes: "Nowhere is perhaps such trust shewn" (p. 37).

possibly comes from the title *logos* in the prologue, as well as its use in Exod 19:8. One must commit oneself to the word of Jesus because, as the reader is aware, Jesus Christ is the Word.

The command of the mother of Jesus to the attendants, which fittingly also has its roots in Israel's experience of God's presence to them at Sinai, is a communication of the Mother's unconditional trust in the word of her son.[29] As once the *děbārîm* ("words") of the Law offered life to a people, so now the mother of Jesus trusts that the *dābār* ("word") of her son will do likewise. But she has no *proof* that such will be the case. As far as the narrative is concerned, the reader, who is meeting this woman for the first time, has been given no indication *why* she should display this trust, repeating the trust of the people of God at Sinai. The mother of Jesus, unable to *know* what would be the result of her command to the servants, is the first to believe in Jesus. Such is the intent of the narrative. She bases her confidence on an unshakable trust that Jesus' word will be efficacious. The response of Jesus in v. 4 should not be forgotten. The reader moves from v. 4 to v. 5. The mother's word to the servants was preceded by a rebuke or, at best, a distancing of Jesus from her. Therefore, her trust in the efficacy of the word of Jesus is even more impressive. It is present despite the rebuke. She places all her trust in the word of Jesus, cost her what it may.

The woman, the mother of Jesus, is the *first* person, in the experience of the reader, to manifest trust in the word of Jesus. Her relationship with Jesus transcends the limitations displayed by the disciples, who attempted to understand him within their own categories in 1:35-51. The mother of Jesus is deliberately shown by the author as the first who commands action based entirely on the word of Jesus, without offering any supporting cultural, religious, or historical motivation for such a command. Indeed, the motivation for her action is a rebuke. The reader encounters a first indication of an answer to the question raised by Jesus' reaction to the faith of the disciples shown in the first days (1:35-51). The mother of Jesus instructs the implied reader that true Johannine faith has to do with a radical trust in the efficacy of the word of Jesus (2:4-5).[30]

The account of the miracle is introduced through the description of six large stone jars (v. 6). Later Jewish texts indicate that stone was useful

---

[29] See, for a more detailed study of this Exodus background, A. M. Serra, *Contributi dell'antica letteratura giudaica per l'esegesi di Gv. 2:1-12 e 19:25-27* (Scripta Pontificiae Facultatis 'Marianum' 31; Rome: Herder, 1977) 139–81. For some earlier suggestions along these lines, see J. A. Grassi, "The Wedding at Cana (John II 1-11): A Pentecostal Meditation?" *NovT* 14 (1972) 134–35.

[30] See Boismard, *Du Baptême*, 159. This is denied by Becker (*Johannes*, 110): "Ihre Reaktion ist . . . unwichtig."

for purificatory purposes because it did not itself contract uncleanness.[31] Each jar contains eighteen to twenty-four gallons.[32] The purpose of the jars was "for the Jewish rites of purification."[33] There is no need to decide whether or not a specific feast is involved, or whether the jars were there for the purifications involved in the cleansing that took place both before and after a ritual meal. It is enough that the reader is told of six jars made out of stone to avoid ritual uncleanness. The choice of the number "six" is probably a further hint to the implied reader that the Jewish world represented by this ritual lacks the perfection of the number "seven."[34]

The reader knows from the prologue that "his own people received him not" (1:11). The implied reader has already met "priests and Levites" sent by the Jews and by the Pharisees from Jerusalem (1:19, 24). These representatives from the heart of Judaism attempted to force John the Baptist into categories they could control and understand, but the Baptist pointed beyond himself (1:19-34). The author has begun his presentation of "the Jews." Now a reader with even clearer ideas on the relationship between Jesus and Judaism is emerging. If "the Jews" showed an inability to accept the testimony of the Baptist, here the author is more explicit. The gift that Jesus gives surpasses the gift of Jewish Law and traditions. The prologue has already said it: "And from his fullness we have all received, a gift in place of a gift" (1:16). The reader is discovering how such things take place in the life story of Jesus.

Jesus commands: "Fill the jars with water" (v. 7a), and these words are obeyed to the letter (v. 7b). The attendants do what the mother told them to do (v. 5). The narrator tells the reader that the jars were filled "to the brim." The author supplies these details to create the impression of superabundance. There is no spectacular instantaneous miracle. That would distract the reader from the real point of the narrative. Jesus instructs the attendants, again through the "words" of direct speech, to draw from

---

[31] See Str-B, 2:406.

[32] For this calculation of *metrētas dyo ē treis*, see among many Barrett, *St John*, 192.

[33] This explanation is provided to develop the information given to the implied reader in 1:17: the perfection of God's earlier gift through the gift of Jesus. It is not there to explain the presence of jars to an uninformed reader. The reader does not need to have Jewish customs explained.

[34] Along with many others, C. K. Barrett rejects this suggestion, as he claims that Jesus does not create a seventh jar to bring the number to perfection (*St John*, 191). This misses the point. The narrator merely wishes to indicate that Judaism, along with its ritual, falls short of the fullness. On this, see M.-E. Boismard, *Moïse et Jésus: Essai de Christologie Johannique* (BETL 84; Leuven: University Press, 1988) 56. The good wine (v. 10) created by openness (v. 5: the mother) and obedience to the word of Jesus (vv. 7-8: the attendants) provides that fullness.

the jars that had been filled, and to take it to the steward (v. 8b). Again, the narrator reports silent obedience to the word of Jesus: "So they took it" (v. 8c). They continue to respond to the mother's imperative (v. 5).

Only now, as the result of a series of actions that depend on the command of the mother of Jesus, does the reader discover, through the reaction of the steward, that the water has become wine. The miracle itself is not reported. The narrative depends on a series of encounters where there are never more than two active characters on stage at the one time.[35] The action unfolds as the result of "words," that is, direct speech:[36]

- The mother *speaks* to Jesus (v. 3).
- Jesus *responds* to his mother (v. 4).
- The mother *speaks* to the attendants (v. 5). This is a crucial turning point in the narrative, as she points toward her son and instructs them to act according to his word. She disappears from the action, and Jesus becomes the leading character.
- Jesus *speaks twice* to the attendants (vv. 7-8).
- Jesus *apparently* disappears from the action, as the steward *speaks* to the bridegroom (v. 10).[37]

The event of the miracle is told only parenthetically.[38] On tasting the water become wine, the steward's concern is to discover "where it came from" (*pothen estin*). He is ignorant of the origins of the wine, although the attendants are not, as they have been reported as obedient recipients of the word of Jesus on two occasions (vv. 7-8). The question of origins, which will play such a large part in the Fourth Gospel, has been raised for the reader who knows the origin of both the word that set the miracle in motion (vv. 7-8) and the Word (1:1-2, 14) who spoke to the attendants.[39]

The encounter between the steward and the bridegroom follows. The reader never meets the bridegroom. He never speaks and the bride is never

---

[35] On this Johannine characteristic, see J. L. Martyn, *History and Theology in the Fourth Gospel* (2nd ed.; Nashville: Abingdon, 1979) 3-16, 49-57.

[36] What follows has been seen by Olsson (*Structure and Meaning*, 86-88), but he misses the role of the word in the passage.

[37] In a structural analysis of the passage, P. Geoltrain has traced the movement from character to character ("Les noces à Cana: Jean 2,1-12: Analyse des structures narratives," *Foi et Vie* 73 [1974] 83-90). M.-E. Boismard has seen the importance of the dialogue between Jesus and his mother (*Du Baptême*, 154-59).

[38] See Olsson, *Structure and Meaning*, 58.

[39] Against Barrett, *St John*, 193. As J. Gnilka puts it: "Das Woher der Gabe ist wie das Woher des Gebers ein vorborgenes (vgl. 4:11; 19:9)" (*Johannesevangelium* [NEchtB 4; Würzburg: Echter-Verlag, 1989] 23).

mentioned. The bridegroom is reprimanded for keeping the best wine *heōs arti*, "until now." Jesus' presence has transformed the rituals of Israel into an unexpected fullness.[40] The next time the reader will encounter the word "bridegroom" (*nymphios*) will be in 3:29, where the term is applied by John the Baptist to Jesus. At this stage of the Gospel (2:9-10), the reader can only wonder at the sudden introduction of a new character, a bridegroom who does nothing but is only spoken to by the steward. A gap has been created for the reader. It will be filled in 3:29 where, in the reader's next (and only other) encounter with the word, it is explicitly applied to Jesus. At one level of the narrative the encounter between the steward and the bridegroom allows the former to instruct the latter in common sense. At another level the encounter raises a question about the source of the fullness provided by the bridegroom. "The steward here seems to be wholly unaware of the supply of wine, of the shortage or of the drawing of water. He merely states that the wine is excellent (*kalos*) and that the bridegroom's actions are not those of ordinary men."[41]

As Jesus told his mother in v. 4, his hour has not yet come. The steward may think it has. The implied reader knows better and will read further, waiting for the hour of Jesus which is "not yet."[42] On the way, the reader will discover that Jesus is the bridegroom (3:29), and the author's strange introduction of that character in 2:9-10 will be clarified. Ironically, the steward is speaking to the one who provided the wine, and thus Jesus is present throughout the whole narrative. This first (*archē*) miracle is also the germ (*archē*) of the messianic gift which Jesus will eventually bring.[44] There is a tension between the *oupō hēkei* of the hour of Jesus (v. 4) and the best of wines kept *heōs arti* (v. 10). The plotted time of the hour of Jesus points beyond the story time of the gift of the wine. They must not be collapsed into story time (v. 10). The *doxa* of Jesus is manifested in the narration, and the disciples come to faith, but there is still a plotted "not yet" which remains outside the narrated "now" of the gift of the wine.

---

[40] The fullness is found in the manifestation of God in the person of Jesus (see 1:14, 51; 2:11). A eucharistic interpretation of the passage reads too much into it. For a survey, see Smitmans, *Das Weinwunder*, 50-54. For the classical statement of this case, see O. Cullmann, *Early Christian Worship* (SBT 10; London: SCM Press, 1953) 66-71.

[41] Olsson, *Structure and Meaning*, 62; see also P. D. Duke, *Irony in the Fourth Gospel* (Atlanta: John Knox Press, 1985) 83-84.

[42] J. L. Staley claims that the implied author has destabilized the implied reader, who is faced with an "earthly" story that has a "heavenly" meaning (*Print's First Kiss*, 87-90). But he has not given the reader all the tools needed for the correct reading.

[43] For the patristic background to this interpretation, see Smitmans, *Das Weinwunder*, 207-17.

[44] See Olsson, *Structure and Meaning*, 60-61, 67-68; R. Kieffer, *Le monde symbolique de saint Jean* (LD 137; Paris: Cerf, 1989) 44.

> The transformation of water into wine . . . is the first act of the Word in the
> world, and a type of the greater transformation to come. Perhaps it is the grace
> beyond grace, the messianic wine of being that replaces the inferior wine of
> the Torah, which is appropriate only to becoming.[45]

The narrator draws back from his reporting of the narrative to comment to the reader (v. 11). This was the first of Jesus' *sēmeia*. It is not simply
a wondrous event. It is a "sign" of something that Jesus both is and is doing.
The days of preparation and the gift of the *doxa* have come to a conclusion, as in this sign Jesus "manifested his glory" (*ephanerōsen tēn doxan
autou*). This is the only place in the Fourth Gospel where the Johannine
word *phaneroun* (see also 1:31; 3:21; 7:4; 9:3; 17:6; 21:1 [twice], 14) is used
with *doxa*.[46] The solemnity of the language indicates to the reader that the
revelation of the glory of Yhwh manifested "on the third day" at Sinai has
been surpassed in the manifestation of the *doxa* of Jesus "on the third day"
at Cana (2:1).[47]

The four days of preparation (1:19-51) have now been crowned with
the revelation of the *doxa* "on the third day." The disciples, who stumbled
toward an understanding of Jesus in terms they could control over the days
of preparation (1:35-51), are now credited with the beginnings of true faith:
episteusan eis auton. What need is there to go any further with the story
of the life of Jesus? The implied reader has traced the journey of the
disciples through failure into their acceptance of the revelation of the glory
in the *sēmeion* of Cana. But the reader has also read two references to time
which point beyond story time to plotted time. The words of Jesus to his
mother spoke of the hour that had not yet come (*oupō*), and the words
of the steward to the bridegroom chided him for keeping the good wine
"until now" (*heōs arti*).

The miracle shows that the presence of Jesus as the *doxa* has been kept
until "now" (v. 10). But the whole narrative is told under the shadow of
a "not yet" (v. 4). The story time of the "now" looks forward to the plotted

---

[45] F. Kermode, "John," in *The Literary Guide to the Bible,* ed. R. Alter and F. Kermode (London:
Collins, 1987) 449; see also J. Marsh, *Saint John* (The Pelican New Testament Commentaries;
Harmondsworth: Penguin Books, 1968) 146; and the remarks of Haenchen, *John 1,* 178-79.
Haenchen also relates 2:1-12 to 1:16-17 and the "greater things" of 1:50.

[46] The verb *phaneroun,* used nine times in the Fourth Gospel, is closely associated with
the Johannine idea of Jesus' revelation of God. See Schnackenburg, *St John,* 1:335-37; W. J.
Bittner, *Jesu Zeichen im Johannesevangelium: Die Messias-Erkenntnis im Johannesevangelium vor
ihrem jüdischen Hintergrund* (WUNT 2, Reihe 26; Tübingen: J. C. B. Mohr [Paul Siebeck], 1987)
97-98.

[47] For a full discussion of the Sinai connection, see Olsson, *Structure and Meaning,* 69-73;
see also M. Theobald, *Die Fleischwerdung des Logos: Studien zum Verhältnis des Johannesprologs
zum Corpus des Evangeliums und zu 1 Joh* (NTAbh N.F. 20; Münster: Aschendorff, 1988) 290-92.

time of the "not yet." The implied reader cannot be totally satisfied with
the story so far. Neither can the reader be satisfied with the response of
the disciples. They may have come to faith, but there is still the time
between the "now" and the "not yet" which must be experienced. As well
as the indications of the Cana story itself, the reader has not found an
answer to questions the prologue raised, especially the response of "his
own" and the judgment which flows from an acceptance of or a refusal
of the light (1:5, 11-13, 16). The next episode in the overall story will develop
the theme (2:13-22). The fact that the *doxa* can be seen in the actions of
Jesus recalls 1:14. But there is a great deal more that was "told" in the
prologue which still has to be "shown" to the reader.

The narrator closes the first Cana story with v. 12.[48] Brown has com-
mented that "it is difficult to treat this verse as a real connective between
Cana and the next scene at Jerusalem, for a journey to Capernaum is a
long detour from the road to Jerusalem."[49] Such observations miss the role
of v. 12 in the narrative in its present form.[50] The major players in the
dramatic narrative which the reader has just read are re-assembled: Jesus,
his mother, his brothers, and his disciples. They journey away from Cana,
and stay in Capernaum "for a few days." The author provides these details
to keep the narrative moving. Within the brief summary there is a gathering of the characters of the story that has just been read (with the addition
of the brothers of Jesus).[51] Also included are an indication of a geographical
journey from one place to another and a final indication of the passing
of time. The narrative axes of character, space, and time gathered in this
way lead the reader into the next event in the life of Jesus.[52]

My reading of the text of 2:1-12 raises a further question. Bultmann
has described this passage as a typical miracle story.[53] A more narrative
approach to the text (whatever its origins may have been) would seem to
indicate that such a description of the event fails to meet Bultmann's own

[48] This verse is generally seen by the commentators as a very clumsy transition with roots
in earlier tradition. See especially Brown, *John*, 112-13; C. H. Dodd, *Historical Tradition in
the Fourth Gospel* (Cambridge: Cambridge University Press, 1963) 235-36. Bultmann suggests
that in the signs source, this verse led on to 4:46-54 (*John*, 114 n. 4). See also Fortna, *Signs*,
102-3; idem, *Fourth Gospel*, 58-59; Boismard, *Moïse ou Jésus*, 44-46.

[49] Brown, *John*, 113; similarly Dodd, *Historical Tradition*, 235.

[50] I am not denying that v. 12 had a prehistory that needs to be considered. The point
of the present study is to determine its present role. Did the author lose control of sources
here, or does v. 12 play an intended role in a narrative that an author is deliberately shaping?

[51] "The brothers" will reappear in 7:1-10, not unknown to the implied reader.

[52] See Schnackenburg, *St John*, 1:342-43.

[53] See Bultmann, *John*, 115; see also Becker, *Johannes*, 106.

description of a typical miracle story. In his *History of the Synoptic Tradition*, Bultmann argues that the Synoptic miracle stories were shaped in the tradition according to the following form:[54]

> (a) A problem is described in some detail, so that the gravity of the situation will be clear.
> (b) A request is made.
> (c) The miracle is performed, and it is accompanied by the description of a gesture, a touch, a word, or a name.
> (d) The miracle and its successful accomplishment are described.
> (e) The miracle closes with the wonder of all who saw it or heard about it.

We have seen that the narrative of John 2:1-12 has a setting, a verbal exchange, the main action, the narrator's comment, and a final scene which moves the main characters on. But embedded within the present Johannine narrative the implied reader encounters a miracle story that is quite untypical:

> 1. *Problem:* "The wine failed" (v. 3a).
> 2. *Request:* "The mother of Jesus said to him, 'They have no wine'" (v. 3b).
> 3. *Rebuke:* "O woman, what have you to do with me? My hour has not yet come" (v. 4).
> 4. *Reaction:* "His mother said to the servants, 'Do whatever he tells you' (*ho ti an legē hymin poiēsate*)" (v. 5).
> 5. *Consequence:* A miracle that leads to the faith of others (the disciples) (vv. 6-11).

There are several elements within this structure that make it non-typical of miracle stories. Particularly important are those elements in which the mother of Jesus plays an important role. Following the normal form, she points out to Jesus that there is a problem.[55] Immediately, however, the form of a miracle story is broken as he rebukes the one who raised the

[54] See R. Bultmann, *The History of the Synoptic Tradition* (Oxford: Blackwell, 1963) 218-31; idem, *John*, 118 n. 2.

[55] Even here, however, G. Theissen claims that such a request is peculiar (*Miracle Stories of the Early Christian Tradition* [Studies of the NT and its World; Edinburgh: T. & T. Clark, 1983] 104). He classifies the Cana story as a "gift miracle" and points out that "gift miracles are never initiated by requests, but always by an act of the miracle worker." In this light, the form of John 2:1-12 is strange indeed.

problem.[56] The Synoptic tradition does not normally report such a personal response to the one making the request.[57] The next step is also foreign to the regular form of miracle stories. Without being instructed in any way by Jesus, his mother is the one who turns and tells the attendants what to do: "Do whatever he tells you" (v. 5). The final element in the Johannine story is also somewhat foreign. One does not read of the wonder of all who see or hear of the miracle. Nothing is said of the effect of the miracle upon the guests, who are never mentioned.[58] The result of the miracle is a manifestation of the glory of Jesus and the faith of the disciples (v. 11). These alterations to the traditional form of a miracle story are also the incidents that shape the implied reader in a special way. There can be no doubt that the author has composed this miracle story in its present form so that the reader, who arrives at 1:51 asking how one should respond to Jesus, will sense that an answer to that question is now being provided.

CONCLUSION

Behind the proposed reading of John 2:1-12 lies a close relationship between these events, which led to the manifestation of the *doxa* of Jesus "on the third day" (2:1), and the former gift of the *doxa* at Sinai "on the third day" (Exod 19:16, 19). At Cana "on the third day" a Jewish woman in a Jewish town at a Jewish celebration shows an unconditional trust and commitment to the word of Jesus. Consequently, Jesus manifests his *doxa* (v. 11). The Evangelist has thus initiated his catechesis on the nature of true faith by presenting the figure of the mother of Jesus responding to the word of her son. Even though the verb *pisteuein* has not been applied to the response of the mother of Jesus in 2:1-12, the implied reader meets it in association with the disciples (v. 11). Because the mother of Jesus,

[56] R. E. Brown, "The 'Mother of Jesus' in the Fourth Gospel," in *L'Evangile de Jean: Sources, rédaction, théologie*, ed. M. de Jonge (BETL 44; Leuven: University Press, 1977) 308. R. F. Collins, "Cana (Jn. 2:1-11)," 83. Collins resolves the problem by judging vv. 3b-4 and 19:25-27 as Johannine additions to a more traditional source (see pp. 86-91). W. J. Bittner claims that in no place in miracle stories in any Gospel does Jesus rebuke those seeking miracles (*Jesu Zeichen*, 129). He does not mention 2:4 and excludes its parallel 4:48.

[57] On occasion within the context of a miracle story there are remarks from Jesus about the faithless generation (see, e.g., Mark 9:19; par. Matt 17:17; Luke 9:41) or, in Matthew, the littleness of the faith of the disciples (Matt 8:26; 14:31; 16:8). Such texts are hardly parallels to the *ti emoi kai soi, gynai* of John 2:4.

[58] Schnackenburg, *St John*, 1:323; P. W. Meyer, "John 2:10," *JBL* 86 (1967) 191-97.

despite the rebuke that her son directed toward her, trusted completely in the efficacy of the word of Jesus, the disciples have come to see the sign, the *doxa,* and they have come to faith.[59]

Here a further element is provided for the emerging implied reader. True Johannine faith – a trusting acceptance of the word of Jesus – is not an end in itself. The implied reader is given a first taste and an initial hint of another element in a correct understanding of faith in Jesus: the first to commit herself totally to the word of Jesus (v. 5) does so that others might believe (v. 11). There is a suggestion that the encounter between the mother and Jesus provides a model response to Jesus which may be understood as an expression of *authentic faith.* Such a suggestion, of course, will be further tested by the reader through the rest of the story.

[59] See R. H. Strachan, *The Fourth Gospel: Its Significance and Environment* (3rd ed.; London: SCM Press, 1941) 123: "All is accomplished by His creative 'Word' (cf. v. 5)."

Chapter Five

A Journey of Faith in Israel: John 2:13—3:36

❡ THE NARRATIVES and the discourses in 2:13–3:36 reflect encounters between Jesus and representatives of Judaism: "the Jews" (2:13-22), Nicodemus (3:1-21), John the Baptist (3:22-36), and, as lesser characters, John's disciples and a Jew (3:25-26). Although Aenon (see 3:23) may be in Samaria,[1] leading the reader toward 4:1-42, the narrative is set in a Jewish world. If the implied reader emerges from 1:1-51 asking what is needed for a fruitful response to Jesus, the first Cana miracle (2:1-12), set within a Jewish world of Jewish characters and customs provides the beginnings of an answer to that question. The presence of Jesus to Israel, and further responses from its representatives now follow.

I. JESUS, "THE JEWS," AND THE TEMPLE (2:13-22)

The Shape of the Narrative

Whatever may have been the prehistory of the passage,[2] narrative criteria point to a carefully shaped account: an introduction (v. 13) and a

---

[1] For the Samaritan location of Aenon, see M.-E. Boismard, "Aenon, près de Salem," *RB* 80 (1973) 218–29.

[2] Why is the event reported so early in Jesus' ministry? For the discussion, see R. E. Brown,

conclusion (vv. 23-25) from the narrator, the description of Jesus' activity in the Temple (vv. 14-17), highlighted by his words (v. 16), the subsequent reaction of "the Jews," again marked by direct speech (vv. 18-20), and a closing comment on the action from the narrator (vv. 21-22). The narrative, therefore, has been shaped as follows:

(a) *Verse 13:* The scene is set. After the "few days" in Capernaum (v. 12) Jesus is again in motion, this time going up to Jerusalem. The motivation for Jesus' going up to Jerusalem is indicated: "The Passover of the Jews was at hand."[3]

(b) *Verses 14-17:* A description of Jesus' action in the Temple follows. The motivation for Jesus' action is given toward the end of the section, in the words of Jesus: "You shall not make my Father's house a house of trade" (v. 16). It concludes with the disciples' understanding of the action in terms of LXX Ps 68:10: "Zeal for thy house will consume me."

(c) *Verses 18-20:* A verbal exchange is narrated. The whole of this section is marked by direct speech: "The Jews said" (v. 18); "Jesus answered" (v. 19); "The Jews said" (v. 20).

(d) *Verses 21-22:* The narrator draws back from the action to make a comment for the implied reader on the correct meaning of the words of Jesus and to inform the reader of the faith of the disciples.

(e) *Verses 23-25:* A concluding passage indicates that Jesus stays in Jerusalem for the feast and describes the response of many to his signs and his response to them.

There are close links between this account and the shape of 2:1-12.[4] At Cana the exchange of words between the mother of Jesus and her son took place *before* the action; in Jerusalem the action leads to the exchange of words. This is the only major difference between the shape of the two narratives. I bracket 2:23-25 because this passage serves both as a conclusion to the episode of the purification of the Temple and a narrative comment that will lead into the next episode: Jesus' encounter with Nicodemus.[5] In terms of the shape of the narrative, it belongs to 2:13-22

The Gospel According to John (2 vols.; AB 29, 29A; Garden City, N.Y.: Doubleday, 1966, 1970) 116–20. How does it relate to its context? For example, X. Léon-Dufour regards it as "un texte isolé" (*Lecture de l'évangile selon Jean* [Parole de Dieu; Paris: Seuil, 1988] 248.

[3] This is a very Johannine expression; see 6:4; 7:2; 10:22; 11:55.

[4] The close relationship between the two narratives is often noticed; see especially C. Koester, "Hearing, Seeing and Believing in the Gospel of John," *Bib* 70 (1989) 327–48.

[5] It is a "bridge" passage; see L. J. Topel, "A Note on the Methodology of Structural Analysis in Jn 2:23–3:21," *CBQ* 33 (1971) 216–17.

as a concluding passage. But for the purpose of our study, it will be considered in its own right. It plays a role as commentary for the implied reader.

There is a strong concentration on the Jewish context of all that happens in this scene. The time setting is the approaching Jewish feast of Passover (v. 13a).[6] This is the motivation for the place in which the narrative happens: Jesus goes to Jerusalem and is in the Temple (vv. 13b-14a). Conflict ensues. This first angry encounter serves as a paradigm for the growing tension between Jesus and "the Jews." To this point in the narrative there has been no encounter between Jesus and "the Jews" as such. Although they had sent the priests and Levites from Jerusalem (1:19) who interrogated John the Baptist (1:19-28), the reader meets "the Jews," as active characters in the story, for the first time in 2:18. After the model of complete faith provided by the mother of Jesus, a Jewish woman at a Jewish celebration in a Jewish town, the next example of a reaction to the revelation of Jesus through his word is that of "the Jews."[7]

The Passover is mentioned in the frame of the action, in 2:13 and 2:23. Feasts are often used throughout this Gospel, and there has been considerable discussion over their significance for both the theology and the structure of the Fourth Gospel as a whole.[8] The feast of the Passover is mentioned in v. 13, and v. 23 has no immediate connection to the systematic use of the feasts of the Jews in chaps. 5–10 or with the Passover, which dominates chaps. 11–20. It serves here as a link with the traditional practices of Israel and "the Jews," who play a central role within the context of 2:13-25.

Reading the Narrative

After the pause in Capernaum (2:12), action returns as Jesus "went up" (*anebē*) to Jerusalem because the Passover of the Jews was at hand. The

---

[6] Many commentators point to the author's stressing "of the Jews" as a polemic against a Passover feast no longer celebrated in the Christian community. See, among many, J. Becker, *Das Evangelium des Johannes* (2 vols.; ÖTK 4/1-2; Gütersloh: Gerd Mohn; Würzburg: Echter-Verlag, 1979, 1981) 1:123. I disagree. The narrator's main purpose is to set what follows firmly within a Jewish world and a Jewish feast.

[7] Against Léon-Dufour (*Lecture*, 250), who plays down the importance of "the Jews" and argues that the passage has no role to play in a supposed Cana to Cana grouping (see p. 250 n. 9).

[8] For example, R. Schnackenburg, *The Gospel according to St John* (3 vols.; HTCNT 4/1-3; London: Burns & Oates; New York: Crossroad, 1968-82) 1:1-2; Léon-Dufour, *Lecture*, 31-32, 252-53. R. E. Brown rightly sees the three Passovers as "setting for a particular narrative," and not "signposts for a division of the Gospel" (*John*, cxxxix).

reader is familiar with the importance of the Temple-centered celebration of the Passover. Jesus discovers merchants in the Temple area (v. 14, *kai heuren en tō hierō*) who were selling oxen, sheep, and pigeons and were changing Roman money into Tyrian money so that people might pay the Temple tax (v. 14).[9] He drives out of the Temple (*exebalen ek tou hierou*) with a whip of cords those selling oxen and sheep;[10] he scatters the coins and overturns the tables of the money changers (v. 15). Throughout this opening description of Jesus' activity the author uses the same word for the Temple building twice: *to hieron* (vv. 14, 15).[11]

The action is briefly reported so that the narrator can move to the direct speech of Jesus.[12] He speaks to those who sold pigeons, giving reasons for his action.[13] The words of Jesus attack the abuse of *to hieron*. The Temple should never be an *oikos emporiou*. For Jesus it is not a building where people gather (*to hieron*); it is "the house of my Father" (*ton oikon tou patros mou*).[14] The *hieron* is now called an *oikos*. It is not only an area where people gather to honor God, but a place among men and women where the God of Israel, whom Jesus calls "my Father" has his dwelling. It is an important part of Jewish belief that the God of Israel dwells in the Temple, on the Temple mount.[15] The crucial aspect of these words of Jesus is not the claim that the Temple is the dwelling place of God, but the claim that it is the dwelling place of "my Father."[16] A very Johannine feature has been added to

[9] See E. Haenchen, *John 1-2* (2 vols.; Hermeneia; Philadelphia: Fortress Press, 1984) 183; Schnackenburg, *St John*, 1:346 n. 13; G. R. Beasley-Murray, *John* (WBC 36; Waco: Word Books, 1987) 38.

[10] Reading, with most commentators, *pantas* as including the human beings as well as the beasts.

[11] With many others, R. E. Brown simply affirms that *hieron* means the outer court of the Temple, while *naos* refers to the sanctuary (*John*, 115). On the basis of the evidence supplied by BAGD (p. 372, s.v. *to hieron*), the expression refers to the Temple as a whole, *including the sanctuary*. This, I would maintain, is the meaning intended by the author in 2:14-15. It makes more sense of the misunderstanding that occurs in vv. 19-21.

[12] R. Bultmann sees the importance of the direct speech (*The Gospel of John: A Commentary* [Oxford: Blackwell, 1971] 125–26).

[13] One cannot drive out cages of pigeons; thus Jesus orders the pigeon sellers: "Take these things away." So also B. F. Westcott, *The Gospel According to Saint John* (London: John Murray, 1908) 41; M.-J. Lagrange, *Évangile selon saint Jean* (Ebib; Paris: Gabalda, 1936) 66.

[14] There is a probable contrasting play on the two "houses," the *oikos emporiou* and the *oikos tou patros mou* and a hint of Zech 14:21. See C. H. Dodd, *The Interpretation of the Fourth Gospel* (Cambridge: Cambridge University Press, 1953) 300.

[15] On this, see R. de Vaux, *Ancient Israel: Its Life and Institutions* (London: Darton, Longman & Todd, 1961) 325-30.

[16] Some commentators draw too much from this early stage of the narrative, claiming that the replacement of the Temple is the point of Jesus' words. See, e.g., Beasley-Murray, *John*, 39–40. The introduction of "my Father" is thus missed. Rightly, see J. H. Bernard, *A Critical*

the narrative.[17] The reader learned from the prologue that the key to understanding who Jesus is and what he does lies in his relationship with God. In the Synoptic report of this event, all the evangelists have Jesus cite Isa 56:7, whereby he claims that the Temple is "my house" (see Mark 11:17; Matt 21:13; Luke 19:46). Such a claim would not rest easy in the Johannine presentation of Jesus. While Israel relates to God through its Temple, Jesus now challenges such a relationship by claiming that even their Temple belongs to him in a special way, as it is the house of his Father.

The direct speech of Jesus in v. 16, laying claim on the Temple as his Father's house and insisting that all objects of trade and commerce must be banned from it, is the turning point of the narrative. The *hieron*, which had become an *oikos emporiou*, has now been claimed by Jesus as *ton oikon tou patros mou* (v. 17).[18] It is the relationship with his Father that enables Jesus to change the theme of the discussion with "the Jews" from a Temple building (vv. 13-16) to a sanctuary which is his body (vv. 19-21). Another theme known to the implied reader from the prologue is mentioned for the first time in the prose narrative of the Gospel story: the relationship between Jesus and his Father (see 1:14, 18). The *telling* of the poetic narrative is now receiving its *showing* in the human story of Jesus. The order and logic of the relationship spelled out in the hymn are being realized within the context of "the wayward paths of human freedom."[19]

Jesus' revelation of God as his Father—on this occasion of the Temple as the house of *his Father*—produces two reactions. The implied reader has also been told in the prologue (see 1:11-13) that this would happen. For the first time, the reader is now shown how it happens. The disciples accept what has been said, and they interpret Jesus' actions by recalling LXX Ps 68:10 (v. 17).[20] But the reader is expected to notice the difference between what is said in the LXX Psalm and what is said by the disciples, as they

---

and Exegetical Commentary on the Gospel according to St John (2 vols.; ICC; Edinburgh: T. & T. Clark, 1928) 1:91.

[17] Against Becker, who argues (via Luke 2:49) that the saying is traditional, lacking the Johannine Son-title (*Johannes*, 124).

[18] It is sometimes pointed out that, while not particularly praiseworthy, there was nothing intrinsically wrong with the Temple trade. Indeed, it was essential for the proper organization of the Temple cult. See especially I. Abrahams, *Studies in Pharisaism and the Gospels* (Cambridge: Cambridge University Press, 1917) First Series, pp. 82-89.

[19] R. Alter, *The Art of Biblical Narrative* (New York: Basic Books, 1981) 26.

[20] The disciples appear in the narrative rather unexpectedly, as it was not said that they traveled from Capernaum (v. 12) to Jerusalem (v. 13). The Psalm is used elsewhere in the New Testament in passion apologetic (see Rom 11:9; 15:3; Matt 27:48; John 15:25; 19:28-29; Acts 1:20). For an assessment of its Johannine use, see B. Lindars, *New Testament Apologetic: The Doctrinal Significance of the Old Testament Quotations* (London: SCM Press, 1961) 104-8.

interpret Jesus' gesture, explained by his words to the pigeon sellers. The tense of the verb is changed. LXX Ps 68:10 explains the sufferings of the person at prayer in the aorist tense: "Zeal for your house *has consumed (katephagen) me*." But the Johannine disciples recognize, through their use of the future tense of the verb, that this encounter between Jesus and "the Jews" announces some future experience that is yet to come: "Zeal for your house *will consume (kataphagetai) me*" (v. 17).[21]

As characters in the story, they can only guess that the actions Jesus has performed, and his explanation of those actions in terms of the Temple's being the home of *his Father*, will eventually lead to a life-and-death struggle. The disciples are able to recognise in Jesus a figure committed to the honor of God unto death, like Phineas, Elijah, or Mattathias (see Num 25:11; 1 Kgs 19:10, 14; Sir 48:2; 1 Macc 2:24-26).[22] As it has happened with these figures in the past, so will it happen with Jesus. At the first meeting of Jesus and "the Jews" an echo of a future passion is heard by the reader.[23] At this stage, however, the reader only knows the story thus far. The disciples accept, insofar as the author will permit them to understand at this stage of the story, Jesus' claim that his authority in the Temple (*to hieron*) arose from that building being the house of his Father (*ho oikos tou patros mou*). But "the Jews" seek further evidence for such claims. The Evangelist introduces them through the pleonastic construction: "Then 'the Jews' answered and said (*apekrithēsan oun hoi Ioudaioi kai eipen*) to him" (v. 18).

With this solemn entry of "the Jews" into a dialogue with Jesus the narrative enters a new phase. From v. 18 to v. 20 the narrator provides the reader with a verbatim report of an encounter between "the Jews" and Jesus. They demand that Jesus give them a "sign" (*sēmeion*).[24] As in the parallel dialogue between the mother of Jesus and her son in 2:3-5, so here the use of "words" is important for the author's shaping of the emerging reader of the Gospel. Jesus' reply is equally solemn: "Jesus answered and said (*apekrithē Iēsous kai eipen*) to them . . ." (v. 19).

---

[21] See Brown, *John*, 123–24. There are variants in the textual traditions. The tense of the verb in the LXX is sometimes future, and the tense of the verb in John 2:17 is sometimes aorist. For discussion, supporting the text as we have it, see Bernard, *St John*, 1:92; Lagrange, *Saint Jean*, 66–67; C. K. Barrett, *The Gospel according to St John* (London: SPCK, 1978) 198–99.

[22] For this suggestion, see E. C. Hoskyns, *The Fourth Gospel*, ed. F. N. Davey (London: Faber & Faber, 1947) 194; Léon-Dufour, *Lecture*, 256–58.

[23] See Schnackenburg, *St John*, 1:341.

[24] Here the word means a miraculous proof to guarantee belief. Jesus never works such "signs"; see Brown, *John*, 115. For the reasonableness of this request from "the Jews" that such a prophetic act of zeal be authenticated, see Lagrange, *Saint Jean*, 67–68.

The reader encounters a further shift in the expression used for the sacred place of worship: "Destroy this Temple (*ton naon*) and in three days I will raise it up" (v. 19).[25] More than a building is in question. The words *hieron* and *naos* may mean much the same, but Jesus distinguishes between them. This puzzles both "the Jews" and the reader. "The Jews" will destroy it and Jesus will raise it up "in three days."[26] The use of the future tense "I will raise it up in three days" can only be a mystery for the reader.[27] There has been nothing in the narrative so far that would give the reader any indication of what "raising up" might mean. For the first time in the narrative, the implied reader is given advance notice of an event that will prove to be crucial to the story. As yet the reader is almost as ignorant as "the Jews" about what the future tense may refer to, but the word of Jesus is at stake here. How trustworthy is that word?

The reader is not in the same position as "the Jews"; the implied reader has read the prologue. Is Jesus' raising up of his body victory of the light over the darkness (see 1:5, 11-12)? On whose side will the reader remain at the close of this encounter: on the side of "the Jews" who approach the whole question with a great deal of practical sense; or on the side of Jesus who points out of the story time into some future plotted time, as yet closed to the knowledge of the emerging reader? Jesus is not speaking about the destruction of the Jerusalem Temple nor of his raising up a Temple made of stone. He is alluding to some future event, when, in a very brief period of time after its destruction, he will raise up the Temple. Which Temple? How can he personally raise it up in three days?[28] The reader can only

---

[25] BAGD (pp. 533-34, s.v. *ho naos*) gives documentation for the use of the word to speak of the whole Temple area, as well as the sanctuary itself.

[26] As Schnackenburg (*St John*, 1:349), among many, points out, the verbs used for "destroy" (*lyein*) and "raise up" (*egeirein*) can be applied equally well to the tearing down and reconstruction of a building, or the destruction and resurrection of the body of Jesus.

[27] I argued above (p. 77 n. 1) that the use of the expression "on the third day" in 2:1 was not a reference to the resurrection of Jesus. The same thing must be claimed here *for the implied reader*. The expression *en treis hemerais* does not have the same resurrection links as the more traditional *tē hēmerą tē tritę* (see 1 Cor 15:4; Matt 16:21; 17:23; 20:19; Luke 9:22; 18:33; 24:7, 46). It is a conventional expression for a short period of time. As B. Lindars puts it: "Even if the temple be destroyed, I will build it up in a trice" (*The Gospel of John* [NCB; London: Oliphants, 1972] 143). It is in this way that the implied reader takes it. This is not to deny the possibility that the intended readers may have seen the connection with a resurrection tradition, as is almost unanimously claimed by the commentators. However, "three day" language never appears in the Johannine resurrection accounts of chaps. 20-21. The Johannine community may not have been familiar with such a tradition.

[28] Against Léon-Dufour, *Lecture*, 258-62. He argues for the basic historicity of this encounter and claims that Jesus spoke of the destruction of the Jerusalem Temple, which would be caused by Israel's continuing sinfulness. In its place there would be a new Temple.

ask these questions, but will find no answer for them. The narrator will provide the beginnings of an answer shortly (see v. 21), but before the reader is let into the secret the direct speech continues in the response of "the Jews" to the words of Jesus.

The reply of "the Jews" shows the implied reader that there are serious implications in the shift from *to hieron*, via *ho oikos*, to *ho naos*. Both *hieron* and *naos* can refer to the building of the Temple, but the context shows that Jesus distinguishes between them. The narrative places "the Jews" in a situation where they are not prepared to go beyond the building of the Temple (*to hieron/ho naos*) to the use of *naos* by Jesus. For "the Jews" there can be no distinction, as they logically see the words as identical.[29] "The 'Jews' take Jesus' words at their face value, as always happens in the Johannine 'misunderstandings'; and apply them literally to the visible temple of stone which rises before their eyes."[30] "The Jews" are being used by the narrator to show an inability to accept the word of Jesus. Is the reader sensitive to the implicit commentary involved in this shift of direction by Jesus' use of the expression *ho naos*, or is the reader still identifying it with *to hieron*, the Temple building made of stone? If the latter, then the implied reader is in the company of "the Jews."[31]

Although they use the same word as Jesus (*ho naos*), "the Jews" speak of the forty-six years that have elapsed during its building.[32] They identify the Temple (*to hieron*) with the sanctuary (*ho naos*). The reader sees that "the Jews" have misunderstood the "sign" that Jesus offered as his authority. The implied reader may not understand what that sign will be, but it will not be the destruction and the rebuilding of the whole of the Temple structure "in three days." Something more is involved. The reader trusts in the word of Jesus that there is something in plotted time that will explain this. Rather than settle for the ridicule which "the Jews" aim at Jesus, the reader reads on into plotted time.

Jesus has replied *in direct speech*. "The Jews" are addressed by the words of Jesus. They reject his words. They throw his "words" back at him, refusing to take the leap outside the categories of the stones of their Temple building. Not only do they misunderstand Jesus' shift from a Temple

---

[29] Thus the need to insist that it is incorrect to read *to hieron* as the whole building and *ho naos* as only the sanctuary area.

[30] Schnackenburg, *St John*, 1:350; see also Barrett, *St John*, 200.

[31] On 2:19-21 as implicit commentary, see R. A. Culpepper, *Anatomy of the Fourth Gospel: A Study in Literary Design* (Philadelphia: Fortress Press, 1983) 155.

[32] As the period of forty-six years does not fit the facts, the figure has been interpreted symbolically: Jesus' age, the numerical value of the name "Adam," gnostic numerical speculations, etc. See Lagrange, *Saint Jean*, 69; Brown, *John*, 115–16.

building (*to hieron*), via his reference to that building as his Father's house (*ho oikos*), to a different Temple (*ho naos*); they reject the words that he offers as his authority: "and in three days I will raise it up" (v. 19). The narrator reports the response of "the Jews" on the basis of the words Jesus had said. The sign he offered was: "Destroy this Temple and in three days I will raise it up" (v. 19). "The Jews" reply: "It has taken forty-six years to build this Temple, and you, will you raise it up in three days?" (v. 20). In an insolent use of the personal pronoun "you," they make a mocking question of the words of Jesus:

Jesus	"The Jews"
kai en trisin hēmerais	*kai su en trisin hēmerais*
egerō auton.	*egereis auton;*

If the response of the mother of Jesus to her son was trust in the efficacy of his word, the response of "the Jews" is the exact opposite. They have formally rejected the word of Jesus. As at the Cana encounter between Jesus and his mother, so here the narrator has reported the "words" of Jesus. The rhetoric of the passage demands that we see the failure of "the Jews" in their rejection of the word of Jesus.

The narrator, as in 2:11, draws back from the action of the narrative to guide the reader to a correct reading of 2:13-20. What is the reader to make of the shift from the aorist to the future in the disciples' interpretation of Jesus' actions and words in the Temple: "Zeal for thy house *will consume me*" (v. 17)? What is this Temple which will be destroyed, and yet be raised up after three days (v. 19)? A partial answer is provided for the implied reader as the author comments: *ekeinos de elegen peri tou naou tou sōmatos autou* (v. 21). The use of *ekeinos* is emphatic, and the reader senses a deliberate contrast between the reply of "the Jews" in v. 20 and the narrator's point of view expressed in v. 21. The reader already knows that Jesus Christ is the gift that replaces a former gift (1:17), and his changing water from the jars used for the Jewish rites of purification was a first "sign" (see 2:11) of this gift. But there is more to be seen. In the plotted time of vv. 17, 19-20, the reader was informed that Jesus' passion for the ways of his Father will lead to his being consumed and that after a very short time he would raise up the Temple of his body (v. 21). The presence of God to Israel in the Temple will be replaced by the presence of the Temple of the body of Jesus.[33] Trusting in the reliability of the narrator, the reader

---

[33] See R. Kieffer, *Le monde symbolique de saint Jean* (LD 137; Paris: Cerf, 1989) 45. R. Bultmann rightly points out that the genitive is either appositional or explicative (*John*, 127 n. 5).

can only read on through the story time into the future of the plotted time.[34]

But before leaving the episode, the narrator reports the eventual experience of the disciples of Jesus. The reader is not alone in the perplexing tension between story time and plotted time. In v. 17 the disciples "remembered" the word of the Scriptures which spoke of a holy man's passion for the House of God leading to his all-consuming suffering. The reader discovers in v. 22 that this is not enough. Jesus is not another Phineas, Elijah, or Mattathias. The disciples' remembering in v. 17, while not entirely wrong, falls short of a full understanding of the passion which Jesus has for the ways of his Father. The disciples are still unable to articulate a correct understanding of Jesus. But there will be a time, "when therefore he was raised from the dead," when they will come to believe, understand, and interpret both the word of Jesus and the Scriptures. The reader encounters a further prolepsis, repeating that there will be a raising from the dead sometime in the future. Only then the disciples' present limited understanding of the word of Jesus and the Scriptures will be overcome. On arrival at the *tē graphē* of v. 22, the reader naturally thinks of the *hoti gegrammenon estin* of v. 17. Whatever the implied reader makes of the narrator's reflection on the "remembering" of the disciples in v. 17, the reader now knows that they do not, as yet, "believe the Scripture" of LXX Ps 68:10. They did not understand the Scripture in the story time. But there will be a future plotted time, outside the present story, when they will understand this passage from Scripture, and the strange word of Jesus about the raising up of his destroyed body.

The author is shaping a reader in the text to speak to the intended readers of the text. The members of the Johannine community, living their Christian lives after the destruction of the Jerusalem Temple, are able to look to the presence of the risen Lord as their "Temple."[35] In terms of the

---

[34] C. H. Dodd takes the opposite view (*Interpretation*, 209). Referring to 6:30, he argues that the *sēmeion* of a destroyed and restored Temple has already taken place in the expulsion of the sacrificial animals.

[35] See Schnackenburg, *St John*, 1:356–57; Bultmann, *John*, 128–29; Beasley-Murray, *John*, 42–43; P. Perkins, *NJBC*, 954. This christological interpretation is often wrongly taken further, via the Pauline notion of the body of Christ, into an ecclesiological interpretation. The rebuilt Temple is the church. See, e.g., Westcott, *St John*, 42; R. H. Strachan, *The Fourth Gospel: Its Significance and Environment* (3rd ed.; London: SCM Press, 1941) 127; Dodd, *Interpretation*, 302–3; H. van den Bussche, *Jean: Commentaire de l'Évangile Spirituel* (Bruges: Desclée de Brouwer, 1976) 156–59; G. Zevini, *Vangelo secondo Giovanni* (2 vols.; Commenti Spirituali del Nuovo Testamento; Rome: Città Nuova, 1984, 1987) 1:122–24. It has been further claimed that the expression "the Temple of his body (*tou sōmatos autou*)" refers to the eucharistic experience

story time, however, that is yet to come. The disciples, whose initial favorable reaction had still not been a full understanding of Jesus' earlier actions (vv. 13-17) will later come to true Johannine faith (v. 22). Attention must be paid to this final comment from the narrator. Caught within the story of Jesus' action, the disciples are not able to go further than their initial expectations of 1:19-49. The sight of the glory which began at Cana and which led to an initial faith (2:11) is still insufficient. Only "the hour," the death and resurrection of Jesus, will produce true Johannine faith in the first group of disciples. The narrator indicates the criteria for the true faith which the disciples eventually experienced. Looking back to the past, to the beginnings of the Johannine community's story as an authentic community of faith, the narrator tells of a past event: "They believed the Scripture and *the word which Jesus had spoken (kai tǭ logǭ hon eipen ho Iēsous)*" (v. 22).

The narrator is able confidently to claim this experience for the original disciples. The narrator claims to have been one of them, belonging to the first person plural of 1:14: "We have looked upon his glory" and 1:16: "From his fullness we have all received." It is the desire of the real author that, through the implied reader emerging in the narrative, the intended readers will join the real author and the original disciples of Jesus in their faith in and experience of Jesus Christ. As a conclusion to a narrative which was highlighted by the rejection of "the word which Jesus spoke" (vv. 18-20), this final comment to the implied reader on the eventual faith experience of the disciples of Jesus is an indication for the reader of the nature of authentic faith: one must believe in the word which Jesus spoke.

The experience of the mother of Jesus will eventually be matched by the experience of the hesitant disciples. As yet, however, they must stumble forward. The actors in the story have not yet come to true faith, but the reader who is emerging in the narrative has a growing and deepening understanding of true faith as belief in the word of Jesus. The narrative is beginning to articulate the criteria for true Johannine faith. The question posed by the reader at the close of 1:19-51 is being answered: true belief calls for openness to the word of Jesus. This has been evidenced by the mother of Jesus: "Do whatever he tells (legǭ) you" (2:5) and will eventually form the basis of the Johannine community (2:22). Only after his death and resurrection do disciples abandon their own expectations: "They believed the scripture and the word (tǭ logǭ) which Jesus had spoken" (2:22).[36]

---

of the community. See O. Cullmann, *Early Christian Worship* (SBT 10; London: SCM Press, 1953) 71-74. However, the eucharistic passage of 6:51-58 uses the word *sarx* rather than *sōma*.

[36] See Schnackenburg, *St John*, 1:349.

But what of "the Jews"? In the light of their mocking rejection of the words of Jesus himself they must be judged as failing in faith. The reader has experienced the story of a Jewish woman at a Jewish wedding trusting completely in the word of Jesus (2:5) and a further story of "the Jews" who totally reject that word (2:13-22). In the midst of the revelation of Jesus as the new Temple, "the Jews" settle for the status quo of *to hieron/ho naos*, formally rejecting the promise of the *naos* of the body of Jesus. Their rejection of the word of Jesus indicates to the implied reader that "the Jews," gathered in Jerusalem to celebrate a Jewish feast, are to be understood as placing themselves in a relationship with Jesus which can only be described as a relationship of *non-faith*.

II. THE NARRATOR'S COMMENT (2:23-25)

The first days of Jesus have been marked by a "sight" which promised well, as the disciples gathered around Jesus. But Jesus demanded a greater faith, as a necessary condition for the promise of a greater "sight" (1:19-51). In 2:23-25 the narrator returns to this theme by drawing back from narrative to speak directly to the reader in a commentary on the quality of a faith based on the "sight" of the miracles of Jesus.[37] While serving as a conclusion to the events that took place in the Temple, reported in vv. 13-22, this commentary also enables the author to lead the reader into the next example of faith in Israel: Nicodemus (3:1-21).

Reading the Narrative

In many ways, the account of the purification of the Temple is rounded off by a return to the themes first raised in v. 13: the presence of Jesus in Jerusalem for the Passover feast (v. 23a).[38] The Jewish context is strongly maintained. The reader next learns of the movement of many people *toward* Jesus in an action of belief (*polloi episteusan eis to onoma autou*) because they saw the signs (*ta sēmeia*) which he did. Strangely, no signs have been reported, and the initial reaction of "the Jews" (v. 20) would seem to discourage such a mass movement of "believers" toward Jesus. The reader

---

[37] The narrative "slows down" as the narrator speaks directly to the reader; see G. Genette, *Nouveau discours du récit* (Collection Poétique; Paris: Seuil, 1983) 22-25.

[38] J. Jeremias reads *en tē heortē* as "in the festival crowd" (*The Eucharistic Words of Jesus* [London: SCM Press, 1971] 71-73). He is followed by Barrett, *St John*, 202. I would be prepared to accept this suggestion, because it continues to insist on the Jewish feast.

must accept the word of the narrator.[39] Warned by Jesus' reaction to Nathanael's initial faith (see 1:49-51), the reader is now wary of a quality of faith in Jesus based on "the signs which he did." Such faith may not be enough. They may lead to belief in Jesus (see 2:11), but such signs are not requested; they are given.[40] The reader has already learned this from "the Jews'" request for a sign, and their inability to accept the sign they are offered (see 2:18-20). A faith inspired by the wonders worked by Jesus often stops at the sign itself. As we have already seen in 1:19-51, the Fourth Evangelist asks more from those who would be followers of Jesus.[41]

The narrator uses the verb *pisteuein* twice to report Jesus' response to a faith based on signs. The double use of the verb, once to speak of the movement of many in faith toward him (v. 23), and then again to refer to Jesus' refusal to move toward them in similar trust and faith (v. 24),[42] indicates to the implied reader the dynamic quality of true faith. There is a reciprocity between Jesus and the believer already expressed in 1:12: "To all who received him . . . who believed in his name." As the implied reader has already had occasion to discover, there is a close parallel between receiving (*lambanein*) and believing (*pisteuein*). The Fourth Gospel never uses the noun "faith" (*pistis*), whereas it uses the verb "to believe" (*pisteuein*) ninety-eight times. The reader is now on the way to understanding the relational quality of true faith. The careful use of the verb *pisteuein*, on the one hand to refer to those who moved toward Jesus because of his signs (v. 23), and on the other hand to indicate that he did not move toward them in the same way (v. 24), shapes the emerging reader along these lines.[43]

[39] In some ways this is a Johannine version of what G. Genette would call "anachrony" (*Narrative Discourse: An Essay in Method* [Ithaca, N.Y.: Cornell University Press, 1980] 35-47). The story has not reported the "signs" in Jerusalem, and these "signs" upset the numbering of a first and a second miracle at Cana (see 2:11; 4:54), but the ongoing narrative takes it for granted that they happened. The reader can only accept this uncomfortable situation. See the apt remarks of Schnackenburg, *St John*, 1:342.

[40] The criticism that the implied author aims at many people in Jerusalem does not mean that they can go no further in their journey of faith. See F. Hahn, " 'Die Juden' im Johannesevangelium," in *Kontinuität und Einheit: Für Franz Mussner*, ed. P.-G. Müller and W. Stenger (Freiburg: Herder, 1981) 432-34.

[41] X. Léon-Dufour puts it well: "Caractérisée par un 'voir', elle n'est pas encore un 'croire' qui est acceuil de la Parole et du mystère du Révélateur" (*Lecture*, 285).

[42] The second use of *pisteuein* (in v. 24) is a reflexive use of the verb found only here in the New Testament. It is, however, found outside the New Testament. See Barrett, *St John*, 202; Schnackenburg, *St John*, 1:359. For the author, the important issue was the repetition of *pisteuein*, but it was difficult to speak of Jesus' "faith" in others. Thus the rather singular use of the reflexive.

[43] B. F. Westcott rightly points out: "There is at the same time a contrast of tenses. The first verb marks a definite, completed, act: the second a habitual course of action" (*St John*, 45).

Having made this point through commentary to the reader, the narrator continues with general statements about Jesus' knowledge of all people. Jesus was not able to give himself in faith to those who believed because of the signs. Such faith would not be a sufficient response to meet the profoundest needs of a human being. Jesus knew this.[44] He had no need for further witness concerning the human situation ("man"), for he knew what was in man (v. 25). The repetitions— "he knew all *men* . . . bear witness of *man* . . . what was in *man*" —leads the reader into the next major scene: Jesus' encounter with Nicodemus: "There was a *man* of the Pharisees" (3:1).[45]

III. JESUS AND NICODEMUS (3:1-21)

The Shape of the Narrative

While the basic unit of 3:1-21 does not create problems, the determination of its internal shape often does.[46] As with 2:1-12 and 13-22, the encounter between Jesus and Nicodemus is communicated to the reader through the use of direct speech. "Words of Jesus" and a response in direct speech highlight 3:1-10. Only in the following discourse (vv. 11-21) does the author separate Jesus from a one-to-one encounter where a representative of the Jewish world hears the word of Jesus and responds to it. At best Nicodemus remains in the background in vv. 11-21, as Jesus speaks directly to the reader of the Gospel. Closely linked with Jesus' revelation of himself through his words to Nicodemus, and Nicodemus's inability to accept this revelation, the discourse speaks directly to the reader about the revelation that takes place in Jesus, and the consequences of the acceptance or refusal of such revelation.

The narrative of 3:1-21 has the following shape:

I. *Verses 1-2a:* Introductory passage, setting the scene at night, presenting the two characters involved in the discussion that follows: Jesus and Nicodemus.

[44] The reader can be credited with this knowledge from the prologue's insistence, in 1:3-4 and 1:10, that the Word who became flesh in Jesus Christ stands behind the creation of all things. See A. Loisy, *Le quatrième évangile* (Paris: Emile Nourry, 1921) 154. C. K. Barrett is rightly critical of all attempts to find parallels for 2:24 (*St John*, 202).

[45] See F. J. Moloney, *The Johannine Son of Man* (2nd ed.; Biblioteca di Scienze Religiose 14; Rome: LAS, 1978) 46-47.

[46] For an attempt to reconstruct the development of 3:1-21, 31-36, see M.-E. Boismard and A. Lamouille, *L'Evangile de Jean* (Synopse des Quatre Evangiles en Français III; Paris: Cerf, 1977) 112-17. For more general surveys, see Brown, *John*, 135-36; Barrett, *St John*, 203-4; H. Thyen, "Aus der Literatur zum Johannesevangelium," *TR* 44 (1979) 110-18. On the unity of John 3, see D. Rensberger, *Johannine Faith and the Liberating Community* (Philadelphia: Westminster Press, 1988) 58-61.

II. *Verses 2b-11/12:* The dialogue between Jesus and Nicodemus:

(a) *Verse 2b:* Nicodemus's opening statement, reflecting his understanding of Jesus' person and role.

(b) *Verses 3-8:* Jesus' teaching on rebirth in the spirit, marked by Nicodemus's misunderstanding (v. 4) enabling a further development of the theme.[47]

(c) *Verses 9-10:* Nicodemus's final intervention, reflecting his inability to comprehend the teaching of Jesus. Jesus responds to Nicodemus's incomprehension.

(d) *Verses 11-12:* Bridge: words from Jesus which both close the discussion of vv. 2b-12 and open the discourse of vv. 11-21.[48]

III. *Verses 11/12-21:* The discourse of Jesus. After the bridge passage of vv. 11-12, the discourse develops two basic themes:[49]

(a) *Verses 11-12:* Bridge: words from Jesus which both close the discussion of vv. 2b-12, and open the discourse of vv. 11-21.

(b) *Verses 13-15:* Theme one: the revelation of the heavenly in the Son of Man.

(c) *Verses 16-21:* Theme two: the salvation or condemnation that flows from the acceptance or refusal of this revelation.

As with 2:1-12 and 2:13-25, there is an insistence on the Jewishness of the character who meets Jesus. Nicodemus is described as "a Pharisee . . . a ruler of the Jews" as the passage opens, and Jesus' final words to him call him "the teacher of Israel" (v. 10: *sy ei ho didaskalos tou Israēl*).[50] The setting, although not explicitly given, must be taken as Jerusalem, as there has been no indication of movement away from the city since Jesus' arrival there (see 2:13, 23).

---

[47] Within this section, the Johannine double "amen" —in v. 3 to open Jesus' response and in v. 5 to carry the discussion further—marks the introduction of a new idea closely related to what went before. See Westcott, *Saint John,* 48; Bernard, *St John,* 1:67. G. Rossetto, "Nascere dell'alto: Gv 3:3-8," in *Segni e Sacramenti nel Vangelo di Giovanni,* ed. P. R. Tragan (Studia Anselmiana 66; Rome: Editrice Anselmiana, 1977) 50.

[48] On vv. 11-12 as a bridge ("cerniera"), see G. Segalla, *Giovanni* (NVB 36; Rome: Edizioni Paoline, 1976) 174. The double "amen" is again found in v. 11. Some change in the shape of the narrative is marked by the double "amen" in v. 11. The use of *oidamen* in v. 2 and v. 11 also links this section.

[49] J. H. Neyrey has shown that vv. 1-10 treat Johannine epistemology, vv. 11-17 Christology, and vv. 18-21 judgment ("John III—A Debate over Johannine Epistemology and Christology," *NovT* 22 [1981] 118-23).

[50] J. M. Bassler claims that already in the narrative the term "Jew" has acquired the connotation of unreceptivity and even hostility toward Jesus ("Mixed Signals: Nicodemus in the Fourth Gospel," *JBL* 108 [1989] 636-37). But the reader has not yet been furnished with sufficient material to equate "Jew" with such sentiments.

Reading the Narrative

The Jewish setting of the incident needs no further stressing. Nico-demus, "a Pharisee . . . a ruler of the Jews" (v. 1) is a new character for the reader. Nicodemus comes to Jesus "by night." A Jewish leader approaches Jesus in a context of darkness. Even at this early stage of the narrative the reader is able to look back to the conflict between the *phōs* and the *skotia* of 1:5. On this basis, Nicodemus's first impression on the reader is favorable. He is moving out of the darkness toward the light.[51]

The discussion that follows is initiated by Nicodemus. The author reports Nicodemus's words: "Rabbi, we know that you are a teacher come from God; for no one can do these signs that you do, unless God is with him" (v. 2). It is on the basis of this confession of faith that the following discussion develops.[52] The reader senses in these words a repetition of sentiments found in the expressions of insufficient faith based on signs criticized by the Evangelist in 2:23-25. Indeed, the implied reader can look further back, to recall the limited response of the first disciples in 1:35-51. These two passages provide the reader with the means to understand the limitations of Nicodemus's confession. Thus, despite the positive first impressions of his coming from the darkness, Nicodemus approaches Jesus from within his own world, with all its cultural and religious limita-tions. The term of honor, "Rabbi," has already been used by the first two disciples who followed Jesus (1:38), and by Nathanael (1:49). As Jesus' final response to the accumulation of titles of honor in 1:35-49 has shown, there are "greater things" in store for those who can see beyond the signs (1:50-51).

A telltale note of self-confidence, based on the traditions and culture

---

[51] As the narrative unfolds, the implied reader will associate Nicodemus with a move-ment from darkness to light, against D. Rensberger, who claims that Nicodemus, a figure who represents the crypto-Christians of 12:42-43, never moves beyond his inability to believe in Jesus as it is expressed in 3:1-11 (*Johannine Faith*, 37-41, 54-59). So also M. de Jonge, "Nicodemus and Jesus: Some Observations on Misunderstanding and Understanding in the Fourth Gospel," *BJRL* 53 (1970-71) 341-46; and Culpepper, *Anatomy*, 135-36. For an overoptimistic understanding of the role of Nicodemus in the Gospel, see J. N. Suggit, "Nicodemus—The True Jew," *Neotestamentica* 14 (1981) 90-110. J. M. Bassler argues that Nicodemus is neither "in" nor "out" by the time the reader comes to the end of the story ("Mixed Signals," 635-46). Thus he is a *tertium quid* whose ambiguity is never resolved.

[52] On this "dialogue form," see C. H. Dodd, "Dialogue Form in the Gospels," *BJRL* 37 (1954-55) 54-67, esp. pp. 60-67. J. H. Neyrey shows that v. 2 sets the agenda of correct knowledge and correct Christology ("John III," 118-19).

of Israel appears in his affirmation, "We know. . . ."[53] The reading of 1:35-51 has again prepared the reader to recognize that this expression reflects an unsatisfactory understanding of Jesus (see 1:41, 45). Out of his knowledge Nicodemus is prepared to accept Jesus as a teacher from God and a prophet. He even goes so far as to say that no one could do these signs unless God was with him, a dignity reserved for the great figures of Israel.[54] As with the first disciples, Nicodemus falls short of an authentic act of faith. He has been well introduced by 2:23: "Many believed in his name when they saw the signs which he did."[55]

> Men like Nicodemus have identified themselves with definitions they know too exactly. They want someone new to confirm a notion already fixed inside the heads of those who know best. For them revelation has become, quite unconsciously, a kind of technology.[56]

But if Nicodemus's opening confession falls short of being totally adequate, the reader is nevertheless aware that there has been a progression from the open hostility shown toward Jesus by "the Jews" who arrogantly rejected his word (2:18-20). Now Nicodemus comes out of the night, attempting to find, through an encounter with Jesus, a confirmation of his convictions (3:1-2). The reader's greater sympathy for Nicodemus is reinforced. There is no conflict or rejection.[57] Jesus attempts to draw Nicodemus beyond his own expectations. He does this through a play on a double-meaning word which the reader understands. Without any clarification Jesus responds: "Unless one is born anōthen (anew/from above), he cannot see the kingdom of God" (v. 3).[58] The reader is expected to understand the play on the double-meaning word anōthen, but the association of a rebirth anōthen in order to see (idein) the kingdom of God introduces a new idea to the narrative.

---

[53] G. Gaeta claims that the expression indicates not a personal opinion but a doctrinal declaration (Il dialogo con Nicodemo [Studi Biblici 26; Brescia: Paideia, 1974] 45). As is often pointed out, the plural is used to indicate Nicodemus's representative status.

[54] LXX Exod 3:12 applies this title to Moses. In Jer 1:8 the prophet is told that YHWH is "with him." J. H. Bernard claims that this phrase "expressed the general belief of Judaism" about great Israelites (St John, 101). See also Barrett, St John, 205.

[55] Some commentators deny this; see the summary in Moloney, Son of Man, 46 n. 28.

[56] J. Bishop, "Encounters in the New Testament," in Literary Interpretations of Biblical Narratives, ed. K. R. R. Gros Louis (Nashville: Abingdon, 1982) 2:292.

[57] J. M. Bassler overstates her case when she writes of Jesus' "surprisingly acerbic response" ("Mixed Signals," 535) and "clear and emphatic rebuke" (p. 537).

[58] Jesus' words ou dynatai (v. 3) pick up Nicodemus's oudeis dynatai (v. 2). Among others, R. E. Brown (John, 130) and G. R. Beasley-Murray (John, 45) claim that the best translation is "be begotten." I am using "born" so that I can later speak of "rebirth from above" to maintain both the temporal and the spatial possibilities of anōthen. "Re-begotten" hardly suits.

Jesus' claims are not an affirmation of the traditional understanding of God as a King whose sovereignty stood at the basis of Jewish thought and practice. Jesus speaks of a rebirth that enables the one reborn *to see* the kingdom of God. However familiar the reader is with a Jewish notion of God as King, something different is being introduced by these words of Jesus to Nicodemus. He finds himself confronted with an affirmation from the man he approached as a rabbi and a miracle worker which is beyond his comprehension.[59] However, instead of opening himself to the mystery of the words of Jesus, Nicodemus falls back on what he can control. He asks of Jesus: "How can a man be born when he is old? Can he enter a second time (*deuteron*) into his mother's womb and be born?" (v. 4). Here we have the Johannine misunderstanding technique. For Jesus, there must be a further birth which comes from above. This is expressed in v. 3 by means of the double-meaning word *anōthen*. But Nicodemus reduces Jesus' teaching to purely temporal dimensions by using the word *deuteron*, which can only mean "a second time." The connection with "from above" has been entirely lost. He responds to Jesus in terms he can grasp. The concrete experience of "a second time" is within his comprehension but physically impossible. A rebirth "from above" is beyond his control and is thus simply ignored. Jesus' words to Nicodemus combine both the horizontal experience of time and the vertical experience of the inbreak of God. Nicodemus's response is limited to the horizontal, and he does not even raise the question of seeing the kingdom of God.[60]

Both the temporal (again) and the spatial (from above) meaning of the word *anōthen* must be accepted if one is to see the kingdom of God.[61] Nicodemus's inability to move outside his own knowledge and experience affords a further opportunity for the author to have Jesus clarify what is meant by "rebirth."

Jesus continues the dialogue by repeating the same message in more concrete terms: "Unless one is born of water and the Spirit, he cannot enter the kingdom of God" (v. 5). The word *anōthen* has been replaced by "of water and the Spirit." The reader's difficulty with the association of a rebirth

---

[59] See J. Bishop, "Encounters in the New Testament," 293: "He (Jesus) leaps ahead, out of the game Nicodemus had begun to play."

[60] See Kieffer, *Le monde symbolique*, 46–47.

[61] The implied reader, at home in Koine Greek, knows the double meaning of *anōthen*. Translation loses this, unless both words are given. See J. L. Staley, *The Print's First Kiss: A Rhetorical Investigation of the Implied Reader in the Fourth Gospel* (SBLDS 82; Atlanta: Scholars Press, 1988) 36–37. Many commentators claim that Jesus' use of *anōthen* only means "from above" and that Nicodemus misunderstands this as *deuteron*. Rightly C. K. Barrett comments that "*anōthen* is capable of two meanings and here it probably has both" (*St John*, 205).

that is both temporal (again) and spiritual (from above) is clarified by the words Jesus addresses to Nicodemus. There is a human experience "of water," which refers to a temporal dimension, and a spiritual experience "of the Spirit," which refers to the rebirth from above. Nicodemus does not have to make a choice for one or the other of the meanings, as they are both involved.[62] There is a quality of faith which exceeds human control and comprehension and which one can only receive from the Spirit. But there is more. There is also some form of rebirth "of water" (*ex hydatos*). Nicodemus has come to Jesus prepared to accept him as a part of his own world. On the basis of the narrative to this point the implied reader knows that such an understanding of Jesus falls short of the ideal. For the first time in the narrative Jesus himself, in direct speech, tells Nicodemus what is required: a twofold rebirth. Through the implicit commentary of the misunderstanding, the reader senses that more than an inner experience is involved and also that something more than the traditional notion of God as King is at stake.

There is a rebirth "of water and the Spirit" that understandably puzzles Nicodemus; but the reader has already learned of a close association between water and the Holy Spirit from the reliable witness of John the Baptist. The second day of 1:29-34 was marked by the absence of a specified audience. This indicates that the narrator is speaking, through the words of the Baptist, to the reader. Within that context, the Baptist spoke of his own baptism as "with water, that he (Jesus) might be revealed to Israel" (v. 31). The mission of the Baptist, to baptize with water, is a God-given task (v. 33b), but Jesus brings more than a baptism with water. He "baptizes with the Holy Spirit" (v. 33d). The implied reader must associate the rebirth from above with the continuation of the God-given task of a baptism of water, but now perfected with the baptism of the Spirit brought by Jesus.[63] The idea of a heavenly rebirth is not new to the reader either. In 1:12-13 the implied reader was told: "But to all who received him, who believed in his name, he gave power to become children of God; who were born not of blood, not of the will of the flesh nor of the will of a human being but of God." Nicodemus, the character in the story, has not been

---

[62] Against, among many, Lindars (*John*, 150–52), who eliminates the temporal meaning completely. It is here that R. Bultmann's widely accepted explanation of the Johannine misunderstanding technique is imprecise (*John*, 135 n. 1). Bultmann claims that it is a question of seeing the right meaning of the word but thinking "that its meaning is exhausted by the reference to earthly matters." But it is more than that. *Both* meanings must be maintained.

[63] See Hoskyns, *Fourth Gospel*, 213–14.

informed of this birth from above for those who believe in Jesus, nor did
he hear the Baptist's witnessing to baptism with water and Jesus' baptism
of the Spirit. But the reader is equipped with such knowledge.

Nicodemus may be baffled, but the reader is aware that the prophecies
of John the Baptist and the promises of the prologue are being realized
in the demands Jesus makes of Nicodemus. Thanks to Jesus' further
clarification of what the expression *anōthen* (v. 3) means (v. 5), the reader
is now able to associate the water and the Spirit with baptism. This also
enables the reader to appreciate the change of verb found in v. 5d, and
further light is shed on Jesus' use of the expression "the kingdom of God."
In v. 3 Jesus spoke of being born *anōthen* so that one might see (*idein*) the
kingdom of God. In v. 5 he replaces *anōthen* with "water and the spirit,"
so that one might enter (*eiselthein*) the kingdom of God. The reader knows
only what has been read so far, but the reader has been armed with
sufficient information to suspect strongly that there is a baptismal rite,
similar to the water baptism of John the Baptist (1:31), now transformed
by the Spirit which began with the coming of Jesus (see 1:33). By means
of this rite one "sees" (v. 3) and "enters into" (v. 5) the kingdom of God.[64]
The kingdom is no longer an invisible presence of YHWH as King. It is a
place into which one enters through a new rite, a rebirth through a baptism of both water and the Holy Spirit.

Most commentators on the Fourth Gospel rightly remark that the
author's use of "the kingdom of God" reflects contact with earlier Gospel
traditions.[65] Having made that remark, they simply affirm that for this
Evangelist, the kingdom of God is to be identified with eternal life,[66] or
"the heavenly realm on high to which the divine envoy leads."[67] In speaking of the kingdom of God, the author had good traditional background
to speak of the kingdom as a present reality (see, e.g., Mark 1:15; 9:1; Matt
5:10; 6:10, 33; Luke 9:2, 11; 17:21; Rom 14:17). Yet despite the "present"
indications of some of the traditional kingdom language, the narrator
adapts what was basically eschatological imagery into more realized terms.

---

[64] It is generally claimed that there is no real difference between *idein* and *eiselthein* in this
context, as "seeing" means to experience. See, e.g., Strachan, *Fourth Gospel*, 130; Barrett,
St John, 207; and the discussion in M. Vellanickal, *The Divine Sonship of Christians in the Johannine
Writings* (AnBib 72; Rome: Biblical Institute Press, 1977) 207.

[65] For a detailed analysis, see Boismard and Lamouille, *Jean*, 118–19; and B. Lindars, "John
and the Synoptic Gospels: A Test Case," *NTS* 27 (1980-81) 287–94.

[66] See, e.g., Lagrange, *Saint Jean*, 74; Bernard, *St John*, 1:101–2; Bultmann, *John*, 152 n. 2;
R. H. Lightfoot, *St John's Gospel*, ed. C. F. Evans (Oxford: Oxford University Press, 1956) 130–31;
Vellanickal, *Divine Sonship*, 208–13.

[67] Schnackenburg, *St John*, 1:366–67.

The kingdom of God refers to a community that professes and attempts to live the Johannine understanding of Jesus.[68] The members of the Johannine community would be aware of their passage from Temple or synagogue into a Christian community, solemnized by water.

The experience of Baptism within the Johannine community (through water) is a gift from above (in the Spirit).[69] Both the gift of the Spirit and the passage through water have been part of the intended reader's experience. The members of the Johannine community are aware that the passage through water and the Spirit has formed them into a Christian community. The traditional understanding of "kingdom of God" has been altered. Some sort of liminal experience, marked by a rebirth of water and the Spirit, guides the believer into the kingdom of God. As Nicodemus is being challenged to make that journey, the reader is being asked to recognize the transcendent nature of the events that lead to true Johannine faith. Again there is a suggestion that Johannine faith also involves others (see

[68] This case was cogently argued by B. F. Westcott (*St John*, 48–50), but has been largely ignored since. For a strong case linking v. 5 with the entry into the Johannine community through a gift of the Spirit, worked out in discussion with Judaism, see H. Leroy, *Rätsel und Missverständnis: Ein Beitrag zur Formgeschichte des Johannesevangeliums* (BBB 30; Bonn: Peter Hanstein, 1968) 129–36; see also Rossetto, "Nascere dell'acqua," 56–58. Recent structuralist studies have restated Westcott's position (without acknowledgment). See M. Michel, "Nicodème et le non-lieu de vérité," *RevScRel* 55 (1981) 231–36; Gaeta, *Il dialogo*, 49; and especially D. Patte, "Jesus' Pronouncement about Entering the Kingdom like a Child: A Structural Exegesis," *Semeia* 29 (1983) 41: "The realm of the kingdom is nothing else than the Johannine community of faith." Without reference to the kingdom of God (or Westcott), D. Rensberger has recently argued for 3:5 as a reference to the ritual of baptism through which a person crossed a social barrier upon entering into the Johannine community (*Johannine Faith*, 55–56, 58, 66–70). See, along similar lines, T. Onuki, *Gemeinde und Welt im Johannesevangelium: Ein Beitrag zur Frage nach der theologischen und pragmatischen Funktion des johanneischen "Dualismus"* (WMANT 56; Neukirchen-Vluyn: Neukirchener Verlag, 1984) 63–64; and C. H. Cosgrove, "The Place where Jesus is: Allusions to Baptism and the Eucharist in the Fourth Gospel," *NTS* 35 (1989) 522–39, especially pp. 530–39.

[69] There is considerable diachronic debate over 3:5. The rest of 3:5-8 concentrates on "spirit," and "water" never again appears. Was it added to the text by later scribes, in an attempt to render a "spiritual" text more ecclesial (so Bultmann, *John*, 138 n. 3)? I accept that historically it was added to the text at some stage of the journey of the Johannine community. The earliest form of this text spoke only of a rebirth in the spirit as necessary for entry into the community. However, the community's break with the synagogue and its growing awareness of its uniqueness led to the introduction of an explicit reference to the ritual of water baptism, a public sign that *externally* marked their *internal* experience and commitment to the beliefs of the Johannine community. In my opinion, this involved both the temporal and the spiritual meaning of *anōthen*. See the comprehensive study of I. de la Potterie, "Naître de l'eau et naître de l'Esprit," *ScEccl* 14 (1962) 351–74. See also F. J. Moloney, "When is John Talking about Sacraments?" *AusBR* 30 (1982) 10–33. For a good presentation of the intersecting vertical and horizontal perspective involved here, see J. Calloud and F. Genuyt, *L'Evangile de Jean (I): Lecture sémiotique des chapitres 1 à 6* (Lyon: Centre pour l'Analyse du Discours Religieux, 1989) 61–62.

2:5, 11). The Johannine baptismal experience of water and the Spirit introduces a believer into a community of believers: the kingdom of God.

In terms of the narrative, who makes more sense to the reader—Jesus
with his extraordinary word about a rebirth from above through water and
the Holy Spirit in order to enter the kingdom of God (vv. 3, 5), or
Nicodemus with his "commonsense" reply (see v. 4)? The reader must
make a decision, but already has sufficient information and experience
to be aware that the right decision is to commit oneself to the word of Jesus.
The absence of the conflict and rejection that marked 2:13-22 is obvious
to the reader as Jesus perseveres with Nicodemus. He affirms that there
is a distinction between birth by flesh and birth by the spirit (v. 6). "Flesh"
here has a neutral meaning. To be born of the flesh means to be happy
with what one can observe and control and, above all, to make judgments
on the basis of what one senses (see especially 8:15 and then 7:24). Birth
in the Spirit leads into a different way of seeing and understanding things.[70]

On the basis of that affirmation, Jesus tells Nicodemus not to marvel
over his word (*mē thaumasēs hoti eipon soi*) that the rebirth must take place
through a gift "from above" (v. 7; *anōthen* is again used). After this
imperative insisting that the attitude which created Nicodemus's confession (v. 2) and subsequent misunderstanding (v. 4) should cease,[71] Jesus
teaches "the teacher" (see v. 11) by means of a brief parable on "the wind/the
Spirit" (v. 8). The same Greek word (*pneuma*) is used for "the wind" and
"the Spirit," as Jesus moves from the experience of the wind to instruct
Nicodemus about the Spirit. Jesus starts by speaking of something within
Nicodemus's understanding: the wind. The wind (*to pneuma*) is a mystery:
one can experience it, it is a part of life, but one can never pin down its
origins or its end (see Qoh 11:5; Sir 16:21).[72] Having made this objective
and observable point about the wind (*to pneuma*), Jesus moves on to affirm
that it is thus with those born of the Spirit (*to pneuma*). "The Spirit, like
the wind, is entirely beyond both the control and the comprehension of

---

[70] See Schnackenburg, *St John*, 1:372.

[71] After *mē* one would have expected the present imperative, forbidding the continuation
of such an attitude. Instead, we find the aorist subjunctive, making the imperative more vivid
and absolute. See ZBG, 80 (§246) and p. 83 (§254). W. Bauer comments: "eine gewisse Hast
und Ungeduld zum Ausdruck kommt" (*Das Johannesevangelium erklärt* [HKNT 6; Tübingen:
J. C. B. Mohr (Paul Siebeck), 1933] 55).

[72] I am interpreting v. 8abc as referring to the natural wind, and only v. 8d as an application to the Spirit. Some commentators claim that v. 8abc has a double meaning, wind and
Spirit, particularly on the basis of the use of the word *phōnē*.

man: it breathes into this world from another."[73] Those born of this Spirit have their origin and destiny in the mystery of God.

At this stage, Jesus' attempts fail to draw Nicodemus beyond his own categories. But his response in v. 9 is not one of refusal: "How can this be?" It is a stunned inability to step out of his own categories into the mysterious life in the Spirit which Jesus is offering him.[74] It is beyond him. Thus far in the narrative Nicodemus has shown three different responses to Jesus. He began with a confession that showed the limitations of his understanding of Jesus (v. 2). From there he progressed to a misunderstanding of Jesus' words (v. 4). Finally, he comes to a stunned puzzlement (v. 9).

Jesus' response to Nicodemus's question indicates that he, "the teacher of Israel," should have been able to grasp what Jesus has said so far (v. 10).[75] As Jesus will say in v. 12, all the things he has said so far are "earthly things" (*epigeia*). The idea of a life in "the Spirit" which transcends all that the human spirit can control or understand was not new in Israel. It was already a part of its religious tradition (see Exod 15:8; Isa 40:7; 44:3; 59:21; Ezek 11:19-20; 36:26-27; Joel 28:29; Job 34:14; Pss 18:15; 51:10; Wis 9:16-18; 1QS 3:13–4:26). The covenanted community at Qumran had assimilated such a tradition (see esp. 1QS 4:20-22).[76]

Jesus can now move beyond the one-to-one dialogue with Nicodemus to a more wide-reaching commentary on all that has taken place in the narrative. Through the use of the double "amen," Jesus closes his words to Nicodemus. If we can speak of "bridge" scenes in the Fourth Gospel, we must also speak of "bridge" verses. Not only does the literary unit of vv. 11-12 close the story of Jesus' encounter with Nicodemus ("I say to *you*": singular); it also opens Jesus' commentary which is for both Nicodemus and the readers of the Gospel ("*you* do not receive": plural). Thus far Jesus and Judaism have been the two parties in the discussion, but now one senses the presence of two larger groups: the community of Jesus speaks

---

[73] Barrett, *St John*, 211.

[74] See Bultmann, *John*, 143 n. 2: "The *pōs* of this question is typical of the 'common sense' point of view."

[75] The use of the definite article (*ho didaskalos*) is rhetorical. It indicates an important teacher, but not the only one. See the discussion in Bultmann, *John*, 144 n. 2. On the irony involved in Jesus' question, see P. D. Duke, *Irony in the Fourth Gospel* (Atlanta: John Knox Press, 1985) 45–46.

[76] See Brown, *John*, 139–41.

to Israel but they are unable to grasp *ta epigeia*. What will happen when Jesus speaks to them of *ta epourania*?[77]

Jesus has been open with his interlocutor throughout the dialogue. In the following commentary on the dialogue Nicodemus and all that he represents may still be present, along with the reader. But through this commentary a wider audience is addressed. The point of vv. 11-12 is not so much to show how Judaism is wrong but, more positively, to tell the reader, who may be happy to settle for Jesus' use of the best of Israel's religious traditions (earthly things), that more is necessary (heavenly things) for salvation.[78] There is a newness made possible because of the revelation that comes from above. This discourse provides the reader with a synthesis of the Gospel message on Jesus as the unique revealer of the "heavenly things" (vv. 11-15)[79] and the subsequent salvation or condemnation which follows from an acceptance or refusal of this revelation (vv. 16-21).[80]

Concluding the encounter, Jesus comments on what has happened thus far (v. 11). Nicodemus's response to the discourse has shown an inability to accept Jesus' authoritative revelation of what he has seen.[81] Jesus' words do not come from hearsay. He speaks out of a direct contact with God. The reader has already been informed that the Logos is "the true light" (1:9), making known the God whom no one has ever seen (1:18). Nicodemus, who does not know these truths, has been unable to set himself free from the bonds in which his own "knowledge" ties him (see vv. 2 and 4). So damaging are those bonds that he is unable to grasp a traditional concept of rebirth in the Spirit (v. 9). Having reflected on the encounter so far (v. 11), Jesus then looks forward to what he is about to announce (v. 12). Jesus' further disclosures reach beyond all that the best of Israel's thought had produced. Jesus has used such teaching to speak

---

[77] See among many who follow this explanation Barrett, *St John*, 202-3, 211-12; Dodd, *Interpretation*. R. E. Brown objects, asking why Jesus returns to the singular in v. 12 (*John*, 132). In terms of the narrative, it is possible that while a debate over the meaning of *ta epigeia* has been part of the conflict between community and synagogue (v. 11), the revelation of *ta epourania* comes only from Jesus, and thus the singular "I" returns (v. 12).

[78] See D. Patte, "Jesus' Pronouncement," p. 41: "The readers are invited to become the addressees of the discourse and to become listeners"; see also pp. 18-19.

[79] I am including the bridge of vv. 11/12 in the discourse, which it has linked with the dialogue of vv. 1-11/12.

[80] There is uncertainty among scholars over the speaker of this discourse. I am taking it to be Jesus. For a summary of the discussion, also concluding that Jesus is the speaker, see Brown, *John*, 149.

[81] As happens often, the verb *lambanein* is used to speak of the response to Jesus' revelation.

to Nicodemus about "earthly things" (*ta epigeia*): rebirth in water and in the Spirit. Jesus is now about to speak of "heavenly things" (*ta epourania*), which surpass "earthly things." Will Judaism (Nicodemus, the Pharisee, the ruler of the Jews and the teacher of the Jews [vv. 1 and 10], now addressed as "you" in the plural) ever be able to grasp these "heavenly things" (vv. 11-12)?[82]

The bridge out of the encounter between Jesus and Nicodemus has been crossed. The discourse proper begins with the first affirmation since the prologue of the uniqueness of the revelation of God in Jesus (vv. 13-15). Jesus affirms the uniqueness of his revealing role in terms of the Son of Man (v. 13). In strong contradiction (*oudeis*) of any suggestion that the great revealers of Israel had been to heaven to learn the secrets they eventually revealed, Jesus affirms that only the Son of Man has come down from heaven (v. 13). Only he is able to reveal the things he has seen (see vv. 11-12).[83] For those who have not read the prologue, this is a remarkable claim. For the reader it is a restatement, in terms of the Son of Man, of what was said of the Son in 1:18: "No one has ever seen God; the only Son, who is turned toward the bosom of the Father, he has told his story." The reader also recalls Jesus' promise of a future vision of the Son of Man, made to the first disciples in 1:51.

However, it is not enough to affirm the authoritative heavenly origins of all that the human story of Jesus, the Son of Man, will make known. Where and how will it take place?[84] The reader will not find all the answers so early in the narrative, but is now provided with basic Johannine truths about the way in which God will be revealed in Jesus (vv. 14-15). As Moses physically raised (*hypsōsen*) the serpent on a stake, so must the Son of Man be lifted up (*hypsōthēnai*) (v. 14). As Israel in the desert gazed upon the raised serpent to be restored to health (see Num 21:8-9), so eternal life will come to the one who, gazing upon the elevated Son of Man, believes.

The reader is expected to grasp the author's use of the double-meaning verb *hypsōthēnai*. It means both a physical lifting up and an exaltation. What this event might be is, however, a puzzle. The reader's puzzlement is increased by the further affirmation that belief in a God made known

---

[82] See J. Blank, *Krisis: Untersuchungen zur johanneischen Christologie und Eschatologie* (Freiburg: Lambertus Verlag, 1964) 62-63.

[83] For a detailed study that has led to this understanding of v. 13, see Moloney, *Son of Man*, 52-59. For a recent study of the wisdom background, supporting my view, see M.-E. Boismard, *Moïse ou Jésus: Essai de Christologie Johannique* (BETL 84; Leuven: University Press, 1988) 78-79.

[84] See Brown, *John*, 145.

through the gift of a Son in a "lifting up" will bring life (v. 15).[85] But the reader is not totally unprepared for Jesus' words in vv. 13-15. The implied reader knows of the conflict between light and darkness that does not overcome the light (1:5); he or she knows that Jesus will be rejected by "his own" (1:11), has heard of some future "hour of Jesus" which has not yet come (2:4), and has had the first hints of a conflict between Jesus and "the Jews" (2:18-20). But that is all the implied reader knows.[86]

As far as the author is concerned, an acceptance of Jesus' being "lifted up" as the place where God is made known is essential for correct faith. The author is leading the reader toward an acceptance of such truths. The introduction of the lifting up of Jesus as the place of his exaltation may produce a puzzled reader, but he or she reads further. The author's introduction of the theme of salvation (v. 15) leads into a development of that theme throughout vv. 16-21.

The saving love of God stands behind the mystery of the lifting up of the Son. God has "given" the Son, "sent" him to bring the possibility of eternal life and the salvation of the world (vv. 16-17). The immediate context of the "lifting up" (vv. 13-15) still lingers strongly enough for the reader to grasp some initial understanding of the dimensions of God's loving gift of the Son.[87] God loves the world so much that the Son was sent that the world might be saved, not judged.[88] Although the narrative to this point has been carefully set within a Jewish world, and all the responses to Jesus have come from Jews, the universal saving will of God is made explicit here: "God so loved the world" (v. 16); "God sent the Son into the world" (v. 17). This recalls the prologue (1:10-13) and prepares the reader for a narrative dedicated to Samaritans and a Gentile (4:1-54).

[85] For a detailed study of vv. 14-15, see Moloney, Son of Man, 59–65.

[86] The Christian implied reader (see 20:30-31) knows of the cross, but the Johannine description of it as a hypsōsis is unknown.

[87] A link between the cross and the "gift" of the Son in v. 16 is sometimes seen in the use of the verb didōmi. See, e.g., Brown, John, 134. But the Gospels use the technical term paradidōmi for the cross. See Mark 9:31; 10:33; 14:21, 41; Matt 17:22; 20:18; 26:2, 24, 25; Luke 18:32; 22:22; 24:7. See, however, Gal 1:4. It is better to see the link between God's love and the cross from the immediate context of vv. 13-15. This point is also made by Brown (John, 147).

[88] The reader is now encountering language very typical of later gnostic thought: the Son speaks of what he has seen (v. 11); the revelation of earthly and heavenly things (v. 12); the descent of the Son of Man (v. 13); the "lifting up" of the Son of Man (v. 14); the Father sends the Son to save the world (vv. 16-17). See Lindars, John, 147–48: "It is this passage more than any other which supports Bultmann's theory of adaptation from a pre-Gnostic source. . . . It is more reasonable to suppose that John presents what is basically Jewish and Christian teaching, in words that may be expected to be meaningful to a Gentile audience familiar with the ideas of Hellenistic religious aspirations."

Judgment there will be, however, and this theme is developed in the final verses of the discourse (vv. 18-21).

The reader has been provided with sufficient information to be aware that the loving gift of the Son for the salvation of the world will raise a fundamental question. One is called to a decision to accept or refuse the saving revelation of the Father who sent the Son. The narrative telling of the experience of Nicodemus challenges the reader to recognize that a decision must be made. Nicodemus may have been left puzzled and wavering, but the author, through the latter part of the discourse of Jesus aimed at the reader, is able to draw upon the familiar language of the prologue to develop the theme of judgment. Using the language of "life," "light," and "darkness" (see 1:4-8), the author presents the importance of decision: a commitment to belief or unbelief, which leads to life or death (v. 18).[89] Neither God nor the Son acts as judge. To refuse belief brings self-condemnation, shown in evil deeds and the presence of the darkness (vv. 18-19). It depends on the acceptance or refusal *now* of the believer faced with the revelation of God in the Son. Johannine realized eschatology stresses the importance of the response of the believer, not the sovereign action of God.[90]

As he comes to the conclusion of Jesus' commentary on the encounter between himself and Nicodemus, the implied reader is growing in awareness that one cannot be indifferent. Yet the reader is told that decisions will be made as a result of a long-standing preparedness to accept the revelation of God (vv. 20-21).[91] The doing of evil or the doing of good is not the *result* of living in the light. One does evil because one loves the darkness and therefore chooses it, hiding one's own ambiguity in the darkness (v. 20). In a parallel fashion, good deeds lead to one's coming to the light. It is not as if one lives in the light and simply basks in the blessedness of such an existence. To live in the light involves a continual doing of good deeds to become more deeply a part of the light, and indeed a part of the ongoing revelation of that light: "his deeds have been wrought by God" (v. 21).[92]

---

[89] The important Johannine expressions *krinein* and *krisis* appear here (vv. 18-19) for the first time in the narrative. See especially Blank, *Krisis*, 75-108; Dodd, *Interpretation*, 208-12.

[90] See Blank, *Krisis*, 41-52; see also pp. 91-108.

[91] Verses 19-21 contain a suggestion of predestination. For a discussion, see Barrett, *St John*, 218-19, and the more detailed commentaries of Schnackenburg, *St John*, 1:403-8; Blank, *Krisis*, 75-108; and G. Stemberger, *La symbolique du bien et du mal selon saint Jean* (Paris: Seuil, 1970) 26-33. Helpful reflections are also found in Bultmann, *John*, 159-60; and Lindars, *John*, 161.

[92] See Schnackenburg, *St John*, 408.

Nicodemus has not been able to accept Jesus' revelation of "earthly things" (v. 11); however, his response to Jesus has not been one of conflict or rejection. He is simply unable to move beyond what he knows and controls as he stumbles from self-confidence to misunderstanding to stunned silence (vv. 2, 4, 9). The narrative so far suggests that some in Israel have rejected Jesus' word (2:18-20), but Nicodemus does not belong to that group. The author is directing the narrative to the reader, moving from one example of the response to the word of Jesus in Israel (2:13-22) to another (3:1-21). This section of the Gospel has been called "the Johannine kerygma,"[93] because it depends on themes already provided for the reader in the prologue[94] and summarizes themes that will be developed at a later stage in the narrative: the love of God in the gift of the Son, the judgment which the presence of Jesus brings, the themes of light and darkness.[95] Many of the author's main themes already touched on have now been further developed. The reader has been made more aware that one cannot be indifferent.

The hesitations of Nicodemus, and especially his desire to keep his acceptance of Jesus within the limitations of his own understanding and experience (see vv. 2, 4, 9), certainly do not match the requirements of Jesus' discourse found in vv. 11-21. Yet from within the heart of Judaism (see vv. 1, 10) a faltering movement toward Jesus has been initiated. At no stage of the narrative does Nicodemus take the word of Jesus and reject it. The ongoing reading experience of the reader will eventually reveal that Nicodemus will make his own journey into faith (and into the Johannine community: 19:38-42). The figure of Nicodemus is used by the storyteller as an example for the implied reader of *partial faith*.

But the passage is not only the story of a leading figure from Judaism who can only come to a partial faith because of his inability to forsake his own criteria. It is, above all, a dense instruction for the reader on the uniqueness of the revelation that Jesus brings and the consequences of accepting or refusing such revelation. The presentation of the partial faith

---

[93] Blank, *Krisis*, 53.

[94] See especially Neyrey, "John III," 124–26.

[95] As we will see, the same themes are repeated in vv. 30-36, the commentary on the Baptist episode (vv. 22-29); however, the language there is less overtly "Johannine." From a diachronic point of view, vv. 31-36 probably formed the basic tradition from which vv. 11-21 had their origin. This has been convincingly shown in the detailed study of Boismard and Lamouille (*Saint Jean*, 113–17); see also C. H. Dodd, *Historical Tradition in the Fourth Gospel* (Cambridge: Cambridge University Press, 1963) 281–87; M. Black, *An Aramaic Approach to the Gospel and Acts* (3rd ed.; Oxford: Clarendon Press, 1967) 146–49.

of Nicodemus within this setting in the narrative serves to throw the limitations of such faith into relief. Again there may well be a hint of the lived experience of the Johannine community in this fearful initial approach, particularly in the light of Nicodemus's growing preparedness to stand publicly for Jesus as the narrative progresses. He objects to the judgments of the chief priests and the Pharisees in 7:50-52 and he accompanies Joseph of Arimathea to request the body of Jesus for a royal burial in 19:38-42.[96] In many ways, the journey of Nicodemus through the whole Gospel parallels the journey of the man born blind in John 9.[97] However, Nicodemus's further journey of faith lies ahead of the implied reader. At this stage of the narrative, Nicodemus is clearly seen as not rejecting Jesus but still falling short of belief in his word.[98]

IV. JESUS AND JOHN THE BAPTIST (3:22-36)

The Shape of the Narrative

Critics point to many difficulties in this passage, especially in its opening and closing sections (vv. 22-24, 31-36), but in narrative terms these passages serve to focus the reader's attention firmly on the central issue: the right relationship which must exist between Jesus and the Baptist. Jesus' going into Judea seems strange, as the Jerusalem encounter with Nicodemus was already in Judea. Yet the narrator needs to shift Jesus and his disciples away from the scene of the Baptist's activity. The indication that Jesus was baptizing, which has strong roots in history, links him with the Baptist. The latter, not yet imprisoned, is baptizing but in another place (vv. 23-24).[99] The imperfect tense of the verb *baptizein* in both v. 22 and v. 23

[96] J. N. Suggit makes much of the use of *elabon* in 19:40 ("Nicodemus—The True Jew," 102-4). He claims that it indicates Nicodemus's total acceptance of Jesus, and even that there is an indication of the reception of the Eucharist in the Johannine community. See also B. Hemelsoet, "L'ensevelissement selon Saint Jean," in *Studies in John: Presented to Professor Dr. J. N. Sevenster on the Occasion of His Seventieth Birthday* (NovTSup 24; Leiden: Brill, 1970) 47-65. Given the important parallel between *pisteuein* and *lambanein* in the Fourth Gospel (see especially 1:12), the first suggestion is just possible, but the latter asks too much of the evidence. See Bassler, "Mixed Signals," 640-43.

[97] See J. L. Martyn, *History and Theology in the Fourth Gospel* (2nd ed.; Nashville: Abingdon, 1979) 110-11, 122-27; W. A. Meeks, "The Man from Heaven in Johannine Sectarianism," *JBL* 91 (1972) 54-55.

[98] See Bauer, *Johannesevangelium*, 61.

[99] For a reconstruction of the historical background, which I accept, see J. Murphy-O'Connor, "John the Baptist and Jesus: History and Hypotheses," *NTS* 36 (1990) 359-74; see also S. Légasse,

indicates the habitual practice of Jesus and John the Baptist in their different locations.[100]

Having set the scene in this way, a discussion of "purification" leads the disciples of the Baptist to raise the question of the relationship between Jesus and the Baptist (see vv. 25-26). While the disciples of the Baptist are puzzled over the two baptizers, the reader is aware that the Baptist himself will not be (see 1:6-8, 15, 19-34). Yet after the failure of "the Jews" to accept the word of Jesus (2:13-22), a comment on the limitations of a faith based on signs (2:23-25), and Nicodemus's inability to abandon his own categories and knowledge (3:1-12), the narrator reports this encounter between John the Baptist and his disciples to conclude his account of Israel's response to the appearance of Jesus Christ.

As with the encounter with "the Jews" (2:23-25) and with Nicodemus (3:11-21), the narrator concludes the scene by standing back from events and speaking directly to the reader (vv. 31-36). There has been considerable discussion over the speaker of the words reported in vv. 31-36. Many suggest that the Baptist is still speaking,[101] while others claim that Jesus has entered the scene.[102] It appears that the narrator addresses the reader here.[103] In the end, whether the speaker be the Baptist, Jesus, or the narrator, the point of view of the author is being expressed. "We must never forget that though the author can to some extent choose his disguises, he can never choose to disappear."[104]

The narrative has been shaped as follows:

I. *Verses 22-24:* Introductory passage, setting the scene by describing the time (John is not yet in prison) and the two places (Judea and

---

"Le Baptême administré par Jésus (Jn 3,22-26; 4,1-3) et l'origine du baptême chrétien," *BLE* 78 (1977) 17-25; B. Witherington, "Jesus and the Baptist—Two of a Kind?" in *SBL 1988 Seminar Papers,* ed. D. Lull (Atlanta: Scholars Press, 1988) 225-44; on John 3:22-4:3, see pp. 242-43. I am disregarding symbolic interpretations of the place-name of Aenon near Salim and the scene as a whole. See, e.g., N. Krieger, "Fiktive Orte der Johannes-Taufe," *ZNW* 45 (1953-54) 121-23.

[100] See Bauer, *Johannesevangelium,* 62; Murphy-O'Connor, "John the Baptist and Jesus," 363.

[101] See, e.g., Bauer, *Johannesevangelium,* 63-65; Barrett, *St John,* 224; J. Wilson, "The Integrity of John 3:22-26," *JSNT* 10 (1981) 36-38.

[102] See, e.g., Schnackenburg, *St John,* 380-81. Schnackenburg, however, has transposed vv. 31-36 to follow v. 12. It is, in turn, followed by vv. 13-21; see further, R. Schnackenburg, "Die situationsgelösten Redestücke in Joh 3," *ZNW* 49 (1958) 88-99.

[103] See, e.g., Westcott, *St John,* 60; Lagrange, *Saint Jean,* 96; Dodd, *Interpretation,* 308-11; Brown, *John,* 159-60.

[104] W. C. Booth, *The Rhetoric of Fiction* (2nd ed.; Chicago: University of Chicago Press, 1983) 20. For the centrality of the narrator in the Gospels, see S. D. Moore, *Literary Criticism and the Gospels: The Theoretical Challenge* (New Haven: Yale University Press, 1989) 25-40.

Aenon near Salim) of the respective baptizing activities of the major characters in the narrative: Jesus and John the Baptist.[105]

II. *Verses 25-30:* The discussion between John the Baptist and his disciples:

   (a) *Verses 25-26:* The opening statement from the disciples of the Baptist, raising the question of the nature of the relationship between Jesus and the Baptist.

   (b) *Verses 27-30:* The response of the Baptist, describing himself as the friend of the bridegroom, rejoicing in the bridegroom's voice.

III. *Verses 31-36:* The discourse-commentary of the narrator, developing two basic themes:

   (a) *Verses 31-35:* Theme one: the revelation of the heavenly in the Son.

   (b) *Verse 36:* Theme two: the salvation or condemnation that flows from the acceptance or refusal of this revelation.

This narrative, made up of an introduction to a discussion which leads into a discourse repeats the shape of 3:1-21.

The various narratives that form 2:1–3:36 are closely related. Both 2:1-12 and 2:13-25 have an identical shape, as do 3:1-21 and 3:22-36.[106] When one adds to these formal observations the fact that the narrator has told of the way in which Jews (the Mother of Jesus, "the Jews," Nicodemus and John the Baptist) have responded to Jesus, the literary and thematic unity of 2:1–3:36 emerges.

Reading the Narrative

The narrator moves Jesus and his disciples away from the action (v. 22). There is a clear break in time (*meta tauta*) as Jesus is shifted away from the city of Jerusalem *eis tēn Ioudaian gēn.*[107] He does not move away from Judea,

---

[105] I claim that Jesus is a "major character in the narrative," even though he never takes part in the events. The whole discussion is about him.

[106] The parallel structures (slightly different from the one I am suggesting) have been noticed and discussed by Y. Ibuki ("*kai tēn phōnēn autou akoueis:* Gedankenaufbau und Hintergrund des 3. Kapitels des Johannesevangeliums," *Bulletin of Seikei University* 14 [1978] 9–33), H. Thyen ("Aus der Literatur zum Johannesevangelium," *TR* 44 [1979] 112), and W. Klaiber ("Der irdische und der himmlische Zeuge: eine Auslegung von Joh 3.22-36," *NTS* 36 [1990] 211-13, 232-33). J. Wilson argues that John 3 can be divided into two parallel scenes: 3:1-21 (Jesus as protagonist) and 3:24-36 (the Baptist as protagonist) with vv. 22-23 as a literary bridge ("Integrity of John 3:22-26," 38–40).

[107] This is a difficult expression that is often read as a clumsy remnant of a source. For a discussion of the difficulty and the interpretation I have followed, see Westcott, *St John,* 57; Bultmann, *John,* 170 n. 3; Barrett, *St John,* 220.

but he is no longer in the city. The reader is informed that he was baptizing there. Armed with this information, the reader is told that John the
Baptist was also baptizing, but in a different place (v. 23). For the first time
since 2:1-12 the scene shifts away from Jerusalem. Although the exact location has not been established, there is growing agreement that the site
is in Samaria.[108] The reader is aware of its location. This is a hint to the
reader that the long section devoted to the Jewish response to Jesus is drawing to a conclusion. A further hint is given when the narrator reports that
the events took place before the Baptist's imprisonment.

The reader approaches the following episode knowing that the two
major characters in the story so far, Jesus and John the Baptist, are both
engaged in a baptismal ministry.[109] However, Jesus is in Judea and the
Baptist is in Aenon, in the period before the Baptist was imprisoned.
Although Jesus will not personally play a part in the action that follows,
the scene focuses on the relationship between Jesus and the Baptist, both
exercising a baptismal ministry. It is on the basis of the information
provided in vv. 22-24 that the reader understands the discussion between
"John's disciples and a Jew over purifying" (v. 25). Whatever the historical
origins of the discussion over "purifying" (see 2:6), it must be read as a
discussion over the issue of baptism.[110] So much attention has been given
to the two baptizers in vv. 22-24 that the reader immediately understands
there is some unsolved problem over the question of their respective baptisms.[111]

The disciples of the Baptist are faced with a problem concerning the
baptism of Jesus and the baptism of John. The implied reader knows of
their relative merits, as the Baptist clarified the issue (see 1:29-34). But the
Baptist's witness on the second day of preparation for the revelation of
the glory (1:29-34) had no specific audience. Their master's positive witness
to Jesus as the Lamb of God and the Son of God (1:29-34) remains unknown
to the disciples of the Baptist. It is thus not part of John's witness referred
to in v. 26, as they have only heard the more public negative witness to

[108] For a survey of possible sites, see Brown, *John*, 151. On its Samaritan location, see
Boismard, "Aenon, près de Salem," 219–22; Murphy-O'Connor, "John the Baptist and Jesus,"
363–66.
[109] The text shows no interest in affirming the superiority of Jesus' baptism. Historically
it would have been parallel to that of the Baptist. See Légasse, "Le Baptême administré par
Jésus," 25–29; Murphy-O'Connor, "John the Baptist and Jesus," 367–74.
[110] See Barrett, *St John*, 219.
[111] C. K. Barrett suggests that the discussion probably arose from the Baptist's lack of concern, in his baptismal ministry, to observe the details of Jewish ablutions (*St John*, 221).

Jesus (see 1:15, 19) reported in 1:19-28. The characters in the narrative, therefore, know less than the reader, who was part of both the negative (1:19-28) and positive (1:29-34) witnessing of John the Baptist.[112] Even though the scene may be set in Samaria, the characters in the narrative must be understood as belonging to the Jewish world. The Baptist and his disciples have their origins there (see 1:19-28, 36), and the unnamed figure discussing purification with the disciples is simply called "a Jew."[113] The disciples address their master with the Jewish title "Rabbi." The reader has encountered this salutation on three earlier occasions: twice in the first days of Jesus, when he was addressed in this way by his newly found disciples (1:38, 49), and very recently in Nicodemus's confession of Jesus (3:2). A title of honor that has been given only to Jesus is now applied to John the Baptist by his disciples. From the perspective of the reader, a parallel is being drawn between Jesus and the Baptist. This is further reinforced as the disciples of the Baptist ask about Jesus, who had been with the Baptist on the other side of the Jordan, to whom the Baptist had borne witness (v. 26).[114] They are puzzled by the fact that someone who was once a follower of the Baptist now seems to be attracting more attention. The disciples of the Baptist remark (complain?) that "all are going to him" (v. 26). The reader has been told that "people came and were baptized" at Aenon near Salim (v. 23). The implied reader is now informed that "all are going" to Jesus (v. 26).[115] Therein lies the problem for the disciples of the Baptist, although the reader, well informed by the narrative so far, has no doubts about the nature of the relationship.

The Baptist's response to these queries is to shift the discussion into a context of revelation (v. 27).[116] The reader has read enough to be aware that the truth about both Jesus and John the Baptist will not be discovered in messianic gestures, precursors, messianic titles, and "signs." The authority of both comes from God (1:1-2, 3:13-14, 16-17 [Jesus]; 1:6, 33 [the Baptist]), and thus the disciples are directed away from their perspective of who is

---

[112] For other attempts to resolve this difficulty see Brown, *John*, 153-55.

[113] Reading *meta Ioudaiou*. There is excellent ancient textual witness for *tōn Ioudaiōn* and a popular, but unattested, reading of *Iēsou*. For a survey, see Barrett, *St John*, 221. R. Schnackenburg suggests that "the Jew" may have come from Judea, where Jesus was baptizing (*St John*, 1:413-14). This would make sense of the disciples' statement in v. 26.

[114] For a description of Jesus' association with the Baptist on the other side of the Jordan, see Murphy-O'Connor, "John the Baptist and Jesus," 367-76.

[115] It is often pointed out that the *pantes* of v. 26 is an exaggeration, possibly produced by anger. However, in terms of the narrative, it creates a tension between the *pareginonto* of v. 23 and the *pantes erchontai* of v. 26.

[116] The pleonastic *apekrithē kai eipen* is used.

the more important baptizer to the source of all true gifts: "No one can receive anything except what is given to him from heaven" (v. 27).

The reader finds that the Baptist is associating himself with the point of view expressed by Jesus in his discussion with Nicodemus (see vv. 3, 5, 7-8, 11-12). It is on the basis of what has been received from the only source of authentic revelation, "from above," that anyone can be in a proper relationship with God (v. 27).[117] On the basis of this affirmation, the Baptist is able to remind his disciples of his earlier witness (see 1:19-28): he is not the Christ, but the one sent before him (v. 28). The reader is aware that there is more to the use of the verb "sent" than the disciples would realize, because he or she has read 1:6: "There was a man, sent by God, whose name was John" (see also 1:33).[118] Although "the Jews" totally refused the words of Jesus (2:13-22) and although Nicodemus, the leader and teacher of the Jews, was unable to go beyond his own criteria (3:1-21), another Jew, John the Baptist, is now laying himself open to all that comes "from above."

From this perspective he describes his relationship with the Christ. The background of the Baptist's description of his relationship with Jesus is twofold. On the one hand there is an Old Testament presentation of Israel as the bride of God (see Isa 62:4-5; Jer 2:2; 3:20; Ezek 16:8; 23:4; Hos 2:21) and a New Testament reflection of the same theme in speaking of the church as the bride of Christ (see 2 Cor 11:2; Eph 5:25-27, 31-32; Rev 21:2; 22:17). Out of this background, "the Baptist is made to indicate that not he but Christ is the head of the New Israel."[119] But as well as the biblical image, the narrator has the Baptist use language that reflects the marriage practices of the time. He describes himself as "the friend of the bridegroom who stands and hears him (*akouōn autou*)" and as one who "rejoices greatly at the bridegroom's voice (*tēn phōnēn*).[120] Because of this "hearing" of the bridegroom's "voice," the Baptist is full of joy, prepared to decrease as Jesus comes upon the scene (vv. 29-30).[121]

---

[117] Verse 27 is a general statement about the source of ultimate truth for anyone (*ou dynatai anthrōpos lambanein*). Against, e.g., Becker, who applies v. 27 only to the Baptist (*Johannes*, 154).

[118] Against Bultmann (*John*, 167-72) and others, I claim that the Baptist plays a positive role each time he appears or is referred to in the narrative (see 1:6-8, 15; 1:19-34; 3:22-29; 5:33-36).

[119] Barrett, *St John*, 222-23.

[120] Str-B 1:45-46, 500-504. See especially *Tosefta Ketuboth* 1:4 (J. Neusner, *The Tosefta Translated from the Hebrew: Third Division Nashim [The Order of Women]* [New York: Ktav, 1979] 61). See A. van Selms, "The Best Man and the Bride—from Sumer to St. John," *JNES* 9 (1950) 65-75; M.-E. Boismard, "L'ami de l'époux (Jo III, 29)," in *A la Rencontre de Dieu: Mémorial Albert Gelin*, ed. A. Barucq, J. Duplacy, A. George, and H. de Lubac (Le Puy: Xavier Mappus, 1961) 289-95.

[121] On the use of increasing and decreasing as an image of the waxing and waning of the

The Baptist is presented as one who sees his relationship to Jesus as one of listening. Although there is no use of the expression *logos* or related words, they are paralleled by the word *phōnē* in v. 29. We can never be certain why an author chooses certain words, and "it is highly probable that we are here in touch with precanonical tradition."[122] I would suggest that as the tradition already said what the real author had in mind, he left these words as he found them.[123] John the Baptist demonstrates openness to the word of Jesus, even though it means he must disappear from a scene which, up to this stage in the story, he has occupied so significantly. The passage culminates in v. 29. It is here that the *nature of the relationship* between Jesus and John the Baptist is articulated in John's direct speech. He is the friend of the bridegroom, rejoicing greatly as he hears the voice of the bridegroom, even though it means he must now disappear from the scene (v. 30).[124] This leads to a comment from the narrator (vv. 31-36).

There are close parallels between vv. 31-36 and vv. 11-21.[125] Both speak of Jesus as the authoritative revealer whose revelation is not accepted (vv. 31-32; see vv. 11-12). The uniqueness and authenticity of the revelation brought by Jesus come from his being "from above" (v. 31; see v. 13). Life comes from belief in the revelation brought by the Son and cannot be provided by any person or institution that belongs to "the earth." The question of origins emerges as the one from above brings a revelation of the truth that is beyond the limited truths the world and its knowledge can offer.[126] The narrative of 2:13–3:30 stands behind such an affirmation, as "the Jews" and Nicodemus must be judged as being "of earth" in this sense.[127] Failure to accept the witness of Jesus has marked much of the

---

sunlight, indicating a turning point where the old gives way to the new, important for the patristic reading of the passage, see Schnackenburg, *St John*, 1:417–18.

[122] Dodd, *Historical Tradition*, 287. Dodd, however, suspects that *phōnē* may be Johannine, although he admits that one cannot be sure (see p. 282).

[123] Augustine said it beautifully: "Ego sum in audiendo, ille in dicendo, ego sum illuminandus, ille lumen; ego sum in aure, ille Verbum" (*In Joannem* 13.12; CCSL 36, p. 137).

[124] Commentators give little attention to the culminating importance of vv. 29-30 in the narrative. R. Infante sees it as crucial "L'amico dello sposo, figura del ministero di Giovanni Battista nel Quarto Vangelo," *RivBib* 31 [1983] 12–14). However, he argues that the central issue is the Baptist's joy. I am arguing, from the whole context of 2:1–3:36, that it is his openness to the voice (word) of Jesus.

[125] See Brown, *John*, 159–60; Segalla, *Giovanni*, 185–87; Moloney, *Son of Man*, 44–45.

[126] See Westcott, *St John*, 60–61. I am not accepting that "from above" refers to Jesus while "of the earth" refers to the Baptist. See, e.g., Barrett, *John*, 224–25; Klaiber, "Der irdische," 205–33.

[127] So also W. Loader, "The Central Structure of Johannine Theology," *NTS* 30 (1984) 189.

narrative from 2:12–3:30, even though he has revealed what he has heard
(v. 32; see v. 11).[128] The risk of such refusal is made clear in the author's
insistence that the one who accepts Jesus' revelation of God is attesting
to the ultimate truth, authorized by God who is true.[129] God makes the
"word" known through the spoken "word" of the sent one, pouring
out the Spirit without reserve (vv. 33-34; see v. 17).[130] The basis of this
authoritative revelation of God is the love that unites the Father and the
Son, leading the Father to give the Son the task of making God known
(v. 35; see v. 16). By now the reader is aware that this is the fullness from
which we have all received (1:16). Although the major part of vv. 31-36
has been devoted to the theme of Jesus as the revealer (vv. 31-35), the
themes of death and judgment are stated in v. 36. Belief produces eternal
life, while the wrath of God is the fruit of a refusal to accept this revelation
(v. 36; see vv. 20-21).

Although the message of revelation and salvation found in vv. 11-21
is repeated in vv. 31-36, it is not told in the same way. Here there is no
reference to the christological theme of the Son of Man as the unique
revealer who must be lifted up on a cross (vv. 13-15). The stress is more
on the one sent from above who "speaks" (v. 31), who "bears witness"
(v. 32), who gives authentic testimony (v. 33), who "utters the words of
God" (v. 34). It is likely that vv. 31-36 reflect an earlier version of what eventually formed vv. 11-21. The author has retained the more traditional
passage, with its insistence on the word of the authoritative revealer,
deliberately placing it at the end of his narratives on the response of Jews
to the revelation of Jesus. As the reader comes to the end of this section
he or she finds a reflection showing interest in "the word" rather than the
person of Jesus.[131]

At the end of a triptych of faith experiences within Judaism, found
in the encounters which "the Jews," Nicodemus, and John the Baptist have
had with Jesus, the theme of "the word" is central. The saving revelation

---

[128] R. Schnackenburg points out that the *kai* is adversative (*St John*, 1:384). Jesus reveals
from direct access to God, *but* this is refused.

[129] Again the verb *lambanein* is used for the commitment of faith: "He who accepts his
testimony." See Schnackenburg, *St John*, 1:389.

[130] There is a long-standing discussion over who gives the Spirit, the Father or Jesus. Both
are possible. Because I understand the Gospel as primarily theological rather than christological
(see *NJBC*, 1420-21), I would opt for God, but the difference is not great. See also W. Loader,
The Christology of the Fourth Gospel (BBET 23; Frankfurt: Peter Lang, 1989) 25-26; and the survey
of Brown, *John*, 161-62.

[131] On the question of the development of vv. 11-21 from vv. 31-36, see Moloney, *Son of
Man*, 50-51; and especially Boismard and Lamouille, *Jean*, 113-17.

of God takes place in "the word" of Jesus.[132] This has been the criterion for the reader who by now has judged that "the Jews" demonstrated a total lack of faith, while the faith of Nicodemus is limited by his determination to understand Jesus according to his own categories. But John the Baptist saw himself as the friend of the bridegroom, rejoicing to hear his voice. He shows an openness to the word of Jesus cost what it may: "He must increase, but I must decrease" (v. 30). The reader rightly sees John the Baptist as an example of *authentic belief*, laying himself open to the word of God (3:29), as the mother of Jesus had done (2:5).

CONCLUSION

The real author has assembled four different narratives which have provided the material for this section of his story of Jesus. The narratives of the first miracle at Cana (2:1-12) and the purification of the Temple (2:13-22) were shaped in an identical fashion: a setting, verbal exchange, action, and a final comment on the scene from the narrator. Jesus' nocturnal encounter with Nicodemus (3:1-21) and the discussion over the right relationship between the Baptist and Jesus (3:22-36) were also shaped in the same way: a setting, a dialogue reflecting the response of a major character to Jesus, leading into a discourse reflecting on that response.

The narrative is further unified by the presence of Jews throughout: the mother of Jesus, "the Jews," Nicodemus, and John the Baptist. Only the first Cana miracle (2:1-12) does not conclude with commentary directed toward the reader (but see v. 11). The purification of the Temple leads into a comment on a faith based on signs (2:23-25), while both the encounter between Jesus and Nicodemus and the response of John the Baptist lead into parallel discourses presenting Jesus as the unique revealer of God, bringing either salvation or condemnation to those who accept or refuse such revelation (3:11-21, 31-36).

Leaving aside 2:1-12, which I will later regard as A] in the narrative shape of 2:1–4:54, the narrative of 2:13–3:36 unfolds as follows:

B] After the purification of the Temple, "the Jews" refuse to accept Jesus' word on the raising of the temple of his body. The author presents "the Jews" to the reader as models of a lack of faith, rejecting the very words of Jesus (2:13-22).

---

[132] See especially Bultmann, *John*, 161-66.

X] *Drawing back from the narrative, the author speaks directly to the reader, criticizing the quality of a faith that draws people to Jesus because of the signs he did (2:23-25).*

C] The nocturnal discussion with Nicodemus is used by the author to show the reader an example from the story of Jesus of the people described in 2:23-25. While there is much that is positive in Nicodemus's approach to Jesus and Jesus' patient attempts to draw Nicodemus beyond his own "knowledge," he fails at this stage of the narrative. His failure is rooted in his inability to accept Jesus' word about rebirth from above. He can only raise questions about a second birth and thus is only partially open to the newness that is produced "from above." Nicodemus is presented to the reader as an example of imperfect and partial faith, caught within the limitations of his own knowledge and control, not open to the word of Jesus (3:1-21).

D] In a final scene where Jewish characters play a major role, John the Baptist describes his relationship to Jesus as one of listening for the voice of the bridegroom, rejoicing in the sound of his voice, even though he himself must now decrease. The author has taken the reader a step further in his description of a possible response to Jesus. He has used John the Baptist as a model of authentic belief (3:22-36).

C. K. Barrett has claimed that this section of the Gospel, dedicated entirely to Jewish characters and situations, is a presentation of Jesus as the fulfiller of Judaism.[133] There is much that is true in the claim, but there is more to it. My tracing of the implied reader through the narrative has shown that the reader has met a series of responses to Jesus, and reflections on those responses. Many major themes of the Gospel have already been initiated in 2:1–3:36. But, above all, the careful interweaving of these narratives, commentaries, and discourses teaches the reader that the criterion for authentic belief is openness to the word of Jesus. The implied reader has come to *know* that important Johannine truth. However, the reader has now also had an *experience* of a journey of faith within Israel. Using "the word" of Jesus as the criterion, and regularly addressing the reader directly (see 2:23-25; 3:11-21, 31-36), the author leads the reader to an understanding of authentic faith and its importance for life and salvation. The author tells the reader that there are three possible reactions to the revelation Jesus brings: no faith ("the Jews"), partial faith (Nicodemus), and complete faith (John the Baptist).

[133] Barrett, *St John,* 219–20.

The intended readers of this Gospel, however, no longer belonged to the world of Judaism. Through the implied reader, the real author has addressed them on the possibility of a journey from no faith to authentic faith within Judaism. It is important that the author show the possibility of true faith within Judaism. This is the birthplace of the community. The Johannine community exists at the time of the final writing of the Fourth Gospel because such acceptance has already been part of its story: "When therefore he was raised from the dead, his disciples remembered that he had said this; and they believed the Scripture and the word which Jesus had spoken" (2:22).

It is a comfort for the Johannine community to know that its roots in Judaism are based in an experience of authentic faith and that such faith is always possible in Israel.[134] But what of the wider world into which the community is being sent? The narrative will turn next "to the world on and beyond the borders of Judaism."[135]

[134] Many commentators see this first section of the Gospel as the transcending of Israel. It must be observed that two Jews, the mother of Jesus and John the Baptist, are presented to the reader as models of authentic faith.

[135] Barrett, St John, 220.

Chapter Six

A Journey of Faith
in Samaria: John 4:1-42

¶ IN 4:1-6 THE AUTHOR moves Jesus away from Judea, on a journey to Galilee, via Samaria. Located in a non-Jewish world,[1] Jesus encounters Samaritans (the Samaritan woman [vv. 7-30] and the Samaritan townsfolk [vv. 39-42]), and a Gentile (vv. 43-54).[2] The introduction to the narrative contains a number of literary and historical problems, but once the scene is set, Jesus encounters a Samaritan woman. There are two moments in his discussion with her. The first discussion concerns thirst, wells, and water (vv. 7-15), and the second is initiated by Jesus' questioning her marital situation (vv. 16-30).[3]

---

[1] I will use the expression "non-Jewish" in the sense of the Samaritans' being a people of mixed blood (see 2 Kgs 17:24-41), no longer accepting a cult centered on Jerusalem and having broken with the Jews who returned from Babylon (see the different but equally hostile reports of the events in Nehemiah 13 and Josephus, _Antiquities_ 11.297-347). This situation had worsened by the time of Jesus. For a survey of the evidence, coming to the same conclusion, see J. Jeremias, _Jerusalem in the Time of Jesus_ (London: SCM Press, 1969) 352-58. See also F. M. Cross, "Aspects of Samaritan and Jewish History in Late Persian and Hellenistic Times," HTR 59 (1966) 201-11.

[2] On my understanding of the _basilikos_ of v. 46 as a Gentile, see below, pp. 182-83.

[3] For this position, reading Jesus' encounter with the Samaritan woman down to vv. 29-30, see below. See also the study of A. Lenglet, "Jésus de passage parmi les Samaritains," _Bib_ 66 (1985) 493-503, especially pp. 496-97; and H. Boers, _Neither on This Mountain Nor in Jerusalem_ (SBLMS 35; Atlanta: Scholars Press, 1988) 2-5.

As other Samaritans come toward Jesus (v. 30), the narrator draws back from the encounters that are taking place between Jesus and the Samaritans, to report an interlude in which Jesus converses with his disciples (vv. 31-38). Action returns to the narrative as the Samaritan villagers come to him (vv. 39-42) and eventually confess that Jesus is the savior of the world (v. 42).[4] Parallels between 2:13 – 3:36 can be sensed. As in 2:13 – 3:36 we find three different reactions to Jesus: the Samaritan woman goes from uncomprehending perplexity (vv. 7-15) to a question about Jesus' being the Messiah (vv. 16-30), and the Samaritans express their faith in him as the savior of the world (vv. 39-42). As in 2:13 – 3:36 the author drew back from the narrative to speak directly to the reader in 2:23-25, a similar technique is used in the words directed to the disciples in 4:31-38.[5]

The section of the Gospel dedicated to the encounters between Jesus and Jews shifted quite dramatically from encounter to encounter through clearly indicated and typically Johannine introductory and linking passages (2:13; 3:1-2a; 3:22-24). This is not the case in 4:1-42. All the encounters between Jesus and the Samaritans, as well as the discourse directed toward the disciples, happen in the one place, with only a slight displacement at the end of the passage (v. 40). These encounters follow a lengthy introduction (vv. 1-6). The temporal axis of the narrative is sequential. As the disciples go into the town to buy food (v. 8), Jesus talks with the Samaritan woman. As the disciples come back, she returns to the town (v. 28), and her fellow townsfolk begin to come to Jesus (v. 30). While they are on their way Jesus addresses his disciples (vv. 31-38). The Samaritans arrive, ask him to stay with them (v. 40), and eventually come to faith in him. After his two days with the Samaritans, he departs for Galilee (v. 43).[6]

---

[4] For a helpful analysis of the flow of the narrative, part of which I am adopting here, see Groupe de Jura, "Jean 4: Jésus en Samarie," *Sémiotique et Bible* 12 (1978) 38-40. See also H. Boers, "Discourse Structure and Macro-Structure in the Interpretation of Texts: John 4:1-42 as an Example," in *Society of Biblical Literature 1980 Seminar Papers*, ed. P. Achtemeier (Chico, Calif.: Scholars Press, 1980) 159-82; and P. J. Cahill, "Narrative Art in John IV," *Religious Studies Bulletin* 2 (1982) 41-48.

[5] Recent attempts to structure John 4 chiastically miss the important narrative relationship it has with John 2-3. See, e.g., F. Roustang, "Les moments de l'acte de foi et ses conditions de possibilité. Essai d'interpretation du dialogue avec la Samaritaine," *RSR* 46 (1958) 352; C. Hudry-Clergeon, "De Judée en Galilée: Etude de Jean 4:1-45," *NRT* 103 (1981) 830; Cahill, "Narrative Art," 42.

[6] On the temporal aspect of the narrative, see the analysis of B. Olsson, *Structure and Meaning in the Fourth Gospel: A Text-Linguistic Analysis of John 2:1-11 and 4:1-42* (Coniectanea Biblica, New Testament Series 6; Lund: Gleerup, 1974) 147-49.

I. JESUS AND THE SAMARITAN WOMAN (I)
(4:1-15)

The Shape of the Narrative

After the preparatory vv. 1-6 and the introduction of the Samaritan woman in v. 7, the reader finds direct speech dominating the narrative as one partner in a dialogue either addresses or questions the other.[7] However, in the encounter between Jesus and the Samaritan woman, even though no new character enters the story, there are indications in the dialogue that the narrative can be divided into two moments. Jesus initiates dialogue with the woman through the use of an imperative in v. 7 (*dos moi*) and v. 16 (*hypage phōnēson*).[8] Once the dialogue is under way, the issues discussed change.[9] From vv. 7-15 Jesus and the Samaritan woman are at cross-purposes over thirst, wells, water, and life.[10] These themes disappear completely in vv. 16-30, where the issues are the person of Jesus (prophet or Messiah?) and true worship.

The narrative of vv. 1-15 is shaped as follows:

I. *Verses 1-6:* General introduction and setting for 4:1-42.[11]

II. *Verses 7-15:* The report of a discussion between Jesus and a Samaritan woman. The dialogue has three moments.

---

[7] The analysis of B. Olsson (*Structure and Meaning*, 173-218) is based on an appreciation of the text as a dialogue. See also G. Friedrich, *Chi è Gesù? Il messagio del quarto evangelista nella pericopa della samaritana* (Biblioteca Minima di Cultura Religiosa; Brescia: Paideia, 1975) 20-24; and the more comprehensive study of E. Leidig, *Jesu Gespräch mit der Samaritanerin und weitere Gespräche im Johannesevangelium* (ThD 15; Basel: Friedrich Reinhardt, 1981) especially pp. 190-202. See also L. Eslinger, "The Wooing of the Woman at the Well: Jesus, the Reader and Reader-Response Criticism," *Literature and Theology* 1 (1987) 171.

[8] See G. R. O'Day, *Revelation in the Fourth Gospel: Narrative Mode and Theological Claim* (Philadelphia: Fortress Press, 1986) 52-53.

[9] Most commentators see this, but not all regard it as important. G. R. Beasley-Murray has the first stage of Jesus' encounter with the Samaritan woman run to v. 18 (*John* [WBC 36; Waco: Word Books, 1987] 61). Olsson shows the unity of vv. 7-26 (*Structure and Meaning*, 193-208). There is no break at v. 15.

[10] Many scholars see v. 15 as a climax to the first section of the narrative. See, e.g., C. H. Dodd, *The Interpretation of the Fourth Gospel* (Cambridge: Cambridge University Press, 1953) 311; T. Okure, *The Johannine Approach to Mission: A Contextual Study of John 4:1-42* (WUNT 2, Reihe 32; Tübingen: J. C. B. Mohr [Paul Siebeck], 1988) 79, 92. C. Hudry-Clergeon calls v. 16 a "changement brusque" ("De Judée en Galilée," 819).

[11] Some critics have vv. 1-4 as the introduction, making vv. 5-6 part of the encounter. B. Olsson has shown how an interweaving of vv. 1-4 and vv. 5-6 form a unified introduction (*Structure and Meaning*, 134).

(a) *Verses 7-9:* In an initial encounter, the ground for Jesus' teaching on water and life is prepared through Jesus' request for water. Jesus initiates the dialogue, but the word of the woman is dominant. She raises a surprised and mocking question to Jesus.

(b) *Verses 10-14:* Jesus shifts the discussion away from the request for a drink into a gift from God which he can give. Although the woman speaks in this section, the words of Jesus lead the discussion into a line of argument that perplexes her. As she falters, Jesus is the dominant partner in this dialogue.

(c) *Verse 15:* The woman rejects Jesus' offer because she misunderstands his words.

Reading the Narrative

One of the first impressions the reader has from 4:1-2 is the reference to the "disciples" as both receiving and administering baptism. The Pharisees have heard that Jesus is making and baptizing more disciples than John.[12] If the reader only read v. 1 and then progressed to discover that for this reason Jesus left Judea and set out for Galilee (v. 3), the reader might wonder why. In itself, the greater reception being given to Jesus' baptizing ministry should not be sufficient reason for Jesus to move away from Judea. On the contrary. Why should Jesus leave a place where he is very successful? There is nothing in vv. 1 and 3, in their present place in the narrative, to suggest that the Pharisees had any objection or were opposed to Jesus. Perhaps the difficult v. 2, rather than being the stumbling block for a synchronic reading of the passage, is the solution to the problem.[13] Must we assume that here, at least, the author has lost control

[12] There is a textual problem in v. 1. Equally ancient witnesses give either *ho kyrios* (Bodmer papyrus, Codex Alexandrinus, etc.) or *ho Iēsous* (Codex Sinaiticus, Codex Bezae, Codex Koridethi, etc.). It is difficult to decide. It is possible that originally there was no noun, and thus both would be secondary. For this reading, see R. E. Brown, *The Gospel According to John* (2 vols.; AB 29, 29A; Garden City, N.Y.: Doubleday, 1966, 1970) 164. I am hesitantly choosing *ho Iēsous* supposing that *ho kyrios* was supplied to avoid the clumsy twofold use of *ho Iēsous* in the one sentence. For this, see also M.-E. Boismard and A. Lamouille, *L'Evangile de Jean* (Synopse des Quatre Evangiles en Français III; Paris: Cerf, 1977) 128.

[13] I have no doubt that our present 4:1-6 has had a long history and that v. 2 is a late part of that story. So careful a scholar as C. H. Dodd has argued that the same person cannot have written 3:22 and 4:2 (*Historical Tradition in the Fourth Gospel* [Cambridge: Cambridge University Press, 1963] 237, 285–86). I am sure that is the case. For an analysis of the data, see Boismard and Lamouille, *Jean,* 128–32. Yet someone is responsible for the text as we now

of his sources? Is it impossible to make sense out of the present state of the text?[14]

The reader is aware, from 3:22-36, that the Baptist is prepared to stand aside as Jesus appears on the scene. What is at stake in the Johannine narrative is the person of Jesus and his "voice," which the Baptist waits to hear and receives with joy (see 3:29). The immediately following passage now found in 4:1-3, continues that theme.[15] Not only is the Baptist disappearing, but so is his role in salvation history as witness (see 1:6-8, 15, 19-34; 3:27-30). He is being replaced by Jesus. But in the Johannine narrative, Jesus must not be regarded as a baptizer. The author does not present the Baptist as debating the relative merits of his and Jesus' baptism, even though the question raised by his disciples required him to do so (3:25-30). The discussion shifts from the issue of baptism to speak of Jesus as the bridegroom who takes possession of the bride (3:29). It is not a question of what he does but who he is.

The Baptist's final witness to Jesus (3:27-30) and the narrator's commentary on that witness (vv. 31-36) remind the reader that Jesus is the authentic revelation of God. Thus, the narrator, who has told of Jesus' baptizing ministry in 3:22, decides that the reader must experience Jesus' withdrawal from a baptizing ministry. It is now the disciples of Jesus who baptize. Through the rite of a baptism presently administered by the disciples of Jesus, more and more people are attaching themselves to Jesus.[16]

Such a proliferation of baptismal ministries which point beyond themselves to the recognition of the importance of Jesus poses a threat to the established religious authority in Judea. There is a "Jesus baptism" which is replacing the "John baptism." A new and more dangerous feature has been added to a traditional rite. Rather than repeating John's baptism of repentance, Jesus' person and message are being accepted by the many who go through the baptismal rite administered by his disciples. The reader understands that ritual baptisms can no longer be a task for Jesus. Jesus

---

have it. For a complete and critical survey of source and redactional theories, defending the unity of the text as it stands, see Leidig, *Jesu Gespräch*, 1–77.

[14] There are many indications of the secondary nature of vv. 1-3 in its present form. It is a long and unwieldy sentence, made so by the introduction of the parenthesis of v. 2, which opens with *kaitoi ge*, a *hapax legomenon* in the New Testament, and uses the name "Jesus" without an article.

[15] See Olsson, *Structure and Meaning*, 135–38.

[16] T. Okure claims that whereas Jesus baptizes and makes disciples, the disciples only baptize (*Johannine Approach to Mission*, 80–83). Thus "Jesus does not win people by the baptismal activity of the disciples" (p. 82).

is not a baptizer; he is much more. Baptism is now being administered by an increasing number of disciples as a means by which more and more people are drawn toward the *person* of Jesus.[17] Here we have the reason for Jesus' departure for Galilee. The Pharisees have heard of Jesus' growing stature and significance, made evident by the proliferation of a rite now administered by his disciples, leading larger crowds to Jesus. Thus Jesus sets out for Galilee.[18]

The details of vv. 4-5 reflect first-century practice accurately. There were two ways to make the south-north journey: via Samaria or via the other side of the Jordan. The former was shorter and, under Roman rule, the unified country made it an easier passage, although it was still fraught with danger (see Josephus, *Antiquities* 20.118; *War* 2.232). The reader, who is presumed to know the topography, would nevertheless be somewhat surprised to read in v. 4 *edei de auton dierchesthai dia tēs Samareias* (despite the oft-cited texts from Josephus, *Life* 269, where *edei* appears, and *Antiquities* 20.118).[19] It is not true that Jesus *had to* pass through Samaria. He could have taken the longer route, if he had wished. The use of the verb *edei* informs the reader that Jesus *must* pass through Samaria. This is an indication that some divine necessity lies behind the journey.[20]

Whatever might be the exact location of Sychar,[21] Jacob themes emerge with the reference to his gift of the field to Joseph (see Gen 48:22; see also Gen 33:19; Josh 24:32).[22] Two themes of importance to the following narrative emerge here: the theme of a gift and that of a well.[23] A further theme has been adumbrated with the mention of Jacob's well. There are Jewish traditions concerning Jacob's gift of a well from which he miraculously

---

[17] See the perceptive remark of A. Loisy, *Le quatrième évangile* (Paris: Emile Nourry, 1921) 177. He refers to 1 Cor 1:14-17 and comments: "C'est pour faire valoir la dignité du Christ." So also G. Segalla, *Giovanni* (NVB 36; Rome: Edizioni Paoline, 1976) 188.

[18] It is often objected that there would be Pharisees in Galilee. But as E. Haenchen points out: "The Fourth Gospel thinks of the Pharisees rather as officials residing in Jerusalem alongside the high priests (so John 1:24, 7:32 [twice], 45-48, 8:13, 9:13, 15, 11:46f, 57, 12:19, 42)" (*John 1-2* [2 vols.; Hermeneia; Philadelphia: Fortress Press, 1984] 1:218).

[19] The use of *edei* in *Life* 269 simply states: "for rapid travel it was essential to take that route." *Antiquities* 20.118 associates the shorter journey toward Jerusalem with the celebration of festivals in the city. Neither applies to John 4:4.

[20] This interpretation of the verb *edei* in v. 4 is disputed. For a summary and a convincing presentation of the above position, see Okure, *Johannine Approach to Mission,* 83-86.

[21] For the discussion, see J. Briend, "Puits de Jacob," *SDB* 9, cols. 386-98.

[22] The text of Gen 48:22 reads: "I have given to thee one portion above thy brethren," but the word for "portion" is *šĕkem,* and the author reads this as the city of Shechem, as did the LXX. See C. K. Barrett, *The Gospel according to St John* (London: SPCK, 1978) 231.

[23] Okure, *Johannine Approach to Mission,* 89-90.

produced flowing water.[24] All three themes will be fully exploited in the narrative where Jesus reverses the roles of the one who receives the water from a well that has its origins in a gift from Jacob to the one who gives a living water, which has its origins in God.

Jesus sits down to rest at Jacob's well.[25] The exact hour is given as "the sixth hour" (v. 6). It is thus the middle of the day, the time of greatest heat after a morning's travel.[26] Hence vv. 4-6 make excellent sense, providing an evocative setting for the encounters with Samaritans which now follow, introducing the reader to the themes of a gift and the refreshment afforded by a well.[27]

The reader is introduced to a *gynē ek tēs Samareias*, who comes to the well to draw water (v. 7a).[28] She is a woman and she is a Samaritan. On both accounts Jesus should not speak to her.[29] With considerable care the

[24] With the exception of X. Léon-Dufour (Lecture de l'évangile selon Jean [Parole de Dieu; Paris: Seuil, 1988] 347–49) and P. Perkins (*NJBC*, 956–57) this evidence is largely ignored by the commentators. See A. Jaubert, "La Symbolique du Puits de Jacob. Jean 4,12," in *L'Homme devant Dieu: Mélanges offerts au Père Henri de Lubac* (3 vols.; Théologie 56; Lyon: Aubier, 1963) 1:63–73; J. R. Diaz, "Palestinian Targum and New Testament," *NovT* 6 (1963) 76–77; Olsson, *Structure and Meaning*, 168–73; J. H. Neyrey, "Jacob Traditions and the Interpretation of John 4:10-26," *CBQ* 41 (1979) 421–25. The most important evidence is found in the targums on Genesis 28–29 and Num 21:16-18 and in *Pirke de Rabbi Eliezer* 35–36.

[25] The expression *ekathezeto houtōs epi tę̄ pēgę̄* expresses a genuine settling down for a rest. J. H. Bernard claims that *"kathezomai* in the N.T. is always used in the durative sense" (*A Critical and Exegetical Commentary on the Gospel according to St John* [2 vols.; ICC; Edinburgh: T. & T. Clark, 1928] 1:135). See also M.-J. Lagrange, *Évangile selon saint Jean* (Ebib; Paris: Gabalda, 1936) 104.

[26] C. K. Barrett points out that one cannot be certain about John's use of enumerating the hours, but he agrees that noon is probably meant (*St John*, 231). R. A. Culpepper argues that the hours of the day in the Fourth Gospel (see also 1:39; 4:52; and 19:14) are better calculated according to the Roman system, starting from noon (*Anatomy of the Fourth Gospel: A Study in Literary Design* [Philadelphia: Fortress Press, 1983] 219). Thus, 4:6 indicates 6:00 P.M.

[27] Why do all the disciples need to go to the town to purchase food, leaving Jesus alone? Why does the woman come to the well at the hottest time of the day? The dramatic structure of the narrative should be allowed to stand as it is. See H. van den Bussche, *Jean: Commentaire de l'Évangile Spirituel* (Bruges: Desclée de Brouwer, 1976) 184; Friedrich, *Chi è Gesù?* 28–29.

[28] This expression is often read as an indication that the woman represents all Samaritans. Although this idea is present, the main thrust of 4:7-30 is to show the response or lack of response of *this woman* to the word of Jesus. See especially Okure, *Johannine Approach to Mission*, 111 n. 63 and pp. 129–31. The passage *as a whole* (i.e., vv. 1-42) is directed toward the response of the Samaritans. But the reader will become aware of that only at the end of the narrative.

[29] See R. H. Strachan, *The Fourth Gospel: Its Significance and Environment* (3rd ed.; London: SCM Press, 1941) 151. Many critics see evocations of Old Testament well scenes here (see Gen 24:10-19: Isaac's servant and Rebekah; Gen 29:1-14: Jacob and Rachel; Exod 2:15b-21: Moses and Zipporah). See especially the comparison between Genesis 24 and Jean C in Boismard and Lamouille, *Jean*, 136. See also P. Dagonet, *Selon Saint Jean: Une Femme de Samarie*

narrator first reports Jesus' imperative – "Give me a drink" (v. 7b) – adding that the disciples had already left the scene (v. 8). They are not there to witness their master taking the initiative, speaking to a Samaritan woman. They will return in v. 27 and manifest their shock, and the woman will immediately depart (v. 28).[30]

The reader, well versed in matters Jewish, would be aware of the outrage that Jesus has just committed. This is reinforced by the words of the woman and the following comment from the narrator. The question she asks raises the issue of how Jesus, a Jew, could speak to a Samaritan, who is a woman. Only here in the Fourth Gospel is Jesus called a *Ioudaios*. At the level of the woman's question the expression has a nuance of mockery. She begins her approach to Jesus, from a Samaritan point of view, by calling him an insulting name. The implied reader will come to discover, however, that Jesus' Jewish origins are important for the development of the dialogue. The distinction between Jesus and the Samaritan woman is further reinforced by a comment from the narrator: "For Jews use nothing in common with Samaritans" (v. 9).[31] The narrator insists on two issues at this stage of the narrative. The first addresses the immediate pericope, where Jesus shows himself willing to share with a Samaritan woman.[32] Second, at the beginning of this section of his narrative dedicated to a non-Jewish world, the narrator's fourfold insistence on the Samaritan element in the dialogue (vv. 7, 9 [three times]) makes clear to the reader that the world of the Samaritans is not the world of Judaism (see Sir 50:25-26; Josephus, *Antiquities* 9.288-90; 10.184).[33]

The initiative now shifts to Jesus, who does not answer her question.

(Paris: Cerf, 1979) 47-53; P. D. Duke, *Irony in the Fourth Gospel* (Atlanta: John Knox Press, 1985) 101-3; C. M. Carmichael, "Marriage and the Samaritan Woman," *NTS* 26 (1979-80) 332-46. There is insufficient evidence in the text for such a reading. For a summary, coming to this conclusion, see Okure, *Johannine Approach to Mission*, 87-88.

[30] On the importance of vv. 7 and 28 for the shape of the whole narrative, see G. R. O'Day, *Revelation*, 50-53. J. L. Staley argues that the reader, who has been "victimized" in v. 2, is now raised to heights "which go far beyond even the intimate relationship implied by the Fourth Gospel's prologue" (*The Print's First Kiss: A Rhetorical Investigation of the Implied Reader in the Fourth Gospel* [SBLDS 82; Atlanta: Scholars Press, 1988] 98-103; quotation from p. 103). For a similar approach, see L. Eslinger, "Wooing of the Woman," 167-83.

[31] The verb *synkraomai* is generally translated as "to have dealings with." D. Daube (*The New Testament and Rabbinic Judaism* [London: Athlone, 1956] 373-82), followed by C. K. Barrett (*St John*, 232-33) has argued for the translation given above. In defense of the traditional translation, see, among others, Haenchen, *John 1-2*, 1:219-20. B. Lindars suggests a compromise: "do not eat and drink" (*The Gospel of John* [NCB; London: Oliphants, 1972] 181).

[32] See Str-B. 2:438; see also Friedrich, *Chi è Gesù?* 29-30.

[33] See G. R. O'Day, "Narrative Mode and Theological Claim: A Study in the Fourth Gospel," *JBL* 105 (1986) 665-66; idem, *Revelation*, 58-59.

There is a reversal of roles and a statement of a truth that can be understood by the reader but not by the Samaritan woman. The author reports Jesus' response to her in direct speech. She hears "the words of Jesus" as he tells her of two realities of which she is, as yet, ignorant. The first is the gift of God, and the second is that the person "who is speaking to her" (*ho legōn soi*)[34] is the one who can give this gift to her (v. 10ab).[35] The words of Jesus promise a gift that has its origins in God. The genitive (*tēn dōrean tou theou*) is objective, indicating that the gift comes from God, is sent by God. The gift is further described as "living water." The gift is living water, but there is a play on the meaning of the expression *hydōr zōn* (v. 10c). As with the use of *anōthen* in Jesus' discussion with Nicodemus, the expression "living water" has two possible meanings. On the one hand it can mean flowing water from a fresh stream or spring, as opposed to still water in a cistern or a pond. However, it has a rich history in the biblical and in other traditions which point beyond the physical reality of water.[36] The gift of God is a gratuitous gift of life to all who would receive it. The reader recalls that Jesus is the fullness of the gift of the truth (1:14), from whose fullness we have all received (1:16), a new and perfect gift which replaces the former gift of the Law (1:17). Jesus alone makes known the God whom no one has ever seen (1:18). The reader has also already learned of the need to be born again of water and the Holy Spirit to see and enter the kingdom of God (3:3, 5). Above all, the implied reader recalls Jesus' words: "For God so loved the world that he *gave* his only Son, that whoever believes in him should not perish but have eternal life" (3:16). A loving God who freely gives his Son stands behind the gift which is the living water.

The discussion of the meaning of "the gift of God" and its relationship to "living water" is never ending,[37] but the reader can only understand

---

[34] See Olsson, *Structure and Meaning*, 179: "The wording *ho legōn soi* would also seem to allude to a basic feature in John: Jesus as the Word, he who speaks. The idea of *the speaking God*, which permeates the entire Gospel, hardly needs confirmation here." See also O'Day, *Revelation*, 59–60.

[35] T. Okure attractively suggests that v. 10a ("If you know the gift of God") is the basis for the message of vv. 11-15, which describe the gift of God, and that v. 10b ("and who it is that is saying to you) is the basis for vv. 16-26 which deals with who Jesus is (*Johannine Approach to Mission*, 92). See also L. Schmid, "Die Komposition der Samaria-Szene Joh 4:1-42: Ein Beitrag zur Charakteristik des 4. Evangelisten als Schriftsteller," *ZNW* 28 (1929) 150. I extend the second section to v. 30.

[36] See Haenchen, *John 1-2*, 1:220; Barrett, *St John*, 233 (see pp. 233–34 for a long list of biblical, Jewish, Christian, and Hellenistic uses of this and parallel expressions).

[37] For a survey, see Okure, *Johannine Approach to Mission*, 96–97. The main question is: Does it refer to Jesus himself or the gift of the Spirit? For the case in defense of the Spirit, see

it as implicit commentary, in terms of what has been read so far.[38] Jesus himself is the gift of God (1:14, 16-17). He makes God known (1:18) and thus offers the possibility of eternal life to those who are born again in water and the spirit (3:5). As the fruit of the saving love of God, the gift of Jesus offers the possibility of eternal life to humankind (3:16). Thus, the reader concludes, the revelation of God in Jesus is the gift of God, the living water.[39] But the Samaritan woman has no access to such information.[40] Yet in her objection she unwittingly poses a question that strikes the reader as providing its own answer. Given the depth of the well and Jesus' not possessing a bucket to drop into the well, she logically, and by now more respectfully, asks: *kyrie . . . pothen oun echeis to hydōr to zōn;* (v. 11). The mocking title of "a Jew" has been replaced by "Sir" (*kyrie*), and the question is legitimate.[41] She herself has raised the inevitable Johannine question of origins—but she answers her own question in terms she can control.[42] The water in the well has its origins in the gift of the patriarch Jacob. He, his family and his entourage drank from it. They were all satisfied with the water of this well. It is here that the Jewish background to Jacob's gift of a well from which living water flowed in abundance becomes important. The giver of the gift was Jacob. He cannot be surpassed.

Given that background, the origins of the well at which they stand cannot be matched by this Jew: "Are you greater than our father Jacob?" (v. 12).[43] Not only is she unable to go beyond ordinary wells and ordinary

---

F. M. Braun, "Avoir soif et boire (Jn 4,10-14; 7,37-39)," in *Mélanges Bibliques en hommage au R. P. Béda Rigaux*, ed. A. Descamps and A. de Halleux (Gembloux: Duculot, 1970) 249-51.

[38] See, therefore, the conclusion of G. R. Beasley-Murray based on 6:35, 51 and 7:37-39, that it is "life mediated by the Spirit" (*John*, 60), or similarly that of B. Olsson that it is the revelation of Jesus, giving life through the action of the Spirit (*Structure and Meaning*, 212-18). Such a combination, depending on later words of Jesus in the narrative, is as yet outside the reader's knowledge and experience. At this stage, the reader can only understand it to refer to the revelation of God that takes place in and through Jesus' word and person. On 4:10-15 as implicit commentary, see Culpepper, *Anatomy*, 155-56.

[39] My interpretation excludes a sacramental reading of the passage. For such a reading, see O. Cullmann, *Early Christian Worship* (SBT 10; London: SCM Press, 1953) 80-84. T. Okure accurately summarizes the meaning of "the gift of God" (*hē dōrea*) as "something which is inseparably linked with the person of Jesus, [and] belongs in the order of revelation and proclamation" (*Johannine Approach to Mission*, 98).

[40] See especially O'Day, *Revelation*, 59-61.

[41] Friedrich, *Chi è Gesù?* 35. The movement from "a Jew" to "Sir" begins a process that will culminate in her suspicions that he might even be the Christ (see vv. 25 and 29).

[42] See R. Schnackenburg, *The Gospel according to St John* (3 vols.; HTCNT 4/1-3; London: Burns & Oates; New York: Crossroad, 1968-82) 428; Léon-Dufour, *Lecture*, 355-56; O'Day, *Revelation*, 61-62.

[43] The woman's question, which begins with *mē*, expects a negative answer. It is unthinkable that anyone could be greater than Jacob. On Jacob as the "father" of the Samaritans, see

water. She is unable to accept any origin for "living water" beyond Jacob, the donor of the well she frequents (see vv. 5-6a).[44] "Her reply in vv 11-12 is, in effect, a defense of the ancestral water."[45] But it is more. It is defense of the significance of Jacob as a giver of a living water which cannot be surpassed. She cannot accept that Jesus surpasses both the gift and the giver which she associates with Jacob's well.[46] The implied reader knows of the origins of all that Jesus has come to reveal (see especially 1:18, 51; 3:12-14, 31-35). The reader is thus aware that the first Samaritan encountered is not open to the word of Jesus.[47] The reader's understanding of the woman as someone who fails is confirmed by Jesus' words in vv. 13-14 and her inability to accept them in v. 15.

Jesus continues to speak to the woman in terms that build upon what he said to her in v. 10. However, in vv. 13-14 there is an important shift in the subject and object of the sentence. Whereas the reported words of Jesus in v. 10 spoke of the giver of the gift in the third person, addressing the woman in the second person singular, now Jesus speaks of himself in the first person as the giver of the gift to "everyone" (v. 13b: *pas ho*) and "whoever" (v. 14a: *hos d'an*). The reader encounters Jesus' revealing word, promising the gift of a water that transcends the water from the well of Jacob. There is a progression from the interpersonal discussion between Jesus and the Samaritan woman, where the possibility of a greater gift than thirst-quenching water is communicated to her, to the greater promise directed to all who would accept the revelation of God in Jesus. This promise contains, for the first time in vv. 7-15, the plotted time of a prolepsis, pointing to a future gift.

Through the words addressed to the woman, the revelation of a universal truth is made known to the reader. Water from a well only leads to the further experience of thirst, but Jesus offers a water that will assuage

---

Olsson, *Structure and Meaning,* 139-41. In v. 10 Jesus spoke of "who it is that is saying to you," and then "he would have given you living water." The woman reverses the order in v. 11, speaking first of the water and then asking how Jesus relates to Jacob. See Léon-Dufour, *Lecture,* 355.

[44] It is often claimed that there is no known tradition about Jacob and his sons and his cattle or entourage (*thremmata* is a *hapax legomenon* and may also mean his slaves) at the well. The Jewish traditions, especially as they are found in the targums on Genesis 28-29, go part of the way in providing such background.

[45] Okure, *Johannine Approach to Mission,* 99.

[46] It is Jesus who replaces and surpasses Jacob. There is no question of the Spirit in such a contrast (see n. 37 above).

[47] G. R. O'Day points to the irony at work here, as the reader and the woman are working at different levels (*Revelation,* 62-63).

all needs.[48] It will never lead to the desire for more water. The water Jesus gives will touch the depths of the human spirit, resolving its desires and questions once and for all.[49] In the gift of living water which Jesus has to offer, everyone can find the fullness of God's gift, a fullness of a gift which is the truth (see 1:14, 16-17). But the reader is still being told *that* Jesus is the gift of God (see v. 10), the living water; the implied reader is yet to discover *how* this will take place.[50] Jesus' *words* make this promise. There are two basic elements in the offer Jesus makes to the Samaritan woman: a water that quenches all thirst forever, and a spring that wells up to eternal life inside the believer.[51] To understand the rhetoric of vv. 14-15, one needs to pay close attention to "the words" used by Jesus. He has spoken to the woman of the water he will give: "Whoever drinks *ek tou hydatos hou egō dōsō autǭ ou mē dipsēsei*" (v. 14a),[52] and of the spring this water will produce: "The water that I shall give him *genēsetai en autǭ pēgē hydatos hallomenou eis zōēn aiōnion*" (v. 14b).[53]

The Samaritan woman responds by means of Jesus' words. Repeating the same two elements that stood at the center of Jesus' promise, water and a spring, she transforms them into her words.[54] Like "the Jews" in Jesus' earlier encounter (see 2:20), she speaks Jesus' words in an uncomprehending way.[55] The Samaritan woman responds to his offer of water: "*kyrie,*

---

[48] The Johannine expression *eis ton aiōna* (see also 6:51, 58; 8:35, 51-52; 10:28; 11:26; 12:34; 13:8; 14:16) is not a promise of eternal bliss after death. It promises a fullness of life, beginning now. See Schnackenburg, *St John,* 1:430-31.

[49] See Schnackenburg, *St John,* 1:431-32; and Haenchen, *John 1-2,* 1:220. The centrality of the theme of the fulfillment of human searching has been well identified by A. Lenglet ("Jésus de passage," 497-98). The image of "living water" as a spiritual gift is widespread in ancient religions. See W. Bauer, *Das Johannesevangelium erklärt* (HKNT 6; Tübingen: J. C. B. Mohr [Paul Siebeck], 1933) 68-69. It has strong links, although in a somewhat contrasting fashion, with the Wisdom tradition. See, among many, Bernard, *St John,* 1:140-42.

[50] R. H. Lightfoot sees a number of hints in 4:1-15 that point toward the passion: Jesus' weariness (see 19:1-2), his desire for water (19:28), and "the sixth hour" (19:14) (*St John's Gospel,* ed. C. F. Evans [Oxford: Oxford University Press, 1956] 121-22). See also G. Zevini, *Vangelo secondo Giovanni* (2 vols.; Commenti Spirituali del Nuovo Testamento; Rome: Città Nuova, 1984, 1987) 1:156; Hudry-Clergeon, "De Judée en Galilée," 821-23. The implied reader may be expected to make the connection—but not yet.

[51] For a detailed analysis of this, see Okure, *Johannine Approach to Mission,* 101-3.

[52] The use of the aorist subjunctive (*piǫ ek*) hints at a once-and-for-all drinking; see Barrett, *St John,* 234.

[53] Two words have been used for "well" and "spring": *phrear* (vv. 11, 12) and *pēgē* (vv. 6, 14). Some commentators see theological nuances in these words: one used by the narrator or Jesus (vv. 6, 14) and the other by the woman (vv. 11-12). It is probably only stylistic.

[54] See O'Day, *Revelation,* 64-66.

[55] See also E. C. Hoskyns, *The Fourth Gospel,* ed. F. N. Davey (London: Faber & Faber, 1947) 236.

dos moi touto to hydōr, hina mē dipsō" (v. 15a). Responding to his words on
a spring of water which wells up to eternal life,[56] she says: *"mēde dierchōmai
enthade antlein"* (v. 15b). The contrast can best be seen by placing the words
of Jesus and the words of the woman beside one another:

Words of Jesus	Words of the Woman
ek tou hydatos hou egō dōsō	*dos moi touto to hydōr*
autǭ ou mē dipsēsei.	*hina mē dipsō.*
genēsetai en autǭ	*mēde dierchōmai*
pēgē hydatos hallomenou eis	*enthade antlein.*
zōēn aiōnion.	

The words of Jesus have been taken up by the woman, understood
in a physical and selfish sense, and used in her response to him.[57] Thus,
we must conclude that the words of Jesus in vv. 13-14 have not been
accepted by the Samaritan woman in v. 15, as they were rejected by "the
Jews" in 2:20. However, there is a difference between the exchange that
takes place between Jesus and "the Jews" in 2:13-22 and Jesus and the
Samaritan woman in 4:7-15. The end result of the response of "the Jews"
and the Samaritan woman is the same, as the words of Jesus are rejected.
But the hostility of the response of "the Jews" is not found in the inability
of the Samaritan woman to comprehend either the water or the spring
that Jesus offers.[58]

The reader can only conclude that, like "the Jews," the Samaritan
woman does not accept the word of Jesus. But while "the Jews" disappeared
from the narrative after 2:13-22, to return, publicly hostile, in 5:16-18, the

---

[56] In fact, more than "welling up" is implied in the use of the verb *hallesthai*. It generally
refers to quick leaping movements of human beings. Only here is it used of the movement
of water. B. Olsson sees in the use of this verb a further link with the Jewish tradition of
Jacob's gift of an overflowing well (*Structure and Meaning*, 182). The targums use the Aramaic
verb *sālaq*, which means "to go up," "to pile up."

[57] B. Olsson reads v. 15 as positive (*Structure and Meaning*, 182–83). The woman shows a
readiness to abandon Jacob's well. See also C. M. Carmichael, "Marriage and the Samaritan
Woman," 337–43; M. Vellanickal, *Studies in the Gospel of John* (Bangalore: Asian Trading Corporation, 1982) 90. See, among others, Boers, *Neither on This Mountain*, 169: "The first round
in the conversation ends in complete failure. The woman remains level-headed, incredulous."

[58] In some ways, there is a parallel between the response of the woman and the response
of Nicodemus, but there are important differences. See M. Pazdan, "Nicodemus and the
Samaritan Woman: Contrasting Models of Discipleship," *BTB* 17 (1987) 145–48. Nicodemus
comes to Jesus with a partial confession of faith on his lips (3:2), but is unable to go beyond
his own knowledge. At this stage of the narrative, the Samaritan woman shows no belief
at all in Jesus. The most that can be said for her is that her esteem for him grows, as she
shifts from calling him "a Jew" (v. 9) to "Sir" (v. 11). But she refuses the word of Jesus, and
thus parallels "the Jews" in 2:20.

reader discovers that the Samaritan woman remains in the narrative. Her refusal of the word of Jesus in vv. 7-15 does not bring her role in the narrative to a conclusion. She will eventually wonder whether Jesus is the Christ (see vv. 25 and 29b) and will point other Samaritans toward Jesus (v.29a).

The experience of the intended reader forms the background for this narrative. Cast out of the synagogue, the members of the Johannine community have experienced a postwar official Judaism that has rejected the revelation of God in Jesus. The Samaritan woman, on the other hand, reflects the community's missionary experience. An initial revelation of the word of Jesus would often meet puzzlement, ignorance, and rejection — but not hostility and a final decision that his word can have no part in one's life. In the (Samaritan?) mission, the task goes on. The preaching of the word of Jesus has not been angrily rejected, and perseverance eventually produces fruit, as it does in the story of Jesus' paradigmatic first missionary encounter with the non-Jewish world.[59]

At this stage of the narrative, matching the response of "the Jews" in 2:13-23, the Samaritan woman rejects the words of Jesus himself. She is presented to the reader as a model of the absence of faith.[60]

II. JESUS AND THE SAMARITAN WOMAN (II)
(4:16-30)

The Shape of the Narrative

The first part of the dialogue between Jesus and the Samaritan woman (4:7-15) developed the theme stated in v. 10a — "If you knew the gift of God (*tēn dōrean tou theou*)"—in Jesus' offer of living water. The second part of the dialogue unfolds the theme of v. 10b: "Who it is that is saying to you

---

[59] Rightly Schnackenburg, *St John*, 1:419: "We could thus see the actual setting in the life of the communities in which the tradition was handed on." See also H. Leroy, *Rätsel und Missverständnis: Ein Beitrag zur Formgeschichte des Johannesevangeliums* (BBB 30; Bonn: Peter Hanstein, 1968) 97–99. T. Okure notices the difference between the hostile encounters between Jesus and "the Jews" and the absence of hostility in the present encounter, but resorting to the categories of Greek rhetoric she misses the possible missionary background (*Johannine Approach to Mission*, 100–101).

[60] Against Léon-Dufour (*Lecture*, 360), who reads v. 15 as the symbolic beginning of the woman's true understanding of Jesus. H. Boers (*Neither on This Mountain*, 7–22), using A. J. Greimas's narrative schema and narrative programs, shows that the woman arrives at a stage of nonperformance in v. 15. His subsequent analysis of the syntactic deep structure (pp. 36–49) leads to the same conclusion.

(*tis estin ho legōn soi*)." A smooth transition into vv. 16-30 is established by means of the link words *dierchōmai enthade* (v. 15) and *elthe enthade* (v. 16) and the fact that the same characters continue in conversation. Jesus' second use of the imperative "go . . . call . . . come" (v. 16) rescues the faltering encounter and enables further discussion.[61] Most critics close the literary unit with the so-called self-revelation of Jesus in v. 26: "I who speak to you am he."[62] However, the place of vv. 27-30 creates problems for scholars who close it off from vv. 16-26. They find that it is linked neither with the encounter between Jesus and the Samaritan woman (vv. 16-26) nor with what follows (vv. 31-38). Most resolve the difficulty by pointing out that Jesus' words to the disciples in vv. 31-38 are an intrusion into the text, which would read better if v. 30 was followed immediately by v. 39.[63]

Two remarks need to be made. First, the disciples' silent wonder on discovering Jesus in discussion with a Samaritan woman continues the theme of v. 10b (who is this man?). As the woman departs and comes to her townsfolk, the identity of Jesus is still the issue. Her words in v. 29 repeat her hesitant approach to Jesus in v. 25. There she raised the question of the person and role of Jesus as a possible Messiah-Christ. She puts the same question to other Samaritans: "Can this be the Christ?" (v. 29). This question sets the Samaritans in motion toward Jesus. But the narrator leaves them, to present the reader with Jesus' discussion with the disciples (vv. 31-38). As Jesus talks to his disciples, the reader (although not the disciples) is aware that the Samaritans are approaching.[64] Second, there are good indications that the narrator's presentation of the second moment in the Samaritan woman's discussion parallels the first. Although the theme shifts from the gift of living water (see v. 10a) to the identity of the person of Jesus (see v. 10b), the overall structure of vv. 16-30 largely repeats that of vv. 7-15.

---

[61] See Okure, *Johannine Approach to Mission*, 106-7.

[62] For the moment I will use the RSV translation of *egō eimi ho lalōn soi*. I will suggest a different version below.

[63] See, e.g., Lindars, *John*, 192-93; Becker, *Johannes*, 179. G. Zevini says "Il colloquio si interrompe . . . serve da ponte" (*Giovanni*, 167). X. Léon-Dufour comments twice on v. 28 – once in connection with vv. 16-26 and again with vv. 27-30 (*Lecture*, 377-80). Among the commentators consulted, only R. Bultmann reads vv. 27-30 as the conclusion to Jesus' encounter with the Samaritan woman (*The Gospel of John: A Commentary* [Oxford: Blackwell, 1971] 192-93).

[64] G. R. O'Day sees the close link between vv. 4-26 and vv. 27-30 (*Revelation*, 53). She points out that vv. 27-30 are "a 'narrative hinge' that serves to end the first dialogue and to provide a context out of which a second dialogue can operate."

(a) *Verses 16-19:* Through a new initiative of Jesus, the encounter is saved. The woman's response to Jesus opens the question of Jesus' role and person. As in the first encounter, although Jesus initiated the dialogue, the woman makes the statements on the person of Jesus (vv. 9, 19).

(b) *Verses 20-26:* Jesus again takes the initiative. He shifts the discussion away from prophecy into the theme of true worship of God in spirit and in truth. The woman progresses in her confession of faith. She suggests that he might be the Messiah – Christ. Jesus attempts to enlarge on this suggestion, revealing himself to her as *egō eimi* (vv. 25-26).

(c) *Verses 27-30:* As the encounter between Jesus and the Samaritan woman began with the departure of the disciples (v. 8), it now draws to a close with their return (v. 27). The departure and return of the disciples in vv. 8 and 27 hold the whole of vv. 7-30 together.[65] The woman has not been able to grasp all that Jesus has revealed, but there is no rejection. She is prepared to suggest to her fellow Samaritans that Jesus might be the expected Messiah (v. 29). The Samaritans set out to make their own discovery (v. 30).

Only this final remark from the narrator, telling the reader that the Samaritans "were coming to him," is not paralleled in vv. 7-15. It has been placed here in the narrative to shift the reader's attention away from the Samaritan woman, to provide background for vv. 31-38, and to hold the reader's interest in the Samaritan question until it is resolved in vv. 39-42.

The two stages in the dialogue between Jesus and the Samaritan woman (vv. 7-15 and 16-30) are parallel:[66]

1. A relationship is established, initiated by a command from Jesus (vv. 7-9//vv. 16-19).
2. Jesus' words transcend the apparent basis of the relationship (v. 10//vv. 21-24).
3. The woman makes an intermediate response to Jesus' words (vv. 11-12//v. 25).
4. A final intervention from Jesus (vv. 13-14//v. 26).
5. The woman's concluding response (v. 15//vv. 28-29).

---

[65] See Okure, *Johannine Approach to Mission,* 133–36; Lenglet, "Jésus de passage," 498–99; O'Day, *Revelation,* 50-53.

[66] For a partial recognition of some of these parallels, see Brown, *John,* 181.

But there is a difference in the two responses of the woman. In her first encounter with Jesus, she rejects his word (vv. 13b-15). In the second she is prepared to suggest that he fits *her* categories of Messiah-Christ (vv. 25, 29).

Reading the Narrative

Jesus' series of imperatives to the woman gives life to a dialogue that the woman seems ready to terminate. He tells her to "go . . . call . . . come." The theme changes from water to the woman's marital situation. The woman is told to go back to the town, call her husband, and return to the well. She responds that she has no husband (v. 17a). There is every possibility that she is responding honestly to Jesus, as she regards herself as not married to the man with whom she is currently living.[67] It is for this reason that Jesus can compliment her for telling the truth: "You say well (*kalōs eipas*) 'I have no husband'" (v. 17b).

In a way parallel to his revelation of Nathanael's private life (see 1:48), Jesus, a complete stranger, knows her marital situation, both past and present. Although critics generally dwell on the detail of her sinful situation,[68] this does not appear to be the point of the narrative. Certainly, she is living in a sinful situation and has lived an irregular married life. But her sinfulness never again appears in the narrative,[69] and Jesus concludes his revelation of her situation by again complimenting her on her truthfulness: "This you said truly (*alēthes*)." The point of v. 18 is not to lay bare the sinfulness of the woman but to let her know that Jesus possesses supernatural powers that enable him to know her secrets. The story of the woman is understood by the reader as a statement of fact. She has had five husbands and is now living with a man who is not her husband.[70] Jesus'

---

[67] P. Dagonet, *Selon Saint Jean*, 91–92. J. Bligh suggests that her reply is an indication that she has marital designs on Jesus ("Jesus in Samaria," *HeyJ* 3 [1962] 335–36). There is insufficient evidence in the text for this claim. T. Okure suggests that it is her way of trying to bring the discussion to a close (*Johannine Approach to Mission*, 108–10).

[68] See, e.g., Lagrange, *Saint Jean*, 110; R. Schnackenburg, *St John*, 1:433; Vellanickal, *Studies*, 90–93.

[69] Unless one regards her passing remarks in v. 29 about "everything I ever did" as an important reference to her sinful state. I do not.

[70] Much is made of the five husbands, beyond the possibilities allowed by Jewish practice (see Str-B 2:437), as a possible symbolic use of the number five to refer to the five gods of Samaria (see Josephus, *Antiquities*, 9.288), or the five books of the Samaritan Pentateuch (Origen, *In Johannem* 13.8 [PG 14:410–11]), or the five foreign cities who brought their gods (there were in fact seven, but recourse is had to Josephus for the number five) with them

knowledge of these facts is the turning point of the dialogue. Buckets and water from wells are one thing; a man who tells her about her marital situation commands attention. She is now prepared to speak with him.

For the first time in the narrative she shows an openness to the person of Jesus: "Sir, I perceive that you are a prophet" (v. 19). The term "prophet" has no article, and thus is being used in a generic way. Similarly, the woman's use of the verb *theōreō* indicates that she has come to an intellectual perception of Jesus' prophetic qualities from her growing experience of him. There is no deep spiritual insight being shown here.[71] Limited though such a confession may be, she has progressed from her earlier assessment of Jesus in v. 9: "a Jew." Having made this confession, she raises an issue which a Jewish prophet, famous for the defense of the cult of YHWH in Jerusalem, would have to discuss in the unlikely event of a dialogue with a Samaritan. This is not an attempt to steer Jesus' questioning away from her personal secrets.[72] It is "an age-old problem debated between Samaritans and Jews."[73] She says to the man she considers a prophet: "Our fathers worshiped on this mountain; and you say that in Jerusalem is the place where one ought to worship" (v. 20).[74]

(see 2 Kgs 17:27-31). The man with whom she is presently living, who is not her husband, has been identified with Simon Magus. See J. D. Purvis, "The Fourth Gospel and the Samaritans," *NovT* 17 (1975) 193-95. For a summary and criticism of these approaches to v. 18, see Okure, *Johannine Approach to Mission*, 110-13. C. K. Barrett is correct when he comments: "It is quite possible, and may well be right, to take these words as a simple statement of fact, and an instance of the supernatural knowledge of Jesus" (*St John*, 235). The symbolic reading is widespread among scholars who see the Samaritan woman as representing Samaritans as such. See, e.g., A. Loisy, *Quatrième évangile*, 182; O. Cullmann, "Samaria and the Origins of the Christian Mission," in *The Early Church*, ed. A. J. B. Higgins (London: SCM Press, 1956) 187-88.

[71] See BAGD, 360, s.v. *theōreō*, para. 1. Some scholars see this as a reference to the Samaritan messianic interpretation of Deut 18:15-19. See, e.g., M.-E. Boismard, *Moïse ou Jésus: Essai de Christologie Johannique* (BETL 84; Leuven: University Press, 1988) 29-30, 67-68. This is to ask too much of the reader of the present text and of Samaritan messianic expectations.

[72] As is claimed, e.g., by Bernard, *St John*, 1:145; van den Bussche, *Jean*, 190.

[73] Schnackenburg, *St John*, 1:434. See the interesting report of such a discussion in *Bereshit Rabbah* 32.10; see also 81.9.

[74] All interest in the woman's marital situation has gone from the narrative. The person and role of Jesus as "prophet" are now at stake. "As a prophet, He should know" (R. H. Lightfoot, *St John*, 123). See also Boers, *Neither on This Mountain*, 173-76. Samaritan tradition locates Abraham's sacrifice of Isaac and Jacob's vision on Mount Gerizim. The *šekînâ* associated with the Mosaic revelation also dwells there even though, at the time of Jesus, the temple on Mount Gerizim had long since been destroyed (by John Hyrcanus in 128 B.C.). On these and other claims for Mount Gerizim, see J. A. Montgomery, *The Samaritans: The Earliest Jewish Sect: Their History, Theology and Literature* (Philadelphia: John C. Winston, 1907) 236-39; B. W. Hall, *Samaritan Religion from John Hyrcanus to Baba Rabba: A critical examination of the relevant*

Jesus' response to this comment from the Samaritan woman attempts to transcend the limited notion she has of him as a Jewish prophet and her commitment to local traditions attached to Mount Gerizim, in whose shadow the dialogue is taking place. He appeals to her: "Woman, believe me" (v. 21a). There is a real attempt to draw this woman into a deeper understanding of his person and role.[75] His appeal is followed by a promise, a prolepsis that points beyond the story time when both Gerizim and Jerusalem will no longer be the place where one worships the Father. Such a promise is a remarkable challenge to the woman and could only lead her to wonder. She would be waiting for Jesus to name a new place and a new time, but she would also wonder why Jesus has spoken of God as "Father."[76] The reader is aware that Jesus is the authentic revelation of the Father (1:18). But the theme of "father" has already been subtly and ironically introduced earlier in this narrative. In v. 12 the woman spoke of Jacob's gift of water to his sons; in v. 20 she again challenged Jesus to better "the fathers" who worshiped on Gerizim. Such notions of "father" are now eclipsed by Jesus' words on God as "the Father."[77] Yet even the reader wonders where and how this new form of worship will take place.

Instead of immediately resolving the questions about a future time and place of worship, Jesus returns to the current situation. Verse 22 is strongly attached to the story time of the narrative. The woman has called Jesus "a Jew" (v. 9), and so he is. He speaks confidently of the superiority of Jewish traditions, bearing within them the authentic presence of God, and he criticizes the vague Samaritan traditions for not having such authority. Jesus owns his origins among the Jewish people by using the plural "we." His criticism of the Samaritan people and their traditions is framed in the plural "you."[78] In terms of the story time, Jesus claims to be part of a long tradition in which God has made himself known within the story of the Jewish people. Not only is he part of that story, but the man whom the

---

material in contemporary Christian literature, the writings of Josephus, and the Mishnah (Studies in Judaica 3; Sydney: Sydney University Press, 1987) 229–32.

[75] See Schnackenburg, *St John,* 1:435; Dagonet, *Selon Saint Jean,* 98–99. Contrary to J. H. Bernard (*St John,* 1:146) and others, who see this request as replacing the double "amen."

[76] See Bernard, *St John,* 1:147; Schnackenburg, *St John,* 1:436–37; Léon-Dufour, *Lecture,* 368.

[77] O'Day, *Revelation,* 68–69.

[78] E. Leidig has shown that v. 22 reflects the essentially Jewish nature of Jesus' presence to the Samaritan (*Jesu Gespräch,* 103–33). In this she rightly criticizes the interpretation of the "we" in v. 22 as Jesus and his followers rather than Jews and Samaritans. See also Léon-Dufour, *Lecture,* 368–71. I. de la Potterie offers a history and an assessment of the interpretations of the "we" and "you" ("'Nous adorons, nous, ce que nous connaissons, car le salut vient des Juifs': Histoire de l'exégèse et interprétation de Jn 4,22," *Bib* 64 [1983] 78–85).

woman had earlier called "a Jew" is also the one who brings salvation. In the Jew, Jesus, salvation has come. Salvation is from the Jews. The Johannine Jesus speaks in perfect coherence with the rest of the early church, which was never ashamed of the fact that its origins lay within the story of the Jewish people.[79]

But why introduce this reflection here? The narrator has chosen this first moment of genuine communication between Jesus and the Samaritan woman to remind the reader that this is an encounter between Jesus and the non-Jewish world. The narrative opened with strong indications to the reader that the events were taking place in a foreign world (vv. 4, 7, 9). The implied reader must never be allowed to forget that fact. It is for this reason that the traditions of Judaism culminating in the salvation that Jesus himself brings and the traditions of Samaritanism are contrasted. Jesus is revealing himself and the way to his Father to a non-Jewish world. The narrator ensures that the reader stays attuned to this aspect of the narrative.[80]

Having made that clear, however, the narrator then continues the dialogue by returning to the theme first broached in v. 21. There he spoke of the new time and place of worship. In vv. 23-24 the narrator explains that more clearly to the woman. The reader meets, for the first time, the typical Johannine indication of his unique eschatological perspective: "the hour is coming and now is." What Jesus is about to announce is eschatological, but one need not wait till the end of time for its availability: it is present because Jesus is present.[81] Thus, the time of the new form of worshiping God has been resolved.

---

[79] See Brown, *John*, 172; Schnackenburg, *St John*, 1:436; H. Thyen, "Das Heil kommt von den Juden," in *Kirche: Festschrift für Günther Bornkamm zum 75. Geburtstag*, ed. D. Lührmann and G. Strecker (Tübingen: J. C. B. Mohr [Paul Siebeck], 1980) 163–84. Against Bauer (*Johannesevangelium*, 70) and Bultmann (*John*, 189–90 n. 6), who see this verse as a gloss, inconsistent with what John says elsewhere about "the Jews." For a detailed criticism of this position, see Leidig, *Jesu Gespräch*, 49–70. See further F. Hahn, "Das Heil kommt von den Juden: Erwägungen zu Joh 4,22b," in *Wort und Wirklichkeit: Studien zur Afrikanistik und Orientalistik Eugen Ludwig Rapp zum 70. Geburtstag Herausgegeben*, ed. B. Benzing, O. Böcher, and G. Mayer (Meisenheim: Hain, 1976) 67–84; and K. Haacker, "Gottesdienst ohne Gotteserkenntnis: Joh 4,22 vor dem Hintergrund des jüdisch-samaritanischen Auseinandersetzung," in *Wort und Wirklichkeit*, ed. B. Benzing et al., 110–26; O. Betz, " 'To Worship God in Spirit and in Truth': Reflections on John 4:20-26," in *Standing Before God: Studies on Prayer in Scriptures and in Tradition with Essays in Honor of John M. Oesterreicher*, ed. A. Finkel and L. Frizzell (New York: Ktav, 1981) 53–72.

[80] See de la Potterie, "Interprétation de Jn 4,22," 85–115, for a comprehensive presentation of the history of salvation and christological perspectives which I have adopted.

[81] See Barrett, *St John*, 237. Bultmann, *John*, 190. G. R. Beasley-Murray puts it well: the expression "brackets future and present without eliminating either" (*John*, 62).

Such worship has two aspects. The true worshiper worships the Father in spirit and truth, but it is the Father who seeks out such worshipers. The act of worshiping is described by the use of the verb *proskynein*. It implies the act of bending or prostrating oneself in the direction of the one worshiped.[82] In this context, where holy mountains and their sanctuaries are being excluded, true worship is the orientation of oneself toward the Father himself in such a way that he becomes the imperative of one's life. The expression "in spirit and truth" is a combination of terms already familiar to the implied reader. The revelation of the true word (1:9) become flesh is the fullness of a gift which is truth (1:14, 17). From the parallel passage, where Nicodemus was challenged to reach beyond the categories he could control, the reader recalls that those who are born again from above of water and the Spirit (3:3-5) live in the light and do the truth (3:21).[83] No longer is there need to decide between Gerizim and Jerusalem. Jesus reveals a God and Father who is to be worshiped with one's life.[84]

But worship does not take place because of the virtue or initiative of the worshipers. The Father himself seeks them out (*zētei*). "The 'seeking' by the Father signifies, not a passive desire on his part, but his causative action in the individual without which a genuine human response is impossible."[85] The basis for all that Jesus has taught the Samaritan woman is the way in which God himself acts (v. 26). He is not a mountain, a place, or a sanctuary. He is spirit, an all-pervading personal presence to the believer.[86] Such a notion is not new to the reader who has both learned and experienced Jesus' creative life-giving presence (see 1:12-13; 3:3-8). The hour has now come when the only acceptable act of worship (*dei proskynein*) can be the total orientation of one's life and action toward the Father, sharing

---

[82] The use of *proskynein* is closely related to the Hebrew verb *hištaḥāwâ*, used to speak of a cultic inclining of oneself or physical bending down. See H. Greeven, "*proskyneō*," *TDNT* 6:760-61; Okure, *Johannine Approach to Mission*, 116.

[83] E. C. Hoskyns also draws attention to the parallel with Nicodemus (*Fourth Gospel*, 238).

[84] Against C. H. Dodd (*Interpretation*, 314), who reads "spirit and truth" as "on the plane of full reality," as against the "sensible and the material" of the cults of both Gerizim and Jerusalem. For my interpretation, see O. Betz, "To Worship God," 53-72; R. Schnackenburg, "Die 'Anbetung in Geist und Wahrheit' (Joh. 4,23) im Lichte vom Qumran-Texten," *BZ* 3 (1959) 88-94; E. D. Freed, "The Manner of Worship in John 4:23f.," in *Search the Scriptures: New Testament Studies in Honor of Raymond T. Stamm* (Gettysburg Theological Studies 3; Leiden: E. J. Brill, 1969) 33-48.

[85] Okure, *Johannine Approach to Mission*, 116. C. K. Barrett goes so far as to comment: "This clause has as much claim as 20.30f. to be regarded as expressing the purpose of the gospel" (*St John*, 238).

[86] See Barrett, *St John*, 238-39.

already in the gift of the Father (*en pneumati*), a gift that is all it claims to be (*kai alētheiai*).[87]

The brief discussion between Jesus and the Samaritan woman reported in vv. 20-24 leads to further puzzlement on the part of the woman in the story. But it prepares the reader for the immediately following section of the narrative. Although salvation comes from the Jews (v. 22), now incarnated in the person of "the Jew" (v. 9), the time is coming and now is when the debates between Samaritans and Jews (v. 20) will no longer play any part in the true worship of the living God (vv. 21, 23-24). "Jesus is presented as maintaining the Jewish case against the Samaritans, at the same time as asserting that both Jewish and Samaritan aspirations are alike fulfilled in his person."[88] The reader comes away from the words of Jesus better informed, but the Samaritan woman is still struggling to understand who it is that is speaking to her (see v. 10b). The reader follows her struggle, watching her move from the truth toward the whole truth. Her response is to fall back on what she knows. In an exact parallel with Nicodemus (see 3:2: *oidamen hoti*), she says, "I know that (*oida hoti*) Messiah is coming, he who is called Christ; when he comes he will show us all things" (v. 25).[89]

It is often taken that the Samaritan messianic figure of the Ta'eb stands behind her use of the terms "Messiah" and "Christ."[90] In this case, attempts are then made to show how her description of the figure as someone who "will show us all things" matches Samaritan messianic expectation. The understanding of the figure of the Ta'eb within Samaritanism itself is fraught with difficulties.[91] While not discounting the possibility that there

---

[87] J. H. Neyrey draws on rather late traditions to link the well of vv. 7-15 with Jesus' special knowledge, cult, and Spirit in vv. 21-24 ("Jacob Traditions," 432-36).

[88] Lindars, *John*, 176.

[89] Some ancient witnesses read *oidamen*, reflecting the Samaritans generally, but they have probably been influenced by the *oidamen* of v. 22 and/or the *hēmin* at the end of the sentence: these readings are to be rejected in favor of the singular. See Haenchen, *John 1-2*, 223-24; Lindars, *John*, 190.

[90] See, e.g., J. Bowman, "Samaritan Studies I: The Fourth Gospel and the Samaritans" *BJRL* 40 (1958) 299; Lagrange, *Saint Jean*, 115; Schnackenburg, *St John*, 1:441; S. Sabugal, *Christos: Investigación exegética sobre la cristología joannea* (Barcelona: Herder, 1972) 226-32.

[91] The earliest known written source that mentions the figure is the *Memar Markah*, which dates from the fourth century A.D. The earliest manuscript we have of this document comes from the fourteenth century. See J. McDonald, *The Theology of the Samaritans* (London: SCM Press, 1964) 42-43; Purvis, "The Fourth Gospel," 162-68. For a recent survey of John 4, Josephus, and the Samaritans, see Hall, *Samaritan Religion*, 226-327. Hall concludes: "The evidence fails to establish even the probability—although it does not preclude the possibility—that some form of messianic belief existed among the Samaritans at that time" (pp. 298-99; on the *Memar Markah*, see pp. 233-35). See also F. Dexinger, *Der Taheb. Ein "messianischer" Heilsbringer der Samaritaner* (Kairos, Religionswissenschaftliche Studien 3; Salzburg: Otto Müller,

may be some link between the woman's statement to Jesus and Samaritan messianic ideas, I will stay with the internal development of the narrative itself, rather than use background that is speculative.

The use of both "Messiah" and "Christ" is anarthrous and thus must be understood in a generic way, similar to the woman's use of "prophet" in v. 19. Thus, in v. 25 we have on the lips of the woman both the Semitic and the Greek word for an anointed figure.[92] The reader has now followed the woman's developing understanding of Jesus as "a Jew" (v. 9), "Sir" (v. 11), "a prophet" (v. 19), and "Messiah-Christ" (v. 25).[93] Whether or not the mounting respect involved in these titles formed part of the background of a Samaritan mission is difficult to prove; however, they certainly form part of the reader's knowledge and experience. The criterion that the woman offers for the recognition of a coming Messiah is that "he will show us all things."[94] Her experience of Jesus' knowledge of her private life, which he should not have known (v. 18), still dazzles her. His masterly exposure of the whole issue of Gerizim, Jerusalem, and true worship (vv. 21-24) is simply ignored.[95] She suspects that this man might be Messiah-Christ because of the supernatural knowledge he demonstrated in v. 18.[96] Jesus has told her that the hour is coming "and now is." The woman's response ignores the possibilities of the "and now is." She speaks only of the possibilities of the coming of the Messiah.[97] In his earlier encounter with Nicodemus, Jesus did not reject the Jewish leaders' confession of a partial faith (3:2), but he attempted to lead him beyond that which he knew. The same thing happens in v. 26. The majority of critics read the words of Jesus as an identification of himself as "Messiah-Christ," suggested by the woman

---

1986). He concludes that more evidence is needed to link the Samaritan Pentateuch's use of the prophet like Moses in Deut 18:18 and the fourth-century Ta'eb.

[92] I am taking the whole sentence as coming from the woman; so also Bultmann, *John*, 192 n. 2. C. K. Barrett affirms: "John as usual translates" (*St John*, 239).

[93] On the mounting dignity of the titles, see Schmid, "Komposition," 152–53; Segalla, *Giovanni*, 189.

[94] This could also be part of the function of the expected Ta'eb. J. H. Neyrey finds traces of Jacob as the one who would tell all things ("Jacob Traditions," 428–32). Thus, Jesus, prophet and Messiah, has greater knowledge than Jacob.

[95] Critics discuss whether "all things" (*hapanta*) refers to Jesus' knowledge of her marital situation (v. 18), his discussion of true worship (vv. 21-24), or both. The narrative, especially vv. 27-30, 39-42 demands that "all things" refers only to v. 18.

[96] T. Okure draws a parallel between the experience of the woman who is told of her past by a stranger and the similar experience of Nathanael in 1:47-49 (*Johannine Approach to Mission*, 110–13). In accepting the parallel, I would go further to claim that as Nathanael's confession of faith in 1:49 was insufficient, so is the woman's in 4:25.

[97] See O'Day, *Revelation*, 71–72.

in v. 25.[98] There are indications in the narrative that this is not the case. The reader is reading a narrative explanation of v. 10b: *tis estin ho legōn soi*. The narrative now arrives at an important moment, when Jesus answers that question himself: *egō eimi ho legōn soi* (v. 26).[99] Who is this man who is speaking to the woman? The answer Jesus gives is: *egō eimi*.

For the first time the reader meets one of the narrator's major titles for Jesus (see also 8:24, 28, 58; 13:19).[100] The expression has a long history in the literature of Israel. Its distant roots lie in the revelation of God's name to Moses in Exod 3:14, but the expression became particularly important to the prophets (see especially Isa 43:10; 45:18). It has always been used to refer to the living presence of a God who makes himself known among his people. The reader now finds that Jesus Christ (1:17), the Word (1:1-2, 14), the Lamb of God (1:29, 36), the Son of God (1:14, 18, 34), and the Son of Man (1:51; 3:14) also claims "I am he."[101] Jesus is not content to accept the Samaritan woman's "knowledge" about a Messiah-Christ (v. 25). Nor is he prepared to abandon the dialogue. Thus he challenges her to transcend the conclusion which she has reached on the basis of Jesus' telling her about her marital situation and true worship. He does this by resolving the question he himself posed to her in v. 10b: *tis estin ho legōn soi;* with

---

[98] See, e.g., Westcott, *St John*, 73–74; Lagrange, *Saint Jean*, 115; Barrett, *St John*, 239; Segalla, *Giovanni*, 196–97; Leidig, *Jesu Gespräch*, 154–55. R. E. Brown states: "Woman finally recognizes who Jesus is (as far as she is able) and Jesus affirms it" (*John*, 177). Yet on pp. 172–73 and 178 he tends to think "that it is not impossible that this use is intended in the style of divinity" (p. 172). R. Schnackenburg (*St John*, 1:441–42) also seems to argue that v. 26 is Jesus' acceptance of "the Messiah" and "the absolute terms in which Jesus reveals his divine being" (p. 442). See also E. D. Freed, "*Ego eimi* in John 1:20 and 4:25," *CBQ* 41 (1979) 289–90. I do not think it can be both. Jesus either accepts or transcends the woman's suggestion. The narrative as a whole (read down to v. 30) demands the latter. H. Boers offers a third alternative (*Neither on This Mountain*, 178–79). The woman's statement (v. 25) is a "negative sanction," showing her conviction that Jesus is not the expected Messiah. Jesus' reply (v. 26) is to affirm that indeed he is. Only R. Bultmann sees v. 26 as a revelation of the *egō eimi* and follows the narrative down to v. 30.

[99] See Sabugal, *Christos*, 209; O'Day, *Revelation*, 59–60, 72–74.

[100] This freestanding use of the expression, the absolute use, applied by Jesus to speak of himself, is one of several forms in which the expression appears. See F. J. Moloney, *NJBC*, 1423–24. For a somewhat different view, suggesting that the expression is used to articulate Jesus' being a divine figure, "eternal in the past and imperishable in the future," see J. H. Neyrey, *An Ideology of Revolt: John's Christology in Social-Science Perspective* (Philadelphia: Fortress Press, 1988) 213–20.

[101] E. Haenchen writes: "The Evangelist has the woman's perception of Jesus grow steadily (Jew, lord, prophet, Christ) and does not introduce an expression that overpowers everything else into the midst of this development" (*John 1-2*, 1:224). On the contrary, that is exactly what the narrative does. See especially O'Day, *Revelation*, 59–60, 72–74.

his self-revelation as *egō eimi ho legōn soi:* "I AM HE (is) the one speaking to you" (v. 26).[102]

The return of the disciples (v. 27) does not open a new literary unit; it rounds off the discussion between Jesus and the Samaritan woman, which their departure made possible in v. 7. The narrator's linking words show that he wished his reader to read on from vv. 16-26 into vv. 27-30: *kai epi toutō*. The disciples are joining a scene, not initiating a new one. They wonder at what they see. Jesus is talking to a woman. The use of the imperfect tense of the verb (*elalei*) shows that they are aware that this strange situation has been going on for some time. Their wonder is expressed through the strongly emotional verb *thaumazein*.[103] Yet despite their wonder, they say nothing. Here the narrator enters the story to tell the reader what the disciples really would like to have said: "What do you wish?" or "Why are you talking with her?" Behind these questions continues the same problem that has been at the front of the narrative since v. 16: Who is this man Jesus? "The awe of his friends makes the mystery of the revealer stand out more strongly."[104]

The mystery of who Jesus is has not been resolved for the disciples. They were not present to hear his reply to the woman's suggestion that he might be a Messiah-Christ in v. 26. The reader now finds that both the woman and the disciples are perplexed by the person of Jesus. The unresolved christological confession of the Samaritan woman is restated in vv. 28-29. The water jar is left behind. This detail has been the subject of considerable speculation: it tells the reader that she may have departed, but the Samaritan story has not yet come to an end. There will be a continuation of the process that has led a Samaritan woman to suspect that Jesus is a Messiah-Christ. The presence of her water jar is closely linked to v. 30, where the reader discovers that the Samaritans left the town and were coming to him. Their arrival, and the subsequent events which include the Samaritan woman, will resolve the problem of the jar at the well.[105]

---

[102] See Bultmann, *John*, 192: "Whoever hears these words spoken by the Revealer is faced with the ultimate decision: the *egō eimi* lays absolute claims to faith."

[103] See BAGD, 352. Okure renders it as "dumbfounded" (*Johannine Approach to Mission*, 133). For a summary of the Jewish evidence that would make Jesus' discussion so shocking see, among many, Barrett, *St John*, 240.

[104] Schnackenburg, *St John*, 1:443; see also O'Day, *Revelation*, 74-75.

[105] The Samaritan woman's presence in the final scene (vv. 39-42) is shown in the direct speech aimed at her in v. 42. On the jar as a hint of her proximate return, among others, see Westcott, *St John*, 74; Lindars, *John*, 193; Becker, *Johannes*, 179; O'Day, *Revelation*, 75.

What concerns the reader most, however, is not the jar at the well but the question she poses to her fellow Samaritans. She repeats what she said to Jesus in v. 25: "Come, see a man who told me all that I ever did. Can this be the Christ?" (v. 29). She invites them to see "a man." She is not prepared, at this stage, to go beyond that established fact. Yet he is a remarkable man who arouses certain suspicions in her. Recalling Jesus' surprising revelation in v. 18, she repeats her limited response of v. 25, limiting Jesus' showing of "all things" to his knowledge of her marital situation. The omission of any reference to vv. 21-24 in v. 29 has created problems for a diachronic analysis of the text,[106] but it is precisely this omission which shows the limitations of the woman's belief. It is on the basis of his telling her "all things" (*panta*) that she asks the question: "Can this be the Christ?" Her question *mēti houtos estin ho christos* expresses her uncertainty.[107] In a fashion that parallels Nicodemus's inability to go beyond what he knew (3:2: *oidamen hoti*), she repeats in v. 29 what she claimed to know in v. 25 (*oida hoti*). Jesus' revelation of himself as *egō eimi* has not moved her away from the securities of her own knowledge.[108] It is on the basis of the words of the woman, reported in v. 29, repeating what she had said to Jesus in v. 25, that the Samaritans left the town (aorist tense) and set out toward Jesus (imperfect tense).[109]

The Samaritan woman's rejection of the word of Jesus in vv. 7-15 repeated the response of "the Jews" in 2:13-22. Her preparedness to accept Jesus as "a prophet" (v. 19) and possibly the Messiah (vv. 25 and 29) repeats the response of Nicodemus in 3:1-12. He was prepared to accept that Jesus was a rabbi, a teacher from God who did great signs and who had God with him (3:2). However, he was unable to go further than that (3:4, 9). The reader, who knows of Nicodemus's conditioned response to Jesus,

---

[106] E.g., E. Haenchen says that vv. 28-30 immediately followed v. 18 in the Evangelist's source (*John 1-2*, 1:224). Thus she makes no reference to the things she told him about true worship, which was added by the Evangelist (along with the rest of vv. 19-27) to the source.

[107] The use of *mēti* "introduces a hesitant question" (Barrett, *St John*, 240); Bernard, *St John*, 1:152. BDF, 221, (§ 427 [2]) suggests that the question hints at unlikelihood. Against Okure (*Johannine Approach to Mission*, 169), who claims, despite the grammatical difficulties, that v. 29 reflects "complete belief in Jesus." See van den Bussche, *Jean*, 195: "La Samaritaine du texte n'est ni missionaire, ni même vraiment croyante."

[108] O'Day, *Revelation*, 76. Against Okure (*Johannine Approach to Mission*, 121-27, 168-75), who argues that Jesus accepts the fluid concept of Messiah-Christ of the woman, and she thus becomes a missionary witness.

[109] A. Lenglet argues that the theme of 4:1-42 is the gathering of the Samaritans around Jesus ("Jésus de passage," 494-98). This has been achieved by developing two subplots: the Samaritan woman (vv. 7-29) and the Samaritans (vv. 28-42). In this reading, vv. 28-29 form a bridge between the two subplots.

now discovers that the Samaritan woman arrives at a parallel form of conditioned faith in Jesus. The Samaritan woman is unable to accept Jesus'
revelation of himself as *egō eimi* (vv. 25-26, 29). Thus, the author has used
this second moment in Jesus' encounter with a non-Jewish world to present
the reader with the example of a Samaritan woman who comes to a partial,
conditioned belief in Jesus.

III. JESUS' INSTRUCTION – HIS MISSION
AND THE MISSION OF HIS DISCIPLES (4:31-38)

The Shape of the Narrative

While reading vv. 31-38 the reader is aware of two events going on
simultaneously. First, after a brief dialogue between the disciples and Jesus
(vv. 31-33), which, like the earlier dialogues between Jesus and the woman,
begins with an imperative (v. 31: *phage*), Jesus instructs his audience (vv. 35,
37, 38: *hymeis*) on the source and purpose of his own (v. 34) and their
mission (vv. 35-38). Second, because of the narrator's report that the
Samaritans are coming toward Jesus (v. 30), the reader is aware that the
space opened between Jesus and his entourage by the departure of the
woman (vv. 27-28) is now being closed. The disciples are told to lift up
their eyes, to see the advent of the Samaritans (v. 35).

The narrative unfolds as follows:[110]

(a) *Verses 31-33:* The disciples command Jesus to eat something, only
to receive a puzzling answer about another food, which they do
not know. This leads to their query concerning his source for such
food.

(b) *Verse 34:* Jesus' response to the query of the disciples is both the
theological foundation for his own mission and the basis for all
that he has yet to say to them about their mission.[111]

(c) *Verses 35-38:* By means of a proverbial statement on harvesting
(vv. 35-37) and a concluding affirmation (v. 38), the place and function of the missionary activity of disciples of Jesus is taught.

Two further issues need to be raised. Is it proper to call vv. 31-38 a
"dialogue"? I suggest that, like several other passages which the implied

---

[110] The following is generally accepted by commentators, although not all would single
out v. 34, as I have done. On v. 34, see G. Segalla, *Volontà di Dio e dell'Uomo in Giovanni (Vangelo
e Lettere)* (SuppRivB 6; Brescia: Paideia, 1974) 153–58.

[111] See Okure, *Johannine Approach to Mission*, 137.

reader has already met (especially 3:1-21 and 3:22-36), an initial exchange of words leads to a monologue. There is no exchange of direct speech recorded after v. 33. The disciples are not participating in a discussion; they are listening to a discourse, brief though it might be.[112]

On this basis, I would claim that vv. 31-38 must not be interpreted simply in terms of Jesus' speaking to his disciples about their mission.[113] They are not the only ones listening to the words of Jesus. Once the dialogue with the disciples comes to its conclusion (vv. 31-33), the author is primarily interested in addressing the reader, via Jesus' words to the disciples. Thus, while at one level of the narrative the *hymeis* refers to the disciples listening to him, at a more important level, it is the narrator's way of slowing the narrative to insert a commentary on the action *for the reader*. Verses 31-38 serve as a commentary on all that has happened in the Samaritan section.

Reading the Narrative

The episode falls in between two other events: the coming of the Samaritans (v. 30), and their decision concerning his person and role (vv. 39-42). The adverbial use of the expression *metaxy* ("between, in the middle, what lies between")[114] is rare in the New Testament (see Acts 13:42), but it expresses exactly the "in-between" nature of the dialogue discourse of vv. 31-38. The implied reader is aware of everything that has happened thus far. The reader is now aware that something further will happen, related to what he has already read, after the present interlude. The disciples command that Jesus eat something (v. 31). The use of the imperfect *ērōtōn* and the participle *legontes* conveys the idea of a continual insistence. The narrator makes a deliberate link with v. 8. At the start of the narrative, the disciples left an exhausted Jesus at the well (v. 4: *kekopiakōs*), so that they might go to the town to buy food. Now he does not respond to their command to eat.[115]

Jesus' response to them is that he has food to eat of which the disciples do not know. The use of the present tense (*echō*) and the play on words

---

[112] Rightly, Bernard, *St John*, 1:153; Lenglet, "Jésus de passage," 499; Olsson, *Structure and Meaning*, 219-20.

[113] This is the major defect of the otherwise thorough treatment by T. Okure (*Johannine Approach to Mission*, 136-68, 188-91).

[114] BAGD, 513, s.v. *metaxy*, 1b. See also Bauer, *Johannesevangelium*, 72; Lagrange, *Saint Jean*, 116; Barrett, *St John*, 240.

[115] See O'Day, *Revelation*, 77. Léon-Dufour, *Lecture*, 381. Their address, Rabbi, has so far appeared on the lips of people who have not fully understood Jesus: the disciples of the Baptist (1:38), Nathanael (1:49), Nicodemus (3:2).

where the verb explains the noun *brōsin . . . phagein*,[116] indicates a present and ongoing nourishment of Jesus. It is not some occasional eating that may have taken place while they were away. Another link is established for the reader with the earlier part of the narrative. While the disciples were away finding ordinary food, Jesus has said to the Samaritan woman: "If you knew (*ei ēdeis*) the gift of God and who it is that is speaking to you" (v. 10ab). During the course of her two encounters with Jesus she has not been able to come to a proper knowledge of either the gift of God (vv. 7-15) or who it was that was speaking to her (vv. 16-30). The disciples join the company of the Samaritan woman. While they return with food and thus propose a material eating to Jesus, he transcends these categories to speak of a food which they do not know (*hymeis ouk oidate*). Like the Samaritan woman, they are still outside the program that has been set for Jesus. The implied reader is, by this stage of the narrative, more inside Jesus' program than the disciples, although by no means is even the reader fully informed.[117]

Like the Samaritan woman, the disciples fail because their "words" do not respond to Jesus' words. The two parties in the dialogue talk at different levels. They can only debate among themselves whether or not someone else could have brought him food in their absence (v. 33). While Jesus has spoken of some form of nourishment which he receives, beyond their comprehension (v. 32), their discussion refuses to move beyond the level of an ordinary food which must have been provided by some other agent. Even though he has told them that they are unable to understand, they insist that something has happened that is within the realms of their comprehension (v. 33). In their attempt to explain the mystery of Jesus' words to one another, not only are they unable to transcend the level of ordinary food, but they also refuse to listen to the word of Jesus. The disciples are in exactly the same relationship with Jesus as the Samaritan woman. For all their cultural and religious sentiments of superiority (see vv. 8, 9, 27), the disciples are no better than the Samaritan woman. As the reader has followed the response of the Samaritan woman through her story, looking forward toward a suitable conclusion, so now the author creates a parallel relationship between the reader and the disciples.[118]

The discourse begins in v. 34. Jesus' words go to the heart of the disciples' question (v. 33): *emon brōma estin.* The disciples and the reader

---

[116] C. K. Barrett claims that *phagein* is epexegetic (*St John*, 240). See also Bauer, *Johannes-evangelium*, 72.

[117] See O'Day, *Revelation*, 77-79.

[118] See Barrett, *St John*, 240.

are to be told what the mysterious food might be (see v. 32);[119] however, the reader is not about to have all the solutions to the mystery of Jesus' life story solved. He encounters two parallel statements with important words met here for the first time. Jesus' food comes from his performance of two closely related actions:

hina:
(a) *poiō to thelēma tou pempsantos me*[120]
kai
(b) *teleiōsō autou to ergon.*

Reading the *kai* as epexegetical, his nourishment is found in his doing the will of the one who sent him, which means he will bring to perfection the work of that person.

The idea of Jesus' being "sent" is clear to the reader (see 1:14, 18, 34; 2:16; 3:16-17, 35-36), but his doing the sender's will is a notion that the implied reader is hearing for the first time.[121] Having heard it, the reader recalls the use of *edei* in 4:4. It is now clear why Jesus *had to* pass through Samaria.[122] Behind the episodes that take place in a non-Jewish world stands the will of the one who sends him. Jesus' presence to the Samaritan woman *had to happen*, as he does the will of the one who sent him. The reader also recalls Jesus' instructions on true worship in 4:21-24. Jesus is the model of worship in spirit and in truth as all that he does is nourished by the will of the one who sent him.

The reader is discovering that the questions about the true nourishment of Jesus can be resolved only by an attentive reading of the story of Jesus himself. The implied reader has now read enough of the story to be aware of that truth; the disciples, who have been absent during Jesus' encounter with the Samaritan woman (vv. 8-27), are unaware. Through the epexegetical *kai* two further important terms are introduced which the

---

[119] For a detailed study of 4:34, see Segalla, *Volontà*, 149-77 (on *brōsis* and *brōma*, see pp. 162-66).

[120] See Leroy, *Rätsel und Missverständnis*, 148-49. Reading, contrary to the Nestle-Aland text, *poiō* rather than *poiēsō*. There are good witnesses (Codex Sinaiticus, Codex Alexandrinus, Family 13, and Nestle-Aland's *Mehrheitstext*) that read the present *poiō*. See, for its acceptance as the *lectio difficilior,* Schnackenburg, *St John,* 1:447 n. 81; Olsson, *Structure and Meaning,* 224. The present tense links v. 34 with its immediate narrative context, pointing to the present nature of Jesus' acceptance of the Father's will.

[121] Once this is established, however, it will return regularly in explanation both of who Jesus is and what he does. See 5:23-24, 30, 37; 6:38-39, 44; 7:16, 18, 28, 33; 9:4; 12:44-45, 49; 13:20; 14:24; 15:21; 16:5). See Segalla, *Volontà,* 166-69.

[122] See also Boers, *Neither on This Mountain,* 191-92.

implied reader is meeting for the first time: *teleioō* and *to ergon*.[123] The reader is able to look back over the narrative to see what is meant by the first part of the explanation, but this is impossible for the second part. At this stage of the narrative, the reader, like the disciples in vv. 31-33 and the woman in the earlier part of the narrative, is being challenged to accept the word of Jesus. The reader can understand what the words mean, but what do they refer to? The future tense of the verb introduces a prolepsis.[124] It points the narrative forward. There will be a moment in the future when *autou to ergon*, the overall scheme or plan of the task given to Jesus by the one who sent him, must be brought to its perfection, its fulfillment. Therein Jesus will find his nourishment. This is the goal toward which his life is oriented.

Although the perfection of the task given by the Father lies in the future, the reader is not entirely in the dark. There have already been some hints pointing toward the end of the story. The prologue has told of the clash of light and darkness (1:5), and of the Word's rejection by his own (1:10-11). The first days of Jesus led to a promise of a future sight which true believers would have in the Son of Man (1:51). This was further explained by the prophecy of Jesus that the Son of Man must be "lifted up" to make God known (3:13-14). Jesus has spoken of his "hour" which has not yet come (2:4), and the narrator, in an aside to the reader, has spoken of the belief that would be engendered in the disciples "when therefore he was raised from the dead" (2:22). A Christian reader (see 20:30-31) knows of these events, but he has never heard them described as the *teleiōsis tou ergou*.

The implied reader comes away from v. 34 able to look back over the narrative to understand that all that Jesus is and is doing flows from his basic dependence on the will of the one who sent him (v. 34a). The reader has now been made even more aware that there will be some moment in the future when Jesus will bring to completion all that he is and does

---

[123] These terms will play an important role in the shaping of the implied reader. On *teleioō* and the related *teleō*, see 5:36; 17:4, 23; 19:28, 30. On *to ergon*, see 17:4, which announces the completion of the program stated in 4:34. Against Bultmann (*John*, 265) and J. Becker (*Johannes*, 179) Okure rightly distinguishes between *ergon* and *erga* in the Fourth Gospel (*Johannine Approach to Mission*, 141-42). See also Segalla, *Volontà*, 169-73.

[124] For the reading of *teleiōsō* as a future rather than an aorist subjunctive, see Schnackenburg, *St John*, 1:447 n. 81; Olsson, *Structure and Meaning*, 225 n. 34. See also BDF, 186 § 369 (3): "A special case is that in which a future connected by *kai* follows upon *hina* or *mē* with the subjunctive to designate some further consequence." See also 15:8, where the same construction, clearly pointing into the future, is found. Even without the future, the use of the aorist subjunctive after *hina* would still indicate a prolepsis.

(v. 34b). The reader is involved in a life story, a description of a series of events that happened in time and space, which the author regards as the perfect response to the will of God and the final consummation of his plan. Some of that has already been encountered in the story so far. More is still to come, but there have been sufficient hints that the story is heading toward a death which is at the same time an exaltation and which will lead to a resurrection. Jesus' statement in v. 34 looks both backward and forward along the time axis of the narrative. What the hints of his future experience might mean is beyond the control of the implied reader, but the centrality of these *events* to the person and message of Jesus Christ has been made clear: *emon brōma estin*.

The final words of the discourse shift away from Jesus' own response to the one who sent him to the role of the disciples. These verses have created a number of difficulties for traditional exegesis. Are the words of Jesus in v. 35 based on a parable with a universal application, or is it just that the disciples say these things?[125] Does the word "already" (*ēdē*) belong to v. 35, or should it be the first word of v. 36? Who is the sower and who is the reaper in v. 36 and the "one" and "the other" in v. 37? The problem of the disciples entering into the labor of others (plural) to reap what they did not sow in v. 38 has also created a series of hypotheses. Who are these "others"? The thrust of v. 35 demands that the *ēdē* comes as the last word in the sentence. Read in this way, both v. 35 and v. 36 reflect Johannine realized eschatology, where the now and the not yet become one.[126] The words of the proverblike statement of Jesus, whatever its source (it is not known anywhere in antiquity),[127] are directed to the disciples. They are being reminded of the common opinion, probably based on the physical reality of the fields around them (however it has been expressed), that the harvest is still some time away.[128] Jesus contradicts this. It is here already in the Samaritans, who, for the reader, have been coming toward Jesus during the discourse (see v. 30). The disciples are not aware of this, and thus Jesus can tell them to raise their eyes.

Jesus stretches language. A harvest "already white" can only refer to sown fields. Jesus points to the advancing Samaritans, telling his disciples

---

[125] W. Bauer suggests that it may not be original (*Johannesevangelium*, 73).

[126] Following the indication of P⁶⁵. See especially Okure, *Johannine Approach to Mission*, 150-51, but also Bauer, *Johannesevangelium*, 73; Bernard, *St John*, 1:157; Lagrange, *Saint Jean*, 120. Against most critics who rightly see it as better Johannine style to place *ēdē* at the beginning of a sentence. See, e.g., Westcott, *St John*, 76; Schnackenburg, *St John*, 1:449 n. 92; Lindars, *John*, 196.

[127] See the survey of suggestions in Okure, *Johannine Approach to Mission*, 147-49.

[128] See Barrett, *St John*, 241.

that their estimation is incorrect.[129] As the ordinary meanings for temple, birth, water, a well, and food have been transcended to speak of the transformation worked by the presence of Jesus, so now the term "harvest" becomes an image used by Jesus to speak of the newness of life, the eternal life, which he has come to bring (see v. 36). The crop in the fields may well be four months away from harvesting, but the advent of the Samaritans should be sign enough to the disciples that Jesus' presence brings life to all who would "come toward him" (see v. 30). Johannine realized eschatology contradicts the expectations of the disciples. The "not yet" is here already, and the advent of the Samaritans is concrete proof of it.[130]

The disciples had to be removed from the scene, so that Jesus could have his conversation with the Samaritan woman (v. 8). Their presence would have rendered Jesus' revelation of himself to the non-Jewish world impossible, "for Jews use nothing in common with Samaritans" (v. 9). On their return, they are shocked, and the woman departs (vv. 27-28). For a moment their values dominate, but the water jar left behind informs the reader that this may not be the end of the Samaritan story. The *en tǭ metaxy* of v. 30 was yet a further hint. Now the apparent acceptance of the disciples' values is reversed. As Jesus draws them into his response to the Father, the first people he points to are Samaritans![131] Cultural, historical, and religious antipathy must be overcome in order to do the will of the Father. This must be the case for both Jesus (v. 34) and his disciples (v. 35).

The *Sitz im Leben* for this discourse is the Samaritan mission of the Johannine community. Its members are being told that the reception of Samaritans into the community is the result of the initiative of Jesus himself.[132] Thus, Jesus differentiates between the sower and the reaper in v. 36. The disciples are to work as reapers in a harvest that has been sown by Jesus himself through his encounter with the Samaritan woman.[133] She has moved slowly to a stage of imperfect faith (vv. 7-29), but her word has

---

[129] This interpretation of "lift up your eyes" is widely accepted by the critics. Isa 49:18 is close at hand.

[130] On the harvest as an eschatological symbol, see Isa 27:12; Joel 4:13; Mark 4:1-9, 26-29; Matt 13:24-30; Rev 14:14-16. See Friedrich, *Chi è Gesù?* 57; Léon-Dufour, *Lecture*, 386-87.

[131] See O'Day, *Revelation*, 82-83.

[132] See, among many discussions of this setting, Cullmann, "Samaria," 185-92; idem, *The Johannine Circle: Its place in Judaism, among the disciples of Jesus and in early Christianity: A study in the origin of the Gospel of John* (London: SCM Press, 1976) 39-56; Brown, *John*, 175-76; Olsson, *Structure and Meaning*, 233-41; Okure, *Johannine Approach to Mission*, 188-91.

[133] Against R. Schnackenburg (*St John*, 1:450-51), who understands Jesus to be the reaper, thus having "no option but to think of the Father" (p. 451) as the sower, B. F. Westcott sees Jesus as "the Lord of the harvest" and thus not as the sower (*St John*, 76). Thus, the lawgiver, priest, and prophet who "went before" Jesus are the sower.

sent other Samaritans toward Jesus (vv. 29-30). The disciples, in reaping
the fruit of the Samaritans now coming toward them, are paid as they
gather fruit for eternal life.[134] There is no need, in the Johannine view of
things, to do good things now in the hope that this will bring its eventual
reward. The "not yet" is here already. The reaper receives his wage and
gathers fruit for eternal life in the act of reaping. Here and now Jesus who
sows and the disciples who reap rejoice together. The implied reader will
shortly discover that the disciples have nothing to do with the Samaritans'
act of faith (vv. 39-42), but the intended reader, the Johannine community, recognizes that disciples are still reaping the fruits of a harvest sown
by Jesus.[135]

In this interpretation, v. 37 restates what has already been said by
means of a short proverb (*ho logos*) and prepares the way for the final statement from Jesus in v. 38[136] The general principle stated in v. 37 flows from
what has taken place down to v. 36. Whatever the disciples may make of
Jesus' words, the reader who has followed the narrative experiences a
logical and temporal sequence of events leading to the summary statement
of v. 36. Against a background of prejudice (vv. 8, 9, 27), Jesus has gradually
drawn the Samaritans toward himself (vv. 7-30). Prejudice must be overcome, as the disciples are associated with the urgency that stands behind
all that Jesus has done in Samaria (v. 7: *edei*). They have been pointed
toward the Samaritans (v. 35) so that they may become reapers of a harvest
they did not sow and thus enter into the joy that Jesus himself has from
his union with the Father (v. 36). The narrative shows that the proverb
is true (*estin alēthinos*): One sows (Jesus) and another reaps (the disciples)
(v. 37).[137]

Thus the flow of the narrative arrives at the much-debated v. 38: "I
sent you to reap that for which you did not labor; others have labored,

---

[134] See Barrett, *St John*, 241.

[135] This suggests that the *Sitz im Leben* of the passage is the presence of Samaritans in the
community, not the need to initiate a mission to them. See n. 139 below.

[136] On the possible background of the proverb (*ho logos*), see Bauer, *Johannesevangelium*,
75; W. G. E. Watson, "Antecedents of a New Testament Proverb," *VT* 20 (1970) 368-70; A.
Niccaci, "Siracide 6,19 e Giovanni 4,36-38," *BibOr* 23 (1981) 149-53.

[137] There may have been one or several problems associated with the Samaritan mission.
Some Johannine Christians may have opposed it; some may not have seen its need; or, most
probably, some may have wondered about the presence of Samaritans already in the community. The response of the real author is to indicate to his community that they are but
the reapers of a harvest sown by Jesus himself and that this activity forms part of the will
of God. See Hoskyns, *Fourth Gospel*, 246: "To Him and not to them belongs the labour of
salvation." This is one of the main conclusions of Okure, *Johannine Approach to Mission*, passim,
but see especially, pp. 185-88.

and you have entered into their labor." There are two basic affirmations made in these words of Jesus. The first of them is a further development of what has been said so far. The development comes from the repetition of the idea of being "sent." Behind everything that Jesus is and does is the Father who sent him (v. 34). Now this "mission" is passed on to the disciples of Jesus: *egō apesteila hymas therizein*. Although the verb is different (*pempō* was used in v. 34), this is merely stylistic. The aorist tense of the verb in v. 38a is a clarification of two moments in the past, but is intimately associated with the present narrative. Already in v. 2 the reader has learned that Jesus is not baptizing. His disciples are performing that ministry. In the immediate past, Jesus' missionary command to his disciples has become explicit in v. 35b: "I tell you, lift up your eyes, and see how the fields are already white for harvest."[138] In terms of Jesus' statement in v. 38, the two moments of v. 2 and v. 35 are already past. They are reflected in the aorist tense of the verb.

They may not have labored for this harvest, but they are to reap. The one who has labored for this harvest is Jesus himself, and the strange application of the adjective *kekopiakōs* in 4:6 to speak of Jesus' physical condition is now explained. His presence in Samaria, the result of the Father's will, is one of laboring, as the subsequent narrative has shown. But Jesus adds: *alloi kekopiakasin*. In all that has been said so far, there has been only reference to "one sower" (vv. 36-37). Who are the *alloi*? Many attempts have been made to resolve this question,[139] but again the narrative itself provides the solution. The implied reader is able to recall two figures sent by God to perform a specific task, John (1:6) and Jesus (3:17; 4:34). In 1:29-34 the reader also learned of John the baptizer, who spoke of another who was coming to baptize with the Holy Spirit (1:33). The need to be born again of water and the Spirit in order to see and enter the kingdom (3:3, 5) has made it clear to the reader that baptism is the crucial rite through which one must pass in order to enter the life promised by Jesus. Immediately following that instruction, which was beyond Nicodemus, a discussion arose about the relative merits of the baptism of John the Baptist, baptizing at Aenon near Salim, and the baptism of Jesus, baptizing in Judea (3:22-26). The question was never answered.

---

[138] Thus, there is no need to resort to complicated theories about v. 38 being cast in terms of a postresurrection mandate. See, e.g., Schnackenburg, *St John*, 1:452–53; Perkins, *NJBC*, 957. The aorist can be explained by following the temporal axis of the narrative.

[139] For a survey, see Okure, *Johannine Approach to Mission*, 159–60; Olsson, *Structure and Meaning*, 229–33.

The reader has learned from 4:1-2 that the baptism of Jesus was no longer administered by Jesus himself but by his disciples. Both baptizers— John and Jesus—have ceased their baptizing activity (3:24; 4:2). Now the only ones who are baptizing are the disciples. The disciples come at the end of a long process that has its origins in God. The reader knows from the prologue that "there was a man sent from God, whose name was John" (1:6), and has just read the words of Jesus: "My food is to do the will of him who sent me" (4:34; see also 3:17). Only now are the disciples sent by Jesus. They are the next in line in the historical development of a mis- sionary activity that started in the witness of the Baptist, led to the person of Jesus, who now associates his disciples with himself so that they might reap the harvest that they did not sow. There is no need to look beyond the experience of the reader to discover that the "others" who have labored, into whose labor the disciples now enter, are John the Baptist and Jesus.[140]

The reader has now been instructed, through the discourse of Jesus, on the essential place that the appreciation of the life story of Jesus himself must play in the proper response to Jesus. All that Jesus is and does can be seen from the way in which his life reflects his doing the will of the one who sent him (v. 34a); this will be further seen when Jesus eventually brings to completion the task his Father has given him (v. 34b). The follower of Jesus, the disciple, the reader, and the Johannine community belong to that story. All these readers are involved in harvesting a crop they did not sow. John the Baptist and Jesus went before them. They belong to a long story, a series of events willed by God, responded to by the Baptist and by Jesus. As "sent" by Jesus, they form part of his mission. The story goes on.

On two occasions through the narrative from the first Cana miracle down to 4:38 the narrator has drawn back from reporting encounters between Jesus and others, from the Jewish and the non-Jewish world. On the first occasion (2:23-25) the narrator told the reader that it was not enough to believe in Jesus on the basis of the "signs" he did (2:23-24). Jesus knows what is in the human heart; one's response to him must be founded on deeper convictions (v. 25). Yet does this mean that the "events" of the life of Jesus do not tell the story of God? If "signs" are not enough, does

---

[140] See also Léon-Dufour, *Lecture*, 390. He also has the prophets as part of the "others." The temporal axis of the narrative, John the Baptist–Jesus–the disciples, may also reflect what happened historically. For some suggestions along these lines, see J. A. T. Robinson, "The 'Others' of John 4,38," *Studia Evangelica* 1 (1959) 510–15; Boismard, *Moïse ou Jésus*, 156–57; J. Murphy-O'Connor, "John the Baptist and Jesus: History and Hypotheses," *NTS* 36 (1990) 359–74.

Jesus look only to what is in the human heart (2:25)? If such is the case, only "the spiritual" will do. The charge of Gnosticism often leveled against the Fourth Gospel would be true.

In 4:31-38 the narrator returns to this issue. The argument of 2:23-25 needs to be balanced by the firm belief of Christian tradition, as important for the Fourth Evangelist as it was for other witnesses to that tradition.[141] The life, death, and resurrection of Jesus of Nazareth stand at the basis of all Christian life and practice. The implied reader is not fully aware of the Johannine understanding of this central message of Christianity, but the omniscient narrator is. Thus in 4:31-38 the narrator, who has already told the reader of the need to go beyond "signs" (2:23-25), insists on the importance of the "events" of the life of Jesus and the missionary role of the disciples as a consequence of these events.

IV. JESUS AND THE SAMARITANS (4:39-42)

The Shape of the Narrative

There is no further setting for this final encounter between Jesus and the Samaritan world. Jesus has never moved from the well (see v. 6).[142] The disciples disappear into the background, and the Samaritans are described as *ek de tēs poleōs ekeinēs polloi*. Character portrayal and dramatic action are not important for the narrator here. The passage is composed of four affirmations, three of them from the narrator and the final one in the direct speech of the Samaritans, who speak to the woman.

The narrative unfolds in the following fashion:

(a) *Verse 39:* The narrator reports an initial belief of "many" Samaritans based on the word of the woman.
(b) *Verse 40a:* This leads to a request from the Samaritans that Jesus stay with them.
(c) *Verse 40b:* The narrator then reports that Jesus responded positively to their request.

---

[141] H. Leroy sees the Johannine descent Christology behind "the one who sent me" (*Rätsel und Missverständnis*, 149–55). Thus, he helpfully argues, the background of 4:31-34 is the need for the Johannine community to develop an authoritative catechesis, based on the one sent from above, to counter early gnostic tendencies: "Entgegen der gnostichen Vollendungsauffassung geht es um den Gehorsam gegenüber dem sendenden Herrn" (p. 150).

[142] On the importance of this, see O'Day, *Revelation*, 128 n. 9.

(d) *Verse 41:* The narrator tells the reader that "many more" believe because of the word of Jesus.

(e) *Verse 42:* The Samaritans tell the woman that their faith and knowledge transcend her suggestion that Jesus might be the Messiah. They confess that Jesus is the savior of the world.

Augustine has aptly described this episode: *"Primo per famam, postea per presentiam"* ("First by reputation, then by his presence") (*In Johannem* 15.33; CCSL 36:164).[143] In the present narrative shape of the Fourth Gospel this brief scene serves as a climax to Jesus' presence in Samaria.

READING THE NARRATIVE

Explicitly recalling the direct speech of the woman in v. 29, many of the Samaritans from the town believed in Jesus on the basis of the words of the woman: "He told me all that I ever did" (v. 39). A major section of Jesus' earlier encounter with the Samaritan woman has been omitted: the place of true worship, "neither on this mountain, nor in Jerusalem," but in spirit and in truth (vv. 21-24). The narrator links this final part of the narrative with the woman's words in v. 29 so the reader will know that the "many" who believe in Jesus in v. 39 are still asking the same questions as the woman: "Can this be the Messiah?" (see vv. 25 and 29). The promise of a universal worship of the Father and Jesus' revelation of himself as *egō eimi* have not appeared in the words of the woman to her fellow Samaritans, neither in v. 29 nor in v. 39.[144]

Every indication has been given to the reader that, although there is a sense in which the identification of Jesus with the Messiah is not wrong, there is more to it. From 1:35-51 the reader knows that the identification of Jesus with current messianic hopes is insufficient. Such knowledge has been further reinforced in Jesus' attempt to correct Nicodemus's expectations through his teaching on rebirth (3:2-5) and the parallel attempt to correct the Samaritan woman's messianic suggestions through his self-revelation as *egō eimi* (4:25-26). The author desires to lead the reader to a position where he or she sees and understands that Jesus cannot be fully

---

[143] See also Bultmann, *John,* 200. However, too much has been made of firsthand and secondhand hearers of the word, introduced into the discussion, via Kierkegaard, by Bultmann (*John,* 200-202). See also R. Walker, "Jüngerwort und Herrenwort: Zur Auslegung von Joh 4:39-42," *ZNW* 57 (1966) 49-54. T. Okure is rightly critical of this (*Johannine Approach to Mission,* 172-73).

[144] See Boers, *Neither on This Mountain,* 198-99; O'Day, *Revelation,* 85-86.

understood as the Messiah and has promised that the time is coming and now is when there will be a universal worship of the Father (vv. 21-24). The reader finds none of this in the witness of the word of the woman, which, the reader learns in v. 39, has led many Samaritans to believe in Jesus. They come to their faith *dia ton logon tēs gynaikos martyrousēs*. The witness of the word of the woman has led to a response to Jesus among the villagers that matches her own partial faith. The reader knows that the word of the woman cannot be accepted as a totally reliable witness. After reading v. 39, the implied reader is aware that more will be required of the Samaritans if they are to come to authentic Johannine faith.[145] Their partial faith, based on the witness of the word of the woman, leads the Samaritans to come to him and to ask him to remain with them (*meinei par' autois*). Jesus' acceptance of this request reverses the experience of the first disciples. In 1:39 he called the first disciples to "come and see," and they remained with him that day. The reader also recalls that the Samaritan woman attempted to curtail all contact with the Jewish Jesus in v. 9. The question of the conflict between Samaritan and Jew has been forgotten.[146] Here the incipient faith of Samaritans leads them to ask him to remain. The experience of the first disciples led them to tell Simon: "We have found the Messiah" (1:41). The reader, recalling that episode but encouraged by the progress in the overcoming of the Samaritan–Jewish conflict, reads on to discover the results of Jesus' "staying with" the Samaritans.

A bond is set up that had been endangered when the woman left the well. Yet she had left her water jar behind, and so the reader had been warned that the discussions broken by the arrival of the shocked disciples might not have come to their conclusion (v. 28). Jesus is reported as staying there "two days."[147] At this stage, the brief duration of time is simply left with the reader. It will assume a more important role in the near future (see vv. 43 and 46). If "many" (*polloi*) believed in Jesus because of the witness of the word of the woman (v. 39), "many more" (*pollǭ pleious*) believed in him *dia ton logon autou* (v. 41).[148] There is a quantitative and a qualitative

---

[145] Most commentators see that there are two stages of faith reflected in vv. 39-42: a faith based on signs (Jesus' telling the woman her secrets) and a faith based on the word. T. Okure argues the contrary (*Johannine Approach to Mission*, 170–81).

[146] O'Day, *Revelation*, 87.

[147] Schnackenburg points out that the Evangelist's missionary interest may lie behind this staying with the Samaritans (*St John*, 1:455–56). T. Okure links the two days with the stay of the genuine missionary in *Didache* 11.5 (*Johannine Approach to Mission*, 179).

[148] See Westcott, *St John*, 76. The reader is not told that the whole town believed. "Many" (v. 39) and "many more" (v. 41) are reported as believing. As always in John, a choice is made. See Hudry-Clergeon, "De Judée en Galilée," 828–29.

difference between the faith (*episteusan* is used in both v. 39 and v. 41) that is the result of the word of the woman and the faith that is the result of the word of Jesus himself.[149] The nature of that qualitative difference is explained in the direct speech of the Samaritans in v. 42, directed to the woman. Looking back over the brief period of time during which they have believed in Jesus, they recall v. 39 only to disassociate themselves from their initial commitment based on the witness of the woman. There was a time when they believed in Jesus, the Messiah who told the woman everything she ever did. Although the narrator reported their initial experience of faith as *dia ton logon* of the witnessing woman, the Samaritans themselves do not consider her witness as *logos*. In their own words, they speak to her, disassociating themselves from a faith *dia tēn sēn lalian*.

Although the New Testament's use of the word *lalia* may not have the sense of "gossip, common talk," which is its usual meaning in classical literature,[150] it cannot be said to parallel the Johannine use of the expression *logos*.[151] In addition to the change in the noun, the addition of the second person singular possessive pronoun limits the "words" to the woman herself. They are *her* words. There is now another *logos* which transcends the witness of her *lalia*. They now believe because of the word of Jesus (v. 41: *dia ton logon autou*). Thus, the reader is aware, the Samaritans "no longer" (*ouketi*) relate to Jesus as the possible Messiah. Two days have now passed between the original belief in Jesus through the woman's witness and the Samaritans' hearing of the word of Jesus. The reference to a time span separates their two moments of faith: their past sharing in the faith in Jesus as a Messiah who was able to tell the Samaritan woman everything she ever did (v. 39) and their present experience of faith, based on the word of Jesus (v. 41).[152] Looking back to the narrator's statement in v. 41, that they now believed because of the word of Jesus, the words of the Samaritans begin with an affirmation of what has happened to them: "for we have heard (*akēkoamen*) for ourselves."

---

[149] See Schnackenburg, *St John*, 1:456–57; Schmid, "Komposition," 156–57. Much will depend on the distinction between *lalia* and *logos* in v. 42.

[150] See BAGD, 464.

[151] Some scholars see no difference between the *lalia* of the woman and the *logos* of Jesus. See Barrett, *St John*, 243; Walker, "Jüngerwort und Herrenwort," 52–53; Léon-Dufour, *Lecture*, 392. T. Okure argues strongly for an identical meaning for *lalia* and *logos* (*Johannine Approach to Mission*, 171). For my position, see Lagrange, *Saint Jean*, 122; Brown, *John*, 174–75; Segalla, *Giovanni*, 200–201. R. Bultmann distinguishes between the two words but overstates the case (*John*, 201).

[152] The temporal dimension involved in *ouketi* is not discussed in Okure's study (*Johannine Approach to Mission*, 172).

John the Baptist's final appearance in the Gospel was marked by a use of the same verb. He described himself as the friend of the bridegroom who "stands and hears (*akouōn*) him" (3:29). The Samaritans have now had the experience of the presence of Jesus, but they do not refer to miracles or wonders. They simply say that they have heard. Only on the basis of their hearing can they claim to "know (*oidamen*) that this is indeed the savior of the world." Belief in the word of Jesus (v. 41) has produced knowledge (v. 42). The reader recalls that Nicodemus also "knew" about Jesus (see 3:2), but his knowledge came from his own traditions and expectations. The knowledge of the Samaritans comes from their hearing. They believe because they themselves (*autoi*) have heard the word of Jesus.[153]

The expression used by the Samaritans in their confession "the savior of the world" is found only in one other place in the New Testament (1 John 4:14), and the Hellenistic title "savior" (*sōtēr*) is not widespread (see Luke 1:47; 2:11; Acts 5:31; 13:23; Phil 3:20; and the Pastorals). Like John the Baptist's confession of Jesus as the Lamb who takes away the sin of the world (see 1:29, 35), it is a confession that cannot be misunderstood as the fruit of human invention, nor can it be limited to a national expectation. Both Jew and Greek hoped for a "savior," although they thought, spoke, and wrote about such a figure in very different ways.[154] The reader, however, is not surprised by this title on the lips of the Samaritans,[155] as he or she has already learned from the reliable witness of Jesus himself that "God sent the Son into the world, not to condemn the world, but that the world might be saved through him (*hina sōthē ho kosmos di' autou*)" (3:17).

The Son, sent into the world by the love of the Father, to save the world (3:16-17), earlier told the woman that the day would come, and now is, when neither Gerizim nor Jerusalem would be the place of true worship (v. 21). He promised a universal worship of the Father in spirit and truth (v. 23). She has either forgotten or not understood the significance of this promise. She reports to her fellow Samaritans only that "he told me everything I ever did" (vv. 29, 39). Now, even though the Samaritans were not present to hear Jesus' earlier words on the universal worship of the Father, their confession realizes his promise.

---

[153] See O'Day, *Revelation*, 136 n. 112. T. Okure resorts to a poorly attested reading (*autou* rather than *autoi*) to lessen the tension between the reported word of the woman and the firsthand hearing of the word of Jesus (*Johannine Approach to Mission*, 173-74).

[154] For surveys, see Bernard, *St John*, 1:161-63; Schnackenburg, *St John*, 1:457-58.

[155] See Barrett, *St John*, 243: "The Samaritans speak the language of Johannine Christology."

Jesus, the messiah, is neither the savior of the Samaritans nor of the Jews – "an hour comes when neither on this mountain nor in Jerusalem will you worship the Father" (v 21) – but the savior of the world – "the true worshippers will worship the Father in spirit and truth" (v 23). True worship, worship in the spirit, constitutes a community beyond all earthly religious communities, a community of worship in which all of humanity is united. That is what the villagers recognise; it is the point of the story.[156]

This conclusion to Jesus' presence among the Samaritans parallels the final episode which took place between Jesus and a figure from the Jewish world in 3:22-36. There John the Baptist heard the word of the bridegroom, and rejoiced to hear that voice. Here the Samaritans hear the voice of Jesus and confess that this is indeed the savior of the world. After the difficult passage from no faith to partial faith on the part of the Samaritan woman, many of her Samaritan townsfolk believe because of the word of Jesus (vv. 41-42). The Samaritans' openness to the word of Jesus marks them out as examples of authentic Johannine faith.

Despite its brevity, this final scene is read by the implied reader as the climax of a long journey in Samaria. The journey has not been geographical, as once Jesus arrives at the well (vv. 1-6) he never moves from that place. Others come to him (vv. 7, 27, 30, 40) and go away from him (vv. 8, 28). The journey is a steady growth in the experience and the expression of faith. The Samaritan woman does not arrive at true Johannine faith in v. 25. Jesus' response to her in v. 26 is an attempt to transcend her messianic suggestions. He fails, as she goes back to the town, asking "Can this be the Christ?" (v. 29). Only in the final words of the Samaritan episode do non-Jews come to authentic Johannine faith: "We have heard for ourselves and we know that this is indeed the savior of the world" (v. 42). Their hearing of the word of Jesus (v. 41) leads them to true faith (v. 42).[157]

CONCLUSION

After an introduction (vv. 1-6), the narrator has concentrated on the Samaritan world. The theme of the Samaritans is the most obvious unifying feature of 4:1-42. The only exception is found in vv. 31-38, where the disciples listened to Jesus against a backdrop of approaching Samaritans (see v. 30). Throughout 4:1-42 the reader has met people from the non-Jewish world responding to the word of Jesus in different ways. Our

---

[156] Boers, *Neither on This Mountain*, 199-200; see also O'Day, *Revelation*, 88-89.
[157] Schnackenburg, *St John*, 1:456.

investigation has shown that the two encounters between Jesus and the Samaritan woman (vv. 7-15 and vv. 16-30) were structured in an identical fashion: the establishment of a relationship, Jesus' words transcending the basis of the relationship, the woman responding, a final intervention from Jesus, and the woman drawing conclusions on the basis of Jesus' words.

The criterion for true faith that emerged from the first Cana story (2:1-12) was belief in the word of Jesus. We have seen that the same criterion has been used through all Jesus' encounters with potential believers from the Jewish world (2:13–3:36). An identical pattern has emerged from this study of 4:1-42. As with the Jewish story, so also with the Samaritans, the narrator has told of three encounters with Jesus, during which the leading character(s) either refuse the word of Jesus, accept it in their own terms, or come to true faith because of it. During the Jewish story, the narrator paused after his first example (2:13-22: "the Jews") to reflect negatively on the role of Jesus' "signs" (2:23-25). During the non-Jewish story, the narrator paused before the final example (4:39-42: the Samaritans) to reflect positively, through the words of Jesus himself, on the importance of the "sign" of Jesus' life story (4:31-38).

Using sigla that reflect the parallels with 2:13–3:36,[158] an overall shape can now be suggested for the narrative of 4:1-42:

B¹] After an introduction to the section (4:1-6) an initial encounter takes place between Jesus and the Samaritan woman. She is unable to reach beyond her own limitations. When Jesus makes her an offer of a living spring, rising up in her to eternal life, she can only respond, rejecting the word of Jesus, in terms of ordinary water from a well that she must visit. The author presents the Samaritan woman, in the first instance, as a model of a lack of faith, rejecting the word of Jesus (4:7-15).

C¹] Jesus changes the direction of the conversation, establishing a discussion that leads the Samaritan woman to progress in her acceptance of Jesus as a prophet, and even to suggest that he might be the expected Messiah. He does not accept this suggestion but tries to lead her further by revealing himself to her as *egō eimi*. The word from Jesus is more than she can accept at this stage, so she returns to her town, still suggesting that Jesus might be the Christ. In this second encounter, the Samaritan woman is presented as an example of imperfect or partial faith, still caught within the

---

[158] On 2:13–3:36, see above, pp. 129–30.

limitations of her own knowledge and control, and thus not totally open to the word of Jesus (4:16-30).

X^1] *Drawing back from the narrative, the narrator has Jesus address a short discourse to the disciples. Through this discourse, the reader is told of the importance of the life story of Jesus, bringing to completion the task of his Father, and of the important association of the disciples in the ongoing story of a mission they did not initiate (4:31-38).*

D^1] In the final scene, where Samaritans play a major role, the Samaritan townsfolk move away from the partial faith of the woman, which was communicated to them through her word. They hear the word of Jesus and, on the basis of that hearing, come to know and confess that Jesus is the savior of the world. The Samaritans are models of authentic faith (4:39-42).

The implied reader has now been led through two journeys of faith. From 2:13–3:36 the reader encountered Jews who refused the word of Jesus, who accepted it under their conditions, and who opened themselves to it totally. From 4:1-42 the reader discovered that exactly the same journey can take place within the non-Jewish world of Samaria. The criterion behind all stories dealing with a variety of models of faith was provided by the first miracle at Cana (2:1-12). That narrative served as a conclusion to the series of days which opened the public ministry of Jesus (1:19-51), but it also introduced a new character, the mother of Jesus, in a very different setting. Through the miracle at Cana the reader discovered, after the puzzling conclusion to the first four days in 1:50-51, a radical faith in the word of Jesus (v. 5) which led to the revelation of the *doxa* of Jesus and initial faith for the disciples (v. 11). The implied reader has now met, in uninterrupted succession, examples of no faith (2:13-22//4:7-15), partial faith (3:1-21//4:16-30), and authentic faith (3:22-36//4:39-42). The first Cana miracle (2:1-12) provided the criterion for the reader to judge the characters in the ongoing story: belief in the word of Jesus. The reader will now find that the author confirms that criterion in a further encounter between Jesus and a non-Jew which closes this section of the Johannine narrative: the second miracle at Cana (4:43-54).

Chapter Seven

Faith in the Word of Jesus at Cana: John 4:43-54

❡ DOES THE MIRACLE STORY of 4:46-54 conclude the opening section of Jesus' public ministry, or does it introduce the section that follows? Several scholars read 4:46-54 as an introduction to chap. 5. They argue that 4:46-54 is a parabolic action about Jesus' gift of life and the power of the word, which transcends the witness of the old dispensation. The Fourth Evangelist regularly prefaces important discourses with actions (see 5:1-18; 6:1-15; 9:1-7). Thus, these scholars suggest that the miracle in 4:46-54 serves as a Johannine miracle that prefaces the discourse of 5:19-47. There the themes of Jesus as the giver of life and the authority of his word, previously acted out in the miracle of 4:46-54, are developed in discourse.[1]

Themes from chap. 5 may be adumbrated in 4:46-54, especially as Jesus gives life to the son of the official (see especially the repetition of the verb "lives" in vv. 50, 51, 53). The author may be using the familiar "bridge-passage" technique, leading the reader from one section of the narrative to the next. But the author is not primarily concerned with telling a miracle

---

[1] See especially C. H. Dodd, *The Interpretation of the Fourth Gospel* (Cambridge: Cambridge University Press, 1953) 318-19; A. Feuillet, "La signification théologique du second miracle de Cana (Jn IV, 46-54)," in *Etudes Johanniques* (Bruges: Desclée, 1962) 34-46. Feuillet offers a summary of the discussion. R. E. Brown, who opts for a Cana-to-Cana division, also suggests that 4:46-54 serves as an introduction to chaps. 5-10 (*The Gospel According to John* [2 vols.; AB 29, 29A; Garden City, N.Y.: Doubleday, 1966, 1970] cxli, 194-95).

story about the restoration of life. At the center of this account stands an encounter between an official and Jesus, where the miracle of the restoration to life is the result of an encounter in which the official believes in the word of Jesus. The author's main focus is not the miracle itself. There are obvious indications that the author wants the reader to link the two Cana miracles.[2] The implied reader has just read that Jesus stayed two days with the Samaritans (4:40). He now reads on to find "after the two days he departed to Galilee" (v. 43) and then "so he came again to Cana in Galilee" (v. 46). The author has no desire to use the formula "on the third day" here, because in 2:1 it had connections with Sinai traditions which have no place in the following narrative. Nevertheless, the reader is aware that Jesus comes to Cana the day after two days, as earlier he came to Cana on the third day (2:1).[3]

Even if these chronological hints are oversubtle, the narrator reminds the reader that Jesus "came again (*palin*) to Cana in Galilee" (v. 46). There is a repetition of the place, accompanied by the expression *palin*. The narrator then reminds the reader: "where he had made the water wine" (v. 46). As he concludes the story of a second miracle at Cana, the narrator once more recalls the earlier miracle at Cana: "This was now the second (*palin deuteron*) sign that Jesus did when he had come from Judea to Galilee" (v. 54). As well as the close link that exists for the reader between that statement and 2:11 – "This, the first of his signs, Jesus did at Cana in Galilee" – the *palin deuteron* links the whole of this narrative (v. 46 [*palin*] and v. 54 [*palin*]) with 2:1-12. K. Hanhart has remarked: "The curious word order *palin deuteron* implies that this second sign is a reiteration of the first sign or forms its logical complement."[4] The narrator wants the reader to recall the first miracle at Cana. The numbering of these two miracles as the first and the second miracles that Jesus performed at Cana is not the untidy remnant of an original signs source.[5] The reader relates the two miracles

---

[2] As A. Loisy remarks: "Il n'y a pas à se demander pourquoi Jésus revient à Cana, mais pourquoi l'évangeliste l'y ramène" (*Le quatrième évangile* [Paris: Emile Nourry, 1921] 194).

[3] See also M.-E. Boismard and A. Lamouille, *L'Evangile de Jean* (Synopse des Quatre Evangiles en Français III; Paris: Cerf, 1977) 144–45, 151–52. However, they link the three days with the resurrection, via Hos 6:2. I regard this as unlikely. See also R. Schnackenburg, *The Gospel according to St John* (3 vols.; HTCNT 4/1-3; London: Burns & Oates; New York: Crossroad, 1968–82) 1:462 n. 2.

[4] K. Hanhart, "The Structure of John I 35–IV 54," in *Studies in John: Presented to Professor Dr. J. N. Sevenster on the Occasion of His Seventieth Birthday* (NovTSup 24; Leiden: E. J. Brill, 1970) 29.

[5] I am not denying that they may have had their origins in some such source, but they are in the present Johannine text for a purpose. There are a number of indications that the

one to the other.[6] This is a hint that, as the first Cana miracle presented a model of authentic faith which led to a miracle and the faith of others (2:1-12), so might the second Cana miracle (4:43-54).[7]

THE SHAPE OF THE NARRATIVE

The transitional vv. 43-45 come from the narrator as commentary on the story thus far,[8] while some form of v. 46 would have already been part of the narrative of vv. 46-54 in its pre-Johannine stage. In the present text vv. 43-46 combine to provide a typically Johannine introductory statement.[9] The characters, the reason for Jesus' presence, the time, and the place of the following narrative are all provided. Once this has been established, the miracle story is told. However, as with 2:1-12, it cannot be described as a typical miracle story. It may have begun that way in the tradition, but its present form contains a number of elements that differ from the classical miracle story.[10] There is a strong resemblance between the narrative shape of 4:47-54 and that of the immediately preceding encounter between Jesus and the Samaritans (vv. 39-42). The Samaritans came to him on the word of the woman (v. 39), and they made a request of Jesus, to which he responded positively (v. 40). His presence led to a belief in his word (v. 41) and produced a fully Johannine profession of faith (v. 42). Even though the narratives deal with two quite different settings and events, 4:47-54 report the same sequence of events.

Thus, the narrative of 4:43-54 unfolds in the following way:

---

present form of this narrative is the result of a long history. For surveys of the evidence, see Schnackenburg, *St John*, 469-71; idem, "Zur Traditionsgeschichte von Joh 4,46-54," *BZ* 8 (1964) 70-76.

[6] See, for this case, the detailed analysis of F. Neirynck, *Jean et les Synoptiques: Examen critique de l'exégèse de M.-E. Boismard* (BETL 49; Leuven: University Press, 1979) 166-74.

[7] There are many similarities between John 4:46-54 and the Synoptic story of the centurion of Capernaum in Matt 8:5-13; Luke 7:1-10. There must have been contact between the Synoptic tradition (which has its own difficulties) and the Johannine tradition at a preliterary stage. For a survey of the discussion down to 1984, see F. Neirynck, "John 4,46-54: Signs Source and/or Synoptic Gospels," *ETL* 60 (1984) 367-75. Since then, see U. Wegner, *Der Hauptmann von Kafarnaum (Mt 7,28a; 8,5-10.13 par Lk 7,1-10): Ein Beitrag zur Q-Forschung* (WUNT 2, Reihe 14; Tübingen: J. C. B. Mohr [Paul Siebeck], 1985) 18-74.

[8] See C. H. Dodd, *Historical Tradition in the Fourth Gospel* (Cambridge: Cambridge University Press, 1963) 238-41.

[9] In the original story, some form of v. 46 would have been sufficient introduction. The addition of vv. 43-45 have firmly inserted the story from the tradition into its present place in the Gospel. See R. Bultmann, *The Gospel of John: A Commentary* (Oxford: Blackwell, 1971) 206.

[10] See Schnackenburg, *St John*, 1:469.

I. *Verses 43-46:* An introduction that presents the major characters in the subsequent narrative: Jesus (vv. 43, 46) and the official (v. 46); why Jesus goes to Galilee (v. 44); his welcome (v. 45); his presence in Cana of Galilee (vv. 45-46); and the time of his presence (vv. 43, 46).

II. Jesus and the official at Cana in Galilee
   (a) *Verse 47a:* The official goes to Jesus because he has heard about him from the Galileans.
   (b) *Verses 47b-49:* The narrator reports the official's request that Jesus heal his dying son. Despite an initial refusal, he perseveres in his request. His words to Jesus are now reported in direct speech.
   (c) *Verse 50a:* Jesus responds positively, in direct speech, to the official's persevering request.
   (d) *Verse 50b:* The official believes in the word of Jesus and sets out on his way.
   (e) *Verses 51-53:* The result of the official's belief in the word of Jesus is reported. The official "knows," and his household comes to believe in Jesus.
   (f) *Verse 54:* The narrator's closing comment, looking back to 2:1-12.

In comparison with the encounter between Jesus and the Samaritans (vv. 39-42), the request of the official is developed at greater length, for reasons that will emerge below, and the results of the man's faith in the word are also more complex. Yet the parallels are striking. In v. 54 the narrator sends the reader back to 2:1-12. Two different features are well combined here. There is a close link between the first and the second Cana miracle, which the narrator wishes to keep before the implied reader. Yet there is a parallel acceptance of the word of Jesus by the official and by the Samaritans in the narrative that immediately preceded. Although Augustine was commenting on 4:39-42, his words could be applied equally well to 4:47-54: "*Primo per famam, postea per praesentiam*" ("First by reputation, then by his presence") (*In Johannem* 15.33 [CCSL 36:164]).

READING THE NARRATIVE

The first matters raised in the introductory passage (vv. 43-46), widely regarded as "a notorious crux in the Fourth Gospel,"[11] are the questions of time and place. Looking back to v. 40, and forming an excellent transition,

---

[11] Brown, *John,* 187.

after two days he departed to Galilee (v. 43).[12] The problems begin with v. 44, where the narrator recalls a word of Jesus attested in the tradition (see Mark 6:4; Matt 13:57; Luke 4:24; see Luke 13:33-34) and gives the motive for Jesus' journey from Judea, through Samaria, into Galilee by reporting Jesus' testimony that a prophet has no honor in his own country.[13] The problem arises from the fact that the Christian reader takes it for granted that Jesus is from Nazareth (see, e.g., Matt 2:23) and that he is known as a Galilean (see, e.g., Mark 14:67-70).[14] Thus there is no immediate background in the Johannine story for this negative statement, and one wonders how his going into Galilee, which is his own country, can be motivated by such a remark.[15] The Matthean and the Lukan infancy narratives at least situate his birth in Bethlehem, a Judean village, but "this Gospel does not even tell us that Jesus was born in Judea."[16]

The reader is not aware of the traditional Christian background of Jesus. On only one occasion so far in the narrative has the reader been told that Jesus was from Nazareth. In 1:45 Philip told Nathanael: "We have found him of whom Moses in the law and also the prophets wrote, Jesus of Nazareth, the son of Joseph." In our study of that passage, however, we saw that Philip's presentation of Jesus as "of Nazareth" and "of Joseph" was wrong. The well-informed reader was able to reject Philip's statement because he had read of Jesus' origins in the prologue. The only other place in the narrative so far which may have indicated Galilean origins to the reader was the presence of the mother of Jesus at Cana (2:1). But this alone need not necessarily indicate to the reader that Jesus was a Galilean.[17]

---

[12] Most critics rightly point out that v. 43 picks up from v. 3, after the Samaritan interlude.

[13] This proverb is also found in profane literature. See the references in BAGD, 637; and W. Bauer, *Das Johannesevangelium erklärt* (HKNT 6; Tübingen: J. C. B. Mohr [Paul Siebeck], 1933) 77.

[14] See J. W. Pryor, "John 4:44 and the *Patris* of Jesus," *CBQ* 49 (1987) 254-58, for a study of Matt 13:57; Mark 6:4; Luke 4:24; *Papyrus Oxyrhynchus* 1 and the *Gospel of Thomas* 31, which concludes that the saying is derived from a narrative always attached to Nazareth which developed along two strands (represented by Mark and Luke).

[15] For a survey of scholars who understand Galilee/Nazareth as the *patris* of Jesus, see J. Willemse, "La patrie de Jésus selon saint Jean IV.44," *NTS* 11 (1964-65) 350-53.

[16] Brown, *John*, 187.

[17] M.-J. Lagrange writes: "On ne voit donc aucun moyen d'expliquer tout le passage selon les règles d'une logique stricte" (*Évangile selon saint Jean* [Ebib; Paris: Gabalda, 1936] 124). R. Schnackenburg suggests a variety of interpretations (*St Jean*, 462) but is forced to conclude "there is much to be said for the idea that the verse is a redactional gloss" (p. 463). So also J. H. Bernard, *A Critical and Exegetical Commentary on the Gospel according to St John* (2 vols.; ICC; Edinburgh: T. & T. Clark, 1928) 1:163-65; Brown, *John*, 187; J. Becker, *Das Evangelium des Johannes* (2 vols.; ÖTK 4/1-2; Gütersloh: Gerd Mohn; Würzburg: Echter-Verlag,

The Johannine narrative has its own view of Jesus' origins. The reader is aware that Jesus' origins are beyond human control as "in the beginning was the Word and the Word was turned in loving union toward God" (1:1).[18] However, in the light of 1:43, the first three days of Jesus' life story take place in Judea (1:19-42). His presence in Judea is not explicitly stated; it is taken for granted. The fourth day (1:43-51) and the following revelation of the *doxa* take place in Galilee (2:1-12). However, in 1:43 the narrator must explicitly state that Jesus decides to go to Galilee. These Galilean episodes conclude with Jesus and his entourage journeying away from Cana (2:12) and going up to Jerusalem (2:13). Since that time Jesus has been in Judea (2:13 – 3:36) or on his way from Judea to Galilee, via Samaria (4:1-42). Again, however, the reader has met the explicit statement from the narrator that Jesus left Judea and departed for Galilee (4:3, 43). The impression given by the narrative so far is that Jesus' habitual place of presence and activity is Judea, whatever the Synoptic Gospels may say to the contrary. The implied reader knows only what has been read so far in the Johannine story.

In terms of the narrative, Jesus is from Judea.[19] Each time he sets out for Galilee, the narrator tells the reader that Jesus is going on a journey away from his normal place of residence and activity. Once this is accepted, then v. 44 makes excellent sense to the reader. In Judea Jesus has met rejection from "the Jews" (2:13-22); many have come to him looking for miracles, but Jesus has not trusted himself to them (2:23-25); and the Jewish leader, Nicodemus, has been unable to accept Jesus' teaching (3:1-12). Jesus

---

1979, 1981) 1:185. G. R. Beasley-Murray also moves in this direction for both v. 44 and v. 48 (*John* [WBC 36; Waco: Word Books, 1987] 73). These are desperate measures.

[18] A. Loisy claims that the whole of Israel is the *patris* and that v. 44 is to be linked with 1:11: "He came to his own home, and his own people received him not" (*Quatrième évangile*, 192–93). See also G. Reim, "John IV.44 – Crux or Clue?" *NTS* 22 (1975-76) 476–80. R. L. Sturch argues for both Galilee and Judea, pointing out that Jesus has just come from the "foreign" Samaria ("The '*PATRIS*' of Jesus," *JTS* 28 [1977] 94–96). He does not make the link with the prologue. See also Pryor, "John 4:44," 261–63. R. H. Lightfoot (*St. John's Gospel*, ed. C. F. Evans [Oxford: Oxford University Press, 1956] 34–36) and J. Marsh (*Saint John* [The Pelican New Testament Commentaries; Harmondsworth: Penguin Books, 1968] 231–32) point beyond any earthly place to Jesus' real home in heaven. This is attractive, but see B. Lindars, *The Gospel of John* (NCB; London: Oliphants, 1972) 201.

[19] For this position, although on different grounds, see B. F. Westcott, *The Gospel According to Saint John* (London: John Murray, 1908) 77-78; E. C. Hoskyns, *The Fourth Gospel*, ed. F. N. Davey (London: Faber & Faber, 1947) 260–61; C. K. Barrett (*The Gospel according to St John* (London: SPCK, 1978) 246; Dodd, *Interpretation*, 352; Feuillet, "La signification théologique," 67–68. B. Lindars argues for Jerusalem as the meaning of the expression *patris* (see Luke 13:33) (*John*, 200–201). See also K. Matsunaga, "The Galileans in the Fourth Gospel," *Annual of the Japanese Biblical Institute* 2 (1976) 144–50; and especially Willemse, "La patrie de Jésus," 354–64.

has moved away from Judea because of the danger of hostility from the Pharisees (4:1). The implied reader has no difficulty in accepting the sentiments of Jesus, reported by the narrator: "a prophet has no honor in his own country" (v. 44).[20]

Part of the reason for Jesus' setting out for Galilee is because of the rejection and misunderstanding he received in Judea, understood by the reader as Jesus' own country, insofar as the Word who became flesh (1:14) can be regarded as having "his own country." A further reason for Jesus' going to Galilee is the welcome that he is given there (v. 45). However, the motivation for the welcome leaves the reader suspicious. Looking back to the feast of Passover that has just been celebrated (see 2:13, 23-25), the narrator reports that the Galileans had been in Jerusalem for the celebrations and had seen all the things Jesus had done there. The implied reader is aware that the Galileans are responding to Jesus in the same way as the Judeans, who "believed in his name when they saw the signs which he did" (see 2:23-25). The Galileans were at the same feast, and they have responded in the same fashion.[21]

The introduction is now concluded by v. 46. Repeating what he has already said in v. 45,[22] the narrator reports that Jesus came *again* to Cana in Galilee, and reminds the reader of the miracle Jesus had performed there. The reader has 2:1-12 in mind as he or she reads on. The narrator then blandly reports: "At Capernaum there was an official (*basilikos*) whose son was ill."[23] Informed of the time, the place, and the reason for the narrative that follows, the reader now meets the other major character, a *basilikos* whose son was ill. Was the *basilikos* a Jew or a Gentile? The question has been well surveyed in U. Wegner's recent monograph.[24] Wegner documents four possible meanings for *basilikos*: from royal blood, servants to a royal household, soldiers of either the Herodian kings or of the emperor, or royal scribe.[25] The context and the widespread use of the term in Josephus[26]

---

[20] Against C. H. Dodd (*Historical Tradition*, 239-40), who suggests that John may have regarded Judea, and especially Jerusalem, as Jesus' *patris*, but who then claims that "the Prophet had received an embarrassing degree of honour, or at least acceptance, there (IV,1)" (p. 240 n. 2). So also Sturch, "The '*PATRIS*' of Jesus," 95. This hardly fits the facts.

[21] See Schnackenburg, *St John*, 1:464.

[22] An indication that vv. 43-45 have been added by the real author to an already existent story that began with some form of v. 46.

[23] Some witnesses have *basiliskos*, which corresponds to the Latin *regulus*. It is certainly not original. See the discussion in Lagrange, *Saint Jean*, 125.

[24] See Wegner, *Hauptmann*, 57-72.

[25] Ibid., 57-60.

[26] For references, see Wegner, *Hauptmann*, 59 n. 8. See also Bauer, *Johannesevangelium*, 77.

suggest that the third of these meanings is intended by v. 46: a soldier of either Herod or the emperor. However, this solution does not answer the question posed: Jew or Gentile? A soldier in the service of Herod could be either.[27] It is tempting to resolve this problem by claiming that the *basilikos* parallels the Matthean and Lukan centurion, as a *hekatontarchēs* is certainly a Gentile, and most probably a Roman.[28] On the basis of the word itself and the difficult question of the relationship of the Johannine *basilikos* to the *hekatontarchēs* in the Synoptic tradition, a conclusive answer to the question posed cannot be found.[29] What can be claimed is that *both* are possible. The *basilikos* may be either Jewish or Gentile.[30]

The problem does not occur to the implied reader of the Fourth Gospel. In 2:1-12 a Jewish woman played a major role at a Jewish feast in Galilee. From 2:13-36 a series of Jewish people encountered Jesus and his word. From 4:1-42 this concentration on the world of Judaism disappeared. It was replaced by a series of events where Samaritans, people from a non-Jewish world, encountered Jesus and his word. Returning to Cana, the non-Jewish world is still present in the person of the *basilikos*. He is not from Cana, but from the border town of Capernaum. Arriving at v. 46 the reader accepts this figure from Capernaum, a town where a military presence was called for,[31] as a Gentile.[32]

Having thus introduced the narrative, the action begins in v. 47. As the Samaritans had heard from the woman that Jesus was able to tell her all she had ever done (v. 39), so also the official has "heard that Jesus had come from Judea to Galilee." There is a close link between v. 45, where the reader has been told that the Galileans welcomed Jesus because they had been in Jerusalem and had seen what he had done, and this "hear-

---

[27] Wegner, *Hauptmann*, 70. See also A. Schalit, *König Herodes: Der Mann und sein Werk* (Berlin: Walter de Gruyter, 1969) 167-83, on the structure and composition of Herod's army.

[28] See Wegner, *Hauptmann*, 60-69. There is considerable debate concerning which expression was primary in the tradition, *basilikos* or *hekatontarchēs*. See ibid., pp. 71-72 for a summary of current discussion.

[29] See, however, A. H. Mead ("The *basilikos* in John 4.46-53," *JSNT* 23 [1985] 69-72) who claims to muster sufficient evidence to say that the *basilikos* is a Gentile. Yet G. Schwarz ("'*kai ēn tis basilikos* . . .' [Joh 4,46]," *ZNW* 75 [1984] 138) suggests an Aramaic *Vorlage* meaning advisor to the king. K. Matsunaga argues that the man is a representative of the Galileans ("The Galileans," 157-58), and P. Perkins (*NJBC*, 958) simply affirms that he is "presumably a Jewish functionary of Herod's court."

[30] U. Wegner concludes: "ist eine sichere Entscheidung in dieser Frage nicht mehr möglich" (*Hauptmann*, 72).

[31] Brown, *John*, 190.

[32] Against Schnackenburg, *St John*, 1:466: "The evangelist does not seem to take any interest in whether he is a Jew or not."

ing" of the official.[33] The basis of the official's request, which is about to follow, is his hearing from the Galileans of the wonders that Jesus did in Jerusalem: *"primo per famam."* The Galileans also present Jesus on the basis of "all that he had done in Jerusalem at the feast" (v. 45). Because of this hearing, he approaches Jesus and begs him to come to Capernaum to heal his son.

As is typical of miracle stories, the gravity of the situation is accentuated: "for he was at the point of death." His first approach to Jesus is reported by the narrator in indirect speech. But there is more to it. Because of what the official heard from the Galileans, he has initiated his request to Jesus. Jesus responded immediately to the simple request of the Samaritans—who had heard from the woman—that he stay with them (v. 40). Now, in a more urgent situation of life and death, where one would expect that the Son who has been sent into the world as the savior of the world (see especially 3:16-17 and 4:42) would readily accede to the request, Jesus rebukes the official (v. 48).

Although the passage may be the result of a long history, v. 48 plays an important narrative role in the present redaction.[34] The use of the word *oun* in v. 48 makes a logical link between the request of the official (v. 47) and the basis of his request: the report of the Galileans who had come back from Jerusalem, telling about Jesus' works (v. 45). The enthusiasm of the Galileans parallels the faith of the people at the feast in Jerusalem, who believed in Jesus because of the signs he did (2:23-25). The official approaches Jesus with his request because he has heard that he is a wonder-worker.[35] The request of the official provides Jesus the chance to warn against "signs and wonders."[36] He does so, however, by addressing a plural

[33] Against Dodd (*Historical Tradition*, 238), who claims that v. 45 leads nowhere.

[34] E. Schweizer ("Die Heiligung des Königlichen, Joh 4,46-54," *EvTh* 11 [1951-52] 64-71) and E. Haenchen ("Johanneische Probleme," *ZTK* 56 [1959] 23-31) have both suggested that vv. 48-49 have been added to an original miracle story, as they contradict vv. 51-53. For a survey, see Schnackenburg, "Zur Traditionsgeschichte," 62-63. See, however, Boismard and A. Lamouille (*Jean*, 148), who claim that vv. 50b-53 were added to the original story to *reinforce* v. 48! B. Lindars suggests that the story ended at v. 50 and that vv. 51-54 are "a Johannine elaboration of the original story" (*John*, 204-5; quotation from p. 205). For a recent discussion of this question, without a personal conclusion, see G. van Belle, "Jn 4,48 et la foi du centurion," *ETL* 61 (1985) 167-69.

[35] See Schnackenburg, "Zur Traditionsgeschichte," 64-67. W. J. Bittner eliminates Jesus' rebuke (*Jesu Zeichen im Johannesevangelium: Die Messias-Erkenntnis im Johannesevangelium vor ihrem jüdischen Hintergrund* [WUNT 2, Reihe 26; Tübingen: J. C. B. Mohr (Paul Siebeck), 1987] 128-34). He claims that sentences with *ean mē . . . ou* [*mē*] are proverbial, and he thus translates v. 48 as a positive statement: "Wenn ihr nicht Zeichen und Wunder seht, werdet ihr nicht glauben." This strains the grammar and misses the parallel with 2:4.

[36] B. Lindars attractively suggests that this is the johannization of the Matthean version of the tradition: "Only say the word and my servant will be healed" (Matt 8:8) (*John*, 203).

audience: *ean mē sēmeia kai terata idēte* (v. 48b). The official forms part of the larger group, as his approach to Jesus is motivated by what he has heard from the Galileans (vv. 45, 47).[37] Here the reader meets the central theme of the passage. The implied reader is prepared for the theme which the words of Jesus introduce: belief.

The reader is by now aware that the narrator is not simply telling a story for the story's sake. The response of Jesus to the official is untypical of a miracle story, but it enables the author to introduce the central issue into the narrative: a right and fruitful relationship with Jesus is not built on the wonders he performs; it is built on belief in the word of Jesus. The man in the story does not know what that might mean, but the reader does.

The section of the narrative devoted to the request concludes as the official makes an even more urgent petition of Jesus, despite the sharp rebuke he has received (v. 49). "He [the narrator] heightens the narrative by stressing the urgency."[38] He does this by reporting the official's second request of Jesus in direct speech: "Sir, come down before my child dies" (v. 49), and through his introduction of the affectionate word *paidion*, "my little boy," into the words of the official.[39] But this is not the first time the reader has met perseverance in the face of a sharp response from Jesus. The implied reader met it in the first Cana miracle, where the mother of Jesus trusted in the word of Jesus, despite his distancing himself from her (2:4-5).[40] The reader recognizes this and is aware that such perseverance augurs well for a positive outcome from this encounter, as happened in the first Cana story.

Jesus accedes to the request, but he does it in his own way. With increasing insistence Jesus has been asked to "come down" (*katabainein*) to heal the son of the official, but Jesus remains the master of the situation. He responds to the official's request through his word, and not through his presence to the child. In direct speech, Jesus simply proclaims: "Go; your son lives" (v. 50a).[41] The well-informed reader experiences

---

[37] Lagrange, *Saint Jean*, 125–26.

[38] Lindars, *John*, 203.

[39] B. F. Westcott points to the use of the diminutive *paidion* as indicating "a faith, however imperfect, which springs out of fatherly love" (*St John*, 79).

[40] This parallel has been noticed by C. H. Giblin, "Suggestion, Negative Response and Positive Action in St John's Portrayal of Jesus" (John 2.1-11; 4.46-54; 7.2-14; 11.1-44)," *NTS* 26 (1979-80) 205; and X. Léon-Dufour, *Lecture de l'évangile selon Jean* (Parole de Dieu; Paris: Seuil, 1988) 408.

[41] Most English translations (see, e.g., RSV, NEB, NAB, NJB) accommodate the translation to a future tense, but the verb is a declaration rather than a promise (see, e.g., BJ and TOB). See Lagrange, *Saint Jean*, 126.

satisfaction on reading the narrator's report: *episteusen ho anthrōpos tō logō hon eipen autō ho Iēsous kai eporeueto* (v. 50b). After all that the reader has come to know and experience from the series of different responses to Jesus' word, from 2:1 down to these present words in 4:50, he or she is aware that true belief in Jesus is acted out in the description of the response of the man. The verb *pisteuein* opens the sentence. The man believed. There have been various examples of faith in the mother of Jesus, "the Jews," Nicodemus, John the Baptist, the Samaritan woman, and the Samaritan villagers. This man believed "in the word which Jesus spoke to him." The implied reader knows from the reading experience up to this point (see 2:5, 22; 3:29; 4:41-42) that this is a living out of authentic faith. The sentence ends with the man's wordless response, in action, to the command Jesus gave. Jesus commanded: "Go (*poreuou*)." This command has no other support except the word of Jesus: "your son lives." As a result of his unquestioning belief in the word of Jesus, "he went (*eporeueto*)": "*postea per praesentiam.*"[42]

In v. 51 the narrator tells of events that comment on the two parts of Jesus' words in v. 50: "Go; your son lives (*ho huios sou zē*)." The reader experiences the man "going down," confirming that the impression that this official had demonstrated authentic faith is true. The man's servants come out to meet him, announcing that his son lives (*ho pais autou zē*).[43] Should the reader simply wonder at the miracle and not make the connection between the man's belief in the word of Jesus and the fruits of that belief, the narrator has the official verify the details. This is the point of vv. 52-53a.[44] Whatever the background of vv. 52-53a in a possible original

---

[42] See, among many, Bittner, *Jesu Zeichen*, 125. Some scholars solve the tensions in the narrative created by the two moments of faith in vv. 50 and 53 by claiming that *pisteuein* followed by the dative does not reflect true faith. As C. K. Barrett puts it: "The man is not yet a Christian believer; contrast v. 53. He believes that what Jesus has said is true" (*St John*, 248). Within the Cana-to-Cana section of the Gospel it is impossible to say that he is not a Christian believer, if "he believes that what Jesus has said is true." The overall context and especially the parallel with 2:1-12 must be noticed. Although it may be generally true, one cannot claim that *pisteuein eis* always indicates true Johannine faith, while *pisteuein en* or *pisteuein*+dative is *always* a lesser faith. Thus far, for example, the reader has met *pisteuein eis* in 2:23 (incorrect faith), *pisteuein*+ dative in 2:22 (correct faith), *pisteuein en* in 3:15 (correct faith), *pisteuein dia* in 4:39 (incorrect faith), and *pisteuein dia* in 4:41 (correct faith).

[43] Reading *pais*, along with the best manuscripts. Origen and some Western texts read *huios*. This has been accepted by G. D. Kilpatrick ("John IV:51, *PAIS* or *HUIOS*?" *JTS* 14 [1963] 393) but refused by E. D. Freed ("John IV.51, *PAIS* or *HUIOS*?" *JTS* 16 [1965] 448–49).

[44] Most commentators point to vv. 51-53 as creating a tension in the narrative. The "word faith" of v. 50b seems to be compromised by the faith produced by a verified miracle in vv. 51-53. Does this not prove that Jesus' accusation in v. 48 is true? For this position, see Schnackenburg, *St John*, 1:467–68. This problem is eased if v. 50b is not regarded as an act of faith. See

miracle story, it shows the reader that true faith in the word of Jesus bears
fruit. This has already been indicated in the first Cana miracle (2:6-10) and
is repeated here. The official's request of the time when the boy began to
mend receives the response that the fever left the boy at the seventh hour
of the previous day.[45] The Samaritan townsfolk's belief in the word of Jesus
led them to knowledge (see vv. 41-42). The same thing happens with the
official. For the first time in his encounter with Jesus the reader discovers
that he comes to "know." His act of commitment to the word of Jesus (v. 50)
was not based on anything except the word itself. Now he "knows" (*egnō*)
that his response to Jesus' word has initiated the process. As in the experience of the Samaritans (see vv. 41-42) faith in the word produces not only
the miracle but also knowledge.

For a third time, the words of Jesus are repeated: "The father knew
that was the hour when Jesus said to him *ho huios sou zē*" (v. 53). The reader
is aware that the man is developing a right relationship with Jesus that
begins with faith in the word. Only on the basis of a prior unconditional
faith in Jesus' life-giving word does the royal official arrive at knowledge:
the word matches the facts. This is in contrast to the knowledge of the
first disciples ("we have found": 1:41, 45) and Nicodemus ("we know":
3:2). The continual repetition of the words of Jesus' direct speech, "your
son lives," keeps the primacy of the word of Jesus before the reader. Faith
in the word of Jesus has led to knowledge.[46]

The final comment from the narrator creates difficulties, as the reader
is again told: "and he himself believed (*kai episteusen autos*)" (v. 53b). This
is the second time the official is reported to have come to belief. Thus
theories have developed about the various traditions which have con-
fusedly been blended to compose this narrative, leaving behind a clumsy
repetition.[47] It is not possible that there are two moments of faith in the

---

n. 42. In the light of the parallel experience of the Samaritans in vv. 41-42, vv. 51-53a can
be read as a movement from faith to knowledge. M. M. Thompson (*The Humanity of Jesus
in the Fourth Gospel* [Philadelphia: Fortress Press, 1988] 72-75) defends the unity of the passage
claiming, with E. Haenchen (*John 1-2* [2 vols.; Hermeneia; Philadelphia: Fortress Press, 1984]
1:235) that in v. 50 the man believes that his son will live and in v. 53 he believes in Jesus.

[45] Given the difficulty in locating Cana, speculations or symbolic readings on the basis
of the improbable length of the journey are not helpful. See especially Loisy, *Quatrième évangile*,
196-97. See the study of the many suggestions for the interpretation of "seven" in B. P. Robinson, "The Meaning and Significance of 'The Seventh Hour' in John 4:52," in *Studia Biblica
1978: II, Papers in The Gospels: Sixth International Congress on Biblical Studies, Oxford 3-7 April
1978*, ed. E. A. Livingstone (JSNTSup 2; Sheffield: JSOT Press, 1980) 255-62.

[46] See Bittner, *Jesu Zeichen*, 259-82.

[47] Many scholars suggest that the man came to faith because of the miracle, and thus
vv. 50-53 would be original. See, e.g., Schnackenburg, "Zur Traditionsgeschichte," 67-70.

reported experience of the man. He commits himself to faith in the word of Jesus in v. 50. The function of v. 53bc is to close the narrative in a way that parallels 2:11. The first Cana miracle is close to the implied reader throughout his reading of vv. 46-54. The narrator has reminded the reader of it in v. 46. Thus the reader is waiting for the further fruits of the man's act of authentic faith. In 2:1-12 not only does the mother of Jesus place all her trust in the word of Jesus and thus act as the catalyst that produces the wine from the water, but this act of faith leads to the faith of others, the disciples (v. 11). The disciples' belief is reported by the narrator.

Similarly here, the narrator tells the reader that the man himself believed in the word of Jesus (v. 50), but this belief is also shared by all his household. The use of the same main verb *episteusen* for both the official and his whole household is certainly difficult for the interpretation I am following. It suggests that they all came to belief at the same time. However, given the parallel with 2:1-12, the verb must be read as a complexive rather than an ingressive aorist. The whole experience of the official is a reflection of his belief, and through it his household also believed. "The servants have confirmed the official's faith, but in so doing have themselves discovered faith."[48] Giving the *autos* its full value one could paraphrase v. 53b: "Not only did he believe, but also his whole household believed."[49]

A closer reading of the text provides further information in support of this interpretation. Taking a hint from R. H. Lightfoot,[50] one can see a progression in the narrator's presentation of the official. He begins the story as a *basilikos* (vv. 46, 49). This is a description of his political and social function. However, there is more to the *basilikos* than his function, and the use of the affectionate term *paidion* is our first hint of this. When the narrator reports the official's act of faith, he tells the reader that the official is an *anthrōpos* (v. 50). The hint of v. 49b has been carried further through the act of faith. At the end of the story, when his whole household joins him in his belief in Jesus, he is called *ho patēr* (v. 53). "A certain official" (v. 46) who had trusted completely in the word of Jesus to become "the man" (v. 50) is now "the father" (v. 53), whose faith (v. 50) and knowledge (v. 53a) generate faith in others (v. 53b). True Johannine faith is not only a personal commitment to the word of Jesus; it leads others to faith. This has been shown in both Cana miracles, where commitment to the word

[48] Lindars, *John,* 205.

[49] See Schnackenburg, *St John,* 1:461; G. Zevini, *Vangelo secondo Giovanni* (2 vols.; Commenti Spirituali del Nuovo Testamento; Rome: Città Nuova, 1984, 1987) 179-80.

[50] Lightfoot, *St John,* 129; see also Zevini, *Giovanni,* 178 n. 90.

of Jesus (2:5; 4:50) leads to the faith of others (2:11; 4:53c). This truth also lies behind the Samaritan episodes, where faith in the word of the woman (v. 39) has eventually been transcended by faith in the word of Jesus himself (v. 41) to produce knowledge and a confession of true faith (v. 42). Here an initial faith based upon the report of the Galileans (vv. 45-47) has been transcended by faith in the word of Jesus (v. 50) to produce true faith (v. 53).[51]

The final statement from the narrator is, as we have seen, a deliberate attempt to remind the reader of the link between the two Cana miracles. Not only does the narrator's use of *palin deuteron sēmeion* of 4:54 force the reader to recall the *archēn tōn sēmeiōn* of 2:11, but the two Cana stories conclude in contrasting fashion. In 2:12 the narrator gathered all the actors from the miracle story and sent them on their way. The implied reader follows them through the many events reported in 2:13–4:42. In 4:54, however, instead of looking further into the narrative yet to come, the narrator looks back. Thus, 2:1-12 looked forward to 4:43-54, while 4:43-54 looks back to 2:1-12.[52]

CONCLUSION

The link between the two Cana miracle stories is very strong. By now the reader is aware that he or she has been deliberately taken from one Cana story to another, via a series of encounters between Jesus and Jews and a further series of encounters between Jesus and non-Jews. As the first Cana story, which opened the Jewish responses to Jesus, had a Jewish woman as the first example of authentic faith, so now the reader finds that the series of non-Jewish responses to Jesus is terminated by a final example of perfect faith, from a Gentile official.

The author may well be using traditional miracle stories in both Cana accounts, but they have been radically rewritten to suit the purposes of the present narrative. We have seen that the first Cana miracle is untypical of a miracle story. We have also noticed, through our reading of 4:46-54,

[51] The missionary background of this faith of the household is widely recognized; see especially Boismard and Lamouille, *Jean*, 150–51; also J. Gnilka, *Johannesevangelium* (NEchtB 4; Würzburg: Echter-Verlag, 1989) 38.

[52] Most scholars who attempt to reconstruct the signs source link 2:12 with 4:46-54. See, e.g., Bultmann, *John*, 205–6; R. T. Fortna (*The Fourth Gospel and its Predecessor: From Narrative Source to Present Gospel* (Studies in the NT and its World; Edinburgh: T. & T. Clark, 1989) 58–65; Boismard and Lamouille, *Jean*, 146, 149–50. They generally miss the point of v. 54.

that similar problems emerge with this version of the curing of the official's son.[53] The problems that the first Cana miracle created for a typical miracle account reappear: the negative reaction of Jesus to the person making the request; belief in the word as the catalyst that sets the cure in motion; the miracle itself not reported in any way and a lessening of interest in the theme of wonder from the witnesses. Instead, the household comes to share in the faith of the official. Indeed, the parallels between the two Cana miracles are most evident where they differ from the traditional miracle form. The relationship that binds these two miracle accounts can be seen from the following presentation of the narratives in parallel.[54]

	2:1-12	4:43-54
1.	*Problem:* "The wine failed" (v. 3).	*Problem:* "An official whose son was ill" (v. 46).
2.	*Request:* "The mother of Jesus said to him, 'They have no wine'" (v. 3).	*Request:* "He went down and begged him to come down and heal his son" (v. 47).
3.	*Rebuke:* "O woman, what have you to do with me?" (v. 4).	*Rebuke:* "Unless you see signs and wonders you will not believe" (v. 48).
4.	*Reaction:* "His mother said to the servants, 'Do whatever he tells you' (*ho ti an legē hymin poiēsate*)" (v. 5).	*Reaction:* "'Go, your son will live.' The man believed *the word* that Jesus spoke to him (*episteusen ho anthrōpos tō logō hon eipen autō ho Iēsous*)" (v. 50).
5.	*Consequence:* A miracle which leads to the faith of others (the disciples) (vv. 6-11).	*Consequence:* A miracle which leads to the faith of others (the household) (vv. 51-53).

---

[53] Again R. Bultmann, as in his analysis of 2:1-12, claims that the story reflects traditional miracle stories (*John*, 207 n. 1, and 208 nn. 3, 9-10). For some indications of the strangeness of the Johannine form of the account, see Perkins, *NJBC*, 958.

[54] This parallel was noticed by Bauer, *Johannesevangelium*, 78: "Die Geschichte baut sich übrigens ganz auf wie das erste Kanawunder 2:1-12: Bitte, schroffe Abweisung, Fortdauer des Vertrauens, Erhörung."

The two Cana miracles serve as a literary frame around a series of episodes where a variety of people from the life story of Jesus respond to his word. The first of these miracles provided the reader with a suggested criterion for judging authentic faith – faith in the word of Jesus. The second Cana miracle confirms such a suggestion. On arriving at 4:54 the reader is aware that he or she has now been instructed on the nature of a right relationship with Jesus. The implied reader knows that the parallel between "receiving" and "believing" in 1:12 has to happen in real life. It happens when the potential believer abandons his or her absolutes and trusts only in the word of Jesus.

As well as the close link between 2:1-12 and 4:43-54, which thus frames the whole of 2:1–4:54, we have also seen that the internal structure of 4:43-54 repeats that of 4:39-42. In both cases Augustine's words are true: *"primo per famam, postea per praesentiam."* The second Cana miracle not only looks back to the first Cana miracle for its meaning. It is the conclusion of a series of responses to the word of Jesus which has taken place in the non-Jewish world. The reader discovers that not only in Israel but also among the Samaritans and the Gentiles one can refuse the word of Jesus (4:7-15), accept it under one's own conditions (4:16-30), or come to authentic faith by committing oneself unconditionally to Jesus' word (4:39-42, 43-54).[55]

---

[55] See Lightfoot, *St John*, 128. Against the symbolic reading of 4:52 by B. P. Robinson ("Seventh Hour," 259-61). He links the seventh hour of 4:52 with the sixth hour of 4:6, concluding that the faith of the Samaritan woman is symbolized by the strong light of the full sun (midday), while the faith of the official is of a lesser intensity, symbolized by the waning sun (1:00 P.M.).

Chapter Eight

Looking Back

❡ THE IMPLIED READER, having arrived at 4:54, is the product of the process of reading John 1:1–4:54. I am now in a position to summarize the spatial and temporal dimensions of that reading process. The author has brought the implied reader to a point where he or she has both experienced and come to know who Jesus is and how to respond to him. It has not been a simple process. The fight has been athwart, rather than along, ideological boundaries. But the omniscient and omnipotent author has his way.[1] Despite the implied reader's awareness of who Jesus is, provided by the prologue, the reader may be tempted to regard the disciples' messianic confessions of Jesus in 1:35-51 as satisfactory. The prologue does not necessarily suggest that Jesus' followers must reach beyond the highest messianic hopes of Israel. Even in the prologue the Logos, the Son of God (1:14), was given the name "Jesus Christ" (v. 17).

Against a background of four days of preparation (1:19-51) for the gift of the glory "on the third day" (2:1-12), the reader experiences a series of events that mark the general preparation for the gift of the glory (1:19-42: the first three days). The first of the final three days (1:43-51: the fourth day of preparation) was marked by an increasing initiative of Jesus in the

---

[1] See M. Sternberg, _The Poetics of Biblical Narrative: Ideological Literature and the Drama of Reading_ (ILBS; Bloomington: Indiana University Press, 1985) 494–95.

action and a significant confession of faith from Nathanael. It has neverthe-less shown the reader that there must be more to the Christian response than the acceptance of Jesus as the Messiah. The mounting drama of a growing christological confession across these first four days (1:20, 21, 24, 29, 33, 34, 36, 38, 41, 49), coming to a climax in Nathanael's confession of Jesus as a rabbi, Son of God and King of Israel, proves to be an imperfect response to Jesus. Jesus promises the sight of "greater things" (1:50). Explicitly linked to this promise is the need for greater faith: "Because I said to you I saw you under the fig tree, do you believe?" (1:50). But the promise, along with its inherent requirement of faith, is not just for the disciples. The words of Jesus' promise in v. 51 indicate that the reader is part of the present tense of the verb (*kai legei*) and the plural form of address (*amen, amen, legō hymin*).

The author has brought the reader close to a point of acceptance of Nathanael's confession that Jesus is "the Son of God" (1:49), a confession that is superficially coherent with the witness of the prologue (1:14, 18) and the reliable testimony of the Baptist (1:34). He then intrudes Jesus' question to Nathanael: "Because I said to you I saw you under the fig tree do you believe?" (1:50). More than the christological confession of Nathanael and the attachment to Jesus implied thereby is needed from the disciples. A greater faith will produce a greater sight: the revelation of God himself in and through the Son of Man (1:51). In the Johannine narrative the search for truth is best expressed in terms of a quest for a right relationship between the disciple-believer and Jesus. The reader has already been told the conditions for a right relationship. The implied reader has already read in the prologue: "But to all who received him (*hosoi de elabon auton*), who believed in his name (*tois pisteusousin eis to onoma autou*), he gave power to become children of God; who were born, not of blood nor of the will of the flesh nor of the will of a human being, but of God" (1:12-13). Arriving at 1:50-51, the reader is at a point somewhere between a culturally conditioned faith and true believing. The reader asks what more is required from the commitment in faith of disciples who wish to "follow" Jesus.

The real author composes a narrative and shapes an implied reader to create in real readers a desire to "follow" Jesus (see 1:37, 39-40, 43, 46). The prologue has indicated *that* a parallel exists between "receiving" and "believing" (1:12-13), but the reader needs to be shown *how* this takes place. Thus, the reader concludes a reading of the first days asking what more is required. The story of the response of the first disciples shows that "greater things" will be seen, depending on a belief in Jesus that is not based on either a recognition of his messianic role (see 1:20, 21, 25, 38, 41, 45, 49) or his power as a miracle worker (1:48-50). The Sinai background to these first "days" of the story is now clear to the reader. The first four days are *preparation* for the gift of the glory. In the Johannine narrative, disciples are *prepared* for the gift of the glory at Cana (see 2:11), and the reader must read further to discover *how*, in the life of Jesus, the glory is revealed and *how* the disciple is to respond to the revelation of the glory of God in Jesus.

The section of the Gospel that now follows (2:1–4:54) presents some memorable Johannine characters, especially Nicodemus (3:1-21), John the Baptist (3:22-30) and the Samaritan woman (4:7-30).[2] But the author did not write the Gospel to tell stories from the past about the community's significant foundational figures. The author is not interested in them for their own sakes. The theme that unites all the accounts of Jesus' encounters with these characters is the variety of responses his presence and especially his word elicits from them. The reader's understanding and experience of a right relationship with Jesus emerge as the narrative unfolds.

Within the frame of the two Cana miracles, where a Jewish woman (2:5) and a Gentile official (4:50) commit themselves to the word of Jesus and thereby bring others to believe in Jesus (2:11, 4:53), the author has assembled a series of narratives with both a Jewish (2:13–3:36) and a non-Jewish (4:1-42) setting.[3] The story of Jesus' journey from Cana to Cana (2:1–4:54) has been told in the following way:

A] **At Cana the mother of Jesus, a Jewish woman, demonstrates a radical openness to the word of Jesus. This faith triggers a miracle in which Jesus manifests his glory, and the disciples see and believe for the first time. The author has used the mother of Jesus to show the reader a model of authentic faith and to describe the consequences of such belief (2:1-12).**

B] After the purification of the Temple, "the Jews," who ask for a sign, refuse to accept Jesus' word on the raising of the temple of his body. The author presents "the Jews" to the reader as models of a *lack of faith*, rejecting the words of Jesus (2:13-22).

---

[2] On the characters of the Johannine narrative, see the survey of R. F. Collins, "The Representative Figures in the Fourth Gospel," *DRev* 94 (1976) 26–46, 118–32; R. A. Culpepper, *Anatomy of the Fourth Gospel: A Study in Literary Design* (Philadelphia: Fortress Press, 1983) 99–148.

[3] M. M. Thompson remarks that one of the peculiarities of both 2:1-11 and 4:46-54 is "the lack of explicit connection with any discourse, dispute, or debate" (*The Humanity of Jesus in the Fourth Gospel* [Philadelphia: Fortress Press, 143 n. 11]). My suggested shape of the narrative from Cana (2:1) to Cana (4:54) explains this "peculiarity."

X] *Drawing back from the narrative, the author speaks directly to the reader, criticizing the quality of a faith that draws people to Jesus because of the signs he did (2:23-25).*

C] The nocturnal discussion with Nicodemus is used by the author to show the reader an example of the people described in 2:23-25. While there is much that is positive in Nicodemus's approach to Jesus and Jesus' patient attempts to draw Nicodemus beyond his own "knowledge," he falls short of true faith at this stage of the narrative. His failure is rooted in his inability to accept Jesus' word about rebirth from above. He is only able to raise questions about a second birth, and thus is only partially open to the radical newness that is produced "from above." Nicodemus is presented to the implied reader as an example of *imperfect and partial faith*, caught within the limitations of his own knowledge and control, and thus not open to the word of Jesus (3:1-21).

D] In a final scene where Jewish characters play a major role, John the Baptist describes his relationship to Jesus as one of listening for the voice of the bridegroom, rejoicing in the sound of that voice, even though he must now decrease. The author has taken the reader a further step in his description of a possible response to Jesus. He has used John the Baptist as a model of *authentic faith* (3:22-36).

B'] After an introduction to the Samaritan section of the narrative (4:1-6), an initial encounter takes place between Jesus and the Samaritan woman. She is unable to reach outside her own limitations. When Jesus makes her an offer of a living spring, rising up to eternal life, she can only respond, rejecting the words of Jesus, in terms of ordinary water from a well that she must visit. The author presents the Samaritan woman, in the first instance, as a model of a *lack of faith*, rejecting the words of Jesus (4:7-15).

C'] Jesus changes the direction of the conversation, establishing a discussion that leads her to progress in her acceptance of Jesus as a prophet, and even to suggest that he might be the expected Messiah. He does not accept this suggestion but tries to lead her further by revealing himself to her as *egō eimi*. The word from Jesus is more than she can accept at this stage, so she returns to her town, still suggesting that Jesus might be the Christ. In this second encounter, the Samaritan woman is presented as an example of *imperfect or partial faith*, still caught within the limitations of her own knowledge and control, and thus not totally open to the word of Jesus (4:16-30).

X'] *Drawing back from the narrative, the narrator has Jesus address a short discourse to the disciples. Through this discourse, the reader is told of the importance of the life story of Jesus, bringing to completion the task of his Father, and of the association of the disciples in the ongoing story of a mission they did not initiate (4:31-38).*

D'] In the final scene where Samaritans play a major role, the Samaritan townsfolk move away from the partial faith of the woman, which was communicated to them through her word. They hear the word of Jesus, and as a consequence of a belief based on a hearing of the word, they come to know and confess that Jesus is the savior of the world. The Samaritans have been used by the narrator as models of *authentic faith* (4:39-42).

A'] **Jesus returns to Cana, where a royal official, a Gentile, demonstrates a radical openness to the word of Jesus. This faith triggers a miracle in which Jesus' life-giving word is revealed. Faith in the word produces knowledge, and the official's whole household also comes to faith. The author has used the Gentile royal official to show the reader a model of authentic faith and to describe the consequences of such faith (4:43-54).[4]**

Throughout the analysis of 2:1–4:54, it has also emerged that the author not only developed his themes to unfold this simple but effectively shaped narrative; he has made further links within the story to hold the reader's interest and to focus attention on his point of view. The first Cana miracle (A: 2:1-12), beginning a series of events that take place in a Jewish world, and the purification of the Temple (B: 2:13-22) were paired by an identical narrative shape. The same pairing is found in the shape of Jesus' encounter with Nicodemus (C: 3:1-21) and the Baptist's final witness (D: 3:22-36), both of which continued the story of Jesus' presence to Israel. A parallel technique appeared in the section of the story devoted to the non-Jewish world. Jesus' first (B': 4:7-15) and second (C': 4:16-30) encounter with the Samaritan woman were shaped in an identical fashion. The same pairing continued in Jesus' presence to the Samaritans (D': 4:39-42) and

---

[4] I have indicated several times throughout my study that true belief leads to the faith of others. 2:1-12 and 4:43-54 are examples of this. Many studies of the Fourth Gospel that stress the sectarian nature of the Johannine Gospel ignore the presence of a carefully nuanced missionary idea. See, however, the recent studies of T. Onuki, *Gemeinde und Welt im Johannesevangelium: Ein Beitrag zur Frage nach der theologischen und programatischen Funktion des johanneischen "Dualismus"* (WMANT 56; Neukirchen-Vluyn: Neukirchener Verlag, 1984), esp. 83–115; and D. Rensberger, *Johannine Faith and the Liberating Community* (Philadelphia: Westminster Press, 1988) 144–50.

the second Cana miracle (A': 4:43-54).[5] On two occasions the narrator has drawn back from the telling of the story to comment directly to the implied reader. In 2:23-25 (X), immediately *following* the very first example of faith in the Jewish world, the narrator pointed to the limitations of a faith based purely on signs. Then, in 4:31-38 (X'), immediately *preceding* the final example of faith from the non-Jewish world, the narrator has Jesus himself speak about the importance of his own life as a response to the will of his Father and of the future mission of the disciples, continuing the life story of Jesus. The theme of faith in the word is not found in 2:23-25 and 4:31-38, but they relate antithetically to one another and make an important point for the reader.

To believe in Jesus because of the wonderful things he does is insufficient (2:23-25), but anyone who disregards Jesus' life and mission, and especially his self-giving love to accomplish the task of his Father (4:31-38), fails to appreciate the real author's decision to write what we have come to call a Gospel. He attempts to touch real readers through the telling of a story based on the events of the life, death, and resurrection of Jesus.[6]

---

[5] Many others have seen the question of faith as an important element in the structure and theology of 2:1–4:54. See, e.g., R. E. Brown, *The Gospel According to John* (2 vols.; AB 29, 29A; Garden City, N.Y.: Doubleday, 1966, 1970) cxliii–cxliv; G. Segalla, *Giovanni* (NVB 36; Rome: Edizioni Paoline, 1976) 163–64. See also R. H. Strachan, *Fourth Gospel: Its Significance and Environment* (3rd ed.; London: SCM Press, 1941) 128–65; H. van den Bussche, "La structure de Jean I-XII," in *L'Evangile de Jean: Etudes et problèmes* (RechBib 3; Bruges: Desclée de Brouwer, 1958) 76–88; I. de la Potterie, "Structura primae partis Evangelii Johannis (Capita III et IV)," *VD* 47 (1969) 137–39; idem, "Ad dialogum Jesu cum Nicodemo (2.23–3.21): Analysis literaria," *VD* 47 (1969) 141–50. De la Potterie has been followed by S. A. Panimolle, *Lettura Pastorale del Vangelo di Giovanni* (3 vols.; Bologna: Dehoniane, 1978–84) 1:201; and G. Zevini, *Vangelo secondo Giovanni* (2 vols.; Commenti Spirituali del Nuovo Testamento; Rome: Città Nuova, 1984, 1987) 127–28. See the critique of de la Potterie by L. J. Topel ("A Note on the Methodology of Structural Analysis in Jn 2:23–3:21," *CBQ* 33 [1971] 211–20) and the critique of van den Bussche by E. Galbiati, "Nota sulla struttura del 'libro dei segni' (Gv. 2-4)," *Euntes Docete* 25 (1972) 139–44. Both Topel and Galbiati suggest alternative structures.

[6] The problem of the function of the "signs" in the Fourth Gospel emerges. On the basis of 2:23-25 and 4:31-38, which we have seen, and the conclusion of the Gospel in 20:30-31, it can be claimed that there is a deliberately contrived tension in the narrative. Most studies of the signs adopt some form of the Bultmannian position that the Gospel reflects a signs source that is being corrected by the Evangelist. See, for a survey, H.-P. Heekerens, *Die Zeichen-Quelle der johanneischen Redaktion: Ein Beitrag zur Entstehungsgeschichte des vierten Evangeliums* (SBS 113; Stuttgart: Katholisches Bibelwerk, 1984) 17–43. A few take the opposite position that there is no tension. For this latter position, see the study of W. J. Bittner, *Jesu Zeichen im Johannesevangeliums: Die Messias-Erkenntnis im Johannesevangelium vor ihrem jüdischen Hintergrund* (WUNT 2, Reihe 26; Tübingen: J. C. B. Mohr [Paul Siebeck], 1987). I do not accept the Bultmannian position, but I also feel that Bittner has eliminated a tension that is intended by the author. The narrative demands that the reader somehow resolve the tension created by the presence of both the positive and the negative assessment of the signs. See, e.g.,

CONCLUSION

To believe in the "word of Jesus" does not mean to accept the sounds his mouth produces as he forms sentences. That is part of it, but the reader is aware that Jesus Christ *is* the Word. Acceptance of the word of Jesus is unconditional trust and commitment to all that his words and his deeds reveal, cost what it may. The narrative makes that clear. The examples used by the author to open and close 2:1—4:54, the mother of Jesus and the royal official, have trusted in Jesus, despite his rebuke (2:4; 4:48); John the Baptist joyfully listens for the voice of the bridegroom, aware that he must now disappear from center stage (3:29-30). The author involves the reader in the narrative. The reader of the narrative is not simply informed of responses that the word and person of Jesus elicited from a variety of characters from Judaism and in Samaria during his historical presence among us. The reading experience itself challenges the reader with the central significance of belief in the word of Jesus for *anyone* who desires to establish a right relationship with him.[7] The two Cana miracles told the reader about a Jewish woman (2:1-12) and a Gentile official (4:43-54) who believed in the word of Jesus. Stories about Jews (2:13—3:36) and non-Jews (4:1-42) alike who reject Jesus' word, only partially accept it, or accept it unconditionally teach the reader the universal possibility of a right relationship with Jesus.[8]

The reading experience of 1:1—4:54 has been marked by a variety of characters, but at a deeper level it has led the reader into a challenging story about the Son of God who becomes human and the demands he makes upon all those who would be his followers. Yet despite the strangeness of the message, especially for a reader familiar with the traditions of Judaism, the implied reader is now instructed in some of the most

---

M. de Jonge, "Signs and Works in the Fourth Gospel," in *Miscellanea Neotestamentica*, ed. T. Baarda, A. F. J. Klijn, and W. C. van Unnik (SuppNovT 48; Leiden: E. J. Brill, 1978) 107-25; and Thompson, *Humanity of Jesus*, 53–86. For a survey, see R. Kysar, "The Fourth Gospel: A Report on Recent Research," *ANRW* 2.25.3, pp. 2398-2402.

[7] See G. R. O'Day, *Revelation in the Fourth Gospel: Narrative Mode and Theological Claim* (Philadelphia: Fortress Press, 1986) 89-90: "The reader encounters Jesus and his revelation, but . . . he or she does so through the narrative itself. The narrative is therefore not expendable but is a central element of the revelatory experience."

[8] Many scholars contrast the failure of "the Jews" with the success of the Samaritans. See, e.g., R. Kysar, *John's Story of Jesus* (Philadelphia: Fortress Press, 1984) 31. Both Jews and Samaritans have the same experience (no belief, conditioned belief, and true belief). The author is not interested primarily in contrasting Jews and Samaritans but in communicating to the reader the universal possibility of true belief.

important Johannine beliefs. As the reader looks back, he or she can recognize a reading experience that perturbs but that unfolds according to a plotted spatial and temporal design.

The narrative shape that I have traced is extremely simple, but effective.[9] It appears to me, therefore, that E. Haenchen is only partially correct when he claims:

> The Evangelist was not a master storyteller nor an overpowering poet. Whenever possible, he was satisfied to take the tradition that came to him and to make that tradition serve his proclamation by as few intrusions as possible. The Evangelist was not interested in a unified style or in a polished narrative; he wanted only to effect the correct teaching, as he understood it.[10]

It is true that the author is not a master storyteller nor an overpowering poet. Although he has his moments, there are times when perhaps he tries to do too much (see, e.g., 1:29-34; 3:10-15; 4:2, 34-38), and his characters, for all the space he gives to them, are not highly developed.[11] It is also true that he has used the tradition that came to him in order to offer what is, in his judgment, correct teaching. But he has done this with considerable skill, at least for John 1:1—4:54.

[9] I am unable to develop the point here, but the narrative shape of 2:1—4:54 that I have just outlined is an example of synthetic parallelism which matches the structure of the prologue. Also there, framed between the statement and restatement of 1:1 and 1:18, we found threefold development of the same themes (1:1-5, 6-14, 15-18).

[10] E. Haenchen, *John 1-2* (2 vols.; Hermeneia; Philadelphia: Fortress Press, 1984) 1:86.

[11] S. D. Moore rightly states: "Narrative criticism is a story-preoccupied gospel criticism. Being preoccupied with story means, most of all, being preoccupied with *plot* and *character*" (*Literary Criticism and the Gospels: The Theoretical Challenge* [New Haven: Yale University Press, 1989] 14). From what we have seen, R. A. Culpepper is correct when he describes the role of characters in the Fourth Gospel as "(1) to draw out various aspects of Jesus' character successively by providing a series of diverse individuals with whom Jesus can react, and (2) to represent alternative responses to Jesus so that the reader can see their attendant misunderstandings and consequences" (*Anatomy*, 145). The characters are thus "flattened" by their subordination to the author's plot.

Bibliography

REFERENCE WORKS AND SOURCES

Aland, K., and B. Aland, eds. *Novum Testamentum Graece*. 26th ed. Stuttgart: Deutsche Bibelstiftung, 1979.

Aland, K., M. Black, C. M. Martini, B. M. Metzger, and A. Wikgren, eds. *The Greek New Testament*. 3rd ed. Stuttgart: United Bible Societies, 1975.

Bauer, W., W. F. Arndt, and F. W. Gingrich. *A Greek-English Lexicon of the New Testament and Other Early Christian Literature*. 2nd ed. rev. and augmented by F. W. Gingrich and F. W. Danker. Chicago: University of Chicago Press, 1979.

Blass, F., and A. Debrunner. *A Greek Grammar of the New Testament and Other Early Christian Literature*. Rev. and trans. R. W. Funk. Chicago: University of Chicago Press, 1961.

Boismard, M.-E., and A. Lamouille. *Synopsis Graeca Quattuor Evangeliorum*. Leuven/Paris: Peeters, 1986.

Brown, F., S. R. Driver, and C. A. Briggs. *A Hebrew and English Lexicon of the Old Testament with an Appendix containing the Biblical Aramaic*. Oxford: Clarendon Press, 1907.

Brown, R. E., J. A. Fitzmyer, and R. E. Murphy, eds. *The New Jerome Biblical Commentary*. Englewood Cliffs, N.J.: Prentice Hall, 1989.

Colson, F. H., G. H. Whitaker, J. W. Earp, and R. Marcus, eds. *Philo*. 12 vols. LCL. London: William Heinemann; Cambridge, Mass.: Harvard University Press, 1929–1953.

Danby, H. *The Mishnah Translated from the Hebrew with Introduction and Brief Expository Notes*. Oxford: Clarendon Press, 1933.

Elliger, K., and K. Rudolph. *Biblia Hebraica Stuttgartensia*. Stuttgart: Deutsche Bibelgesellschaft, 1983.

Epstein, I., ed. *The Babylonian Talmud*. 35 vols. London: Soncino, 1948–52.

Kittel, G., and G. Friedrich, eds. *Theological Dictionary of the New Testament*. 10 vols. Grand Rapids: Eerdmans, 1964–76.

Lauterbach, J., ed. and trans. *Mekilta de Rabbi Ishmael*. 3 vols. Philadelphia: Jewish Publication Society of America, 1961.

Liddell, H., R. Scott, and A. S. Jones. *A Greek-English Lexicon*. Oxford: Clarendon Press, 1968.

Metzger, B. M. *A Textual Commentary on the Greek New Testament*. London/New York: United Bible Societies, 1971.

Moulton, J. H., W. F. Howard, and N. Turner. *A Grammar of New Testament Greek*. 4 vols. Edinburgh: T. & T. Clark, 1909–1976.

Neusner, J. *The Tosefta Translated from the Hebrew: Third Division Nashim (The Order of Women)*. New York: Ktav, 1979.

Pirot, L., A. Robert, and H. Cazelles, eds. *Dictionnaire de la Bible Supplement*. Paris: Letouzey, 1928–.

Rahlfs, A., ed. *Septuaginta: Id est Vetus Testamentum Graece iuxta LXX Interpretes*. 2 vols. 8th ed. Stuttgart: Württembergische Bibelanstalt, 1965.

Strack, H., and P. Billerbeck. *Kommentar zum Neuen Testament aus Talmud und Midrasch*. 6 vols. Munich: C. H. Beck, 1922–61.

Temporini, H., and W. Hasse, eds. *Aufstieg und Niedergang der römischen Welt*. Berlin: Walter de Gruyter, 1981–.

Thackeray, H. St. J., R. Marcus, A. Wikgren, and L. H. Feldman, eds. *Josephus*. 9 vols. LCL. London: William Heinemann; Cambridge, Mass.: Harvard University Press, 1926–65.

van Belle, G. *Johannine Bibliography 1966–1985: A Cumulative Bibliography on the Fourth Gospel*. BETL 82. Leuven: University Press, 1988.

Zerwick, M. *Biblical Greek Illustrated by Examples*. Rome: Biblical Institute Press, 1963.

COMMENTARIES ON THE FOURTH GOSPEL

Aurelii Augustini. *In Johannis Evangelium.* CCSL 36. Turnhout: Brepols, 1954.

Barrett, C. K. *The Gospel according to St John.* London: SPCK, 1978.

Bauer, W. *Das Johannesevangelium erklärt.* HKNT 6. Tübingen: J. C. B. Mohr [Paul Siebeck], 1933.

Beasley-Murray, G. R. *John.* WBC 36. Waco: Word Books, 1987.

Becker, J. *Das Evangelium des Johannes.* 2 vols. ÖTK 4/1–2. Gütersloh: Gerd Mohn; Würzburg: Echter-Verlag, 1979, 1981.

Bernard, J. H. *A Critical and Exegetical Commentary on the Gospel according to St John.* 2 vols. ICC. Edinburgh: T. & T. Clark, 1928.

Boismard, M.-E., and A. Lamouille. *L'Evangile de Jean. Synopse des Quatre Evangiles en Français III.* Paris: Cerf, 1977.

Brown, R. E. *The Gospel According to John.* 2 vols. AB 29, 29a. Garden City, N.Y.: Doubleday, 1966, 1970.

Bultmann, R. *Das Evangelium des Johannes.* MeyerK. Göttingen: Vandenhoeck & Ruprecht, 1941.

———. *The Gospel of John: A Commentary.* Oxford: Blackwell, 1971.

Calloud, J., and F. Genuyt. *L'Evangile de Jean (I): Lecture sémiotique des chapitres 1 à 6.* Lyon: Centre pour l'Analyse du Discours Religieux, 1989.

Delebecque, E. *Evangile de Jean: Texte Traduit et Annoté.* CahRB 23. Paris: Gabalda, 1987.

Gnilka, J. *Johannesevangelium.* NEchtB 4. Würzburg: Echter-Verlag, 1989.

Haenchen, E. *John 1–2.* 2 vols. Hermeneia. Philadelphia: Fortress Press, 1984.

Hoskyns, E. C. *The Fourth Gospel.* Ed. F. N. Davey. London: Faber & Faber, 1947.

Lagrange, M.-J. *Évangile selon saint Jean.* Ebib. Paris: Gabalda, 1936.

Léon-Dufour, X. *Lecture de l'évangile selon Jean.* Parole de Dieu. Paris: Seuil, 1988. vol. 1.

Lightfoot, R. H. *St. John's Gospel.* Ed. C. F. Evans. Oxford: Oxford University Press, 1956.

Lindars, B. *The Gospel of John.* NCB. London: Oliphants, 1972.

Loisy, A. *Le quatrième évangile.* Paris: Emile Nourry, 1921.

Marsh, J. *Saint John.* The Pelican New Testament Commentaries. Harmondsworth: Penguin Books, 1968.

Panimolle, S. A. *Lettura Pastorale del Vangelo di Giovanni.* 3 vols. Bologna: Dehoniane, 1978–84.

Perkins, P. "The Gospel according to John." In *NJBC*, 942–85.

Schnackenburg, R. *The Gospel according to St John*. 3 vols. HTCNT 4/1–3. London: Burns & Oates; New York: Crossroad, 1968-82.

Segalla, G. *Giovanni*. NVB 36. Rome: Edizioni Paoline, 1976.

Sloyan, G. *John*. Interpretation. Atlanta: John Knox, 1988.

van den Bussche, H. *Jean: Commentaire de l'Évangile Spirituel*. Bruges: Desclée de Brouwer, 1976.

Westcott, B. F. *The Gospel According to Saint John*. London: John Murray, 1908.

Zevini, G. *Vangelo secondo Giovanni*. 2 vols. Commenti Spirituali del Nuovo Testamento. Rome: Città Nuova, 1984, 1987.

OTHER LITERATURE

Abrahams, I. *Studies in Pharisaism and the Gospels*. Cambridge: Cambridge University Press, 1917. First Series.

Abrams, M. H. *A Glossary of Literary Terms*. 5th ed. New York: Holt, Rinehart & Winston, 1988.

Albright, W. F. "Some Observations Favoring the Palestinian Origin of the Gospel of John." *HTR* 17 (1924) 189–95.

Aletti, J.-N. *L'art de raconter Jésus Christ*. Paris: Seuil, 1989.

Alter, R. *The Art of Biblical Narrative*. New York: Basic Books, 1981.

———. *The Art of Biblical Poetry*. New York: Basic Books, 1985.

Alter, R., and F. Kermode, eds. *The Literary Guide to the Bible*. London: Collins, 1987.

Anderson, J. C. "Matthew, Gender and Reading." *Semeia* 28 (1983) 3–27.

Arens, E. *The ELTHON Sayings in the Synoptic Tradition: A Historico-Critical Investigation*. OBO 10. Freiburg: Universitätsverlag; Göttingen: Vandenhoeck & Ruprecht, 1976.

Ashton, J. "The Identity and Function of the *Ioudaioi* in the Fourth Gospel." *NovT* 27 (1985) 40–75.

———. "The Transformation of Wisdom: A Study of the Prologue of John's Gospel." *NTS* 32 (1986) 161–86.

Ashton, J., ed. *The Interpretation of John*. Issues in Religion and Theology 9. London: SPCK, 1986.

Auerbach, E. *Mimesis: The Representation of Reality in Western Literature*. Princeton, N.J.: Princeton University Press, 1953.

Bar-Efrat, S. *Narrative Art in the Bible*. JSOTSup 70, BLS 17. Sheffield: Almond Press, 1989.

Barosse, T. "The Seven Days of the New Creation in St. John's Gospel." *CBQ* 23 (1959) 507–16.

Barrett, C. K. *The Gospel of John and Judaism.* London: SPCK, 1975.

———. "The Prologue of St John's Gospel." In *New Testament Essays,* 27–48. London: SPCK, 1972.

Barton, J. "Reading the Bible as Literature: Two Questions for Biblical Critics." *Literature and Theology* 1 (1987) 135–53.

Bassler, J. M. "Mixed Signals: Nicodemus in the Fourth Gospel." *JBL* 108 (1989) 635–46.

Berlin, A. *Poetics and Interpretation of Biblical Narrative.* Sheffield: Almond Press, 1983.

Betz, O. "'To Worship God in Spirit and in Truth': Reflection on John 4:20-26." In *Standing Before God: Studies on Prayer in Scriptures and in Tradition with Essays in Honor of John M. Oesterreicher,* ed. A. Finkel and L. Frizzell. New York: Ktav, 1981.

Bishop, J. "Encounters in the New Testament." In *Literary Interpretations of Biblical Narratives,* ed. K. R. R. Gros Louis, 2:285–94. Nashville: Abingdon, 1982.

Bittner, W. J. *Jesu Zeichen im Johannesevangelium: Die Messias-Erkenntnis im Johannesevangelium vor ihrem jüdischen Hintergrund.* WUNT 2, Reihe 26. Tübingen: J. C. B. Mohr (Paul Siebeck), 1987.

Black, M. *An Aramaic Approach to the Gospels and Acts.* 3rd ed. Oxford: Clarendon Press, 1967.

Blank, J. *Krisis: Untersuchungen zur johanneischen Christologie und Eschatologie.* Freiburg: Lambertus Verlag, 1964.

Bligh, J. "Jesus in Samaria." *HeyJ* 3 (1962) 329–46.

Boers, H. *Neither on This Mountain Nor in Jerusalem.* SBLMS 35. Atlanta: Scholars Press, 1988.

———. "Discourse Structure and Macro-Structure in the Interpretation of Texts: John 4:1-42 as an Example." In *Society of Biblical Literature 1980 Seminar Papers,* ed. P. Achtemeier, 159–82. Chico, Calif.: Scholars Press, 1980.

Boismard, M.-E. "Aenon, près de Salem." *RB* 80 (1973) 218–29.

———. "L'ami de l'époux (Jo III, 29)." In *A la Rencontre de Dieu: Mémorial Albert Gelin,* ed. A. Barucq, J. Duplacy, and A. George, 289–95. Le Puy: Xavier Mappus, 1961.

———. "'Dans le sein du Père' (Jn 1,18)." *RB* 59 (1952) 23–39.

———. *Du Baptême à Cana (Jean 1,19–2,11).* LD 18. Paris: Cerf, 1956.

———. *Moïse ou Jésus: Essai de Christologie Johannique.* BETL 84. Leuven: University Press, 1988.

——. "Saint Luc et la rédaction du Quatrième Evangile." *RB* 69 (1962) 185–211.

——. *St. John's Prologue.* London: Blackfriars, 1957.

Boismard, M.-E., and A. Lamouille. *Les Actes des deux Apôtres.* 2 vols. Ebib. Paris: Gabalda, 1990.

Booth, W. *The Rhetoric of Fiction.* 2nd ed. Chicago: University of Chicago Press, 1983.

Borgen, P. "Logos was the True Light: Contributions to the Interpretation of the Prologue of John." In *Logos was the True Light and Other Essays on the Gospel of John,* 95–110. Relieff 9. Trondheim: Tapir, 1983.

Bowman, J. "Samaritan Studies I: The Fourth Gospel and the Samaritans." *BJRL* 40 (1958) 298–327.

Braun, F.-M. "Avoir soif et boire (Jn 4,10-14; 7,37-39)." In *Mélanges Bibliques en hommage au R. P. Béda Rigaux,* ed. A. Descamps and A. de Halleux, 247–58. Gembloux: Duculot, 1970.

——. *Jean le Théologien II: Les grandes traditions d'Israel, L'accord des Ecritures d'après le Quatrième Evangile.* Ebib. Paris: Gabalda, 1964.

Braun, H. *Qumran und das Neue Testament.* 2 vols. Tübingen: J. C. B. Mohr (Paul Siebeck), 1966.

Briend, J. "Puits de Jacob." *SDB* 9, cols. 386–98.

Brown, R. E. *The Epistles of John.* AB 30. New York: Doubleday, 1982.

——. "The 'Mother of Jesus' in the Fourth Gospel." In *L'Evangile de Jean: Sources, rédaction, théologie,* ed. M. de Jonge, 307–10. BETL 44. Leuven: University Press, 1977.

Bultmann, R. "Die Bedeutung der neueschlossenen mandäischen und manichäischen Quellen für das Verständnis des Johannesevangeliums." *ZNW* 24 (1925) 100–46.

——. *The History of the Synoptic Tradition.* Oxford: Blackwell, 1963.

Burge, G. M. *The Anointed Community: The Holy Spirit in the Johannine Community.* Grand Rapids: Eerdmans, 1987.

Byrne, B. J. *"Sons of God—Seed of Abraham": A Study of the Idea of Sonship of God of All Christians in Paul against the Jewish Background.* AnBib 83. Rome: Biblical Institute Press, 1979.

Cahill, P. J. "Narrative Art in John IV." *Religious Studies Bulletin* 2 (1982) 41–48.

Cannon, K. G., and E. Schüssler Fiorenza, eds. *Interpretation for Liberation.* Semeia 47. Atlanta: Scholars Press, 1989.

Cantwell, L. "Immortal Longings in Sermone Humili: A Study of John 4.5-26." *SJT* 36 (1983) 73–86.

Carmichael, C. M. "Marriage and the Samaritan Woman." *NTS* 26 (1979–80) 332–46.

Carter, W. "The Prologue and John's Gospel: Function, Symbol and the Definitive Word." *JSNT* 39 (1990) 35-58.

Cassem, N. H. "A Grammatical and Contextual Inventory of the use of *kosmos* in the Johannine Corpus with some Implications for a Johannine Cosmic Theology." *NTS* 19 (1972-73) 81-91.

Chatman, S. *Story and Discourse: Narrative Structure in Fiction and Film.* Ithaca, N.Y.: Cornell University Press, 1978.

Cholin, M. "Le Prologue de l'Evangile selon Jean: Structure et Formation." *ScEs* 41 (1989) 189-205, 343-62.

Collins, A. Y. "Narrative, History and Gospel." *Semeia* 43 (1988) 145-53.

Collins, R. F. "Cana (Jn. 2:1-12) – The first of his signs or the key to his signs?" *ITQ* 47 (1980) 79-95.

———. "Mary in the Fourth Gospel – a decade of Johannine Studies." *Louvain Studies* 3 (1970) 99-142.

———. "The Representative Figures in the Fourth Gospel." *DRev* 94 (1976) 26-46, 118-32.

Combe, M. "Jésus baptise et cesse de baptiser en Judée: Jean 3,22-4,3." *ETR* 53 (1978) 97-102.

Cosgrove, C. H. "The Place where Jesus is: Allusions to Baptism and the Eucharist in the Fourth Gospel." *NTS* 35 (1989) 522-39.

Cross, F. M. "Aspects of Samaritan and Jewish History in Late Persian and Hellenistic Times." *HTR* 59 (1966) 201-11.

Culler, J. *On Deconstruction: Theory and Criticism after Structuralism.* London: Routledge & Kegan Paul, 1983.

Cullmann, O. *Early Christian Worship.* SBT 10. London: SCM Press, 1953.

———. *The Johannine Circle: Its place in Judaism, among the disciples of Jesus and in early Christianity: A study in the origin of the Gospel of John.* London: SCM Press, 1976.

———. "Samaria and the Origins of the Christian Mission." In *The Early Church*, ed. A. J. B. Higgins, 185-92. London: SCM Press, 1956.

Culpepper, R. A. *Anatomy of the Fourth Gospel: A Study in Literary Design.* Philadelphia: Fortress Press, 1983.

———. "Commentary on Biblical Narratives." *Forum* 5,3 (1989) 87-102.

———. "The Gospel of John and the Jews." *RevExp* 84 (1987) 273-88.

———. "The Johannine *hypodeigma*: A Reading of John 13:1-38." *Semeia* 53 (1991) 133-52.

———. *The Johannine School: An Evaluation of the Johannine School Hypothesis Based on an Investigation of the Nature of Ancient Schools.* SBLDS 26. Missoula, Mont.: Scholars Press, 1975.

———. "The Pivot of John's Prologue." *NTS* 27 (1981) 1–31.

Dagonet, P. *Selon Saint Jean: Une Femme de Samarie*. Paris: Cerf, 1979.

Dalman, G. *The Words of Jesus*. Edinburgh: T. & T. Clark, 1902.

Daube, D. *The New Testament and Rabbinic Judaism*. London: Athlone, 1956.

Davies, W. D. *The Setting of the Sermon on the Mount*. Cambridge: Cambridge University Press, 1966.

de Fiores, S., and S. Meo, eds. *Nuovo Dizionario di Mariologia*. Rome: Edizioni Paoline, 1985.

de Goedt, M. "Un schème de révélation dans le Quatrième Evangile." *NTS* 8 (1961–62) 142–50.

de Jonge, M. "Nicodemus and Jesus: Some Observations on Misunderstanding and Understanding in the Fourth Gospel." *BJRL* 53 (1970–71) 337–59.

———. "Signs and Works in the Fourth Gospel." In *Miscellanea Neotestamentica*, ed. T. Baarda, A. F. J. Klijn, and W. C. van Unnik, 107–25. NovTSup 48. Leiden: E. J. Brill, 1978.

de la Potterie, I. "Ad dialogum Jesu com Nicodemo (2.23-3.21): Analysis literaria." *VD* 47 (1969) 141–50.

———. "'C'est lui qui a ouvert la voie'. La finale du prologue johannique." *Bib* 69 (1988) 340–70.

———. "*Charis* paulinienne et *charis* johannique." In *Jesus und Paulus: Festschrift für Werner Georg Kümmel zum 70. Geburtstag*, ed. E. E. Ellis and E. Grässer, 252–82. Göttingen: Vandenhoeck & Ruprecht, 1975.

———. "L'emploi dynamique de *eis* dans Saint Jean et ses incidences théologiques." *Bib* 43 (1962) 366–87.

———. "Jesus et Nicodemus: de necessitate generationis ex Spiritu (Jo 3:1-10)." *VD* 47 (1969) 194–214.

———. "Naître de l'eau et naître de l'Esprit." *ScEccl* 14 (1962) 351–74.

———. "La notion de 'commencement' dans les écrits johanniques." In *Die Kirche des Anfangs: Festschrift für Heinz Schürmann zum 65. Geburtstag*, ed. R. Schnackenburg et al., 379–403. Leipzig: St. Benno-Verlag, 1977.

———. "'Nous adorons, nous, ce que nous connaissons, car le salut vient des Juifs': Histoire de l'exégèse et interprétation de Jn 4,22." *Bib* 64 (1983) 74–115.

———. "*oida* et *ginōskō*: Les deux modes de connaissance dans le quatrième évangile." *Bib* 40 (1959) 709–25.

———. "Structura primae partis Evangelii Johannis (Capita III et IV)." *VD* 47 (1969) 130–40.

———. "Structure du Prologue de Saint Jean." *NTS* 30 (1984) 354–81.

——. "L'emploi dynamique de *eis* dans Saint Jean et ses incidences théologiques." *Bib* 43 (1962) 366–87.

Delling, G. "*plērēs ktl.*" *TDNT* 6:283–311.

Derrett, J. D. M., "Water into Wine." *BZ* 7 (1963) 80–97.

de Vaux, R. *Ancient Israel: Its Life and Institutions.* London: Darton, Longman & Todd, 1961.

Dewey, K. "*Paroimiai* in the Gospel of John." *Semeia* 17 (1980) 81–99.

Dexinger, F. *Der Taheb: Ein "messianischer" Heilsbringer der Samaritaner.* Kairos, Religionswissenschaftliche Studien 3. Salzburg: Otto Müller, 1986.

Diaz, J. R. "Palestinian Targum and New Testament." *NovT* 6 (1963) 75–80.

Dodd, C. H. "Dialogue Form in the Gospels." *BJRL* 37 (1954–55) 54–67.

——. *Historical Tradition in the Fourth Gospel.* Cambridge: Cambridge University Press, 1963.

——. *The Interpretation of the Fourth Gospel.* Cambridge: Cambridge University Press, 1953.

Duke, P. D. *Irony in the Fourth Gospel.* Atlanta: John Knox Press, 1985.

Edwards, R. B. "*Charin anti charitos* (John 1.16): Grace and Law in the Johannine Prologue." *JSNT* 32 (1988) 3–15.

Eslinger, L. "The Wooing of the Woman at the Well: Jesus, the Reader and Reader-response Criticism." *Literature and Theology* 1 (1987) 167–83.

Fennema, D. A. "John 1:18: 'God the only Son.'" *NTS* 31 (1985) 121–35.

Feuillet, A. "La signification théologique du second miracle de Cana (Jn IV, 46–54)." In *Etudes Johanniques*, 34–46. Bruges: Desclée, 1962.

Fish, S. *Is There a Text in This Class? The Authority of Interpretative Communities.* Cambridge, Mass.: Harvard University Press, 1980.

Filoramo, G. *A History of Gnosticism.* Oxford: Blackwell, 1990.

Forestell, J. T. *The Word of the Cross: Salvation as Revelation in the Fourth Gospel.* AnBib 57. Rome: Biblical Institute Press, 1974.

Fortna, R. T. *The Fourth Gospel and its Predecessor: From Narrative Source to Present Gospel.* Studies in the NT and its World. Edinburgh: T. & T. Clark, 1989.

——. *The Gospel of Signs: A Reconstruction of the Narrative Source Underlying the Fourth Gospel.* SNTSMS 11. Cambridge: Cambridge University Press, 1970.

Fowler, R. M. "Postmodern Biblical Criticism." *Forum* 5,3 (1989) 3–30.

——. "Who is 'the Reader' in Reader-Response Criticism?" *Semeia* 31 (1985) 5–23.

Freed, E. D. "*Ego eimi* in John 1:20 and 4:25." *CBQ* 41 (1979) 288–91.

——. "John IV.51, PAIS or UIOS?" *JTS* 16 (1965) 448–49.

———. "The Manner of Worship in John 4:23f." In *Search the Scriptures: New Testament Studies in Honor of Raymond T. Stamm,* 33–48. Gettysburg Theological Studies 3. Leiden: E. J. Brill, 1969.

Freund, E. *The Return of the Reader: Reader-Response Criticism.* New Accents. London: Methuen, 1987.

Friedrich, G. *Chi è Gesù? Il messagio del quarto evangelista nella pericopa della samaritana.* Biblioteca Minima di Cultura Religiosa. Brescia: Paideia, 1975.

Frye, N. *The Great Code: The Bible and Literature.* New York: Harcourt Brace Jovanovich, 1982.

Gaeta, G. *Il dialogo con Nicodemo.* Studi Biblici 26. Brescia: Paideia, 1974.

Galbiati, E. "Nota sulla struttura del 'libro dei segni' (Gv. 2-4)." *Euntes Docete* 25 (1972) 139–44.

Genette, G. *Narrative Discourse: An Essay in Method.* Ithaca, N.Y.: Cornell University Press, 1980.

———. *Nouveau discours du récit.* Collection Poétique. Paris: Seuil, 1983.

Geoltrain, P. "Les noces à Cana: Jean 2,1-12: Analyse des structures narratives." *Foi et Vie* 73 (1974) 83–90.

Gerhart, M. "The Restoration of Biblical Narrative." *Semeia* 46 (1989) 13–29.

Gese, H. "Der Johannesprolog." In *Zur biblischen Theologie: Alttestamentliche Vorträge,* 152–201. Munich: Kaiser, 1977.

Geyser, A. "The Semeion at Cana of the Galilee." In *Studies in John: Presented to Professor Dr. J. N. Sevenster on the Occasion of His Seventieth Birthday,* 12-21. NovTSup 24. Leiden: E. J. Brill, 1970.

Giblin, C. H. "Suggestion, Negative Response, and Positive Action in St John's Gospel (John 2.1-11; 4.46-54; 7.2-14; 11.1-44)." *NTS* 26 (1979–80) 197–211.

Goguel, M. *Jean-Baptiste.* Paris: Payot, 1928.

Grassi, J. A. "The Wedding at Cana (John II 1-11): A Pentecostal Meditation?" *NovT* 14 (1972) 131–36.

Grayston, K. "Who Misunderstands the Johannine Misunderstandings?" *ScrB* 20 (1989) 9–15.

Greeven, H. "proskyneō," *TDNT* 6:758–66.

Grossouw, W. "La glorification du Christ dans le quatrième Evangile." In *L'Evangile de Jean: Etudes et Problèmes,* 131–45. RechBib 3. Bruges: Desclée de Brouwer, 1958.

Groupe de Jura. "Jean 4: Jésus en Samarie." *Sémiotique et Bible* 12 (1978) 36–40.

Haacker, K. "Gottesdienst ohne Gotteserkenntnis: Joh 4,22 vor dem Hintergrund des jüdisch-samaritanischen Auseinandersetzung." In *Wort und*

Wirklichkeit: Studien zur Afrikanistik und Orientalistik Eugen Ludwig Rapp zum 70. Geburtstag Herausgegeben, ed. B. Benzing, O. Böcher, and G. Mayer, 110–26. Meisenheim: Hain, 1976.

Haenchen, E. "Johanneische Probleme." *ZTK* 56 (1959) 19–54.

Hahn, F. "'Das Heil kommt von den Juden': Erwägungen zu Joh 4,22b." In *Wort und Wirklichkeit: Studien zur Afrikanistik und Orientalistik Eugen Ludwig Rapp zum 70. Geburtstag Herausgegeben*, ed. B. Benzing, O. Böcher, and G. Mayer, 67–84. Meisenheim: Hain, 1976.

———. "'Die Juden' im Johannesevangelium." In *Kontinuität und Einheit: Für Franz Mussner*, ed. P.-G. Müller and W. Stenger, 430–38. Freiburg: Herder, 1981.

———. "Die Jüngerberufung Joh 1,25-51." In *Neues Testament und Kirche: Für Rudolf Schnackenburg*, ed. J. Gnilka, 172–90. Freiburg: Herder, 1974.

Hall, B. W. *Samaritan Religion from John Hyrcanus to Baba Rabba: A critical examination of the relevant material in contemporary Christian literature, the writings of Josephus, and the Mishnah.* Studies in Judaica 3. Sydney: Sydney University Press, 1987.

Hamerton-Kelly, R. G. *Pre-Existence, Wisdom and the Son of Man.* SNTSMS 21. Cambridge: Cambridge University Press, 1973.

Hanhart, K. "The Structure of John I 35–IV 54." In *Studies in John: Presented to Professor Dr. J. N. Sevenster on the Occasion of His Seventieth Birthday,* 21–46. NovTSup 24. Leiden: E. J. Brill, 1970.

Hanson, A. T. "John 1:14-18 and Exodus XXXIV." *NTS* 23 (1976–77) 90–101.

Hayward, C. T. R. "The Holy Name of the God of Moses and the Prologue of St John's Gospel." *NTS* 25 (1978–79) 16–32.

Heekerens, H.-P. *Die Zeichen-Quelle der johanneischen Redaktion: Ein Beitrag zur Entstehungsgeschichte des vierten Evangeliums.* SBS 113. Stuttgart: Katholisches Bibelwerk, 1984.

Hemelsoet, B. "L'ensevelissement selon Saint Jean." In *Studies in John: Presented to Professor Dr. J. N. Sevenster on the Occasion of His Seventieth Birthday,* 47–65. NovTSup 24. Leiden: E. J. Brill, 1970.

Hengel, M. *The Zealots: Investigations into the Jewish Freedom Movement in the Period from Herod I until 70 A.D.* Edinburgh: T. & T. Clark, 1989.

Hofius, O. "'Der in des Vaters Schoss ist' Joh 1,18." *ZNW* 80 (1989) 163–71.

———. "Struktur und Gedankengang des Logos-Hymnus in Joh 1:1-18" *ZNW* 78 (1987) 1–25.

Hooker, M. D. "In His Own Image." In *What about the New Testament: Studies in Honour of C. Evans*, ed. C. Hickling and M. D. Hooker. London: SCM Press, 1975.

———. "The Johannine Prologue and the Messianic Secret." *NTS* 21 (1974-75) 40-58.

———. "John the Baptist and the Johannine Prologue." *NTS* 16 (1970) 354-58.

Hudry-Clergeon, C., "De Judée en Galilée: Etude de Jean 4:1-45." *NRT* 103 (1981) 818-30.

Ibuki, Y. *"kai tēn phōnēn autou akoueis:* Gedankenaufbau und Hintergrund des 3. Kapitels des Johannesevangeliums." *Bulletin of the Seikei University* 14 (1978) 9-33.

———. *Die Wahrheit im Johannesevangelium.* BBB 39. Bonn: Peter Hanstein, 1972.

Infante, R. "L'amico dello sposo, figura del ministero di Giovanni Battista nel Quarto Vangelo." *RivBib* 31 (1983) 3-19.

Irigoin, J. "La composition rythmique du Prologue de Jean (1,1-18)." *RB* 78 (1971) 501-14.

Iser, W. *The Act of Reading: A Theory of Aesthetic Response.* London: Routledge & Kegan Paul, 1978.

Jaubert, A. "La Symbolique du Puits de Jacob. Jean 4,12." In *L'Homme devant Dieu: Mélanges offerts au Père Henri de Lubac,* 1:63-73. Théologie 56. Lyon: Aubier, 1963.

Jeremias, J. *The Eucharistic Words of Jesus.* London: SCM Press, 1971.

———. *Jerusalem in the Time of Jesus.* London: SCM Press, 1969.

Käsemann, E. "The Structure and Purpose of the Prologue to John's Gospel." In *New Testament Questions of Today,* 138-67. London: SCM Press, 1969.

———. *The Testament of Jesus according to John 17.* London: SCM Press, 1966.

Keegan, T. J. *Interpreting the Bible: A Popular Introduction to Biblical Hermeneutics.* New York: Paulist Press, 1985.

Kelber, W. H. "Biblical Hermeneutics and the Ancient Art of Communication: A Response." *Semeia* 39 (1987) 97-105.

———. "Gospel Narrative and Critical Theory." *BTB* 18 (1988) 130-36.

———. "Narrative as Interpretation and Interpretation of Narrative: Hermeneutical Reflections on the Gospels." *Semeia* 39 (1987) 107-33.

———. *The Oral and Written Gospel: The Hermeneutics of Speaking and Writing in the Synoptic Tradition, Mark, Paul, and Q.* Philadelphia: Fortress Press, 1983.

Kermode, F. *The Genesis of Secrecy: On the Interpretation of Narrative.* Cambridge, Mass.: Harvard University Press, 1979.

———. "John as Poet." *SNTS* 28 (1986) 3-16.

Kieffer, R. *Le monde symbolique de saint Jean.* LD 137. Paris: Cerf, 1989.

Kilpatrick, G. D. "John IV:51, PAIS or UIOS?" *JTS* 14 (1963) 393.

Klaiber, W. "Der irdische und der himmlische Zeuge: eine Auslegung von Joh 3.22-36." *NTS* 36 (1990) 205-33.

Koester, C. "Hearing, Seeing and Believing in the Gospel of John." *Bib* 70 (1989) 327-48.

——. "Messianic Exegesis and the Call of Nathanael (John 1.45-51)." *JSNT* 39 (1990) 23-34.

Krieger, M. "Fiktive Orte der Johannes-Taufe." *ZNW* 45 (1953-54) 121-23.

Krieger, N. *A Window to Criticism.* Princeton, N.J.: Princeton University Press, 1964.

Kügler, J. *Der Jünger der Jesus Liebte: Literarische, theologische und historische Untersuchungen zu einer Schlüsselgestalt Johanneischer Theologie und Geschichte. Mit einem Excurs über die Brotrede in Joh 6.* SBB 16. Stuttgart: Katholisches Bibelwerk, 1988.

Kuhn, H.-J. *Christologie und Wunder: Untersuchungen zu Joh 1,35-51.* BU 18. Regensburg: Pustet, 1988.

Kysar, R. *The Fourth Evangelist and His Gospel.* Minneapolis: Augsburg, 1975.

——. "The Fourth Gospel: A Report on Recent Research." *ANRW* 2.25.3, pp. 2389-2480.

——. *John's Story of Jesus.* Philadelphia: Fortress Press, 1984.

Lacan, M.-F. "Le Prologue de saint Jean: Ses thèmes, sa structure, son mouvement." *LumVie* 33 (1957) 91-110.

Lamarche, P. "Le Prologue de Jean." *RSR* 52 (1964) 497-537.

Lategan, B. C. "Coming to Grips with the Reader in Biblical Literature." *Semeia* 48 (1989) 3-17.

Légasse, S. "Le Baptême administré par Jésus (Jn 3,22-36; 4,1-3) et l'origine du baptême chrétien." *BLE* 78 (1977) 3-30.

Leidig, E. *Jesu Gespräch mit der Samaritanerin und weitere Gespräche im Johannesevangelium.* ThD 15. Basel: Friedrich Reinhardt, 1981.

Lenglet, A. "Jésus de passage parmi les Samaritains." *Bib* 66 (1985) 493-503.

Lentzen-Deis, F.-L. *Die Taufe Jesu nach den Synoptikern: Literarkritische und gattungsgeschichtliche Untersuchungen.* FThSt 4. Frankfurt: Josef Knecht, 1970.

Léon-Dufour, X. "Towards a Symbolic Reading of the Fourth Gospel." *NTS* 27 (1980-81) 439-56.

Leroy, H. *Rätsel und Missverständnis: Ein Beitrag zur Formgeschichte des Johannesevangeliums.* BBB 30. Bonn: Peter Hanstein, 1968.

Lindars, B. *Behind the Fourth Gospel.* Studies in Creative Criticism 3. London: SPCK, 1971.

——. "John and the Synoptic Gospels: A Test Case." *NTS* 27 (1980-81) 287-94.

——. *New Testament Apologetic: The Doctrinal Significance of the Old Testament Quotations.* London: SCM Press, 1961.

Lindars, B., and P. Borgen. "The Place of the Old Testament in the Formation of New Testament Theology: Prolegomena and Response." *NTS* 23 (1976-77) 23-59.

Loader, W. "The Central Structure of Johannine Theology." *NTS* 30 (1984) 188-216.

——. *The Christology of the Fourth Gospel.* BBET 23. Frankfurt: Peter Lang, 1989.

MacRae, G. W. "The Fourth Gospel and *Religionsgeschichte.*" *CBQ* 32 (1970) 13-24.

——. *Studies in the New Testament and Gnosticism.* GNS 26. Wilmington: Michael Glazier, 1987.

McDonald, J. *The Theology of the Samaritans.* London: SCM Press, 1964.

McHugh, J. *The Mother of Jesus in the New Testament.* London: Darton, Longman & Todd, 1975.

McKnight, E. V. *The Bible and the Reader: An Introduction to Literary Criticism.* Philadelphia: Fortress Press, 1985.

——. *Post-Modern Use of the Bible: The Emergence of Reader-Oriented Criticism.* Nashville: Abingdon, 1988.

McNamara, M. *Targum and Testament: Aramaic Paraphrases of the Hebrew Bible: A Light on the New Testament.* Shannon: Irish University Press, 1972.

Manns, F. *John and Jamnia: How the Break Occurred between Jews and Christians c. 80-100 A.D.* Jerusalem: Franciscan Printing Press, 1988.

Marshall, C. D. *Faith as a theme in Mark's narrative.* SNTSMS 64. Cambridge: Cambridge University Press, 1989.

Martyn, J. L. "Glimpses into the History of the Johannine Community: From its Origin through the Period of Its Life in Which the Fourth Gospel was Composed." In *L'Evangile de Jean: Sources, rédaction, théologie,* 149-75. BETL 44. Gembloux: Duculot, 1977.

——. *History and Theology in the Fourth Gospel.* 2nd ed. Nashville: Abingdon, 1979.

Mastin, B. A. "A Neglected Feature of the Christology of the Fourth Gospel." *NTS* 22 (1975-76) 32-51.

Matsunaga, K. "The Galileans in the Fourth Gospel." *Annual of the Japanese Biblical Institute* 2 (1976) 139-58.

May, E. *Ecce Agnus Dei: A Philological and Exegetical Approach to John 1,29. 36.* Washington: Catholic University, 1947.

Maynard, A. H. "TI EMOI KAI SOI." *NTS* 31 (1985) 582-86.

Mead, A. H. "The *basilikos* in John 4.46-53." *JSNT* 23 (1985) 69-72.

Meeks, W. A. "The Man from Heaven in Johannine Sectarianism." *JBL* 91 (1972) 44–72.

Meyer, P. W. "John 2:10." *JBL* 86 (1967) 191–97.

Michaud, J.-P. "Le signe de Cana dans son contexte johannique." *Laval Théologique et Philosophique* 18 (1962) 239–85; 19 (1963) 257–83.

Michel, M. "Nicodème ou le non-lieu de la vérité." *RevScRel* 55 (1981) 227–36.

Miller, E. L. *Salvation-History in the Prologue of John: The Significance of John 1:3-4.* NovTSup 60. Leiden: E. J. Brill, 1989.

Mlakuzhyil, G. *The Christocentric Literary Structure of the Fourth Gospel.* AnBib 117. Rome: Biblical Institute Press, 1987.

Moloney, F. J. "From Cana to Cana (John 2:1–4:54) and the Fourth Evangelist's Concept of Correct (and Incorrect) Faith." In *Studia Biblica 1978 II: Papers on the Gospels: Sixth International Congress on Biblical Studies, Oxford 3-7 April 1978,* ed. E. A. Livingstone, 185–213. JSNTSup 2. Sheffield: JSOT Press, 1980. Also available in *Salesianum* 40 (1978) 817–43.

———. "The Fulness of a Gift which is Truth." *Catholic Theological Review* 1 (1978) 30–33.

———. "'In the Bosom of' or 'Turned towards' the Father?" *AusBR* 31 (1983) 63–71.

———. *The Johannine Son of Man.* 2nd ed. Biblioteca di Scienze Religiose 14. Rome: LAS, 1978.

———. "Johannine Theology." *NJBC,* 1417–26.

———. "John 6 and the Celebration of the Eucharist." *DRev* 93 (1975) 243–51.

———. "Mary in the Fourth Gospel: Woman and Mother." *Salesianum* 51 (1989) 421–40.

———. *Mary: Woman and Mother.* Homebush: St Paul Publications, 1988.

———. "Revisiting John." *ScrB* 11 (1980) 9–15.

———. "When is John Talking about Sacraments?" *AusBR* 30 (1982) 10–33.

———. *The Word Became Flesh.* Theology Today Series 14. Dublin/Cork: Mercier Press, 1977.

Montgomery, J. A. *The Samaritans: The Earliest Jewish Sect: Their History, Theology and Literature.* Philadelphia: John C. Winston, 1907.

Moore, S. D. "Are the Gospels Unified Narratives?" In *Society of Biblical Literature 1987 Seminar Papers,* ed. K. H. Richards, 443–58. Atlanta: Scholars Press, 1988.

———. "Doing Gospel Criticism as/with a 'Reader.'" *BTB* 19 (1989) 85–93.

———. *Literary Criticism and the Gospels: The Theoretical Challenge.* New Haven: Yale University Press, 1989.

———. "Narrative Commentaries on the Bible: Context, Roots and Prospects." *Forum* 3,3 (1987) 29–56.

———. "Negative Hermeneutics, Insubstantial Texts: Stanley Fish and the Biblical Interpreter." *JAAR* 54 (1986) 401–13.

———. "Rifts in (a reading of) the fourth gospel, or: does Johannine irony collapse in a reading that draws attention to itself?" *Neotestamentica* 23 (1989) 5–17.

Morgan, R., and J. Barton. *Biblical Interpretation*. The Oxford Bible Series. Oxford: Oxford University Press, 1988.

Muñoz León, D. *Dios-Palabra: Memra en los Targumim del Pentateuco*. Institución San Jeronimo 4. Granada: Santa Rita, 1974.

Murphy-O'Connor, J. "John the Baptist and Jesus: History and Hypotheses." *NTS* 36 (1990) 359–74.

Nations, A. L. "Historical Criticism and the Current Methodological Crisis." *SJT* 36 (1983) 59–71.

Neirynck, F. "The Anonymous Disciple in John 1." *ETL* 66 (1990) 5–37.

———. *Jean et les Synoptiques: Examen critique de l'exégèse de M.-E. Boismard*. BETL 49. Leuven: University Press, 1979.

———. "John 4,46-54: Signs Source and/or Synoptic Gospels." *ETL* 60 (1984) 367–75.

Neyrey, J. H. *An Ideology of Revolt: John's Christology in Social-Science Perspective*. Philadelphia: Fortress Press, 1988.

———. "The Jacob Allusions in John 1:51." *CBQ* 44 (1982) 586–605.

———. "Jacob Traditions and the Interpretation of John 4:10-26." *CBQ* 41 (1979) 419–37.

———. "John III – A Debate over Johannine Epistemology and Christology." *NovT* 22 (1981) 115–27.

Niccaci, A. "Siracide 6,19 e Giovanni 4,36-38." *BibOr* 23 (1981) 149–53.

Nicholson, G. C. *Death as Departure: The Johannine Descent-Ascent Schema*. SBLDS 63. Chico, Calif.: Scholars Press, 1983.

O'Day, G. R. "Narrative Mode and Theological Claim: A Study in the Fourth Gospel." *JBL* 105 (1986) 657–68.

———. *Revelation in the Fourth Gospel: Narrative Mode and Theological Claim*. Philadelphia: Fortress Press, 1986.

Okure, T. *The Johannine Approach to Mission: A Contextual Study of John 4:1-42*. WUNT 2, Reihe 32. Tübingen: J. C. B. Mohr [Paul Siebeck], 1988.

Olsson, B. *Structure and Meaning in the Fourth Gospel: A Text-Linguistic Analysis of John 2:1-11 and 4:1-42*. Coniectanea Biblica, New Testament Series 6. Lund: Gleerup, 1974.

Onuki, T. *Gemeinde und Welt im Johannesevangelium: Ein Beitrag zur Frage nach der theologischen und pragmatischen Funktion des johanneischen "Dualismus."* WMANT 56. Neukirchen-Vluyn: Neukirchener Verlag, 1984.

Painter, J. "The Farewell Discourse and the History of Johannine Christianity." *NTS* 27 (1980–81) 523–43.

———. "Quest and Rejection Stories in John." *JSNT* 36 (1989) 17–46.

———. "Quest Stories in John 1–4." *JSNT* 40 (1991).

Pancaro, S. *The Law in the Fourth Gospel: The Torah and the Gospel, Moses and Jesus, Judaism and Christianity according to John.* NovTSup 42. Leiden: E. J. Brill, 1975.

Panimolle, S. *Il dono della Legge e la grazia della verità (Gv 1:17).* Teologia Oggi 21. Rome: Editrice A.V.E., 1973.

Patte, D. "Jesus' Pronouncement about Entering the Kingdom like a Child: A Structural Exegesis." *Semeia* 29 (1983) 3–42.

Pazdan, M. "Nicodemus and the Samaritan Woman: Contrasting Models of Discipleship." *BTB* 17 (1987) 145–48.

Petersen, N. R. *Literary Criticism for New Testament Critics.* GBS.NT. Philadelphia: Fortress Press, 1978.

Pollard, T. E. "Cosmology and the Prologue of the Fourth Gospel." *VC* 12 (1958) 147–53.

———. *Johannine Christology and the Early Church.* SNTSMS 13. Cambridge: Cambridge University Press, 1970.

Potin, J. *La fête juive de la Pentecôte.* 2 vols. LD 65. Paris: Cerf, 1971.

Preisker, H. "Jüdische Apokalyptik und hellenistischer Synkretismus im Johannes-Evangelium, dargelegt an dem Begriff 'Licht.'" *TLZ* 77 (1952) 673–78.

Prickett, S. "The Status of Biblical Narrative." *Pacifica* 2 (1989) 26–46.

———. *Words and the Word: Language, Poetics and Biblical Interpretation.* Cambridge: Cambridge University Press, 1986.

Prince, G. *Narratology: The Form and Functioning of Narrative.* Janua Linguarum Series Maior 108. Berlin/New York/Amsterdam: Mouton, 1982.

Pryor, J. W. "Jesus and Israel in the Fourth Gospel—John 1:11." *NovT* 32 (1990) 201–18.

———. "John 4:44 and the *Patris* of Jesus." *CBQ* 49 (1987) 254–63.

———. "Of the Virgin Birth or the Birth of Christians? The Text of John 1:13 once more." *NovT* 27 (1985) 296–318.

Purvis, J. D. "The Fourth Gospel and the Samaritans." *NovT* 17 (1975) 161–98.

Quast, K. *Peter and the Beloved Disciple: Figures for a Community in Crisis.* JSNTSup 32. Sheffield: JSOT Press, 1989.

Rabinowitz, P. J. "Whirl without End: Audience-Oriented Criticism." In *Contemporary Literary Theory*, ed. D. D. Atkins and L. Morrow, 81–100. London: Macmillan, 1989.

Reim, G. "John IV.44 – Crux or Clue?" *NTS* 22 (1975–76) 476–80.

———. *Studien zum alttestamentlichen Hintergrund des Johannesevangeliums.* SNTSMS 22. Cambridge: Cambridge University Press, 1974.

Reinhartz, A. "Jesus as Prophet: Predictive Prolepses in the Fourth Gospel." *JSNT* 36 (1989) 3–16.

Rensberger, D. *Johannine Faith and the Liberating Community.* Philadelphia: Westminster Press, 1988.

Rhoads, D. M. *Israel in Revolution 6-74 C.E.: A Political History Based on the Writings of Josephus.* Philadelphia: Fortress Press, 1976.

Richard, E. "Expressions of Double Meaning and their Function in the Gospel of John." *NTS* 31 (1985) 96–112.

Richter, G. "Die Fleischwerdung im Johannesevangelium." *NovT* 13 (1971) 81–126; 14 (1972) 256–76.

Ricoeur, P. "The hermeneutical function of distanciation." In *Paul Ricoeur: Hermeneutics and the Human Sciences: Essays on language, action and interpretation*, ed. J. B. Thompson, 131–44. Cambridge: Cambridge University Press, 1981.

———. "Hermeneutics and the critique of ideology." In *Paul Ricoeur: Hermeneutics and the Human Sciences: Essays on language, action and interpretation*, ed. J. B. Thompson, 63–100. Cambridge: Cambridge University Press, 1981.

———. "The task of hermeneutics." In *Paul Ricoeur: Hermeneutics and the Human Sciences: Essays on language, action and interpretation*, ed. J. B. Thompson, 274–96. Cambridge: Cambridge University Press, 1981.

Ridderbos, H. "The Structure and Scope of the Prologue of the Gospel of John." *NovT* 8 (1966) 180–201.

Rimmon-Kenan, S. *Narrative Fiction: Contemporary Poetics.* New Accents. London: Methuen, 1983.

Robert, R. "'Celui qui est de retour dans le sein du Père' (Jean 1,18)." *RevThom* 85 (1985) 457–63.

———. "La double intention du mot final du prologue johannique." *RevThom* 87 (1987) 435–41.

———. "Le mot final du prologue johannique: A propos d'un article récent." *RevThom* 89 (1989) 279–88.

Robinson, B. P. "The Meaning and Significance of 'The Seventh Hour' in John 4:52." In *Studia Biblica 1978: II, Papers in the Gospels: Sixth International Congress on Biblical Studies, Oxford 3-7 April 1978,* ed. E. A. Livingstone, 255–62. JSNTSup 2. Sheffield: JSOT Press, 1980.

Robinson, J. A. T. *The Priority of John.* London: SCM Press, 1985.

Rochais, G. "La Formation du Prologue (Jn 1,1-18)." *ScEs* 37 (1985) 5–44, 161–87.

Rossetto, G. "Nascere dell'alto: Gv 3:3-8." In *Segni e Sacramenti nel Vangelo di Giovanni,* ed. P. R. Tragan, 45–71. Studia Anselmiana 66. Rome: Editrice Anselmiana, 1977.

Roustang, F. "Les moments de l'acte de foi et ses conditions de possibilité: Essai d'interpretation du dialogue avec la Samaritaine." *RSR* 46 (1958) 344–78.

Rowland, C. C. "John 1.51, Jewish Apocalyptic and Targumic Tradition." *NTS* 30 (1984) 498–507.

Rudolph, K. *Gnosis: The Nature and History of an Ancient Religion.* Edinburgh: T. & T. Clark, 1983.

Sabugal, S. *Christos: Investigación exegética sobre la cristologia joannea.* Barcelona: Herder, 1972.

Schalit, A. *König Herodes: Der Mann und sein Werk.* Berlin: Walter de Gruyter, 1969.

Schenke, L. "Die literarische Entstehungsgeschichte von Joh 1,19-51." *BN* 46 (1989) 24–57.

Schmid, L. "Die Komposition der Samaria-Szene Joh 4:1-42: Ein Beitrag zur charakteristik des 4. Evangelisten als Schriftsteller." *ZNW* 28 (1929) 148–58.

Schnackenburg, R. "Die 'Anbetung in Geist und Wahrheit' (Joh 4,23) im Lichte vom Qumran-Texten." *BZ* 3 (1959) 88–94.

——. "Die situationsgelösten Redestücke in Joh 3." *ZNW* 49 (1958) 88–99.

——. "Zur Traditionsgeschichte von Joh 4,46-54." *BZ* 8 (1964) 58–88.

Schneidau, H. N. "The Word against the Word: Derrida on Textuality." *Semeia* 23 (1982) 5–28.

Schottroff, L. *Die Glaubende und die feindliche Welt: Beobachtungen zum gnostischer Dualismus und seiner Bedeutung für Paulus und das Johannesevangelium.* WMANT 37. Neukirchen-Vluyn: Neukirchener Verlag, 1970.

Schürer, E. *The History of the Jewish People in the Age of Jesus Christ (175 B.C.–A.D. 135).* 3 vols. A New English Version Revised and Edited by Geza Vermes, Fergus Millar, and Matthew Black. Edinburgh: T. & T. Clark, 1973–87.

Schüssler Fiorenza, E. "The Ethics of Interpretation: De-Centering Biblical Scholarship." *JBL* 107 (1988) 3–17.

——. "The Function of Scripture in the Liberation Struggle: A Critical Feminist Hermeneutics and Liberation Theology." In *Bread not Stone: The Challenge of Feminist Biblical Interpretation*, 43–63. Boston: Beacon Press, 1984.

——. "Toward a Critical-Theological Self-Understanding of Biblical Scholarship." In *Bread not Stone: The Challenge of Feminist Biblical Interpretation*, 117–49. Boston: Beacon Press, 1984.

Schwarz, G. "'kai ēn tis basilikos . . . ' (Joh 4,46)." *ZNW* 75 (1984) 138.

Schweizer, E. *Ego Eimi . . . Die religionsgeschichtliche Herkunft und theologische Bedeutung der johanneischen Bildreden, zugleich ein Beitrag zur Quellenfrage des vierten Evangeliums.* FRLANT 38. Göttingen: Vandenhoeck & Ruprecht, 1939.

——. "Die Heiligung des Königlichen, Joh 4,46-54." *EvTh* 11 (1951–52) 64–71.

Segalla, G. *Volontà di Dio e dell'Uomo in Giovanni (Vangelo e Lettere).* SuppRivB 6. Brescia: Paideia, 1974.

Serra, A. M. *Contributi dell'antica letteratura giudaica per l'esegesi di Gv. 2:1-12 e 19:25-27.* Scripta Pontificiae Facultatis 'Marianum' 31. Rome: Herder, 1977.

——. "Le tradizioni della teofania sinaitica nel Targum dello Pseudo Jonathan Es. 19.24 e in Giov. 1,19-2,12." *Marianum* 33 (1971) 1–39.

Silberman, L. H., ed. *Orality, Aurality and Biblical Narrative. Semeia* 39. Decatur, Ga.: Scholars Press, 1987.

Smith, D. M. "Judaism and the Gospel of John." In *Jews and Christians: Exploring the Past, Present, and Future*, ed. J. H. Charlesworth, 76–99. Shared Ground among Jews and Christians 1. New York: Crossroad, 1990.

Smitmans, A. *Das Weinwunder von Kana: Die Auslegung von Jo 2,1-11 bei den Vätern und heute.* BGBE 6. Tübingen: J. C. B. Mohr [Paul Siebeck], 1966.

Solomon, A. M. "Story upon Story." *Semeia* 46 (1989) 3–10.

Staley, J. L. *The Print's First Kiss: A Rhetorical Investigation of the Implied Reader in the Fourth Gospel.* SBLDS 82. Atlanta: Scholars Press, 1988.

Steiner, G. *Real Presences: Is there anything in what we say?* London: Faber & Faber, 1989.

Stemberger, G. *La symbolique du bien et du mal selon saint Jean.* Paris: Seuil, 1970.

Sternberg, M. *The Poetics of Biblical Narrative: Ideological Literature and the Drama of Reading.* ILBS. Bloomington: Indiana University Press, 1985.

Strachan, R. H. *The Fourth Gospel: Its Significance and Environment.* 3rd ed. London: SCM Press, 1941.

Sturch, R. L. "The '*PATRIS*' of Jesus." *JTS* 28 (1977) 94–96.

Suggit, J. N. "Nicodemus—The True Jew." *Neotestamentica* 14 (1981) 90–110.

Talbert, C. H. *Reading Corinthians: A Literary and Theological Commentary on 1 and 2 Corinthians.* New York: Crossroad, 1987.

———. *Reading Luke: A Literary and Theological Commentary on the Third Gospel.* New York: Crossroad, 1982.

Tannehill, R. C. *The Narrative Unity of Luke-Acts: A Literary Interpretation.* 2 vols. Philadelphia: Fortress Press, 1986, 1990.

Taylor, V. *The Gospel of St Mark.* London: Macmillan, 1966.

Temple, S. "The Two Signs in the Fourth Gospel" *JBL* 81 (1962) 169–74.

Tenney, M. C. "The Footnotes of John's Gospel." *Bibliotheca Sacra* 117 (1960) 350–64.

Theissen, G. *Miracle Stories of the Early Christian Tradition.* Studies of the NT and its World. Edinburgh: T. & T. Clark, 1983.

Theobald, M. *Die Fleischwerdung des Logos: Studien zum Verhältnis des Johannesprologs zum Corpus des Evangeliums und zu 1 Joh.* NTAbh N.F. 20. Münster: Aschendorff, 1988.

———. *Im Anfang war das Wort: Textlinguistische Studie zum Johannesprolog.* SBS 106. Stuttgart: Katholisches Bibelwerk, 1983.

Thompson, M. M. *The Humanity of Jesus in the Fourth Gospel.* Philadelphia: Fortress Press, 1988.

Thyen, H. "Aus der Literatur zum Johannesevangelium." *TR* 39 (1974) 1–69, 221–52, 289–330; 40 (1975) 211–70; 43 (1978) 328–59; 44 (1979) 97–134.

———. "Das Heil kommt von den Juden." In *Kirche: Festschrift für Günther Bornkamm zum 75. Geburtstag,* 163–84. Tübingen: J. C. B. Mohr [Paul Siebeck], 1980.

Trudinger, L. P. "The Seven Days of the New Creation in St. John's Gospel: Some Further Reflections." *EvQ* 44 (1972) 154–58.

Tobin, T. H. "The Prologue of John and Hellenistic Jewish Speculation." *CBQ* 52 (1990) 252–69.

Tompkins, J. P. "The Reader in History: The Changing Shape of Literary Response." In *Reader-Response Criticism: From Formalism to Post-Structuralism,* ed. J. P. Tompkins, 201–32. Baltimore: Johns Hopkins University Press, 1980.

Topel, L. J. "A Note on the Methodology of Structural Analysis in Jn 2:23–3:21." *CBQ* 33 (1971) 211–20.

Tournay, R. *Quand Dieu parle aux hommes le langage de l'amour: Etudes sur le Cantique des Cantiques.* CahRB 21. Paris: Gabalda, 1982.

Tröger, K. W. "Ja oder Nein zur Welt: War der Evangelist Johannes Christ oder Gnostiker?" *TV* 7 (1976) 61–80.

van Belle, G. "Jn 4,48 et la foi du centurion." *ETL* 61 (1985) 167–69.

van den Bussche, H. "La structure de Jean I-XII." In *L'Evangile de Jean: Etudes et problèmes*, 61–109. RechBib 3. Bruges: Desclée de Brouwer, 1958.

Vanhoye, A. "Interrogation johannique et l'exégèse de Cana." *Bib* 55 (1974) 155–77.

van Iersel, B. M. F. *Reading Mark*. Edinburgh: T. & T. Clark, 1989.

van Selms, A. "The Best Man and the Bride—from Sumer to St. John." *JNES* 9 (1950) 65–75.

Vellanickal, M. *The Divine Sonship of Christians in the Johannine Writings*. AnBib 72. Rome: Biblical Institute Press, 1977.

———. *Studies in the Gospel of John*. Bangalore: Asian Trading Corporation, 1982.

von Wahlde, U. C. *The Earliest Version of John's Gospel: Recovering the Gospel of Signs*. Wilmington, Del.: Michael Glazier, 1989.

Vorster, W. S. "The Reader in the Text: Narrative Material." *Semeia* 48 (1989) 21–39.

Wainwright, E. "In Search of the Lost Coin: Toward a Feminist Biblical Hermeneutic." *Pacifica* 2 (1989) 135–50.

Walker, R. "Jüngerwort und Herrenwort: Zur Auslegung von Joh 4:39-42." *ZNW* 57 (1966) 49–54.

Watson, W. G. E. "Antecedents of a New Testament Proverb." *VT* 20 (1970) 368–70.

Wegner, U. *Der Hauptmann von Kafarnaum (Mt 7,28a; 8,5-10.13 par Lk 7,1-10): Ein Beitrag zur Q-Forschung*. WUNT 2, Reihe 14. Tübingen: J. C. B. Mohr [Paul Siebeck], 1985.

Wengst, K. *Bedrängte Gemeinde und Verherrlichter Christus: Der historischer Ort des Johannesevangeliums als Schlüssel zu seiner Interpretation*. 2nd ed. BTS 5. Neukirchen-Vluyn: Neukirchener Verlag, 1983.

Whitacre, R. A. *Johannine Polemic: The Role of Tradition and Theology*. SBLDS 67. Chico, Calif.: Scholars Press, 1982.

Willemse, J. "La patrie de Jésus selon saint Jean IV.44." *NTS* 11 (1964–65) 349–64.

Wilson, J. "The Integrity of John 3:22-36." *JSNT* 10 (1981) 34–41.

Witherington, B. "Jesus and the Baptist—Two of a Kind?" In *SBL 1988 Seminar Papers*, ed. D. Lull, 225–44. Atlanta: Scholars Press, 1988.

Wuellner, W. "Is There an Encoded Reader Fallacy?" *Semeia* 48 (1989) 41–54.

Zumstein, J. "L'évangile johannique, une stratégie du croire." *RSR* 77 (1989) 217–32.

Index
of Authors

223

Made in United States
Orlando, FL
18 January 2024

42629698R00143

West Academic
Emeritus Advisory Board

a short &happy guide to

Criminal Procedure

Fifth Edition

Leslie W. Abramson
Frost Brown Todd Professor of Law
Louis D. Brandeis School of Law
at the University of Louisville

A SHORT & HAPPY GUIDE® SERIES

WEST
ACADEMIC
PUBLISHING

a short & happy guide series is a trademark registered in the U.S. Patent and Trademark Office.

© 2015, 2017-2019 LEG, Inc. d/b/a West Academic
© 2021 LEG, Inc. d/b/a West Academic
     444 Cedar Street, Suite 700
     St. Paul, MN 55101
     1-877-888-1330

Printed in the United States of America

ISBN: 978-1-63659-282-4

Preface

Criminal Procedure is one of the most interesting law courses. As you were growing up, you watched news reports or television shows like *Crime Stoppers* which described or portrayed how the FBI or local police arrested suspects, searched their homes, interrogated them about their criminal conduct, and placed them in lineups. After a suspect was taken to court, further reports outlined whether she was released pending trial, indicted by a grand jury, pled guilty or asked for a jury trial, and sentenced to prison for a term of years.

The Short & Happy Guide to Criminal Procedure introduces you to the legal side of what you have heard and read about for years. Whether you use this book to cram for your criminal procedure final examination, or as a guide to follow in your role as a prosecutorial or public defender extern, you will learn the basics of how the criminal justice system functions in federal and state courts.

The first half of this book explores the constitutionality of police practices such as the exclusionary rule, arrests and stops of persons, searches of persons and vehicles, seizures of property, interrogation of suspects, and identification of suspects through lineups and showups.

The remainder of this book addresses the issues that arise after the federal or state prosecutor institutes criminal proceedings against the suspect. You will learn the constitutional and rule-based procedures relating to pretrial release, prosecutorial discretion, preliminary proceedings, grand jury practice, joinder of offenses and defendants, speedy trial, pretrial discovery of factual information, pretrial publicity, plea bargaining, jury trials, appeals, double jeopardy, and post-conviction remedies.

Each chapter explores one of the above topics, first defining the "key terms" for the topic. Each chapter then explains why its topic is important to the workings of the justice system and how it interrelates with other topics elsewhere in the book. The balance of each chapter discusses the foundational principles and shows you how they "work," primarily through decisions of the United States Supreme Court or hypothetical situations.

The materials in this book are current through the 2020-2021 Term of the United States Supreme Court and the Federal Rules of Criminal Procedure through August, 2021. New editions of this book will be published approximately every three years, but readers can check www.shortandhappyguides.com for interim updates. Thanks to Kaylee Raymer, a 2020 graduate of the University of Louisville Brandeis School of Law, for her quality editorial assistance in the preparation of the Fourth edition.

LESLIE W. ABRAMSON

September 2021

Table of Contents

A Short & Happy Guide to Criminal Procedure

Fifth Edition

CHAPTER 1

Fourth Amendment Activity

Key Terms

- **Curtilage:** the land "immediately surrounding and associated with the home."

- **Fourth Amendment activity:** police interference with a person's reasonable expectation of privacy or with property rights in her home, papers or effects.

- **Physical intrusion:** into a constitutionally protected area to obtain information constitutes Fourth Amendment activity.

- **Reasonable expectation of privacy:** a person's subjective expectation of privacy that society recognizes as reasonable.

- **Reasonableness Clause:** Fourth Amendment phrase by which courts balance the intrusion on a person's privacy or into protected areas with how necessary a search or seizure is to promote legitimate governmental interests.

- **Search:** a visual observation or physical intrusion that interferes with a person's reasonable expectation of privacy or a person's property rights in her house, "papers and effects."

- **Seizure:** meaningful interference with an individual's liberty (*e.g.*, an arrest or stop) or her possessory interests (*e.g.*, a seizure of property).

- **Warrant Clause:** Fourth Amendment phrase applying to the issuance, content, and execution of arrest and search warrants.

A. Why Fourth Amendment Activity Is Important

Fourth Amendment activity is a threshold issue for analyzing most searches and seizures. *If* police conduct is classified as Fourth Amendment activity, the police must follow constitutional standards, *e.g.*, probable cause, governing their behavior. *If* the conduct is *not* Fourth Amendment activity, law enforcement officials may disregard Fourth Amendment requirements.

B. Fourth Amendment

The Fourth Amendment to the United States Constitution states: "The right of the people to be secure in their persons, houses, papers, and effects, against unreasonable searches and seizures, shall not be violated; and no Warrants shall issue but upon probable cause, supported by Oath or affirmation, and particularly describing the place to be searched, and the persons or things to be seized."

The Fourth Amendment has two parts: the "Reasonableness Clause" and the "Warrant Clause." The Warrant Clause applies to the issuance, content, and execution of arrest warrants and search warrants. Under the Reasonableness Clause, a court decides the legality of a warrantless search by balancing the intrusion on a person's privacy with how necessary the search is to promote legitimate governmental interests. *Wyoming v. Houghton*, 526 U.S. 295 (1999).

- A search is a visual observation or physical intrusion that interferes with a person's reasonable expectation of privacy or a person's property rights in her house, "papers and effects." For example, when police feel the outside of soft luggage, there is a search. *Bond v. United States*, 529 U.S. 334 (2000).

- Police track the movements of a cell phone (and thus the owner of the phone) through acquisition of cell-site location information [CSLI]. Acquisition of the data constitutes a Fourth Amendment search that normally requires issuance of a warrant. *Carpenter v. United States*, 138 S.Ct. 2206 (2018). The decision invalidated the Government's acquisition of cell-site data that proved a robbery suspect's movements.

- A seizure is a meaningful interference with an individual's liberty (*e.g.*, an arrest or a stop) or her possessory interests (*e.g.*, a seizure of property). To constitute an arrest, "the mere grasping or application of physical force with lawful authority, whether or not it succeeded in subduing the arrestee, was sufficient." *California v. Hodari D.*, 499 U.S. 621 (1991). Accord, *Torres v. Madrid*, 141 S.Ct. 989 (2021).

C. When the Police Must Follow Fourth Amendment Standards

Fourth Amendment activity occurs either when police interfere with a person's reasonable expectation of privacy or they trespass on property rights in her home, papers or effects.

1. When a Person Has a Reasonable Expectation of Privacy

A person has a reasonable expectation of privacy if she has a subjective expectation that society recognizes as reasonable. If a person has a reasonable expectation of privacy, law enforcement must follow the Fourth Amendment's standards such as probable cause.

- A person talking on the telephone inside a public telephone booth with the door closed has a reasonable expectation of privacy in his conversations. In order for the Government to listen to that conversation, it must have probable cause to hear or record it. *Katz v. United States*, 389 U.S. 347 (1967). Katz's privacy depended in part on his behavior (*e.g.*, talking loudly in a public place) and in part on the social context (*e.g.*, using a telephone booth to conduct a phone conversation). Talking loudly in a booth makes the person's expectation unreasonable.

2. When a Person Has No Reasonable Expectation of Privacy

a. Information Shared with Third Parties

No reasonable expectation of privacy exists in several common situations when persons share information with third parties. A government agent does not have to satisfy Fourth Amendment standards when she is one of the parties to a telephone conversation. *United States v. White*, 401 U.S. 745 (1971).

b.   Curtilage and "Open Fields"

- Police can observe activity on the curtilage from a public street, but police presence *on* the curtilage itself is Fourth Amendment activity. The curtilage is the land "immediately surrounding and associated with the home," *e.g.*, the front porch. Courts look to a four-factor test to determine whether a particular area is within the "curtilage": 1) its proximity to the home, 2) whether it is enclosed, 3) the nature of its uses, and 4) the steps taken to protect it from observation. *United States v. Dunn*, 480 U.S. 294 (1987).

- Police can stand in an open field and observe what is occurring on the curtilage or in a house. "Open fields," the area beyond the curtilage, can be entered and searched without a warrant, even though it constitutes a trespass and even if the fields are enclosed by a fence and posted with a "No Trespassing" sign. *Oliver v. United States*, 466 U.S. 170 (1984).

3.   *When the Police Physically Trespass in the Person's Home, or on the Person's Papers or Effects*

- The Government cannot intrude in a constitutionally protected area in order to obtain information without satisfying Fourth Amendment requirements.

- Without prior existence of probable cause, police installation of a GPS tracking device on a defendant's vehicle to monitor the vehicle's movements constitutes a "search," and violates a defendant's Fourth Amendment rights. *United States v. Jones*, 565 U.S. 945 (2012). In *Jones*, the majority emphasized the intrusive nature of the secret installation of a GPS device on the defendant's automobile.

- A government-required program for sex offense recidivists to wear a satellite-based monitoring device constitutes a search under *Jones*. *Grady v. North Carolina*, 575 U.S. 306 (2015).

4. *Dog Sniffs for Enhanced Surveillance*

Certain factors are relevant to whether vantage points such as dog sniffs constitute Fourth Amendment activity.

- Dog sniffs by narcotics detection dogs are minimally intrusive and disclose "only the presence or absence of narcotics," thereby protecting innocent citizens from general police "rummaging" in their possessions.

- A court's determination of probable cause is determined by the totality of circumstances about the dog's reliability. Dog sniffs of the exterior of luggage in a public place do not violate a reasonable expectation of privacy. *United States v. Place*, 462 U.S. 696 (1983). A dog sniff of a car's exterior at a roadblock or a traffic stop is not a "search" or a "seizure" under *Place*. *Illinois v. Caballes*, 543 U.S. 405 (2005).

- Relying on an intrusion analysis, police use of a trained drug-sniffing dog on a homeowner's porch to check for drugs inside the home is a Fourth Amendment search, requiring probable cause. *Florida v. Jardines*, 569 U.S. 1 (2013).

5. *Public Access to the Vantage Point*

- When police look through a vehicle windshield to obtain a vehicle identification number, the owner of the vehicle has no privacy interest in that number because anyone can walk by the vehicle and observe that information. *New York v. Class*, 475 U.S. 106 (1986).

- A defendant has no reasonable expectation of privacy in garbage that is placed in opaque trash bags, left on the curb, and searched by police who procure the bags from the garbage collector. *California v. Greenwood*, 486 U.S. 35 (1988). If police go into the garage, *i.e.*, on the curtilage, to take the garbage bags, there is Fourth Amendment activity.

- Aerial surveillance cases indicate no reasonable expectation of privacy from police "fly overs" of property or of a home's curtilage from a helicopter flying as low as 400 feet, or the use of an aerial mapping camera during "fly overs" of commercial property. *Florida v. Riley*, 488 U.S. 445 (1989); *Dow Chemical v. United States*, 476 U.S. 227 (1986).

- However, observing "intimate details connected with the use of the home or the curtilage," *e.g.*, observing private activity in a home through a skylight, is Fourth Amendment activity. *Florida v. Riley.*

6. *Public Access to the Technology Used by the Government*

- Obtaining information about the interior of a home by sense-enhancing technology constitutes a search (requiring a finding of probable cause *prior* to using the imager), at least where the technology used is not available to the general public. *Kyllo v. United States,* 533 U.S. 27 (2001). The thermal imaging device showed that the garage was warmer than the rest of that house and "neighboring homes."

- When police use a device like a flashlight to artificially enhance sensory perceptions, there is no Fourth Amendment activity if the device aids the police in obtaining information that they could have obtained through their own senses, *Texas v. Brown,* 460 U.S. 730 (1983).

While beepers may substitute for visual surveillance to track a car, *United States v. Knotts,* 460 U.S. 276 (1983), police cannot use them to obtain information through visual surveillance *inside* the home. *United States v. Karo,* 468 U.S. 705 (1984).

CHAPTER 2

Search Warrants and Arrest Warrants

Key Terms

- **Affidavit:** a written document used to support issuance of a warrant, and sworn to under oath.

- **Anticipatory warrant:** a search warrant based on evidence that a crime will occur or is likely to occur at some specified time after some specified triggering condition.

- *Franks* **hearing:** a method for challenging an affidavit for a warrant, when some or all statements in the affidavit are false.

- **Information from an informant:** assessed from the totality of circumstances to prove probable cause, how the information was obtained, why the informant is reliable, and police corroboration of the informant's facts.

- **Knock and announce:** a common law doctrine requiring officers who are executing a warrant to act in specific ways.

- **Neutral and objective Judge:** a judge who issues a warrant cannot have a pecuniary or political interest in the issuance of the warrant.

- **Particularity:** Fourth Amendment requirement for specific description of places to be searched, and persons or things to be seized.

- **Probable cause for arrest warrant:** a fair probability that a crime has been committed and that the person to be arrested committed the crime.

- **Probable cause for search warrant:** a fair probability that the specified items sought are evidence of criminal activity and that those items are presently located at the specified place described in the search warrant application.

- **Stale probable cause information:** excessive time between discovery of information supportive of probable cause and when a search warrant is sought.

A. Why Warrants Are Important

Warrants require police to commit to a factual story justifying their issuance, *before* they execute them, either to seek the person named in an arrest warrant or to search the premises described in a search warrant.

B. The Preference for a Warrant

Searches conducted without a search warrant are *per se* unreasonable under the Fourth Amendment, subject to a few well-delineated exceptions. *Thompson v. Louisiana*, 469 U.S. 17 (1984).

For example, given the pervasive types and amounts of cell phone information, "[o]fficers must generally secure a warrant before conducting . . . a search" for digital information. *Riley v. California*, 573 U.S. 373 (2014). Accord, *Carpenter v. United States*, 138 S.Ct. 2206 (2018) (the Government usually needs a warrant to access cell-site records, but exceptions such as exigent circumstances may support a warrantless search).

An arrest warrant is unnecessary for arrests in public. Absent exigent circumstances, an arrest warrant is required in order to arrest a person in her own home. *Payton v. New York*, 445 U.S. 573 (1980). Entry into the defendant's home without a lawful arrest warrant makes any seized evidence inadmissible.

C. Probable Cause

The Fourth Amendment's Warrant Clause requires probable cause for issuance of a search warrant or an arrest warrant.

- For an arrest warrant, the government must prove a fair probability that a crime has been committed by the person to be arrested.

- For a search warrant, the government must prove a fair probability that the specified items sought are evidence of criminal activity and are presently located at the specified place described in the search warrant application.

Probable cause for a warrant is measured by the information available to law enforcement *prior* to an arrest or search. What is learned afterwards is irrelevant to *that* arrest or search.

The issuing judge makes a "common sense decision" about whether the circumstances articulated in the affidavit show a fair probability that evidence of a crime will be found in a particular place. *Illinois v. Gates*, 462 U.S. 213 (1983). A reviewing court must pay "great deference" to the trial judge's conclusion that probable cause existed. *Id.*

1. Totality of Circumstances to Decide Probable Cause

In *Illinois v. Gates*, the Court adopted a "totality-of-circumstances" test to evaluate probable cause based upon informant information. The most important factors are the informant's basis of knowledge, why the informant is reliable, the informant's status, and police corroboration of the informant's facts.

- For example, the totality of circumstances determines probable cause based upon a dog's alert. In *Florida v. Harris*, 568 U.S. 237 (2013), the record supported the trial court's conclusion that the dog's alert gave the officer probable cause to search.

2. Staleness of Probable Cause Information

Probable cause based upon stale information is invalid. Information for a search warrant may become stale, depending on the length of time between discovery of the information and the time that a search warrant is sought. (Because *arrest* warrants may be served anytime, the staleness issue is inapplicable.)

3. Probable Cause and Anticipatory Warrants

In *United States v. Grubbs*, 547 U.S. 90 (2006), the Supreme Court upheld the constitutionality of an "anticipatory warrant," in which a search warrant issues based upon a showing of *prospective* probable cause.

Many anticipatory warrants involve narcotics to be delivered to a certain place and time (the "triggering condition") in the future.

Two prerequisites of probability must be satisfied: 1) probable cause to believe the triggering condition will occur, and 2) if the triggering condition occurs, a fair probability that contraband or evidence of a crime will be found in a particular place. Anticipatory warrants become invalid if the triggering event (*e.g.*, the delivery of narcotics) that established prospective probable cause does not occur (*i.e.*, no delivery is made).

D. Obtaining Warrants

Information supporting the issuance of a search warrant or arrest warrant is disclosed to the issuing judge *ex parte* when she considers the application for a warrant. Ordinarily, the information presented is in the form of written affidavits, sworn to by the affiant under oath. Most jurisdictions require the issuing judge to consider *only* the information in the affidavits in evaluating whether probable cause exists, but some jurisdictions permit the judge to look at other information, *e.g.*, sworn supplemental oral statements made by the affiant or others.

1. Challenging Information in the Affidavits

Affidavits in support of probable cause may be challenged by defense counsel who argues that 1) the facts in the affidavit for the warrant are insufficient to establish probable cause, or 2) some or all statements in the affidavit were false. The latter may lead to what is called a *Franks* hearing. *Franks v. Delaware*, 438 U.S. 154 (1978). To obtain a *Franks* hearing, defense counsel preliminarily must establish two types of proof.

- There are specific false statements in the affidavit, making the warrant defective.

- The false statements were deliberately or recklessly made. If the statements were merely negligent or innocent, no *Franks* hearing is required.

A *Franks* hearing determines whether, *without* those false statements, the affidavit still contains probable cause. If so, evidence seized under the warrant does not have to be suppressed. If not, the evidence seized is not admissible *but* the warrant still is subject to the good faith of officers in executing it, unless *those* officers knew or should have known that the affiant was deliberately or recklessly lying. *See* Chapter 6.

2.   *Issuing Judge Must Be Neutral and Objective*

A judge who issues a warrant cannot have a pecuniary or political interest in the issuance of the warrant. Examples:

- An Attorney General is not sufficiently neutral and detached to issue warrants. *Coolidge v. New Hampshire*, 403 U.S. 443 (1971).

- The judge cannot have a pecuniary interest in issuing warrants, *e.g.*, receiving cash each time he issues a search warrant (and receiving nothing each time that he declines to issue a warrant). *Connally v. Georgia*, 429 U.S. 245 (1977).

3.   *The Particularity Requirement*

The "Fourth Amendment specifies two matters that must be 'particularly describ[ed]' in the warrant: 'the place to be searched' and 'the persons or things to be seized.' " *United States v. Grubbs*, 547 U.S. 90 (2006). If the warrant fails to specify what can be searched or seized, any evidence obtained is inadmissible.

a.   **Particularity of the Person to Be Seized**

An arrest warrant must specify the name of the defendant or otherwise describe the defendant so that she may be identified with reasonable certainty.

b. Particularity of the Search Premises

The description for the search premises must be so specific that it identifies only the premises intended to be searched, and no other place. If the description fails this test, the warrant is constitutionally deficient. Typical forms of descriptive information of the search premises are: street numbers, geographic indicators, or apartment numbers, descriptions of the building by color, style, composition, or size, or the name of the owner and/or residents.

When the warrant authorizes a search of only part of a building, *e.g.*, a single apartment in a multi-unit, residential building, that limitation must be expressed in the search warrant description. Property descriptions may conclude with language such as "any other evidence of the crime" or "together with other fruits, instrumentalities and evidence of crime." *Andresen v. Maryland*, 427 U.S. 463 (1976).

c. Particularity of Things to Be Seized

The description of things to be seized in the warrant must be as particular as the circumstances require, *e.g.*, a description like "narcotics" or "drugs" is sufficiently specific, but a reference to "stolen property" is unconstitutionally deficient.

d. "All Persons" Warrants

Normally, if a person is a search target of a search warrant, she must be particularly described (although not necessarily by name), just as with any non-human search target like a residence, business, or vehicle. The description is proper when the search premises are used for clearly criminal purposes, *e.g.*, for a "crack house."

E. Execution of Warrants

A search or arrest warrant for a specific place may be executed in the buildings and areas within the curtilage.

1. Who Executes the Warrant

A warrant may be executed by specific law enforcement officers directed in the warrant or by any other law enforcement officers authorized by applicable statutes in that jurisdiction. The executing officers are from their own jurisdiction but they may use officers from other law enforcement agencies or, where necessary, private citizens.

2. When the Warrant Is Executed

Search warrants must be executed within the jurisdiction's maximum time limit for execution (established by court rule or by statute) and before the probable cause information becomes stale. Prescribed maximum time limits vary from two to sixty days.

A delay in the execution of an *arrest* warrant does not render the warrant invalid.

3. The Knock-and-Announce Doctrine

The federal exclusionary rule does not apply to law enforcement officers' knock-and-announce violations. *Hudson v. Michigan*, 547 U.S. 586 (2006). Thus, despite the developing case law about how knock-and-announce works, there is no remedy when the process does not proceed smoothly.

The common-law "knock-and-announce" doctrine for warrants requires executing officers to audibly "knock" or otherwise make their presence and their purpose known at the outer door, and then to delay for a period of time sufficient to permit the occupants to reach and to open the door. *Wilson v. Arkansas*, 514 U.S. 927 (1995).

After a sufficient delay when no one answers the door, officers may enter the premises forcibly, if it is necessary and reasonable to enter. *United States v. Ramirez*, 523 U.S. 65 (1998).

4. Post-Execution Requirements

Executing officers must leave a copy of the search warrant and a receipt for items seized at the search premises, and promptly file a "return" with the court, noting when the warrant was executed and specifying precisely what was seized.

F. Seizures Pursuant to Search Warrant

Items particularly described in the warrant as evidence of crime may be seized under the authority of the warrant. In addition, executing officers may seize non-described items that they see in "plain view." *Horton v. California*, 496 U.S. 128 (1990). *See* Plain View, discussed in Chapter 3.

- Executing officers may search anywhere that described items may be hidden.

- A search warrant description for a particular place usually includes permission to search the land, buildings, and vehicles there.

1. The Permissible Scope of a Search

The scope is limited by the nature of the items being sought under the warrant. For example, a warrant authorizing an officer to search for illegal weapons provides authority to open closets, chests, drawers, and containers in which the weapon might be found.

- A warrant to search a vehicle supports a search of every part of the vehicle that might contain the object of the search. *United States v. Ross*, 456 U.S. 798 (1982).

- Occupants on the premises may be detained or searched, even without suspicion about their involvement in a crime. *Michigan v. Summers*, 452 U.S. 692 (1981). Police may frisk the outer clothing of anyone for whom there is reasonable suspicion that he is armed.

- When executing officers know or reasonably should know that property found on search premises belongs to a non-suspect third party, it cannot be searched pursuant to a warrant. This rule is inapplicable to a third-party *vehicle* passenger. *Wyoming v. Houghton*, 526 U.S. 295 (1999).

2. *When Police Must Discontinue the Search*

Once all of the objects particularly described and sought under a warrant have been found or the police leave, no further searches are permissible under the authority of that warrant.

When executing officers reasonably did not realize that a third floor was divided into two separate apartments, and that they were searching the wrong one, the search was upheld if the search ceased as soon as officers discovered that there were two separate units. *Maryland v. Garrison*, 480 U.S. 79 (1987).

CHAPTER 3

Warrantless Searches

Key Terms

- **Administrative probable cause:** one warrant can be sought to inspect all buildings in a particular area based on an assessment of conditions in that area.

- **Area of immediate control:** in searches incident to arrest, an area where the person may reach to help him escape, grab a weapon to harm another, or destroy evidence.

- *Camara v. Municipal Court:* introduced a test for determining whether a search was "reasonable," balancing the governmental interest against the private interest of the person searched.

- **Exigent circumstances:** a warrantless search theory based upon the imminent destruction of evidence, risk of danger to police or others, or hot pursuit of fleeing suspects.

- **Plain view:** items may be seized when police observe them from a place where they have a right to be.

- **Protective sweep:** to ensure safety, a search of areas beyond the person's immediate control.

- **Scope of a search incident to arrest:** the arrestee's person and the area within her immediate control, relatively contemporaneous with the arrest.

A. Why Warrantless Searches Are Important

Despite the judiciary's preference for search warrants, there often is inadequate time for preparing an affidavit and a warrant to present to a judge for her review and approval. As a result, searches and seizures without warrants have become the dominant approach for police in searching arrested or stopped suspects. The variations of warrantless search theories have developed as the need for quicker police response to crime has escalated. This chapter describes warrantless search theories.

B. Plain View Searches

When police are in a place where they have a right to be (*e.g.*, conducting a lawful search), pursuant to a warrant or an exception to the warrant requirement, they may seize items in "plain view" and search them. Plain view applies regardless of whether the police expected to find what they observed when the search began. *Horton v. California*, 496 U.S. 128 (1990).

- Assume that police standing on a public sidewalk look through the window of a residence and see drugs on a kitchen table. The observation in plain view may provide probable cause to obtain a warrant to search the house for drugs. (Without either a search warrant to enter the house or an emergency situation, the plain view observation does not justify immediate entry.)

C. Search Incident to Arrest

A search incident to a legal arrest is a well-established warrantless search theory. Each time that police arrest a suspect, they have the right to conduct a search of the suspect and the area within her immediate control, relatively contemporaneously with the arrest.

- Police cannot conduct a search incident to arrest if the person was given a citation or summons instead of being arrested. *Knowles v. Iowa*, 525 U.S. 113 (1998).

- Even if an arrest is a pretext to allow them to search for evidence they expect to find, police may still arrest the person and conduct the search. *Arkansas v. Sullivan*, 532 U.S. 769 (2001).

1. Scope of a Search Incident to Arrest

The scope of a search incident to arrest is limited to the area where an arrested person can easily obtain the means to escape, to harm another person, or to destroy evidence. *Chimel v. California*, 395 U.S. 752 (1969).

- An arrest outside the home does not justify a search incident of an adjacent home as incident to the arrest. *Vale v. Louisiana*, 399 U.S. 30 (1970).

- Any contraband found during a proper search incident to the arrest is admissible, even if it is unrelated to the reason for the arrest. *United States v. Robinson*, 414 U.S. 218 (1973).

- Police may open and search a smaller container found in a larger container either on the arrestee's person, associated with her (*e.g.*, a purse), or within her immediate control (*e.g.*, a briefcase next to her).

- Because a search incident to arrest for digital information on a cell phone does not further any rationale for a warrantless search, evidence found is inadmissible. *Riley v. California*, 573 U.S. 373 (2014). However, if police need to look at a cell phone to prevent harm to themselves or others, they can rely on the "emergency" exception, discussed below, to obtain evidence. If they are concerned about destruction of evidence, they can turn off the phone or remove the battery.

- The police can automatically, *i.e.*, without probable cause, look in spaces immediately adjoining the place of the arrest. To search beyond *those* adjoining spaces, police must have reasonable suspicion (a lower standard than probable cause) that another person posing a danger is there. During a protective sweep, police may seize evidence in plain view, even if they find no other persons. *Maryland v. Buie*, 494 U.S. 325 (1990).

- A state may not criminalize a person's refusal to take a blood test in the absence of a warrant because warrantless *blood* tests incident to an arrest violate the Fourth Amendment. Blood tests implicate privacy interests because they are invasive and produce a sample that can be preserved to obtain further information. By contrast, warrantless *breath* tests are far less invasive and seek information that is routinely exposed to the public. *Birchfield v. North Dakota*, 136 S.Ct. 2160 (2016).

2. *Scope of a Search Incident to Arrest: In or Near a Vehicle*

Police "may search a passenger compartment of a vehicle incident to a recent occupant's arrest only if the arrestee is within reaching distance of the passenger compartment at the time of the search *or* it is reasonable to believe the vehicle contains evidence of the offense of arrest." *Arizona v. Gant*, 556 U.S. 332 (2009).

- A proper search incident to arrest may extend to items found in containers within the passenger compartment, *e.g.*, the glove compartment.

3. *Time Limits for a Search Incident to Arrest*

Time limits depend upon whether the search incident is of the arrestee *or* the area within her immediate control.

- A search incident of the arrestee's person may occur hours later at the police station. *United States v. Edwards*, 415 U.S. 800 (1974).

- By contrast, a search of the area within the arrestee's immediate control must occur contemporaneously with the arrest. *Preston v. United States*, 376 U.S. 364 (1964).

D. Vehicle Search

When the police have probable cause to believe that a vehicle contains evidence of crime, they may search the vehicle without a warrant as long as the vehicle is capable of moving and therefore has "ready mobility." Probable cause alone justifies an immediate warrantless search "before the vehicle and its occupants become unavailable."

Like drivers, passengers have a reduced expectation of privacy in property they carry in vehicles, because of the same interest in concealing evidence of a crime. *Wyoming v. Houghton*, 526 U.S. 295 (1999).

1. Scope of a Vehicle Search

If police happen to find a container during the search of the vehicle, they may open it to examine its contents (instead of merely securing it) and anything found in the container is admissible under the plain view doctrine.

- The police searched the suspect's car after receiving information that he had completed a drug transaction with drugs from the trunk of his car. In the trunk, police found a brown paper bag containing illegal drugs. The Court upheld the search of the entire car. *United States v. Ross*, 456 U.S. 798 (1982).

- When police have probable cause to seize a paper bag that happens to be in a vehicle, they may search for the contents, or they may store it. If police see evidence in plain view while looking for that bag, they can seize it. *California v. Acevedo*, 500 U.S. 565 (1991).

2. Timing of a Vehicle Search

Probable cause to search a vehicle enables police to search the vehicle on the street or later in a different location. *Chambers v. Maroney*, 399 U.S. 42 (1970).

E. Booking Search

After the police arrest and "book" a suspect at police headquarters, it is reasonable for police or jail officials to search the personal effects as part of the routine administrative procedure. The government's interests are to 1) prevent personal items from being stolen, 2) help protect jail officials from false claims of theft, 3) prevent contraband or weapons from being introduced into the jail, and 4) ascertain a suspect's identity.

- In the case of an arrested person with a backpack, jail officials have the right to take the backpack and search its interior. *Illinois v. Lafayette*, 462 U.S. 640 (1983).

- Warrantless, routine collection by police of DNA samples from individuals arrested for specified serious crimes is a legitimate booking procedure that is reasonable under the Fourth Amendment. *Maryland v. King*, 569 U.S. 435 (2013).

- Police may conduct routine, suspicionless strip searches of all arrestees who end up in the general population, regardless of the seriousness of the crimes charged. *Florence v. Board of Chosen Freeholders of the County of Burlington*, 563 U.S. 917 (2012).

- A booking search nearly ten hours after a defendant's arrest is reasonable. *United States v. Edwards*, 415 U.S. 800 (1974).

F. Inventory Search

Inventory searches may be conducted without probable cause or a warrant. While the rationales for inventory searches are similar to booking searches, an inventory search cannot be *solely* for a criminal investigation; a mixed motive is allowed.

When a vehicle is legally impounded according to local standards that permit officers to exercise discretion, police may search the entire vehicle and any closed containers to list the contents. Any evidence recovered may be used in a later criminal prosecution. *Colorado v. Bertine*, 479 U.S. 367 (1987). An inventory search without written regulations to govern containers found during inventory searches is unconstitutional. *Florida v. Wells*, 495 U.S. 1 (1990).

G. Consent Search

A person can voluntarily (and without coercion) consent to a search, thereby relieving police of having probable cause for the subject area of the search. A "totality of the circumstances" test is applied, using a variety of factors peculiar to the suspect (*e.g.*, lack of education), and factors that suggest coercion (*e.g.*, police demanded the right to search). Police do not have a duty to inform a suspect of her right to refuse consent. *Ohio v. Robinette*, 519 U.S. 33 (1996); *Schneckloth v. Bustamonte*, 412 U.S. 218 (1973).

- Police asked an elderly widow for permission to search her house. One officer lied when he stated, "I have a search warrant to search your house." The search was illegal because the woman acquiesced to a "claim of lawful authority." *Bumper v. State of North Carolina*, 391 U.S. 543 (1968).

- If a person's consent does not place any limitations on its scope, the police may reasonably conclude that there is consent to search closed containers. *Florida v. Jimeno*, 500 U.S. 248 (1991).

1. *Third-Party Consent*

When a third-party consents to a search of property, a court must decide whether it was voluntarily given and the scope of the search, as well as whether the third party had authority to consent.

- A woman consented to the search of a house that she shared with a suspect. The Court held that the woman had "common authority," which rests on mutual use of the property by people with joint access or control. Each person assumes the risk that the other will consent to a search of the common area. *United States v. Matlock*, 415 U.S. 164 (1974).

- The Court upheld third-party consent search because it was reasonable for the police to believe (though mistakenly) that the defendant's girlfriend had authority to consent despite lacking actual "common authority" over the area searched. *Illinois v. Rodriguez*, 497 U.S. 177 (1990).

- A wife's consent to search is not valid because her husband objected. *Georgia v. Randolph*, 547 U.S. 103 (2006). But after an objecting person is removed from the scene for "objectively reasonable" motives, the consenting victim then may provide sufficient authority to search. *Fernandez v. California*, 571 U.S. 292 (2014).

H. Administrative Search

Administrative agencies regularly conduct inspections, *e.g.*, health inspectors enter restaurants to determine whether food preparation and service areas are clean. No Fourth Amendment search occurs when a public official enters and investigates an area that is open to the public because there is no expectation of privacy in that area.

Camara v. Municipal Court, 387 U.S. 523 (1967) balanced governmental and private interests in a manner used by courts in future cases defying categorization. The governmental interest in administrative inspections ensures "city-wide compliance with minimum physical standards for private property" and prevents "the unintentional development of conditions which are hazardous to public health and safety."

- Search of a locked storeroom of a firearms warehouse during reasonable hours is permitted. *United States v. Biswell*, 406 U.S. 311 (1972).

1. *Administrative Warrant*

"Administrative" probable cause applies when one warrant is used to inspect all buildings in a particular area, because many conditions (*e.g.*, faulty wiring) are not observable from outside the building. In emergencies, administrative warrants are unnecessary. *Michigan v. Tyler*, 436 U.S. 499 (1978); *See v. Seattle*, 387 U.S. 541 (1967).

2. *"Closely Regulated" Businesses*

In closely regulated businesses, a substantial government interest supports a regulatory scheme, and warrantless inspections further those schemes. The regulatory statute advises the business owner that a search is being made within a properly defined scope, and limits the inspecting officers' discretion by time, place and scope. Underground and surface mines qualify as closely regulated businesses. *Donovan v. Dewey*, 452 U.S. 594 (1981).

I. Exigent Circumstance Search

The exigent circumstances exception applies when there is probable cause to believe that an emergency situation exists regarding the imminent destruction of evidence, a risk of danger to police or others, or hot pursuit of fleeing suspects.

The following factors are important in assessing the imminent risk of the destruction or loss of physical evidence: 1) the degree of urgency and the amount of time to obtain a warrant, 2) a reasonable belief that evidence is about to be removed or that the suspect has a firearm, 3) the possible danger to police and others, 4) whether the suspect is aware that the police are looking for her and the likelihood of an escape, and 5) whether evidence can be easily destroyed.

1. Exigent Circumstances to Search a Place

Probable cause that an emergency situation exists justifies entry into private premises and an ensuing search only as long as the exigency exists. *Flippo v. West Virginia*, 528 U.S. 11 (1999).

- In a hot pursuit case, the police may search for weapons as they are seeking the suspect for a crime of violence, and the exigency ends when the suspect is captured. *Warden v. Hayden*, 387 U.S. 294 (1967).

- "Flight of a suspected misdemeanant does not always justify a warrantless entry into a home." An officer applies a totality of circumstances test to decide whether "there is a law enforcement emergency." *Lange v. California*, 141 S.Ct. 2011 (2021).

- After smelling marijuana outside an apartment door, law enforcement officers announced their intent to enter and kicked in the door where they saw drugs in plain view. Upholding the search, the Court held that law enforcement officers may rely on the exigent circumstances exception even when they had a role in creating the exigency, as long as they did not engage in, or threaten to engage in, conduct that violates the Fourth Amendment. *Kentucky v. King*, 563 U.S. 452 (2011).

2. *Exigent Circumstances to Search the Suspect's Body*

Other exigent circumstances cases have addressed police attempts to gather evidence from a suspect who is likely to disappear absent prompt or immediate action. Relevant factors include whether the means used were: 1) effective, 2) commonly used, and 3) involved virtually no risk, trauma, or pain, and performed according to accepted medical practices.

- When an unconscious driver cannot be given a breath test, the exigent circumstances doctrine generally permits a blood test without a warrant. *Mitchell v. Wisconsin*, 139 S.Ct. 2525 (2019) (remanded).

- The police instructed doctors to "pump" a suspect's stomach to locate drugs he swallowed. The Court ruled that the officer's conduct was illegal. *Rochin v. California*, 342 U.S. 165 (1952).

- A police officer, who believed that defendant's intoxication caused a vehicular accident, directed a physician to take a blood sample. The Court upheld the search because there was an "emergency" that would have led to the destruction of evidence. *Schmerber v. California*, 384 U.S. 757 (1966).

- The reasonableness of a warrantless blood test of a drunk-driving suspect is determined case by case based on the totality of the circumstances. *Missouri v. McNeely*, 569 U.S. 141 (2013).

J. Special Needs Search

Traditional warrant analysis is unnecessary for "special needs" searches that are beyond the normal need for law enforcement. Using the test articulated in *Camara v. Municipal Court*, 387 U.S. 523 (1967), courts balance the state's interest justifying the search against the intrusion upon privacy of the searched person or property caused by the search.

1. Drug Testing of Employees

- The Court upheld blood and urine tests of railroad employees involved in "major" train accidents. The Court emphasized: 1) the governmental interest "in ensuring the safety of the traveling public and of the employees themselves"; 2) the need to make sure that restrictions on drug and alcohol use are being observed; and 3) the need to act quickly to take samples after an accident. *Skinner v. Railway Labor Executives' Association*, 489 U.S. 602 (1989).

2. Drug Testing Pregnant Mothers

- The Court struck down a hospital policy of drug testing pregnant mothers suspected of cocaine use and turning the results over to police for prosecution. These tests were not "special needs" searches because their "central and indispensable feature" was to promote law enforcement goals. *Ferguson v. City of Charleston*, 532 U.S. 67 (2001).

3. Drug Testing Candidates for Public Office

- Drug testing of candidates is invalid, without information about a demonstrated drug problem. The government must prove that a suspicionless plan is necessary to protect against a public hazard. *Chandler v. Miller*, 520 U.S. 305 (1997).

4. Special Rules for School-Age Children

- A limited search of a high school student was upheld after a teacher found two girls smoking in a lavatory, and the assistant principal found drugs in their purses. The Court emphasized the "reasonableness" of the school's action: 1) "reasonable grounds" to think that a search would yield evidence of legal or school rule violations, and 2) the search was "reasonably related to the objectives of the search and not excessively intrusive in light of the age and sex of the student and the nature of the infraction." *New Jersey v. T.L.O.*, 469 U.S. 325 (1985).

- Drug testing for all middle and high school students in all competitive extracurricular activities is upheld, even without a documented problem of drug abuse among the students. *Board of Education of Independent School District No. 92 of Pottawatomie County v. Earls*, 536 U.S. 822 (2002).

5. Probationers

A state's operation of its probation system presents a "special need" for the "exercise of supervision to assure that [probation] restrictions are in fact observed."

- Knights' probation condition required him to submit to a search by any probation officer or law enforcement officer. A police officer, aware of the condition of Knights' probation, made a warrantless search of Knights' apartment that produced incriminating evidence. Police had the necessary reasonable suspicion to make a warrantless search of Knights' home. *United States v. Knights*, 534 U.S. 112 (2001).

6. *Border Search*

Special rules have always applied to searches conducted at or near the United States border, because of the interest in protecting those borders. *United States v. Montoya de Hernandez*, 473 U.S. 531 (1985).

- Limited searches of those who enter the United States are designed to make sure that entrants 1) are not carrying contraband, 2) do not have dutiable items that they have failed to declare, and 3) are not carrying harmful or dangerous items (*e.g.*, agricultural products with dangerous parasites). *See United States v. Flores-Montano*, 541 U.S. 149 (2004).

K. Stop and Frisk

A stop is proper when an officer reasonably concludes in light of his experience and observation that criminal activity may be afoot *and* that the person to be stopped is armed and presently dangerous. *Terry v. Ohio*, 392 U.S. 1 (1968). Since *Terry*, the case law appears to have de-emphasized the armed and dangerous requirement for a stop.

The reasonable suspicion standard for a stop or a frisk requires less proof than either probable cause or even a preponderance of evidence. Measuring reasonable suspicion is based on an individual assessment of the totality of the circumstances for suspecting the person of criminal activity. Reliance on drug courier profiles does not necessarily amount to reasonable suspicion to justify a stop.

- Efforts to avoid police or being seen by them may contribute to the reasonable suspicion necessary for a valid stop. *Illinois v. Wardlow*, 528 U.S. 119 (2000).

- The reasonable suspicion standard "depends on the factual and practical considerations of everyday life on which reasonable and prudent men, not legal technicians, act." *Kansas v. Glover*, 140 S.Ct. 1183 (2020). A police officer did not violate the Fourth Amendment by initiating an investigative traffic stop after running a vehicle's license plate and learning that the registered owner had a revoked driver's license.

- Other facts that may support reasonable suspicion for a stop are the nature of the suspected crime, what conduct caused the suspicion, whether the area is a high crime area or a luxury home area, whether the suspect is engaged in conduct for which he already has a criminal record, the suspect's age, race, dress, demeanor, and the police officer's experience.

- Reasonable suspicion may be based on a reliable tip from an informant, even an anonymous tipster. *Alabama v. White*, 496 U.S. 325 (1990).

- Reasonable suspicion for a stop may be based upon a reasonable mistake of law. *See, e.g., Heien v.*

North Carolina, 574 U.S. 54 (2014) (proper traffic stop of defendant was based on a reasonable but mistaken belief that a faulty brake lights violation occurred when fewer than all of the lamps were operational).

- The police are not restricted to stopping people for crimes that have not yet been committed. They also may stop a suspect who is found near the scene of a recent or completed crime. *United States v. Hensley,* 469 U.S. 221 (1985).

- A stop must be temporary and last no longer than is necessary to confirm or dispel the initial reasonable suspicion by police. *Florida v. Royer,* 460 U.S. 491 (1983). Extending a traffic stop to conduct a dog sniff requires continuing reasonable suspicion. *Rodriguez v. United States,* 575 U.S. 348 (2015).

1. *Stopping and Frisking People*

- After a stop, if police still suspect that the person seized is about to or has committed a crime, *Terry* permits them to frisk him if they also have reasonable grounds to believe that the person is armed and dangerous. That standard may be satisfied by the nature of the investigation, a bulge in the suspect's clothing, a suspect's sudden movement toward a pocket or other place where a weapon may be hidden, and police awareness that the suspect was armed on a prior occasion.

- A frisk typically begins with a patdown, when the officer is seeking a weapon that the suspect could reach to harm the officer. If the officer feels a weapon, he may reach beneath the surface and retrieve it. If the hard object turns out to be a container, the officer may open it if he still believes that a weapon is inside.

- During the patdown, if the officer feels something soft, he may *not* continue a tactile examination in an effort to determine whether the object is incriminating. *Minnesota v. Dickerson*, 508 U.S. 366 (1993).

2. Stopping and Frisking Vehicles

- A traffic stop requires reasonable grounds to suspect that a crime is or has been committed. The stop is a seizure of the passengers as well as the driver. *Brendlin v. California*, 551 U.S. 249 (2007).

- If the police are determined to find some reason to stop a suspect, they can follow the suspect's car, just waiting for him to do something illegal like running a stop sign. *Whren v. United States*, 517 U.S. 806 (1996). The actual motivations of the police are irrelevant, as long as reasonable suspicion for a stop or probable cause for an arrest exists.

- A frisk may extend beyond the suspect's person, especially during a vehicle stop. A "frisk" of the entire passenger compartment is reasonable, if it is limited to areas where a weapon may be placed or hidden.

3. Vehicle Checkpoints

Courts permit vehicle checkpoints that stop *all* incoming traffic, rather than discretionary spot checks. Courts have treated sobriety checkpoints with more deference, if supervisory personnel rather than officers in the field select when and where to conduct the checkpoints, the checkpoint location is publicized in advance, police stop every approaching vehicle or stop those selected by neutral criteria (*e.g.*, every fourth car), and the standard for detaining drivers suspected of driving while intoxicated is based on the test of reasonable suspicion.

- However, the Court invalidated a checkpoint where the goal was to intercept persons using illegal drugs. *City of Indianapolis v. Edmond*, 531 U.S. 32 (2000). The Court did recognize an exception for police to use a roadblock for ordinary crime control in an emergency or for an imminent terrorist attack.

- In *Illinois v. Lidster*, 540 U.S. 419 (2004), the Court upheld a roadblock conducted to gather information about a recent hit-and-run crime. *Lidster* found that 1) the seizure assisted in finding the perpetrator of a specific and known crime, 2) the checkpoint was at about the same location and time as the crime being investigated, and 3) the intrusion involved a brief wait in line and a request for information.

4. *Stopping Personalty*

The *Terry* analysis extends to investigative seizures of property, supported by reasonable suspicion. As with long detentions of persons, however, a seizure of property at some point requires probable cause to continue. The relevant factors for deciding whether probable cause has replaced reasonable suspicion are 1) the diligence of the investigation, 2) the length of the seizure, and 3) information given to the suspect about the seizure.

5. *Questioning and Fingerprinting*

Between an arrest and an investigative stop, there are other types of seizures.

- Taking a suspect to the police station for questioning or fingerprinting is tantamount to an arrest and requires probable cause. *Dunaway v. New York*, 442 U.S. 200 (1979); *Davis v. Mississippi*, 394 U.S. 721 (1969).

However, in *Hayes v. Florida*, 470 U.S. 811 (1985), the Court suggested that when fingerprinting is done in the field, reasonable suspicion of criminal activity might justify that brief detention.

CHAPTER 4

Police Interrogation and Confessions

Key Terms

- **Custodial interrogation:** questioning by the police after a person is deprived of his freedom of action in any significant way.

- *Miranda* **warnings:** before custodial interrogation, police must notify a suspect about the rights to remain silent and counsel.

- **Prompt arraignment:** supervisory power of federal courts permits suppression of confessions obtained during periods of unreasonable delay in taking arrestees before a judge.

- **Right to counsel:** at or after the beginning of adversary proceedings, defense counsel must be present before police can interrogate suspects.

- **Voluntariness:** coercive police activity is necessary to a finding of an involuntary confession.

- **Waiver:** before confessing, a suspect must voluntarily, knowingly and intelligently understand the constitutional rights he is giving up.

A. Why Police Interrogation Is Important

Often, police officials obtain confessions from criminal suspects. At trial, prosecutors attempt to introduce those statements as evidence against the defendant. In order to evaluate the admissibility of confessions, you must know about the Fifth Amendment privilege against self-incrimination, the Sixth Amendment right to counsel, Due Process, and the trial court's supervisory authority.

B. The Prompt Arraignment Rule

The Supreme Court's regulation of the admissibility of confessions is based on its supervisory power over all federal courts. Under 18 U.S.C. § 3501(c), if a confession is voluntary and was obtained within six hours of arrest, it is admissible and the weight to be given the confession is left to the jury. If the confession occurred before the initial appearance but beyond six hours after the arrest *and* if the court decides that the delay was unreasonable or unnecessary, the confession must be suppressed. *Corley v. United States*, 556 U.S. 303 (2009).

C. The Fifth Amendment and *Miranda*

Miranda v. Arizona, 384 U.S. 436 (1966) created a "Fifth Amendment" right to counsel in order to protect a defendant's access to the privilege against self-incrimination during the interrogation process. *Miranda* is a constitutional rule, *Dickerson v. United States*, 530 U.S. 428 (2000), and cannot be overruled by Congress. If the police violate the *Miranda* rules and obtain a statement during custodial interrogation, that statement generally is inadmissible.

1. Miranda's Safeguards: Warnings and Waiver

Prior to any questioning, police must inform a suspect in custody that he "has the right to remain silent, that anything he says can be used against him in a court of law, that he has the right to the presence of an attorney, and that if he cannot afford an attorney one will be appointed for him prior to any questioning if he so desires." After those warnings, the individual may knowingly and intelligently waive these rights and agree to answer questions or make a statement.

2. Rationales for Miranda

All custodial interrogations create a "potentiality for compulsion." In addition, the "human dignity" value of the Fifth Amendment may be protected only if rules limit the inherent coercion of interrogation so that confessions may be "truly [the] product of free choice."

3. Miranda Custody

Miranda applies only to "custodial interrogation," defined as "questioning initiated by law enforcement officers after a person has been taken into custody or otherwise deprived of his freedom of action in any significant way." By contrast, answers to "general on-the-scene questioning" are admissible because they lack the coercive atmosphere of in-custody interrogation.

- To determine custody, the "relevant inquiry is how a reasonable [person] in the suspect's shoes would have understood [the] situation," applying the totality of circumstances. *Stansbury v. California*, 511 U.S. 318 (1994). An objective standard insures that police officers will not have to "make guesses" about the existence of the particular circumstances. *Yarborough v. Alvarado*, 541 U.S. 652 (2004).

• Under the Court's "totality of the circumstances" approach to custody, relevant factors include the purpose of the investigation, the location and length of the interrogation, the interrogated person's awareness of her freedom to leave the scene, the person's actual freedom from a variety of forms of physical restraint, and the use of coercive interrogation methods.

• While a person at home may be regarded as being in "custody," *Miranda* warnings do not have to be administered to imprisoned defendants. *Maryland v. Shatzer*, 559 U.S. 98 (2010). "[L]awful imprisonment imposed upon conviction of a crime does not create the coercive pressures identified in *Miranda*."

• Certain situations are non-custodial *per se*, absent unusual circumstances. The typical "traffic stop" does not qualify as "custody," *Berkemer v. McCarty*, 468 U.S. 420 (1984), because a temporary detention for receiving a traffic citation is not comparable to the "police-dominated" atmosphere of a station house interrogation.

4. Miranda *Interrogation*

A suspect does not have to be advised of her *Miranda* warnings as soon as she is arrested, as long as she is advised prior to the commencement of interrogation. *Rhode Island v. Innis*, 446 U.S. 291 (1980) established a test for assessing whether a particular police comment or action would qualify as "interrogation."

- *Miranda* interrogation is "express questioning or its functional equivalent," defined as words or actions by the police that they should know are reasonably likely to elicit an incriminating response from the suspect. This definition of interrogation avoids focusing on the police officer's intent.

- Three important *Miranda* exceptions allow police to engage in conduct that would constitute "interrogation" under *Innis without* the duty to give *Miranda* warnings.

- The "routine booking question" exception: questions "normally attendant to arrest and custody" do not count as "interrogation" under *Miranda*. *Pennsylvania v. Muniz*, 496 U.S. 582 (1990). The rationale is that the answers to booking questions are unrelated to the quest for incriminating statements.

- Undercover agents: *Miranda* warnings are not required if a person "is unaware that [she] is speaking to a law enforcement officer." Such an interrogation does not carry the risks of self-incrimination inherent in a coercive, "police-dominated atmosphere." *Illinois v. Perkins*, 496 U.S. 292 (1990).

- "Public safety exception": without first providing *Miranda* warnings, police may ask about the location of a weapon that the arrestee may have abandoned or hidden in a public area near the scene of arrest. *New York v. Quarles*, 467 U.S. 649 (1984).

5. Adequacy of Miranda Warnings

The prosecution must prove that the warnings were given, as the first step for government arguments for a valid *Miranda* waiver. However, *verbatim* recitation of the *Miranda* warnings is unnecessary. The case law focuses instead on either incomplete or misleading warnings, but the Court has not dictated the exact words in which essential information must be conveyed. *Florida v. Powell*, 559 U.S. 50 (2010).

- When police "question first and warn later," such warnings are given "midstream" between two interrogations, and are likely to mislead the suspect about "the nature of his rights and the consequences of abandoning them." *Missouri v. Seibert*, 542 U.S. 600 (2004).

- However, *Miranda* warnings at later periods may be sufficient to offset the *failure* to warn at an earlier period of questioning. *Bobby v. Dixon*, 565 U.S. 23 (2011). After receiving the *Miranda* warnings, the defendant contradicted his prior unwarned statements by confessing to murder. Unlike *Seibert*, there was no earlier confession to repeat.

6. Waiver of Miranda Rights

In addition to the warnings, the prosecution must prove by a preponderance of the evidence that an arrestee waived her *Miranda* rights. *Colorado v. Connelly*, 479 U.S. 157 (1986). Waivers must be "voluntary, knowing and intelligent," based on the totality of the circumstances surrounding the interrogation. *Moran v. Burbine*, 475 U.S. 412 (1986).

- The factors for a voluntary waiver includes "the duration and conditions of [detention]," the "manifest attitude of the police" toward the defendant, the "physical and mental state" of the defendant, [and] the "diverse pressures which sap or sustain" the defendant's "powers of resistance and self-control." *Colorado v. Spring,* 479 U.S. 564 (1987).

- A waiver also must be "knowing and intelligent," through proof that an arrestee understood the *Miranda* warnings; a court may not presume that such an understanding exists, *Tague v. Louisiana,* 444 U.S. 469 (1980).

- A waiver may be implied from oral statements and conduct, and does not have to be in writing, *North Carolina v. Butler,* 441 U.S. 369 (1979), and it also may be inferred from the fact that a suspect eventually confesses to the police. *Berghuis v. Thompkins,* 560 U.S. 370 (2010).

- A conditional waiver may be proper, *i.e.,* if the suspect agrees to talk to police but not make a written statement, the conditional waiver is voluntary, knowing and intelligent. *Connecticut v. Barrett,* 479 U.S. 523 (1987).

7. Invocation of Miranda Rights

Under *Miranda,* police officers must respect an arrestee's invocations of the right to silence, the right to counsel, or both, by ceasing the interrogation. If an arrestee's invocation is ambiguous, police may ignore the invocation and continue to interrogate. Post-*Miranda* cases have resolved issues about a suspect's unambiguous invocation of rights.

- An invocation of either silence or of counsel must be explicit and "unambiguous," *i.e.*, when "a reasonable police officer in the circumstances would understand the statement to be a request for an attorney." *Davis v. United States*, 512 U.S. 452 (1994). When a defendant's invocation interrupts the police officer before all the warnings are administered, the officer should stop the interrogation as soon as the invocation is uttered. *Smith v. Illinois*, 469 U.S. 91 (1984).

- Police may seek a waiver after either type of invocation when the arrestee initiates a generalized discussion about the investigation with the police.

- An invocation of counsel is different from an invocation of silence; police are barred from initiating discussions and seeking a waiver after the former but not after the latter invocation.

8. *Re-Interrogation After Invocation of Rights*

- An invocation of silence does not permanently end the interrogation, but the police must show that they scrupulously honored an accused's invocation, *e.g.*, if they question him about an "unrelated" crime, a two-hour time lapse occurs before the re-interrogation, and the defendant receives a new set of *Miranda* warnings from a different police officer. *Michigan v. Mosley*, 423 U.S. 96 (1975).

- Different rules apply if the suspect in custody invokes his right to counsel. After the invocation, the police cannot interrogate the suspect unless the *suspect* re-initiates the contact. *Edwards v. Arizona*, 451 U.S. 477 (1981). *Edwards* also bars re-interrogation about different crimes unless counsel is present. *Arizona v. Roberson*, 486 U.S. 675 (1988); *Minnick v. Mississippi*, 498 U.S. 146 (1990).

- If a suspect is released from custody after invoking his right to counsel, the prohibition on police questioning lasts for fourteen days. After that time, the police may resume questioning without the suspect re-initiating the conversation. By contrast, if the suspect is not released from jail, the *Edwards* rules remain in effect. *Maryland v. Shatzer*, 559 U.S. 98 (2010).

9. *Impeachment with Defective Statements or with Silence*

- An unwarned statement that violates *Miranda* is admissible during cross-examination to impeach the credibility of the defendant's testimony *if* the statement was not obtained in violation of Due Process, *i.e.*, if it was given voluntarily. *Harris v. New York*, 401 U.S. 222 (1971). *See* Chapter 6.

- By contrast, a prosecutor cannot impeach a defendant at trial with his own post-warning *silence*. Otherwise, the exercise of the "right to remain silent" in the *Miranda* warnings is penalized. *See Doyle v. Ohio*, 426 U.S. 610 (1976); Chapter 6.

D. Sixth Amendment Right to Counsel

The Sixth Amendment right to counsel applies to police interrogation at or after the commencement of adversary judicial proceedings. *Rothgery v. Gillespie County*, 554 U.S. 191 (2008). Thereafter, law enforcement officials or their agents cannot interrogate the accused in the absence of counsel, unless the accused has validly waived that right. A confession obtained in violation to the Sixth Amendment is inadmissible.

1. Rationales for Sixth Amendment Right to Counsel

- Lack of access to counsel during questioning "might deny a defendant 'effective representation by counsel at the only stage when legal aid and advice would help him.' "

- Counsel's investigation and preparation are "vitally important," because defendants are "as much entitled to [the] aid of counsel during that period as at the trial itself."

2. Elements of a Sixth Amendment Violation

The violation of the Sixth Amendment right to counsel requires three elements: the attachment of the right to counsel, the failure of police to obtain a waiver of rights, and finally, the prohibited act of "deliberate elicitation" (equivalent to improper "interrogation") by police that produced incriminating statements. *Brewer v. Williams*, 430 U.S. 387 (1977).

3. Deliberate Elicitation

The Court has not identified any differences between *Miranda* "interrogation" and "deliberate elicitation" under the Sixth Amendment. However, one distinction relates to the treatment of persons who are questioned by undercover police agents. The Sixth Amendment does not allow the "deliberate elicitation" of incriminating statements by undercover agents from persons who possess Sixth Amendment rights, regardless of whether the suspect is incarcerated at the time of questioning.

- "Deliberate elicitation" exists when an undercover informant-cellmate is not a "passive listener" and joins as an active participant in conversations with the defendant. *United States v. Henry*, 447 U.S. 264 (1980). By contrast, "deliberate elicitation" does not occur when a police informant in the defendant's cell merely listens to a defendant's statements, without commenting to stimulate incriminating conversations. *Kuhlmann v. Wilson*, 477 U.S. 436 (1986).

- Statements obtained through "deliberate elicitation" by undercover agents *are* admissible at a trial on offenses *other than* the crime to which the Sixth Amendment right already has attached. *Maine v. Moulton*, 474 U.S. 159 (1985).

4. Waiver

The waiver standards for *Miranda* and Sixth Amendment rights are so similar that the *Miranda* warnings serve as an adequate method for informing a defendant of Sixth Amendment rights. *Patterson v. Illinois*, 487 U.S. 285 (1988).

5. Invocation of Sixth Amendment Right

When a defendant is questioned by police at or after the initiation of "adversary judicial proceedings," she may invoke her Sixth Amendment right to counsel. *Montejo v. Louisiana*, 556 U.S. 728 (2009). The legal consequences of that invocation depend on whether the suspect is in custody when the invocation occurs.

- The police may question and seek a waiver from any suspect who is *not* in custody. If the suspect is in custody and the police have informed him of his *Miranda* rights, a suspect who asserts his right to counsel is protected by the *Edwards v. Arizona* rules, discussed above. If the suspect *in custody* re-initiates contact with the police following the invocation, the police may seek a waiver and question him.

- The invocation of the *Sixth* Amendment right to counsel does not bar questioning for crimes that have not been charged yet. *McNeil v. Wisconsin*, 501 U.S. 171 (1991). The Court adopted the definition of "offense" from the Double Jeopardy context, *i.e.*, whether each crime requires proof of a fact which the other does not." *Texas v. Cobb*, 532 U.S. 162 (2001). *See* Chapter 13.

- The differences between the Sixth Amendment and Fifth Amendment invocations of the right to counsel: a Sixth Amendment invocation may occur even prior to *Miranda* warnings, and the consequences of a Sixth Amendment invocation permit questioning the suspect about uncharged offenses.

6. Impeachment with Defective Statements

Statements taken in violation of the Sixth Amendment may be used to impeach the defendant if she chooses to testify, as long as the statement was obtained voluntarily. *Kansas v. Ventris*, 556 U.S. 586 (2009). *See* Chapter 6.

E. Due Process

In order to be admissible in evidence, a defendant's statement must be voluntary to satisfy Fourteenth Amendment Due Process requirements. The most significant Due Process decisions in the post-*Miranda* era involve defendants whose confessions could not satisfy the Fifth and Sixth Amendment doctrines. For example,

Miranda does not apply to undercover investigations, to impeachment evidence, or to defendants who have waived their *Miranda* rights. The Sixth Amendment is relevant only at or after the start of adversary judicial proceedings when a defendant has been charged with a crime.

1. The Voluntariness Standard

Police coercion determines whether a defendant's confession is voluntary. If a defendant's free will is "overborne" by his mental illness, his confession is not involuntary in the absence of police coercion. *Colorado v. Connelly*, 479 U.S. 157 (1986).

- Where a police officer questioned a wounded arrestee for three hours while he was hospitalized in intensive care, the officer took advantage of the defendant's physical trauma by interrogating him and obtaining a confession illegally from him. *Mincey v. Arizona*, 437 U.S. 385 (1978).

2. Suspect's Personal Characteristics

Assuming that the police have engaged in overreaching conduct, courts also consider the characteristics of the suspect to evaluate his ability to resist the coercive police pressure. The common factors present in both traditional voluntariness as well as *Miranda* waiver cases include the defendant's: age, intelligence, education, experience in the criminal justice system, mental condition, intoxication on alcohol or drugs, physical injury and coercion, threats to others, length of interrogation and number of interrogators.

CHAPTER 5

Identification Procedures

Key Terms

- **Presence of counsel:** under the Sixth Amendment, the right belongs to the defendant at a pretrial confrontation at or after the start of adversary proceedings.

- **Reliability:** under the Due Process approach to the admissibility of a pretrial confrontation, this factor becomes important only if the identification was unnecessarily suggestive.

- **Unnecessarily suggestive:** based on the totality of circumstances, a pretrial confrontation may violate Due Process, depending upon the circumstances, what occurs prior to the confrontation, and the number of confrontations.

A. Why Identification Procedures Are Important

An eyewitness to a crime may be asked to testify that, prior to trial, she identified the defendant as the perpetrator of the crime. That event is frequently called a "pretrial confrontation." In addition, a police officer who was present at the pretrial confrontation may testify at trial about the pretrial identification made by the eyewitness, *i.e.*, an "out-of-court identification." In addition, the eyewitness may identify the defendant in the presence of the jury, *i.e.*, an "in-court identification."

B. Challenging Testimony About Out-of-Court Identifications

There are three possible and distinct challenges to an out-of-court identification.

- The identification may be challenged on the basis of the Sixth Amendment right to counsel rule requiring that defense counsel be present at the pretrial confrontation.

- The out-of-court identification may be challenged on the basis of Fourteenth Amendment Due Process, which excludes a pretrial confrontation between the defendant and the eyewitness that is so impermissibly suggestive as to give rise to a very substantial likelihood of misidentification.

- The third challenge is based on the idea that an in-court identification is the fruit of a pretrial illegality such as an illegal arrest, search or confession.

If the defendant is successful in either of the first two challenges, proof of the out-of-court identification is inadmissible in the prosecution's case-in-chief. If there was a Sixth Amendment violation, an in-court identification by the witness will not be permitted by the court unless the prosecution proves by clear and convincing evidence that the in-court identification is not *tainted* by the out-of-court identification, *i.e.*, the in-court identification will be based on the eyewitness's observations at the crime scene and not at the pretrial confrontation. *United States v. Wade.* The factors considered by the court in deciding whether to permit the eyewitness to make an in-court identification are the same as described in *Neil v. Biggers*, discussed below.

A Fourteenth Amendment violation will also exclude an in-court identification, but the prosecution is *not* permitted to "rehabilitate" the identification.

C. Sixth Amendment Right to Counsel

If adversary judicial criminal proceedings have been initiated against the defendant, he is entitled to have a lawyer present at any state-sponsored pretrial confrontation with an eyewitness, *i.e.*, any lineup or showup. The defense lawyer may later challenge the credibility of the witness' in-court identification at trial, and to eliminate unfair pretrial confrontations resulting in identifications of persons as the perpetrators of crime when they are not. *Kirby v. Illinois*, 406 U.S. 682 (1972).

1. At or After the Start of Adversary Proceedings

The Court has identified a short list of events that qualify as "adversary judicial proceedings," including initial appearance, formal charge, preliminary hearing, indictment or information. The defendant's initial appearance triggers the attachment of the right to counsel. *Rothgery v. Gillespie County*, 554 U.S. 191 (2008).

- If a pretrial confrontation occurs after adversary judicial criminal proceedings have begun without defense counsel's presence, any identification of the defendant at that pretrial confrontation is inadmissible. *United States v. Wade.*

- Even if the confrontation was fairly conducted, the out-of-court identification is inadmissible. This is a *per se* exclusionary rule, *i.e.*, no proof of the out-of-court identification may be presented to the jury. *Gilbert v. California*, 388 U.S. 263 (1967). It is possible, however, that the witness may still be able to identify the defendant in court.

2. Photo Displays

- There is no Sixth Amendment right to counsel's presence when an eyewitness is shown a photographic display that includes the defendant's photo, regardless of whether adversary proceedings have been initiated against the defendant. *United States v. Ash*, 413 U.S. 300 (1973).

D. Due Process

A Due Process constitutional violation may exist where the pretrial confrontation takes place before *or* after adversary judicial criminal proceedings began, and *even if* defense counsel is present. If the pretrial confrontation violates Due Process, proof that the defendant was identified at the pretrial confrontation is inadmissible and the witness cannot identify the defendant at trial. This is a *per se* exclusionary rule.

1. Unnecessarily Suggestive Confrontation

A pretrial confrontation violates Due Process if it is "unnecessarily suggestive and conducive to irreparable mistaken identification," considering the "totality of the circumstances."

Showups (in which the eyewitness is shown a single suspect) were condemned in *Stovall v. Denno*, 388 U.S. 293 (1967).

- To determine the possible unnecessary suggestiveness of a *lineup*, courts have looked to factors such as the circumstances of the lineup, matters that occur prior to the lineup, and the number of lineups. *See Foster v. California*, 394 U.S. 440 (1969).

2. Reliable Identification

Even though a showup is unnecessarily suggestive, the in-court and out-of-court identifications are still admissible if, under the totality of the circumstances, the identification is reliable. *Neil v. Biggers*, 409 U.S. 188 (1972); *Manson v. Brathwaite*, 432 U.S. 98 (1977).

- A preliminary judicial inquiry into the reliability of an eyewitness identification is mandated *only* when the identification occurred under unnecessarily suggestive circumstances arranged by law enforcement. *Perry v. New Hampshire*, 565 U.S. 716 (2012).

- Alternative devices to test reliability, regardless of whether law enforcement has engaged in improper activity include: expert testimony, "counsel at postindictment lineups, vigorous cross-examination, protective rules of evidence, and jury instructions on both the fallibility of eyewitness identification and the requirement that guilt be proved beyond a reasonable doubt." *Id.*

3. Admitting Out-of-Court Identification

If the pretrial confrontation was unnecessarily suggestive, the court looks at whether that suggestiveness is outweighed by the reliability of the identification, based on the five *Neil v. Biggers* factors, discussed below. Expert eyewitness identification testimony is admissible on issues like cross-racial identification, identification after long delays or under stress, and psychological phenomena.

4. Admitting In-Court Identification

For an *in-court* identification by a witness at trial, if the unnecessary suggestiveness of the pretrial confrontation outweighs the reliability of that identification, a trial court must ask itself whether the out-of-court identification is so unnecessarily suggestive as to create a very substantial likelihood of *irreparable* misidentification by the witness in the trial court, using the same *Neil v. Biggers* factors, discussed below.

5. Determining the Reliability of Identification

The courts look to numerous elements included within the five-factor *Neil v. Biggers* test to determine reliability.

- Opportunity of the witness to view the criminal at the time of the crime, *e.g.*, the lighting conditions, the amount of time for the view, and the degree of view by the victim.

- Witness's degree of attention, *e.g.*, whether the witness was a victim or casual observer as well as the training of the witness.

- Prior description of criminal, *e.g.*, any discrepancy between the defendant's appearance at the time of the crime and at the time of identification.

- Witness's certainty at the confrontation, *e.g.*, whether the witness previously observed other physical or photographic displays and has or has not picked out someone else.

Time between crime and confrontation. This is also a variable, but the other factors appear to be given more weight.

CHAPTER 6

Exclusionary Rule

Key Terms

- **Exclusionary rule:** prohibits the admission of evidence during the prosecution's case-in-chief, because of a direct violation of the defendant's rights.

- **Fruit of the poisonous tree:** prohibits the admission of evidence that is the indirect result of law enforcement's unconstitutional activity.

- **Good-faith exception:** the exclusionary rule is inapplicable when the police act in good faith in executing an unconstitutional search warrant, based on what reasonably appears to the executing officer to be a lawful warrant.

- **Standing:** exists when the defendant seeks to remedy a violation of her reasonable expectation of privacy.

A. Why the Exclusionary Rule Is Important

The exclusionary rule prohibits prosecutors from using evidence obtained in violation of a defendant's constitutional rights: Fourth Amendment, *Mapp v. Ohio*, 367 U.S. 643 (1961), Fifth Amendment, *Blackburn v. Alabama*, 361 U.S. 199 (1960) or Sixth Amendment, *United States v. Wade*, 388 U.S. 218 (1967).

The exclusionary rule applies to both federal and state proceedings as a constitutional remedy. *Weeks v. United States*, 232 U.S. 383 (1914); *Mapp v. Ohio*, 367 U.S. 643 (1961). State courts also may apply the exclusionary rule under their own state constitutions.

The purposes served by the exclusionary rule vary according to the nature of the right that has been infringed and the kind of evidence that has been obtained.

- **Fourth Amendment.** Exclusion of illegally seized evidence is intended to deter law enforcement officers' conduct. *Brown v. Illinois*, 422 U.S. 590 (1975).

- **Fifth Amendment.** The rule operates to ensure the voluntariness of incriminating statements and to prevent the use of coercive techniques, thus promoting the integrity both of the fact-finding process and of the judicial process.

- **Sixth Amendment.** The rule is intended to protect against unduly suggestive procedures that might impugn the integrity of the fact-finding process. *Foster v. California*, 394 U.S. 440 (1969).

1. *Exclusionary Rule Is Not a Per Se Rule of Exclusion*

The exclusionary rule does not forbid the use of all illegally obtained evidence in all situations. Courts balance the interest of deterrence against the costs of suppressing probative evidence, concluding that in certain circumstances suppression is inappropriate. *See Massachusetts v. Sheppard*, 468 U.S. 981 (1984). For example, in *United States v. Calandra*, 414 U.S. 338 (1974), the Court held that a prosecutor may ask a grand jury witness questions based upon illegally seized evidence.

B. Limits on the Exclusionary Rule's Application

- Evidence illegally obtained by private persons is admissible, but evidence resulting from cooperative or coercive action between police officers and private citizens is subject to the exclusionary rule. *See Abel v. United States*, 362 U.S. 217 (1960).

- The exclusionary rule does not usually apply in civil cases. *United States v. Janis*, 428 U.S. 433 (1976).

- Unlawful evidence obtained by an agent of one governmental unit does not lose its taint merely because another governmental unit uses it. *Elkins v. United States*, 364 U.S. 206 (1960).

- The exclusionary rule does not apply to Fourth Amendment claims raised in federal *habeas corpus* proceedings where the petitioner had a full and fair opportunity to litigate these issues in her prior state court proceedings. *Stone v. Powell*, 428 U.S. 465 (1976). *See* Chapter 23.

C. Good-Faith Exception to Exclusionary Rule

The exclusionary rule does not apply where police officers act on the basis of what reasonably appears to them (even erroneously) to be a valid and lawful search warrant. They would not ordinarily be deterred by application of the rule. *United States v. Leon*, 468 U.S. 897 (1984).

1. Extending the Good-Faith Exception Beyond Warrants

The Supreme Court occasionally has extended the good-faith exception beyond a search warrant context to otherwise unconstitutional, warrantless actions by law enforcement officers.

- A computerized police record erroneously indicated the existence of an outstanding arrest warrant, *Arizona v. Evans*, 514 U.S. 1 (1995).

- Police reasonably relied upon a statute subsequently found to be unconstitutional, *Illinois v. Krull*, 480 U.S. 340 (1987).

- An officer reasonably relied on negligent recordkeeping by other officers leading to an illegal search, *Herring v. United States*, 555 U.S. 135 (2009).

2. When the Good-Faith Exception Does Not Apply

The good-faith exception is *always* inapplicable in *any* of four situations:

- The judge issuing the warrant was misled by information in an affidavit that the affiant knew was false or would have known was false, except for his reckless disregard of the truth.

- The issuing magistrate wholly abandoned his judicial role, *Lo-Ji Sales, Inc. v. New York*, 442 U.S. 319 (1979).

- An officer's reliance on a warrant was based on an affidavit "so lacking in indicia of probable cause as to render official belief in its existence entirely unreasonable." *Nathanson v. United States*, 290 U.S. 41 (1933).

- A warrant is so facially deficient, *e.g.*, in failing to particularize the place to be searched or the things to be seized, that the executing officers cannot reasonably presume it to be valid.

D. Using Illegally Obtained Evidence for Impeachment

The exclusionary rule applies only to the use of unconstitutionally obtained evidence during the prosecution's case-in-chief. It does not apply to the same evidence introduced by the prosecution at trial to "impeach" the defendant's credibility on cross-examination. *Harris v. New York*, 401 U.S. 222 (1971); *Kansas v. Ventris*, 556 U.S. 586 (2009).

- A defendant's direct or cross-examination testimony can be impeached with illegally obtained evidence bearing *directly* on the current charge, *e.g.*, a confession admitting to the charged offense. *Oregon v. Hass*, 420 U.S. 714 (1975); *United States v. Havens*, 446 U.S. 620 (1980).

- Before a defendant can be impeached with an illegally obtained confession, the prosecution must show that the confession was given voluntarily, *i.e.*, not in violation of Due Process. *Mincey v. Arizona*, 437 U.S. 385 (1978).

- A *witness* cannot be impeached with illegally obtained evidence. *James v. Illinois*, 493 U.S. 307 (1990).

- A defendant's post-arrest silence, after receiving *Miranda* warnings, cannot be used as substantive evidence or for impeachment at trial. *Wainwright v. Greenfield*, 474 U.S. 284 (1986); *Doyle v. Ohio*, 426 U.S. 610 (1976).

- The prohibition on using the defendant's prior silence does not apply to cross-examination that merely inquires into prior inconsistent statements, *Anderson v. Charles*, 447 U.S. 404 (1980); pre-arrest silence, *Jenkins v. Anderson*, 447 U.S. 231 (1980); and post-arrest silence without *Miranda* warnings, *Fletcher v. Weir*, 455 U.S. 603 (1982).

E. Standing

A criminal defendant must have "standing" to raise the issue of unconstitutional law enforcement conduct. Standing exists only where the defendant seeks to remedy a violation of her *own* personal constitutional rights, not the rights of another person. *Alderman v. United States*, 394 U.S. 165 (1969).

- Some applications of the standing rules are self-evident. For example, only the person confessing can challenge her confession. The same approach applies to identifications, and searches, and seizures of her person.

1. Standing = Violation of Defendant's Reasonable Expectation of Privacy

Personal constitutional rights are violated where the constitutional harm is done to that individual personally, at a place (*e.g.*, her home), or to something (*e.g.*, her car or backpack) where and when she possessed a "reasonable expectation of privacy." *Rakas v. Illinois*, 439 U.S. 128 (1978).

- In standing cases, it is important to isolate which police act is objectionable. If the passengers challenge the stop of the car in which they were riding or challenge the seizure of their persons, they all would probably have standing to challenge the evidence seized as a fruit of the violation of their personal rights.

- Despite not being named in the rental agreement as an authorized driver, a defendant driving a rental vehicle when arrested has standing to challenge a search of the interior of the vehicle. *Byrd v. United States*, 138 S.Ct. 1518 (2017).

- A defendant does not have standing to object simply because evidence has been seized unconstitutionally from her co-defendant or co-conspirator, or the container of that other person. *Rawlings v. Kentucky*, 448 U.S. 98 (1980).

- An individual does have standing to challenge the constitutionality of a search of an apartment where he was present as an "overnight guest." *Minnesota v. Olson*, 495 U.S. 91 (1990). However, an individual lacks standing when his presence in an apartment was strictly as part of a commercial transaction. *Minnesota v. Carter*, 525 U.S. 83 (1998).

2. Standing REOP v. Fourth Amendment REOP

An individual's "reasonable expectation of privacy" (REOP) is the same concept used to define when police conduct is subject to Fourth Amendment requirements. *See* Chapter 1. However, unlike Fourth Amendment "activity" that is about whether there is *a* REOP, standing is about whether *the specific defendant* complaining about police conduct has a REOP to challenge the evidence obtained by the police conduct.

3. Proof Necessary for Showing That Defendant's Rights Were Violated

A person asserting *their own* REOP should attempt to prove property ownership, a possessory interest in the thing seized or the place searched, the right to exclude others from that place, or a subjective expectation that the place would remain free from governmental invasion. Some states use an automatic standing rule under their own state constitutions, enabling defendants to challenge *any* evidence introduced against them.

4. Defendant's Testimony to Obtain Standing Is Inadmissible at Trial

The suppression hearing testimony of a defendant about her relationship to evidence in order to prove standing cannot be used against her at trial on the issue of her substantive guilt. *Simmons v. United States*, 390 U.S. 377 (1968). For example, a defendant's suppression hearing admission to possessing illegal drugs to obtain standing is not admissible at trial.

F. Derivative Evidence: "Fruit of the Poisonous Tree"

Evidence derived from law enforcement's unconstitutional activity is inadmissible in criminal proceedings not only when it is obtained as a direct result of that activity, but also when it has been derived as an *indirect* result of the constitutional breach.

This rule is formally referred to as the "derivative evidence rule," but it is more commonly called "the fruit of the poisonous tree" doctrine [FOPT]. *Nardone v. United States*, 308 U.S. 338 (1939). The FOPT doctrine is *not* a mechanistic and broad "but for" type of causation test. Instead, it is an alternative method for challenging the admissibility of evidence.

- Assume that the defendant was arrested and the police subsequently seized contraband from the defendant's briefcase. FOPT doctrine enables the defendant to challenge the admissibility of the contraband by attacking the legality of the arrest, *even if* the search of the briefcase was legal.

- Where police illegally enter the defendant's home, a legally-obtained statement made by the defendant immediately after the illegal entry and drugs discovered based on the information in the defendant's statement are inadmissible against him. The statement is inadmissible, because the statement was derived from the illegal entry. *Wong Sun v. United States*, 371 U.S. 471 (1963).

1. FOPT Step-by-Step Analysis

In order for a defendant to invoke the FOPT doctrine, the issues are whether 1) the defendant has standing to challenge the original violation, *i.e.*, the tree; 2) the original police activity violated her rights; and 3) the evidence sought to be admitted against her, *i.e.*, the fruit, was obtained as a result of the original violation. FOPT analysis specifically addresses the *last* issue.

Using the facts from the most recent example, above, where the police illegally enter the defendant's home and legally obtain a statement from him, the FOPT analysis applies as follows. The first step is satisfied, because the defendant has standing to challenge the illegal entry of his own home. The second step also is satisfied, because the entry was illegal under the Fourth Amendment. The third step is satisfied as well, because police procured the statement through exploitation of the illegal entry, *i.e.*, it was the fruit of the illegal entry. If the answer for any of these posed questions is in the negative, the FOPT analysis fails.

2. *Why FOPT Is Useful*

FOPT is especially useful for defendants who lack standing to challenge the alleged fruit of the original violation. For example, if a confession was obtained from codefendant A in reaction to the illegal arrest of codefendant B, codefendant B cannot directly attack the admissibility of A's confession because B lacks standing.

- However, under FOPT doctrine, B can prevent the admission of A's confession because B has standing to challenge B's own illegal arrest, which violated B's rights, if B can show a direct link between B's illegal arrest and A's confession.

3. *FOPT Analysis Applies to Physical and Testimonial Evidence*

Traditionally, the FOPT doctrine applies both to physical and testimonial evidence. *Wong Sun v. United States.* However, in *United States v. Patane*, 542 U.S. 630 (2004), the Court questioned the application of the FOPT analysis when the fruit is *physical* evidence that was located as a result of a voluntary statement.

4. Exceptions to FOPT Analysis: Independent Source

A court will admit evidence *even if* it is the fruit of the poisonous tree, under three circumstances. First, the FOPT doctrine is inapplicable when the fruit of the illegality was located by an independent source, *i.e.*, by means unrelated to the illegal source. *Silverthorne Lumber Co. v. United States*, 251 U.S. 385 (1920). Example:

- If a trial judge has ruled that the police conducted an unconstitutional out-of-court identification procedure, the prosecutor still has the opportunity to show that the victim or witness can make an in-court identification that is independent of the improper out-of-court identification. *United States v. Crews*, 445 U.S. 463 (1980). *See* Chapter 5.

5. Exceptions to FOPT Analysis: Inevitable Discovery

Second, the inevitable discovery exception applies to evidence seized by illegal activity where the government can prove that it *would* have discovered this same evidence anyway or "inevitably," absent the constitutional violation. Example:

- The defendant's illegally obtained confession led to expedited discovery of the murder victim's body. Because the prosecution proved that a search party was approaching the actual location of the body and would have found her even if the defendant had not confessed, evidence pertaining to the discovery and condition of the victim was properly admitted. *Nix v. Williams*, 467 U.S. 431 (1984).

6. *Exceptions to FOPT Analysis: Attenuation*

Finally, evidence that would not have been discovered except for police misconduct still may be admissible if it is sufficiently separate from the illegal action. For example, three days after his release from custody, the defendant returned to the police station voluntarily to make a statement. The statement was admissible despite the initial illegal arrest because "the connection between the arrest and the statement had become so attenuated as to dissipate the taint." *Wong Sun v. United States.*

- Attenuation criteria include the lapsed time between the "tree" and the "fruit," the presence of intervening circumstances, and the purpose and flagrancy of the police misconduct. *Brown v. Illinois*, 422 U.S. 590 (1975). The *Brown* defendant's statement less than two hours after his illegal arrest was not attenuated and therefore was inadmissible.

- On the other hand, a statement obtained at the station house following an unlawful home entry to arrest is admissible because the statement was not an exploitation of the illegal entry. *New York v. Harris*, 495 U.S. 14 (1990).

- Based on application of the *Brown v. Illinois* factors, when a valid warrant is discovered after an unconstitutional investigatory stop, the connection between the unconstitutional conduct and the discovery of evidence incident to a lawful arrest based on the warrant is sufficiently attenuated. *Utah v. Strieff*, 136 S.Ct. 2056 (2016).

- When a witness freely decides to testify and a long time has elapsed between the illegal search and the witness's testimony, the testimony is sufficiently attenuated to allow its admission. *United States v. Ceccolini*, 435 U.S. 268 (1978).

- When the Court examined a case involving consecutive confessions, the first unwarned and the second warned, it held that a technical *Miranda* violation of failing to warn a suspect did not taint the second statement. *Oregon v. Elstad*, 470 U.S. 298 (1985).

When the police deliberately violated *Miranda* in the hope of obtaining statements that would lead them to physical evidence, the Court held that the physical evidence acquired from the *Miranda* violation was admissible. *United States v. Patane*, 542 U.S. 630 (2004).

CHAPTER 7

Prosecutorial
Discretion

Key Terms

- **Prosecutorial discretion:** deciding when and whether to pursue criminal charges.

- **Selective prosecution:** equal protection violation, based upon the prosecution improperly charging a defendant because of race, religion, or other arbitrary classification.

- **Separation of powers:** the concern that judicial review of executive branch charging decisions is questionable.

- **Vindictive prosecution:** due process violation, based upon the prosecution charging a defendant to penalize the proper exercise of constitutional or statutory rights.

A. Why Prosecutorial Discretion Is Important

Prosecutors have broad discretion about when and whether to pursue criminal prosecutions. They are the executive branch's delegate to help discharge a chief executive's constitutional responsibility to "take Care that the Laws be faithfully executed." *United States v. Armstrong*, 517 U.S. 456 (1996).

B. The Separation of Powers Doctrine

Courts generally refuse to interfere with executive branch prosecutors' decisions (not) to prosecute, based upon the separation of powers doctrine.

- The "decision to prosecute is particularly ill-suited to judicial review." *Wayte v. United States*, 470 U.S. 598 (1985). Prosecutorial discretionary factors include "the strength of the case, the prosecution's general deterrence value, the Government's enforcement priorities, and the case's relationship to the Government's overall enforcement plan." *Id.*

- When conduct violates more than one criminal statute, the prosecutor may charge under either statute, without regard to the severity of the penalty, as long as the prosecution is not discriminatory. *United States v. Batchelder*, 442 U.S. 114 (1979).

C. Selective Prosecution as a Constitutional Defense

It violates equal protection for a prosecutor to charge a defendant improperly because of race, religion, or other arbitrary classification.

1. *Yick Wo v. Hopkins*

When a Chinese businessman attempted to renew his license to run his laundry business, the board of fire wardens told him that he was violating a new city ordinance prohibiting laundries in wooden buildings. The Supreme Court noted that 310 of the 320 San Francisco laundries were housed in wooden buildings. Of 280 people who applied for licenses from the fire warden, all 80 non-Chinese received a license, even though their laundries were in wooden structures, and all 200 Chinese applicants were denied. The ordinance's intent was to discriminate against the Chinese and not simply to regulate the laundries for the public safety. *Yick Wo v. Hopkins,* 118 U.S. 356 (1886).

2. *Proving a Selective Prosecution Claim*

In response to a criminal charge, a defendant alleging selective prosecution must show both discriminatory intent and discriminatory effect.

- To justify an evidentiary hearing, a defendant must make a preliminary showing of "some evidence" that similarly situated persons of a different race, religion or other arbitrary classification were not prosecuted for the same offense. *United States v. Armstrong,* 517 U.S. 456 (1996).

- Circumstantial evidence through statistical disparities (if they exist) is the sole method for proving discriminatory intent, because prosecutors do not keep records of their motives in charging defendants. In addition, it is difficult to obtain information about a comparison of non-prosecuted offenders known to the police to show disparate treatment.

D. Vindictive Prosecution as a Constitutional Defense

Due Process prohibits a prosecutor from using his criminal charging discretion to penalize a defendant's proper exercise of constitutional or statutory rights, *e.g.*, reindicting a defendant on more serious charges as retaliation after a successful appeal.

1. Proving a Vindictive Prosecution Claim

To win a vindictive prosecution claim under Due Process, a defendant must show either 1) a vindictive motive by the prosecution, or 2) the situation poses such a reasonable likelihood of vindictiveness that a court should apply a rebuttable presumption of vindictiveness by the prosecution.

- When a defendant was convicted of a misdemeanor, he exercised the right to a trial *de novo*, but was then charged by the prosecutor with a felony based on the same conduct. Without having to prove prosecutorial bad faith or malice, the Court found that the appearance of vindictiveness alone would chill the defendant's right to appeal. *Blackledge v. Perry*, 417 U.S. 21 (1974).

- When a presumption of vindictiveness arises, the burden shifts to the prosecution to show that independent reasons or intervening circumstances dispel the appearance of vindictiveness and justify the decision to add charges or increase the severity of charges after a successful appeal.

- The Court applies a rebuttable presumption of vindictiveness when the defendant's convictions are reversed on appeal and he receives a longer sentence after a retrial for the same charge. The prosecutor introduces objective information to rebut the presumption and justify the increased sentence, *i.e.*, the higher sentence is the result of information unavailable to the judge at the time of the first trial. *North Carolina v. Pearce*, 395 U.S. 711 (1969).

- Courts do not recognize presumptions of vindictiveness that arise in a pretrial context. For example, when a prosecutor makes explicit threats during plea negotiations to seek more serious charges against a defendant who rejects the prosecutor's offer, no presumption of vindictiveness exists when additional charges are filed after the defendant requests a jury trial. *United States v. Goodwin*, 457 U.S. 368 (1982). Thus, any challenge to the initial decision to prosecute as a vindictive prosecution requires proof from the defendant that a vindictive motive actually exists.

To show actual vindictiveness, defendant must prove objectively that the prosecutor's charging decision was motivated by a desire to punish the defendant for doing something that the law allowed him to do (such as increasing the charges after asking for a jury trial, or increasing the charges from misdemeanors to felonies when felony convictions have more serious collateral consequences than misdemeanors).

CHAPTER 8

Right to Counsel

Key Terms

- **Conflict of interest:** often occurs when an attorney represents more than one codefendant.

- **"Day in jail" rule:** an indigent defendant charged with a misdemeanor cannot be imprisoned for *any* period of time unless she has the opportunity for appointed counsel.

- **Felony defendants:** accused of felony charges have a right to counsel regardless of whether they are sentenced to prison.

- **Ineffective assistance of counsel:** exists because of 1) an error in defense counsel's performance, and 2) prejudice from that error that had an adverse effect on the outcome of the case.

- ***Pro se* representation:** defendants may waive the right to counsel and represent themselves.

- **Waiver of counsel:** must be voluntary, knowing and intelligent.

A. Why the Right to Counsel Is Important

Counsel is a necessity for criminal defendants due to the state's belief that attorneys are essential to the public's prosecutorial interest. Defendants who can afford attorneys hire them. A fair and impartial system can be a reality only if indigents also have the assistance of an attorney. Defendants are entitled to counsel who render effective assistance.

B. Scope of the Constitutional Right

1. When the Right Attaches

The right to appointed counsel attaches before trial, at any "critical stage of the criminal prosecution" at or after the "initiation of adversary judicial criminal proceedings—whether by way of [first appearance,] formal charge, preliminary hearing, indictment, information, or arraignment." *Kirby v. Illinois*, 406 U.S. 682 (1972); *Rothgery v. Gillespie County*, 554 U.S. 191 (2008).

- A "critical stage" occurs when counsel's presence minimizes the imbalance in the adversarial system between the prosecution and the defendant, and assists an uninformed defendant in the criminal justice system. *See United States v. Wade*, 388 U.S. 218 (1967). Besides the right to counsel at trial, the following are examples of "critical stages" to which the right to counsel applies.

- Police interrogation after the start of the adversarial process, *Massiah v. United States*, 377 U.S. 201 (1964).

- Post-indictment lineups, *United States v. Wade*.

- Entry of guilty pleas, *Iowa v. Tovar*, 541 U.S. 77 (2004).

- Appeal as a matter of right, *Douglas v. California*, 372 U.S. 353 (1963).

- The Supreme Court does *not* consider the following to be "critical stages" that require counsel: post-indictment photo identification procedure, *United States v. Ash*, 413 U.S. 300 (1973); most discretionary appeals, *Ross v. Moffitt*, 417 U.S. 600 (1974); collateral review of any criminal conviction, *Murray v. Giarratano*, 492 U.S. 1 (1989).

2. *Choice of Counsel*

- Indigent defendants have no right to choose the attorney appointed to represent them, *Wheat v. United States*, 486 U.S. 153 (1988).

- A defendant with funds to hire an attorney has the constitutional right to hire that attorney. *United States v. Gonzalez-Lopez*, 548 U.S. 140 (2006).

3. *"Day in Jail" Rule*

Indigent defendants facing *felony* charges have a Sixth Amendment right to appointed defense counsel, regardless of whether they are sentenced to prison. *Johnson v. Zerbst*, 304 U.S. 458 (1938); *Gideon v. Wainwright*, 372 U.S. 335 (1963).

An indigent defendant charged with a *misdemeanor* cannot be imprisoned for *any* period of time unless she had the opportunity to have appointed counsel. *Argersinger v. Hamlin*, 407 U.S. 25 (1972).

- *Argersinger* also requires appointed counsel for defendants who receive suspended sentences (*i.e.*, cases where imprisonment is imposed but may not actually occur), rather than actual, immediate incarceration, because a suspended sentence may ultimately result in incarceration. *Alabama v. Shelton*, 535 U.S. 654 (2002).

- The "day in jail" rule does not mean, however, that an indigent defendant has a right to counsel when she is charged with an offense that *could* result in imprisonment. *Scott v. Illinois*, 440 U.S. 367 (1979).

- An uncounseled misdemeanor conviction that is valid because there was no imprisonment may be used to enhance the sentence for a later offense, even one that does entail imprisonment. *Nichols v. United States*, 511 U.S. 738 (1994).

4. Retained Counsel

Counsel must be admitted to practice law in the place of the criminal proceedings, unless counsel is specially admitted to the Bar of that jurisdiction to represent the defendant in only that criminal proceeding (*"pro hac vice* admission").

- The trial court's authority is discretionary: "the Constitution does not require that because a lawyer has been admitted to the bar of one state, he or she must be allowed to practice in another." *Leis v. Flynt*, 439 U.S. 438 (1979).

C. Waiver of the Right to Counsel

1. Knowing and Intelligent Waivers

A criminal defendant may waive her Sixth Amendment right to counsel, if that waiver is voluntary, knowing and intelligent. The trial court must ensure that the defendant understands the waiver's significance and consequences. *Brewer v. Williams*, 430 U.S. 387 (1977); *Johnson v. Zerbst*, 304 U.S. 458 (1938).

- For an intelligent waiver, the relevant factors include "the defendant's education or sophistication, the complex or easily grasped nature of the charge, and the stage of the proceeding." *Iowa v. Tovar*, 541 U.S. 77 (2004). A voluntary waiver is relevant to the topic of self-representation.

2. *Representing Oneself*

Defendants may waive counsel and represent themselves. *Faretta v. California*, 422 U.S. 806 (1975). First, a defendant must make an unequivocal and timely request. In response, the trial court holds a hearing to determine whether the defendant is competent to waive the right to counsel completely or partially, and whether to appoint standby counsel.

- The standard for waiving the right to counsel begins with satisfying the same competency standard for standing trial. *Godinez v. Moran*, 509 U.S. 389 (1993). The defendant also must indicate competence to conduct the trial proceedings alone. *Indiana v. Edwards*, 554 U.S. 164 (2008).

- A trial court may deny *pro se* representation where the defendant's mental illness interferes with self-representation, even if he is mentally competent to stand trial and understands the disadvantages of self-representation. For the waiver to be intelligent and knowing, the defendant's "technical legal knowledge" is irrelevant. *Id.*

- A trial court may appoint a "standby counsel" for the defendant who requests help, and to represent him if it terminates the defendant's self-representation. The standby counsel cannot make or substantially interfere with 1) significant tactical decisions, 2) the questioning of witnesses, or 3) the defendant on any matter of importance. *McKaskle v. Wiggins*, 465 U.S. 168 (1984).

D. Ineffective Assistance of Counsel

A criminal defendant's Sixth Amendment right to counsel includes the right to the "effective" assistance of counsel. The right applies to trial proceedings, guilty pleas, sentencing, and a first appeal of right. Whether a defendant has a right to effective assistance of counsel during state post-conviction proceedings is still an open question after *Martinez v. Ryan*, 565 U.S. 1 (2012). If there is no right to counsel, no right to effective assistance exists. The remedy for ineffective assistance is automatic reversal of the conviction.

1. Per Se *Ineffectiveness*

A criminal defendant who claims that his defense counsel was guilty of "extrinsic ineffectiveness" alleges that some factor(s) *extrinsic* to counsel's *actual* performance created a permissible inference of Sixth Amendment ineffectiveness.

- Generally, ineffectiveness can be proved extrinsically in only two situations: 1) a complete failure of counsel at a critical stage of the trial, or 2) "counsel entirely fails to subject the prosecution's case to a meaningful adversarial testing." *United States v. Cronic*, 466 U.S. 648 (1984).

- Extrinsic claims commonly focus on counsel's age, inexperience overall or in criminal cases, disability, personal or emotional problems, alcoholism or substance abuse problems, problems with the law, insufficient preparation time, or Bar disciplinary issues.

- An appellate court rarely reverses a conviction due to extrinsic ineffectiveness, *e.g.*, defense counsel's concession of the client's guilt does not rank as a " 'fail[ure] to function in any meaningful sense as the Government's adversary.' " *Florida v. Nixon*, 543 U.S. 175 (2004).

- Allegations of counsel's failures (*e.g.*, failure to introduce mitigating evidence, waiver of closing argument) may raise issues of *actual* ineffectiveness under *Strickland* (discussed in the next section), but not under *Cronic*.

2. Actual Ineffectiveness

Strickland v. Washington, 466 U.S. 668 (1984) established the criteria for ineffective assistance of counsel when claims of *actual* ineffectiveness are alleged.

- In *Strickland*, during the penalty phase of a capital case in which defendant was sentenced to death, defense counsel did not seek character witnesses or request a psychiatric examination, because conversations with his client gave no indication that Washington had psychological problems. The Court concluded that Washington had *not* proved ineffective assistance of counsel.

- The federal constitutional standard for reviewing an allegation of ineffective assistance of counsel involves: 1) a finding of an error in counsel's performance, and 2) prejudice from that error, adversely affecting the outcome, *i.e.*, but for counsel's unprofessional errors, a reasonable probability exists that the result of the proceeding would have been different or that the defendant would have chosen a different course of action. *Strickland v. Washington*, 466 U.S. 668 (1984); *Hill v. Lockhart*, 474 U.S. 52 (1985).

- For example, in *Lee v. United States*, 137 S.Ct. 1958 (2017), the defendant, a South Korean national, pled guilty to drug possession after his lawyer told him that he would not be deported. Following *Hill v. Lockhart*, the defendant established a reasonable probability that he would have rejected the plea had he known that it would lead to mandatory deportation. The bad advice violated the defendant's Sixth Amendment right to effective assistance.

- The performance and prejudice portions of the test are independent of one another. A defendant must show both that defense counsel performed deficiently and that the deficient performance actually prejudiced her defense.

3. Performance Prong

Defense counsel's performance is assessed from his perspective and the professional standards prevailing in the state at the time of the trial. *Bobby v. Van Hook*, 558 U.S. 4 (2009). For example, an appellate court cannot examine defense counsel's conduct based on contemporary views of ballistic evidence rather than how that information was viewed at the time of defendant's trial. In *Maryland v. Kulbicki*, 577 U.S. 1 (2015), because there was no reason for counsel to have questioned the credibility of such evidence at the time of trial, defense counsel was not ineffective for having failed to question that evidence even though it has become viewed as questionable.

No one specific task by defense counsel qualifies counsel as effective, and the Court rejected using a "checklist for judicial evaluation of attorney performance." However, the Court defined general duties that defense counsel *must* assume for the client.

- "[C]ounsel owes the client a duty of loyalty, as well as a duty to avoid conflicts of interest," to advocate the defendant's cause, to consult with the defendant on important decisions, to inform the defendant about important developments in the case, to use her skills and knowledge in order to "render the trial a reliable adversarial testing process," and to make reasonable investigations or reasonable decisions to make such investigations unnecessary. *Kimmelman v. Morrison*, 477 U.S. 365 (1986).

- In general, a defendant can likely prove incompetency where the alleged errors are attributable to a lack of diligence rather than the exercise of judgment.

- In *Wiggins v. Smith*, 539 U.S. 510 (2003), defense counsel decided not to expand the penalty phase investigation beyond a presentence investigation report and a social services report. Counsel knew from the latter report about defendant's alcoholic mother and his problems in foster care; the decision to cease investigating was unreasonable. A reasonably competent attorney would have known that those leads would assist in making an informed choice among possible defenses.

- By contrast, in *McCoy v. Louisiana*, 138 S.Ct. 1500 (2018), the Court held that counsel was ineffective when he admitted that his client had committed the murders. Instead of being strategic to avoid the death penalty, the concessions violated defendant's express instructions not to admit the crimes, and violated his Sixth Amendment right to choose the objective of his defense.

- A finding of ineffective assistance may be based upon the *cumulative* effect of counsel's errors. *Rompilla v. Beard*, 545 U.S. 374 (2005).

4. *Strategic Decisions*

A strategic exercise of judgment, *e.g.*, deciding whether to 1) investigate, 2) file a motion to dismiss the charge or to suppress evidence, or 3) raise substantive defenses, is not deficient performance. However, defense counsel *is* subject to an ineffectiveness claim when strategic choices are made after less than complete investigation.

- In *Florida v. Nixon*, 543 U.S. 175 (2004), for example, defense counsel is not presumptively ineffective by failing to obtain client's express approval of a strategy to concede guilt to a capital offense and focus instead on urging mercy during the penalty phase.

- Defense counsel's recommendation that the client withdraw his insanity defense was based on counsel's reasonable belief that the insanity defense was doomed because medical testimony had been rejected and the defendant's parents were unavailable to testify. *Knowles v. Mirzayance*, 556 U.S. 111 (2009).

- Counsel's strategic decisions include objecting to evidence, *Wainwright v. Sykes*, 433 U.S. 72 (1977), or selecting witnesses.

- "Fundamental rights" decisions such as pleading guilty, having a jury trial, appealing a conviction, and whether to testify belong to the defendant. *Jones v. Barnes*, 463 U.S. 745 (1983).

5. *Prejudice Prong*

In addition to defective performance, a defendant must prove prejudice from the attorney's ineffectiveness. Prejudice focuses on "whether counsel's deficient performance renders the result of the trial unreliable or the proceeding fundamentally unfair." *Lockhart v. Fretwell*, 506 U.S. 364 (1993). Unlike performance, the assessment of prejudice is not limited to standards in effect at the time of defense counsel's deficient performance. *Id.*

- Prejudice is *presumed* when 1) there is an actual or constructive denial of counsel, *e.g.*, where counsel is asleep for long periods of time during the proceeding or where counsel is not a member of the bar), 2) the state interferes with the lawyer's assistance (as where there is a late appointment of counsel or where the judge denies defense counsel the right to cross-examine witnesses), or 3) defense counsel is burdened by an actual conflict of interest (*See* Section E, *infra*).

- When deficient performance costs a defendant an appeal that the defendant would have otherwise pursued, prejudice to the defendant is presumed "with no further showing from the defendant of the merits of his underlying claims." The presumption of prejudice applies even if the defendant has signed an appeal waiver. *Garza v. Idaho*, 139 S.Ct. 738 (2019); *Roe v. Flores-Ortega*, 528 U.S. 470 (2000).

- If prejudice is *not* presumed, a defendant must show a reasonable probability that, but for defense counsel's errors, the results of the case would have been different. If the evidence against the defendant is overwhelming, a conviction will be affirmed no matter how fundamental is counsel's performance error.

- In decisions since *Strickland*, the Court has found no prejudice where defense counsel 1) threatened to withdraw if his client perjured himself at trial, *Nix v. Whiteside*, 475 U.S. 157 (1986), 2) failed to make an objection in a capital sentencing hearing that would have (then) been supported by a decision that was subsequently overruled, *Lockhart v. Fretwell*, 506 U.S. 364 (1993), and 3) misinformed his client of his parole eligibility date in explaining the consequences of his contemplated guilty plea, *Hill v. Lockhart*, 474 U.S. 52 (1985).

- On the other hand, the defense counsel's failure to object to a legal error that affected the calculation of a prison sentence, thereby resulting in additional incarceration, is prejudicial to a defendant. *Glover v. United States*, 531 U.S. 198 (2001).

- Arguing against the death penalty, defense counsel introduced evidence showing that his client was liable to be a future danger because of his race. Counsel's defective performance prejudiced the defendant and constituted ineffective assistance of counsel. *Buck v. Davis*, 137 S.Ct. 759 (2017).

6. Ineffective Assistance in Plea Bargaining

Defense counsel is ineffective if he fails to properly inform the defendant of a beneficial plea agreement offered by the prosecution, or if he incorrectly advises the defendant on the state of the law, leading the defendant to reject a beneficial plea agreement. *Missouri v. Frye*, 566 U.S. 133 (2012); *Lafler v. Cooper*, 566 U.S. 156 (2012).

- Defense counsel has a constitutional duty to communicate formal plea offers from the prosecution. In *Lafler*, counsel's assistance was prejudicially ineffective: 1) but for the ineffective advice of counsel, there was a reasonable probability that the defendant would have accepted the plea offer, 2) the court would have accepted its terms, and 3) the conviction and sentence would have differed from what was imposed at trial. The proper remedy is for the prosecution to re-offer the plea and, if the defendant accepts it, the trial court can decide how to amend the original sentence.

7. Ineffective Assistance of Counsel on Appeal

If a state provides an automatic right to an appeal of a defendant's criminal conviction, he has a constitutional right to effective assistance of counsel. Appellate counsel "must play the role of an active advocate." *Evitts v. Lucey*, 469 U.S. 387 (1985).

- For example, counsel's failure to follow a simple court rule about filing a statement of appeal with an appellate brief constitutes ineffective assistance of counsel rather than an exercise of judgment. *Id.*

- When counsel withdraws from appellate representation because the appeal is frivolous, he must offer more than a bare conclusion that the appeal has no merit. *Anders v. California*, 386 U.S. 738 (1967). He must also file a brief "referring to anything in the record that might arguably support the appeal. A copy of counsel's brief should be furnished [to] the indigent and time allowed him to raise any points he chooses." *Id.*

8. When Ineffective Assistance Claims Can Be Brought

"[A]n ineffective assistance of counsel claim may be brought in a collateral proceeding," whether or not the defendant could have raised the claim on direct appeal. *Massaro v. United States*, 538 U.S. 500 (2003). In addition, a defendant may claim that state counsel in a collateral proceeding was ineffective in failing to raise his ineffective-assistance-at-trial claim. *Martinez v. Ryan*, 566 U.S. 1 (2012).

E. Conflicts of Interest

The constitutional right to effective assistance of counsel entitles the defendant to the "undivided loyalty" of counsel. Defense counsel's conflict of interest can amount to ineffective assistance of counsel. *Glasser v. United States*, 315 U.S. 60 (1942). The situation producing the most frequent conflict claims is the representation of more than one codefendant by the same attorney.

• A lawyer may also be placed in a conflict situation when there is a professional relationship with both the defendant and a third party with some interest in the case, or when someone with an interest in the case pays the legal fees of defense counsel. *Wood v. Georgia*, 450 U.S. 261 (1981).

- With conflicting interests, "the evil . . . is in what the advocate finds himself compelled to refrain from doing, not only at trial but also as to possible pretrial plea negotiations and in the sentencing process." *Holloway v. Arkansas*, 435 U.S. 475 (1978).

- When trial counsel *timely* alerts the trial court to the risk of a conflict of interest, the trial judge must "either [appoint] separate counsel or [take] adequate steps to ascertain whether the risk was too remote to warrant separate counsel." *Id.* Where the trial court fails to either grant the motion or hold a hearing, appellate reversal is "automatic," even without a showing of prejudice. *Mickens v. Taylor*, 535 U.S. 162 (2002).

- "[A] defendant who raised *no objection* at trial must demonstrate that an actual conflict of interest adversely affected his lawyer's performance." *Cuyler v. Sullivan*, 446 U.S. 335 (1980).

- A defendant may waive a conflict of interest, and a trial judge must recognize a presumption in favor of a defendant's counsel of choice. However, a demonstration of either an actual conflict or a serious potential for conflict rebuts the presumption. *Wheat v. United States*, 486 U.S. 153 (1988).

- A trial judge has the discretion to refuse waivers of conflicts of interest in both actual and potential conflict situations, without violating a defendant's Sixth Amendment right to her counsel of choice.

F. Access to Justice for Indigents

The government has a constitutional obligation to redress the consequences of indigency in the criminal justice system.

- "The duty of the state under our cases is . . . only to assure the indigent defendant an adequate opportunity to present his claims fairly. . . ." *Ross v. Moffitt*, 417 U.S. 600 (1974). Thus, indigents undertaking discretionary appeals (as opposed to appeals as of right) are not entitled to the appointment of counsel, even though a non-indigent would have the resources and, hence, could retain such appellate counsel. *Id.*

- However, a defendant *is* entitled to have access to a psychiatrist and a psychiatric examination when raising an insanity defense, because those services are a necessary, basic tool when the issue of sanity is raised. *Ake v. Oklahoma*, 470 U.S. 68 (1985); *McWilliams v. Dunn*, 137 S.Ct. 1790 (2017).

Indigents also have constitutional rights to: 1) a trial transcript to collaterally attack a conviction, *United States v. MacCollom*, 426 U.S. 317 (1976); 2) a transcript of a *habeas corpus* proceeding for use on appeal, *Eskridge v. Washington State Bd. of Prison Terms and Paroles*, 357 U.S. 214 (1958), or in filing a second *habeas* petition, *Gardner v. California*, 393 U.S. 367 (1969); and 3) a preliminary hearing transcript to prepare for trial, *Roberts v. LaVallee*, 389 U.S. 40 (1967). Similarly, filing fees for appeals and post-conviction proceedings do not apply to indigent defendants. *Burns v. Ohio*, 360 U.S. 252 (1959); *Smith v. Bennett*, 365 U.S. 708 (1961).

CHAPTER 9

Pretrial Release

Key Terms

- **Excessive bail:** pretrial release (usually financial) conditions are more onerous than reasonably necessary to ensure defendant's appearance at trial.

- **Preventive detention:** court's decision not to release a defendant pending trial, because of assessment about whether the defendant would appear for trial or would endanger the safety of the community or individuals.

A. Why Pretrial Release Is Important

The modern purposes of the pretrial release decision are to ensure the defendant's appearance at trial and to prevent the accused from committing crimes against either witnesses in the pending case or others in the community. To the accused, pretrial release enables him to resume his daily routine. Moreover, the ability to assist his counsel in locating witnesses to prepare his case is important to a fair trial.

B. Eighth Amendment Prohibition Against Excessive Bail

"Excessive bail shall not be required." *U.S. Const. amend. VIII.* Bail determinations take into account the facts and circumstances of the offense, as well as information about the defendant. The amount of bail must be no more than is reasonably necessary to assure his appearance at trial. Bail set at a higher amount is excessive under the Eighth Amendment. *Stack v. Boyle*, 342 U.S. 1 (1951).

- While state constitutions at least implicitly recognize the fundamental nature of the right to bail by the express prohibition of excessive bail, *United States v. Salerno*, 481 U.S. 739 (1987) found that there is no *federal* constitutional right to bail. Therefore, the Eighth Amendment is not violated by the use of pretrial detention due to the dangerousness of the defendant.

C. Statutory Attempts to Regulate Pretrial Release

In a federal felony prosecution, if a judge decides that a recognizance or unsecured release (neither of which depends upon a defendant's financial assets) will not reasonably assure the defendant's presence at trial, the judge must consider several factors about the defendant and the charged offense in order to tailor conditions for release. 18 U.S.C. § 3142(g).

- In addition to the boilerplate conditions of not committing additional offenses and avoiding contact with the victim or persons known to engage in criminal activities, a defendant may be released, subject to conditions such as being instructed not to leave the jurisdiction, to find employment, to comply with a curfew, and to contact a pretrial services official on a daily basis.

D. Preventive Detention

In response to a growing problem of defendants committing crimes during the period of pretrial release, some state legislatures and the Congress enacted laws prohibiting pretrial release due to either a defendant's criminal history or the nature of the pending charges. Detention is authorized if the prosecution persuades the court that, *e.g.*, no set of conditions "will reasonably assure the appearance of [the defendant] and the safety of any other person and the community." 18 U.S.C. § 3142(f).

- Preventive detention is constitutional, violating neither Due Process nor the Eighth Amendment, as long as the detention 1) serves a compelling state interest; 2) does not impose punishment before an adjudication of guilt; and 3) is implemented in a fair, non-arbitrary manner. *United States v. Salerno*, 481 U.S. 739 (1987).

- The regulatory goal of preventing defendants on pretrial release from endangering the community by continuing to engage in criminal activity outweighs a defendant's liberty interest. *Id.*

- Typically, eligibility requirements for preventive detention are based on the defendant's current charge or prior criminal conduct. When a defendant poses a flight or safety risk, the trial judge must consider whether the risk can be minimized by releasing the defendant under the conditions previously described.

- The government has the burden of proof by a preponderance of the evidence to show that the defendant is a flight risk. Its burden of proof that the defendant should be detained as a result of being a safety risk is clear and convincing evidence. 18 U.S.C. § 3142(f).

To aid the prosecution in sustaining its burdens of proof at the detention hearing, the federal statute establishes two rebuttable presumptions upon which the prosecution may rely. However, a court may order detention even if neither of the statutory presumptions applies. 18 U.S.C. § 3142(e).

CHAPTER 10

Preliminary Proceedings

Key Terms

- *Gerstein* **hearing:** "promptly determines" whether there was probable cause for having arrested a defendant without a warrant, and is a prerequisite to continued detention; it usually occurs at the defendant's initial appearance in court.

- **Initial appearance:** is the first time that an accused appears before a judge, without unnecessary delay after her arrest.

- **Preliminary hearing:** an adversarial proceeding where the stated purpose is to determine whether probable cause exists to refer the case to a grand jury or for trial.

A. Why Preliminary Proceedings Are Important

Although nothing that happens prior to the attachment of jeopardy at trial is dispositive, early court appearances have the potential for helping each side prepare for later events, such as plea bargaining or trial.

B. Initial Appearance

Most jurisdictions require that the arresting officer bring an accused before the nearest available judge without unnecessary delay. *See, e.g.*, Fed.R.Crim.P. 5(a)(1)(A).

- Confessions obtained during periods of unnecessary delay *prior to* the initial appearance may be inadmissible. *See* Chapter 4.

- At the initial appearance, by rule the judge must inform the accused about the pending criminal charges, the right to remain silent, the right to request or retain an attorney, that any statement made may be used against the accused, the general circumstances under which the accused may secure pretrial release, the right to a preliminary hearing, and a reasonable time to consult with an attorney.

- The initial appearance is a "critical stage" at which the Sixth Amendment grants a right to counsel.

C. *Gerstein* Hearing

When the accused is arrested without an arrest warrant or a grand jury indictment, a *Gerstein* hearing is necessary prior to the continued detention of an accused. The hearing must be conducted promptly after arrest, and is usually held at the time of the initial appearance. *Gerstein v. Pugh*, 420 U.S. 103 (1975).

- The only issue determined at a *Gerstein* hearing is whether there is probable cause to believe that the accused committed an offense. The hearing is nonadversarial in nature, with the accused having no right to 1) counsel, 2) be present, or 3) question witnesses. Hearsay and written testimony are admissible. If a court determines that there is no probable cause, immediate release from custody is the proper remedy but that finding does not foreclose a later prosecution.

- The determination of probable cause ordinarily must occur within 48 hours of the warrantless arrest. When the probable cause determination does not occur within 48 hours, the burden shifts to the prosecution "to demonstrate the existence of a bona fide emergency or other extraordinary circumstance" to justify the delay. *County of Riverside v. McLaughlin*, 500 U.S. 44 (1991).

D. Preliminary Hearing

Statutes, rules, and court decisions provide for preliminary proceedings involving *felony* charges, but there is no constitutional right to a preliminary hearing. If a preliminary hearing is held, the defendant has a right to the assistance of counsel at this "critical stage" of the proceedings. *Coleman v. Alabama*, 399 U.S. 1 (1970).

- The purpose of a preliminary hearing is to determine whether there is probable cause that a crime was committed and that the defendant committed the crime. Without a finding of probable cause, the accused is released from custody.

- Besides screening cases, other functions of a preliminary hearing are to obtain pretrial discovery, lay the foundation for future impeachment of witnesses, perpetuate testimony for future proceedings, alter the conditions of pretrial release, and facilitate future plea bargaining.

There is no necessity for a preliminary hearing after a grand jury first has returned an indictment, *i.e.*, where an accused is first arrested *after* indictment. The rationale is that the grand jury has already made the same probable cause determination that is the primary purpose of the preliminary hearing.

Grand Jury Proceedings

Key Terms

- **Indictment:** formal charge against a defendant, issued by a grand jury.

- **Information:** formal charge against a defendant, submitted by a prosecutor.

- **Secrecy:** traditional prohibitions against disclosures of grand jury information by prosecutorial personnel and grand jurors.

- **Subpoena:** document commanding a person to give testimony or documents to a grand jury.

- **Use/derivative use immunity:** protection from prosecution for a person, based upon her testimony, documents, and any derivative evidence.

A. Why Grand Jury Proceedings Are Important

In more than half the states, the grand jury is the primary means by which prosecutors bring formal charges against a suspect. A grand jury may consider formal charges against an accused after a preliminary hearing, regardless of whether there was a finding of probable cause at that hearing, or when the prosecution wants to proceed in secret, in which case the indictment issued by the grand jury may be the first occurrence in a case known by the public or by the named defendant.

B. Constitutional Requirement for a Grand Jury to Indict a Defendant

The Fifth Amendment to the United States Constitution, in part provides: "No person shall be held to answer for a capital, or otherwise infamous crime, unless on a presentment or indictment of a Grand Jury. . . ." The Fifth Amendment phrase "infamous crimes" is construed to apply to all felonies. However, this provision is not applicable to the states through the Fourteenth Amendment.

- A presentment is a formal charging document issued by a grand jury when the prosecutor's office did not initiate consideration of the defendant's case. An indictment is the more common charging instrument for cases brought by the prosecutor. Both documents have the same legal effect, with both having been approved by the grand jury.

- Half the states have eliminated grand juries and permit prosecution by a verified document known as an information (by which charges are prepared by the prosecutor). Some states allow the prosecutor to choose between a grand jury indictment and submitting an information. Federal defendants may waive the right to indictment and proceed by information. Fed.R.Crim.P. 7(b).

C. Composition and Selection of Grand Jury

Federal grand juries consist of 16-23 jurors, 12 of whom must agree to indict the defendant. Fed.R.Crim.P. 6(a)(1). States often use smaller grand juries. Proper grounds for objecting to the composition of the grand jury are: one or more of the grand jurors failed to meet statutorily prescribed qualifications for service, or the selection process violated constitutional standards.

- For example, states cannot deliberately and systematically exclude individuals because of race, gender, or national origin. *Taylor v. Louisiana*, 419 U.S. 522 (1975). A defendant does not have to be a member of the excluded group to challenge the selection process. *See Campbell v. Louisiana*, 523 U.S. 392 (1998).

D. Grand Jury Secrecy

Unlike most stages of a criminal prosecution, grand jury proceedings are conducted in secret. *See* Chapter 16; *United States v. Procter & Gamble Co.*, 356 U.S. 677 (1958). Most jurisdictions impose an obligation of secrecy upon the prosecutor and grand jury personnel, but *not* upon grand jury witnesses.

E. Evidence Presented to the Grand Jury

Evidentiary standards that govern the admissibility of evidence at trial do not apply to a grand jury proceeding. For example, a grand jury may rely exclusively on hearsay evidence to support an indictment. *Costello v. United States*, 350 U.S. 359 (1956). In addition, a grand jury witness may be questioned about illegally seized evidence. *United States v. Calandra*, 414 U.S. 338 (1974).

- A federal prosecutor has no constitutional duty to present exculpatory evidence to the grand jury. However, many state courts rely on their state constitutions to impose a duty on prosecutors to disclose exculpatory evidence to the state grand jury. *United States v. Williams*, 504 U.S. 36 (1992).

- Prosecutorial misconduct that has a "substantial effect on the jury's assessment of the testimony or its decision to indict" may lead to dismissal of an indictment. *Bank of Nova Scotia v. United States*, 487 U.S. 250 (1988).

F. Grand Jury Subpoenas for Witness Testimony

A subpoena may issue for a witness to give oral testimony. The witness "must appear before the grand jury to answer" questions, or risk being punished for contempt. *Branzburg v. Hayes*, 408 U.S. 665 (1972). Any grand jury witness subpoenaed to appear may assert the Fifth Amendment privilege against self-incrimination, which applies to statements that 1) are in themselves incriminating, *or* 2) "furnish a link in the chain of evidence needed to prosecute. . . ." *Hoffman v. United States*, 341 U.S. 479 (1951).

- A target of the investigation has no right to receive *Miranda* warnings prior to grand jury questioning. *United States v. Mandujano*, 425 U.S. 564 (1976).

G. Grand Jury Subpoenas for Documents or Objects

The grand jury also may issue a subpoena *duces tecum* that commands a person to produce writings or objects described in the subpoena. As with a person's testimony, production of existing documents may lead to incriminating evidence or provide a link in the chain of evidence needed to prosecute. The subpoena is not a court order, but unless it is withdrawn or quashed, failure to comply with a court's order to comply with a subpoena may be punished as contempt.

- The recipient of a subpoena has the burden to show that there is "no reasonable possibility that the category of material the Government seeks will produce information relevant to the general subject of the grand jury's investigation." *United States v. R. Enterprises*, 498 U.S. 292 (1991).

- A subpoena *duces tecum* cannot compel the *preparation* of a document; it compels only the *production* of an existing document. When the government seeks documents previously created by the defendant, the contents of the document are legally irrelevant. *United States v. Doe*, 465 U.S. 605 (1984).

- A person served with a subpoena *duces tecum* may file a motion to quash the subpoena on Fifth Amendment grounds. To prevail, the prosecutor must show that, *when* the subpoena issued, she was aware that the documents sought were 1) in existence, 2) in the recipient's possession, and 3) the documents described (known as authentication) in the subpoena. If the prosecutor cannot prove all three elements, the court will grant the motion to quash. At that time, the prosecutor will have to decide whether to seek a judicial grant of immunity for the production of the documents or give up the quest for the documents.

- A taxpayer's rights are not violated by enforcing a subpoena directed to her accountant and requiring production of the taxpayer's records possessed by the accountant. *Couch v. United States*, 409 U.S. 322 (1973). Similarly, a taxpayer cannot shield her accountant's papers by giving them to her lawyer. *Fisher v. United States*, 425 U.S. 391 (1976).

- Subpoenas for voice exemplars and handwriting samples do *not* violate the Fifth Amendment, because they relate to physical characteristics "constantly exposed to the public." *United States v. Mara*, 410 U.S. 19 (1973). *United States v. Dionisio*, 410 U.S. 1 (1973).

H. Immunity for Witnesses

The prosecutor may seek an immunity order from the judge granting the witness immunity from prosecution to force a response. The common types of immunity are transactional and use/derivative use.

- Transactional immunity protects the grand jury witness from prosecution based upon any transaction about which he is questioned and testifies, or about a document he discloses.

- Federal statutes authorize use/derivative use immunity. The witness's grand jury testimony and any information derived from that testimony cannot be used against the witness. *See, e.g.*, 18 U.S.C. § 6002. Its scope is narrower than transactional, because the witness may still be prosecuted.

- In the case of a subpoena *duces tecum*, after the prosecutor obtains an order granting use/derivative use immunity, that immunized person produces the documents. However, the prosecutor cannot introduce those documents into evidence or use leads from them as proof against the person. *United States v. Hubbell*, 530 U.S. 27 (2000).

- If an immunized witness refuses to testify or turn over documents, the court may issue an order to the witness requiring him to show cause why he should not be held in contempt of the court's immunity order.

- Regardless of the type of immunity order, a witness may be prosecuted for perjury based upon his false grand jury testimony.

I. Fifth Amendment and Subpoenas: The Collective Entity Doctrine

Because they are not persons, corporations and other entities have no Fifth Amendment privilege to avoid producing potentially incriminating documents for a grand jury's investigation. The custodian of records of any collective entity such as a corporation cannot claim the privilege *on behalf of the corporation* against a compelled act of production, even though the act of production may amount to personal incrimination by associating the custodian with the corporate conduct.

- Although the prosecution cannot inform the jury about who produced the documents, the prosecutor can prove that they came from the custodian's organization, thereby allowing the trial jury to infer that the custodian knew about the documents. *Braswell v. United States*, 487 U.S. 99 (1988).

A corporate employee may claim Fifth Amendment protection to avoid giving *oral* testimony. *Curcio v. United States*, 354 U.S. 118 (1957).

CHAPTER 12

The Charging Instrument

Key Terms

- **Bill of particulars:** fuller disclosure about the nature of the criminal charge when a charging document is incomplete.

- **Equal Protection:** any distinction in treatment of persons similarly situated must be rational and reasonable.

- *Ex post facto* **laws:** imposition of punishment for an act which was not punishable at the time it was committed or adds punishment, or changes the rules of evidence by which less or different testimony is sufficient to convict than was previously required.

- **First Amendment:** statutes may violate constitutional protections of speech, press, or religion.

- **Police powers:** legislative regulation of conduct that is related to the public welfare and safety.

- **Separation of powers:** one branch of government exercises authority in an area over which another branch has inherent authority.

- **Vagueness:** defining a criminal offense with insufficient clarity so that ordinary people cannot understand what conduct is prohibited.

A. Why the Charging Instrument Is Important

The charging instrument is the jurisdictional document filed in the trial court. The indictment or information is brought in the name of the sovereign, and ordinarily concludes that the offense was against the peace and dignity of the sovereign. The charging document gives the defendant notice of the charge in order to prepare a defense, and protects her from surprise during the criminal prosecution. The document must state an offense that is within the power of the court to adjudicate.

B. Bill of Particulars

Defendants often file a motion for a bill of particulars to provide fuller disclosure about the nature of the charge when they perceive that a charging document is incomplete.

- An indictment's defect in stating the charge cannot be cured by providing information in a bill of particulars, because the defendant has a right to have an adequately informed grand jury return the indictment rather than have the indictment effectively rewritten by the prosecutor. *Russell v. United States*, 369 U.S. 749 (1962).

C. Motions to Dismiss Based on the Unconstitutionality of the Crime Charged

A defendant may move to dismiss an indictment or information on the ground that the statute the defendant is charged with violating is unconstitutional. Motions to dismiss may include the following grounds:

- Separation of powers: One branch of government cannot exercise authority in an area over which another branch has inherent authority.

- Vagueness: A criminal statute must define the criminal offense with sufficient clarity that ordinary people can understand what conduct is prohibited. *See, e.g., Kolender v. Lawson*, 461 U.S. 352 (1983).

- *Ex post facto* laws: A statute is deemed an *ex post facto* law when it imposes punishment for an act which was not punishable at the time it was committed or adds punishment, or changes the rules of evidence by which less or different testimony is sufficient to convict than was previously required. *See, e.g., Stogner v. California*, 539 U.S. 607 (2003).

- First Amendment: Statutes may violate constitutional protections of speech, press, or religion. *See, e.g., Texas v. Johnson*, 491 U.S. 397 (1989).

- Equal protection: Any distinction in treatment of persons similarly situated must be rational and reasonable.

- Police powers: Legislatures have broad powers to regulate conduct that is related to the public welfare and safety.

D. Amended Pleadings and Variance

In federal courts, Fed.R.Crim.P. 7(e) limits the amendment of formal charges with permission of the court. The amendment may be made at any time before verdict or findings, or even after proof has been taken.

- The amendment may include elements originally omitted from the charge or may correct facts incorrectly stated in the original charge.

- The amendment may not charge a new or different offense that prejudices the substantial rights of the defendant. *Stirone v. United States*, 361 U.S. 212 (1960).

- Amending the charge may also be appropriate when the evidence presented at trial differs from the allegations in the charging instrument. Such a variance is allowed as long as it does not deprive the defendant of fair notice about the charge or create the possibility of being placed in jeopardy twice for the same offense. *Berger v. United States*, 295 U.S. 78 (1935).

On the other hand, a Due Process violation occurs if a defendant is convicted on a charge that was not alleged *or* supported by the proof. *Dunn v. United States*, 442 U.S. 100 (1979).

CHAPTER 13

Joinder and Severance

Key Terms

- **Collateral estoppel:** a factual issue in a defendant's favor at one proceeding may preclude the prosecution from disputing that fact in another proceeding against the same defendant.

- **Consolidation:** when charges against a defendant that had been in separate instruments are combined into the same charging document.

- **Joinder:** when charges and/or defendants are combined in one charging document.

- **Prejudicial joinder:** otherwise permissible joinder of offenses or defendants is prejudicial based upon spillover of evidence, guilt by association, inconsistent defenses, or self-incrimination problems.

- **Same offense:** when only one of multiple offenses requires proof that the other offense does not.

- **Separate offenses:** when each of multiple offenses requires proof that the other offense does not.

- **Severance:** multiple offenses separated for trial based on allegations of prejudicial joinder.

A. Why Joinder and Severance Are Important

Most procedural rules allow a prosecutor to combine offenses or defendants by charging multiple offenses or defendants in the same indictment or information.

In addition to joinder and severance issues, the exercise of prosecutorial discretion to join offenses or defendants may have constitutional consequences relating to Fifth Amendment Double Jeopardy and collateral estoppel issues, as well as Sixth Amendment Confrontation Clause problems.

B. Joinder and Severance of Offenses

Fed.R.Crim.P. 8(a) is typical of joinder rules, allowing but not requiring joinder of offenses. Two or more offenses may be charged together against a defendant if they are based upon the same act or transaction (*e.g.*, a rape and an assault), or a series of acts or transactions constituting a common scheme (*e.g.*, armed robbery, auto theft, possession of weapon), or the offenses being of similar character (*e.g.*, bank robberies in the same neighborhood two months apart).

1. Motion to Dismiss for Misjoinder of Charges

A violation of Rule 8 "requires reversal only if the misjoinder results in actual prejudice because it had a substantial and injurious effect or influence in determining the jury's verdict." *United States v. Lane*, 474 U.S. 438 (1986).

2. Motion to Consolidate Multiple Charges

Because Rule 8 is permissive rather than mandatory, a defendant has no right to have all alleged offenses tried together. However, a defendant's motion to consolidate charges under Fed.R.Crim.P. 13 may succeed if the charges initially could have been brought together.

3. Motion to Sever Otherwise Properly Joined Charges

Even if joinder satisfies Fed.R.Crim.P. 8(a), the defendant may seek a severance of the offenses from what is described as prejudicial joinder, *e.g.*, Fed.R.Crim.P. 14, because of a spillover of evidence, guilt by association, inconsistent defenses, or self-incrimination problems.

C. Double Jeopardy Implications for Joinder of Offenses

When the prosecution charges a defendant with multiple offenses, either in simultaneous or successive prosecutions, the Double Jeopardy Clause of the Fifth Amendment shields a defendant from even the risk of being punished twice for the same offense.

1. Double Jeopardy in Simultaneous Prosecutions

In a simultaneous prosecution, suppose a defendant is charged with killing a victim in one count and for assaulting the same victim at the same time. If the defendant is charged with two offenses constituting the same offense, there are two options for how the court is able to address the double jeopardy issue.

- The jury instructions may direct the jury that it can convict the defendant of the homicide or the assault but not both offenses.

- Local laws instead may require the prosecutor to elect which of the two charges should be submitted to the jury so that the jury is not confused by jury instructions that it must make the election.

2. Double Jeopardy in Successive Prosecutions

In successive prosecutions, following an acquittal *or* a conviction for one offense prior to the second trial for the "same" offense, the defendant will seek dismissal of the latter charge because it is the same offense as the offense for which he has already been tried.

3. The "Same Offense" and the Blockburger Test

Double jeopardy protections depend on whether two offenses are considered to be the "same offense." That decision is important both for successive prosecutions for related acts and in a single prosecution involving multiple offenses and punishments.

- A constitutional violation does not occur if there is proof that the legislature intended to impose cumulative punishments for a single act that constitutes more than one crime. Courts generally infer a legislative intent when the offenses are set forth in different statutes or in distinct sections of a statute, and each provision or section unambiguously sets forth punishment for its violation. *Missouri v. Hunter*, 459 U.S. 359 (1983).

- However, because the issue of legislative intent is usually ambiguous, a court must decide whether the two offenses are the "same." Two offenses do *not* constitute the same offense when *each* offense requires proof of an element that the other offense does not. The test may be satisfied despite substantial overlap in the evidence used to prove the offenses. *Blockburger v. United States*, 284 U.S. 299 (1932).

a. Defining the Same Offense

Two offenses constitute the *same offense* when *only one* of the offenses requires proof that the other offense does not. The latter offense is known as a lesser-included offense; it is the same as the greater offense because by definition the greater offense includes all the elements of the lesser. Multiple punishments following a single prosecution for both offenses are barred, without explicit legislative intent to the contrary. Example:

- Because rape is a lesser-included offense of felony-murder committed in the course of that rape, double jeopardy prohibits convictions in the *same* trial for both offenses. Only the felony-murder requires evidence that proof of the rape does not: killing the same victim in the perpetration of the crime of rape. The same principle applies in *successive* trials of rape and felony-murder. *Whalen v. United States*, 445 U.S. 684 (1980).

b. Multiple Victims

When a single act affects multiple victims, separate offenses are committed. If one person is killed and another is wounded by the same bullet, multiple criminal offenses have been committed.

c. Different Time Periods

The legislature may divide a continuous course of conduct into separate offenses, even for conduct that occurs within a short period of time. *Brown v. Ohio*, 432 U.S. 161 (1977). For example, when the defendant fires six gunshots at police during a chase, the result is six different charges of reckless endangerment.

d. Exception for Subsequent Events

When all the events needed for the greater crime of homicide have not occurred when the trial for the lesser crime of assault began, a defendant convicted of assault can still be convicted for that person's death if he died after the assault trial began. *See Diaz v. United States*, 223 U.S. 442 (1912).

D. Collateral Estoppel and Joinder of Offenses

Collateral estoppel provides that determination of a factual issue in a defendant's favor at one proceeding may preclude the prosecution from disputing that same fact in another proceeding against the same defendant.

The most difficult problem in applying collateral estoppel is ascertaining which facts were established in the defendant's favor in the earlier case. Because juries render general rather than special verdicts in most criminal cases, a determination of which facts were essential to the verdict requires careful analysis of the trial record.

In addition to determining that the fact issue was litigated in defendant's first trial, the nature of the reason for acquitting defendant in the earlier trial determines whether collateral estoppel applies in the current case.

- Assume that Defendant is charged with assaults against two victims at the same time and place, but the offenses are not joined for trial. If she is acquitted at the first trial for assaulting Victim #1 because there is doubt as to whether she was present at the time of the assaults, her acquittal acts as a collateral estoppel defense to the second assault charge.

- On the other hand, if the acquittal at the first trial resulted from doubt about whether Defendant actually assaulted Victim #1, the prosecutor can later try to prove that she assaulted Victim #2. *See Ashe v. Swenson*, 397 U.S. 436 (1970).

E. Joinder and Severance of Defendants

In most jurisdictions, joinder of defendants is permitted when the prosecution alleges that the defendants participated either in the same act or transaction or in the same series of acts or transactions. *See, e.g.*, Fed.R.Crim.P. 8(b). Like joinder of offenses, joinder of defendants is permissive. In addition, each defendant does not have to be charged in each count.

- Example: When defendants A and B are charged with committing two robberies in the same week, they are charged with committing both robberies, and their cases may be joined.

- However, if the prosecutor cannot prove that A and B committed both robberies together, there are two options for the prosecution. Under Fed.R.Crim.P. 8(a), the prosecutor may charge defendant A with both robberies in one indictment and charge defendant B with both robberies in a separate indictment. Under Fed.R.Crim.P. 8(b), the alternative for the prosecutor would be to charge both A and B with one robbery in one indictment and to charge A and B with the other robbery in a second indictment.

1. Motion to Dismiss for Misjoinder of Charges

A defendant may seek dismissal of joined charges because of the failure to satisfy the procedural rules for joinder, such as Rule 8(b). Misjoinder is subject to a harmless error analysis.

2. *Motion to Consolidate Multiple Defendants*

While a defendant has no right to have a trial of all alleged offenses tried together with another defendant, a motion to consolidate charges under Fed.R.Crim.P. 13 may succeed if the defendants' charges could have been brought together.

3. *Motion to Sever Joined Charges*

If the joinder satisfies Rule 8(b), one or more of the joined defendants may still seek a severance from what is described as prejudicial joinder, per Fed.R.Crim.P. 14, based upon specific allegations of prejudice in a joint trial. Example:

- An allegation of inconsistent defenses is not *per se* prejudicial. Courts grant a severance only if a "joint trial would compromise a specific trial right of one of the defendants, or prevent . . . a reliable judgment about guilt or innocence." *Zafiro v. United States*, 506 U.S. 534 (1993).

F. Sixth Amendment Issues for the Joinder of Defendants

In a joint trial, the Sixth Amendment Confrontation Clause controls the admissibility of a non-testifying codefendant's pretrial statement, in order to prove the culpability of the other defendant.

- Assume that in a joint trial of defendant A and defendant B, A's pretrial confession *directly* incriminates B. The admission into evidence of A's entire pretrial confession violates B's Sixth Amendment right to confrontation if A does not testify at trial, because B does not have the opportunity to cross-examine A about the pretrial confession.

- Where A later testifies during the defense case-in-chief, there is no confrontation issue because A is subject to cross-examination by B (regardless of whether A admits or denies making the confession). *Bruton v. United States*, 391 U.S. 123 (1968).

- If A's pretrial confession merely inferentially (*e.g.*, "me and some other guys committed the crime") implicates B, the trial court must admonish the jury that the confession does not implicate B. *Richardson v. Marsh*, 481 U.S. 200 (1987).

- Regardless of whether A's pretrial confession implicates B directly or inferentially, in order to introduce the pretrial statement into evidence during the prosecution's case-in-chief, the version of A's statement heard by the jury must delete all references to B. Redaction that merely substitutes a blank space, "delete," a neutral pronoun, or a symbol is not permitted. *Gray v. Maryland*, 523 U.S. 185 (1998).

- If A later testifies during the defense case-in-chief, thereby eliminating the Confrontation Clause issue, the prosecutor then may introduce the full, unabridged version of A's pretrial statement.

When *both* A and B in a joint trial give pretrial confessions incriminating each other, the Confrontation Clause bars the admission of a nontestifying codefendant's confession incriminating the defendant, even if the defendant's own confession is admissible against him. *Cruz v. New York*, 481 U.S. 186 (1987).

CHAPTER 14

Speedy Trial

Key Terms

- **Federal Speedy Trial Act:** establishes specific time limits for completing stages of a criminal prosecution.

- **Post-charge delay:** is determined from the earlier of a defendant's arrest or formal charge (an indictment or information) until the beginning of trial.

- **Pre-charge delay:** is determined from the commission of a crime until the earlier of the defendant's arrest or formal charge (an indictment or information).

- **Right to speedy trial:** is analyzed under a four-part balancing test to assess the existence of a Sixth Amendment constitutional violation.

A. Why Speedy Trial Issues Are Important

Time limitation issues apply to all criminal charges, *e.g.*, statutes of limitations, constitutional Due Process for pre-charge delay, Sixth Amendment speedy trial rights for post-charge delay, and statutory speedy trial guarantees. In every case, courts and parties must be aware of these constitutional and statutory requirements.

B. Pre-Charge Delay in Charging the Defendant

Due Process may protect a defendant from delay between commission of the crime and the earlier of the arrest, indictment or information. However, proving a constitutional violation is difficult.

1. *United States v. Lovasco*

In *United States v. Lovasco*, 431 U.S. 783 (1977), the indictment was filed seventeen months after an investigator's report about the crime. The Court held that the delay was not a Due Process violation even if the defendant was somewhat prejudiced, as long as the delay ensures that the correct charges are brought against the appropriate defendants.

To establish a federal constitutional Due Process violation, a defendant must show:

- A long delay between the crime and the earlier of the defendant's arrest or his formal charge.

- Actual prejudice to the defendant's case, because witness testimony and other evidence are no longer available.

- The delay was motivated by the prosecutor's intent to gain a tactical advantage over the defendant.

- The defendant need not demand a speedy arrest or charge.

A sufficient showing of prejudice requires that the defendant show that the witness would have 1) been available at an earlier time, 2) testified for the defendant, and 3) aided the defense without the testimony being merely cumulative.

C. Post-Charge Delay in Bringing the Defendant to Trial

The Sixth Amendment right to a speedy trial attaches from the earlier of the date of the indictment or information, or the date of the arrest, *i.e.*, when the person becomes "accused" of a crime. Once the right to a speedy trial attaches, it continues until the charges are resolved or the defendant is convicted after a guilty plea or a trial. *See Betterman v. Montana*, 578 U.S. 968 (2016), where the Court ruled unanimously that there is no Sixth Amendment right to speedy sentencing.

1. How Speedy Trial Rights Differ from Other Rights

Society has an interest in a speedy trial to prevent the accused from endangering public safety by committing other crimes. Violating the right may work to the defendant's advantage, because the passage of time results in witness unavailability and fading witness memories. Because the speedy trial right is a vague concept, courts apply a balancing test.

2. Barker v. Wingo

In *Barker v. Wingo*, 407 U.S. 514 (1972), the Court held that any inquiry into a constitutional speedy trial claim requires a balancing of four factors: 1) the length of the delay, 2) the reasons for the delay, 3) whether and how the defendant asserted the speedy trial right, and 4) the amount of prejudice suffered by the defendant.

a. Length of the Delay

A delay of at least twelve months serves as a "triggering mechanism" for examining the other speedy trial factors, because that delay is presumptively prejudicial. Further, the time between dismissal of an indictment and a defendant's reindictment is excluded from the length of delay. *United States v. Loud Hawk*, 474 U.S. 302 (1986).

b. Reason for the Delay

Courts weigh delays intended to gain a trial advantage more heavily against the prosecution than unintentional delays resulting from institutional dysfunction.

- In the absence of a showing of bad faith, the prosecution is not responsible for delays attributable to its own acts.

- Neutral reasons such as negligence and overcrowded calendars weigh less heavily, but are still considered because responsibility for such conditions rests with the prosecution.

- A period of delay attributable to tactics by the defendant is deemed a waiver of the right to a speedy trial for that period of delay.

c. Demand for Speedy Trial

Despite the view that a defendant does not have the duty to bring himself to trial, the defendant's failure to demand a speedy trial undercuts the defendant's constitutional argument. By contrast, a vigorous and timely assertion provides strong evidence that the defendant is interested in a speedy disposition.

d. Prejudice to the Defendant

A court must weigh any prejudice that limits impairment to the defense. *Reed v. Farley*, 512 U.S. 339 (1994) suggested that a "showing of prejudice is required to establish a violation of the Sixth Amendment Speedy Trial Clause."

- *Doggett v. United States*, 505 U.S. 647 (1992) suggested a relationship between the reason for the delay and the burden of proof on the prejudice issue.

- When the reason for the delay is attributable to reasonable diligence by the prosecution, the defendant must show specific prejudice. When the reason for the delay is intentional misconduct by the prosecution, a presumption of prejudice is "virtually automatic," with the burden of proof on the government to overcome the presumption.

- It is uncertain which party has the burden of proof when the reason for the delay is governmental negligence.

e. Remedy for Sixth Amendment Violation

Barker expressly stated that dismissal *with prejudice* to reprosecution is the only remedy for a violation of the Sixth Amendment speedy trial right.

f. Speedy Trial Rights for Incarcerated Defendants

An inmate in one jurisdiction has a Sixth Amendment right to a speedy trial on charges pending in another jurisdiction. *Smith v. Hooey*, 393 U.S. 374 (1969).

g. Speedy Trial Rights Detach After Conviction

Once a defendant is convicted, the presumption of innocence no longer shields her from postconviction sentencing delays. *Betterman v. Montana*, 578 U.S. 968 (2016). However, a defendant retains a diminished due process liberty interest in a fair sentencing process.

D. Statutory Rights to a Speedy Trial

Many state legislatures and the Congress have enacted speedy trial legislation that establishes specific time limits for completing stages of a criminal prosecution.

For example, the federal Speedy Trial Act (18 U.S.C. § 3161 et seq.) provides that an arrested defendant must be formally charged within thirty days after the arrest and the defendant's trial must begin within seventy days after the formal charge is filed. To compute whether there is a statutory violation, the court calculates the gross elapsed days and subtracts the number of days attributable to statutory periods of excludable time, leaving the number of *net elapsed days* for determining a violation.

1. Excludable Periods of Time

- Certain types of pretrial delays are automatically excluded from the computation of time limits, *e.g.*, the absence or unavailability of the defendant. *Id.*

- The running of the seventy-day period from indictment to trial stops upon the filing of a pretrial motion regardless of whether it actually causes or is expected to cause a delay in starting the trial. *United States v. Tinklenberg*, 563 U.S. 647 (2011).

2. Remedies for Violation of Speedy Trial Act

The Speedy Trial Act is not self-executing. To avoid a waiver of her rights, a defendant must file an appropriate motion. *Zedner v. United States*, 547 U.S. 489 (2006). If the Speedy Trial Act's time limits are not met, the charges against a defendant must be dismissed. The key determination for the trial judge is whether the dismissal must be *with or without* prejudice.

- The judge must consider three factors in exercising discretion to dismiss charges with or without prejudice: 1) the seriousness of the offense, 2) the circumstances leading to dismissal, and 3) the effect of reprosecution on the administration of justice and the legislation. 18 U.S.C. § 3162(a)(1)-(2); *United States v. Taylor*, 487 U.S. 326 (1988).

3. Statutes of Limitation

Federal statutory crimes and almost all states have statutes that precisely define limits for bringing a criminal prosecution. *See e.g.*, 18 U.S.C. § 3282, imposing a five-year limitations period after commission for prosecuting felonies. While the length of the period often increases with the seriousness of the crime, many states have no time limitation for charging felonies or capital crimes.

However, even if there is a statute of limitations, a defendant cannot raise it as a defense for the first time on appeal. *Musacchio v. United States*, 577 U.S. 237 (2016).

CHAPTER 15

Discovery

Key Terms

- **Duty to disclose:** prosecution must turn over impeachment evidence and exculpatory evidence favorable to the accused; Due Process is violated when the evidence is material either to guilt or punishment.

- **Duty to preserve evidence:** government's failure to preserve evidence or the loss or destruction may be a Due Process violation.

- **Materiality:** of evidence to be disclosed by the prosecution is determined by whether there was "a reasonable probability that, had the evidence been disclosed to the defense, the result of the proceeding would have been different."

- **Reciprocity:** if the defendant obtains some types of information from the prosecution, he must turn over related information in return.

A. Why Discovery Is Important

Discovery is the pretrial process of exchanging factual information between the prosecution and the defense. Prior to using the discovery rules, the defense may use informal methods for obtaining information from the prosecution. Prosecutors primarily look to police departments and grand jury investigations to uncover relevant facts.

B. Discovery Outside the Rules of Criminal Procedure

Although discovery is not a purpose of preliminary hearings, it is an inherent byproduct of the requirement that the prosecution present at least a *prima facie* case. See Chapter 10.

The grand jury offers prosecutors many of the advantages that civil litigants obtain through discovery depositions. Prior to the return of an indictment, the grand jury has the power to compel testimony and documents in an *ex parte* atmosphere. See Chapter 11.

Discovery may occur as part of the give-and-take of plea bargaining, where the prosecutor voluntarily discusses the nature of the government's case and makes documentary and other evidence available for inspection by the defense, hoping that the defendant will decide to plead guilty. See Chapter 17.

C. Prosecution's Duty to Disclose Exculpatory Evidence

Due Process requires disclosure of information possessed by the government when it is favorable to an accused and is material either to guilt or punishment. *Brady v. Maryland*, 373 U.S. 83 (1963). Prosecutorial good faith at the time of nondisclosure is irrelevant. *Cone v. Bell*, 556 U.S. 449 (2009).

- A prosecutor's duty to disclose includes both impeachment evidence and exculpatory evidence. *United States v. Giglio*, 405 U.S. 150 (1972).

- Regardless of whether there is no request, a general request, or a specific request for information by the defense, the materiality of undisclosed evidence is based on how the undisclosed information would have changed the trial result. *United States v. Bagley*, 473 U.S. 667 (1985).

- There is greater potential for prejudice from nondisclosure in a specific request case, because an incomplete response by the prosecution might cause the defense to abandon lines of investigation, defenses or trial strategies that it otherwise would have pursued. *Id.*

- The constitutional determination of materiality is made collectively, not item-by-item, requiring the prosecutor to inquire in every case what, if any, evidence is undisclosed and to disclose when she believes that the materiality standard is satisfied. *Kyles v. Whitley*, 514 U.S. 419 (1995).

- Example: when evidence from the only prosecution witness links the defendant to the crime scene, withholding contradictory pretrial statements by that witness satisfies the standard of materiality. *Smith v. Cain*, 565 U.S. 73 (2012).

- The prosecutor's failure to disclose witness statements casting doubt on the credibility of the state's *main* witness violated Due Process, because those statements were sufficient to undermine confidence in the verdict. *Wearry v. Cain*, 577 U.S. 385 (2016).

- The prosecution's theory was that a large group had murdered the victim, and no defendant rebutted the prosecution's group attack theory. After their convictions became final, defendants claimed that the prosecution had withheld evidence at trial that was material to their guilt. The evidence included the identity of one man seen running into the alley after the murder and stopping near the victim's body. The Supreme Court held that the withheld evidence was not material, citing *Agurs* and looking at the withheld evidence "in the context of the entire record." Because virtually every witness at trial agreed that a group killed the victim, it was not reasonably probable that the withheld evidence could have led to a different result at trial. *Turner v. United States*, 137 S.Ct. 1885 (2017).

- The Supreme Court has also addressed the prosecution's knowing failure to disclose perjured testimony. The standard of materiality in these cases is different: whether "there is any reasonable likelihood that the false testimony could have affected the judgment of the jury." *United States v. Agurs*, 427 U.S. 97 (1976).

- Despite the government's duty to disclose, the defendant has no constitutional right to search through government's files free of court supervision to search for exculpatory evidence. *Pennsylvania v. Ritchie*, 480 U.S. 39 (1987).

- A defendant also has no constitutional right to disclosure of *impeachment* information prior to a guilty plea. The Court left open whether pre-guilty plea disclosure of *exculpatory* material is required. *United States v. Ruiz*, 536 U.S. 622 (2002).

D. Prosecution's Duty to Preserve Potentially Exculpatory Evidence

Evidence must be preserved when its exculpatory value was apparent before the evidence was destroyed *and* the defendant would be unable to obtain comparable evidence by other reasonably available means. Unlike the duty to disclose, discussed above, the defendant must also prove bad faith on the part of the police. *California v. Trombetta*, 467 U.S. 479 (1984).

- The failure to preserve evidence that is merely potentially useful does not violate a defendant's Due Process rights. *Arizona v. Youngblood*, 488 U.S. 51 (1988). Negligent police work does not prove bad faith. Further, the police do not have a duty to perform specific tests that may exonerate the defendant. *Id.*

- When lost or destroyed evidence no longer exists, the court must 1) suppress test results from the destroyed or lost evidence, or 2) instruct the jury to draw adverse inferences from the loss or destruction of the evidence.

E. Discovery Standards for All Parties

1. Reciprocity

Ordinarily, discovery must be reciprocal, *i.e.*, if the defendant obtains some types of information from the prosecution, he must turn over related information in return. *Wardius v. Oregon*, 412 U.S.

470 (1973). Fed.R.Crim.P. 12.1, 12.2, and 16 provide reciprocal discovery.

2. *Continuing Duty to Disclose*

If a court orders discovery, the parties have a continuing duty to disclose additional evidence as it becomes available.

3. *Pretrial Statements*

Fed.R.Crim.P. 26.2 permits both parties to obtain any pretrial statement of any witness in the possession of the opposition, *after* the witness testifies at trial on direct examination. The key to applying the rule is the definition of a "statement," which can be made and signed or adopted or approved by the witness, *or* a substantially *verbatim* recital of an oral statement (recorded contemporaneously and contained in a recording or transcription of a recording).

4. *Work Product*

Discovery provisions commonly exempt some form of prosecution work product, *e.g.*, the discovery or inspection of reports, memoranda, or other internal government documents made by an attorney or investigating agent for the defense or the government.

5. *Protective Orders*

The trial court may order that discovery or inspection be denied, restricted, or deferred by issuing a protective order when a party's right to pretrial discovery may conflict with the privacy rights of victims or others.

6. Sanctions

For discovery violations, the trial court may order counsel to make further disclosure, grant a continuance of the trial to allow for additional discovery, prohibit counsel from introducing at trial any undisclosed evidence, or enter any other order that is just under the circumstances. The remedies depend on the degree of the violation and the prejudice that the offended party suffered. *Taylor v. Illinois*, 484 U.S. 400 (1988).

F. Defense Discovery

In addition to the constitutional duty to disclose, each state may set discovery requirements. In the absence of voluntary disclosure, the parties either ask the court to order pretrial discovery, or conduct discovery through informal requests of each other.

Most discovery rules require the government to disclose prior statements of the defendant, the defendant's prior criminal record, documents and tangible objects the prosecution will use at trial, and scientific reports and tests such as autopsy reports and fingerprint analysis.

Discovery provisions commonly extend only to discoverable items within the prosecutor's possession, custody or control. This concept clearly encompasses the files of the police department working with the prosecutor in a particular case, but the question may be whether "control" extends to any prosecutor or law enforcement officer to whom the prosecution might have access.

G. Prosecutorial Discovery

Discovery by the prosecution may occur with general discovery rules, such as Fed.R.Crim.P. 16(b), or by specific rules discussed below. Pretrial discovery rules requiring defendants to disclose information that they will present at trial do not violate his Due Process rights. The truth-seeking function of pretrial discovery is more important than enabling a defendant to delay disclosure until trial. *Williams v. Florida*, 399 U.S. 78 (1970).

If a defendant obtains discovery of information, the prosecution is entitled to seek reciprocal discovery of similar information. The prosecution may discover information that the defendant intends to use during her case-in-chief at trial. Fed.R.Crim.P. 16(b)(1)(A)-(C).

Most state rules and Fed.R.Crim.P. 12.1 mandate the disclosure of defendant's intent to raise the defense of alibi without violating the Fifth Amendment, even though the defendant must accelerate the timing of his disclosure. *Williams v. Florida*. The prosecution must disclose rebuttal information after the defendant initially discloses his intent.

Fed.R.Crim.P. 12.2 requires a defendant to give advance notice about the intent to rely on a defense of insanity, or the intent to introduce expert testimony about the mental state for the offense.

Freedom of the Press and Fair Trial

Key Terms

- **Change of venue:** relocating a trial due to fair trial concerns resulting from media publicity.

- **Jury selection:** a method to evaluate the validity of a defendant's claim that the community would be unable to give him a fair trial.

- **Public trial:** Sixth Amendment right, based on whether there is a tradition of openness and the functional value of openness.

A. Why Freedom of the Press and Fair Trial Issues Are Important

In the context of the criminal justice process, freedom of the press may promote or undermine significant societal interests. Public access to legal proceedings promotes self-government by exposing judicial or prosecutorial corruption or incompetence.

Presence of the press may be disruptive and can undermine the fairness of the trial process.

B. Failure of Courts to Control the Press

A trial judge can impose restraints on news reporters who are in or near the courtroom. The failure of the judge to take steps to restrict such behavior may deprive the defendant of his right to a fair trial.

- *Sheppard v. Maxwell*, 384 U.S. 333 (1966) found a denial of the defendant's fair trial rights based on totality of circumstances: reporters' proximity made "confidential talk among Sheppard and his counsel almost impossible during the proceedings;" during recesses, television and photographs were taken of the parties, witnesses and jurors, and newsmen handled and photographed trial exhibits.

C. Pretrial Publicity and the Right to a Fair Trial

During trial, a judge has broad discretion to sequester the jury and caution the jurors to avoid media accounts of the proceedings. She also may consider a change of venue or a continuance.

To prove juror partiality, a defendant must show that the publicity *either* actually prejudiced a juror *or* so pervaded the proceedings that it raised a presumption of inherent prejudice. *Skilling v. United States*, 561 U.S. 358 (2010).

1. Change of Venue

When publicity has already occurred, a trial court will consider a change of venue to ensure a fair trial, *i.e.*, removal of the case to another judicial district within the same system, and beyond the reach of the publicity. *Groppi v. Wisconsin*, 400 U.S. 505 (1971).

- Two months prior to trial, a local television station broadcast a twenty-minute film of the defendant admitting commission of the charged offenses. It was a denial of Due Process for the trial court to refuse the defendant's request for a change of venue, which is constitutionally required even if the jury *voir dire* does not establish an "inference of prejudice." *Rideau v. Louisiana*, 373 U.S. 723 (1963).

- Several factors may lead to a presumption of prejudice: the nature of the pretrial publicity, the size and character of the community, the length of time between the publicity and the trial, whether the defendant was acquitted on any of the charges, and actions by the trial court which reduced the risk that the defendant would not receive a fair trial. *Skilling v. United States*.

2. *Jury Selection*

Frequently, a trial judge will postpone ruling on a motion for a change of venue until after she tries to seat an unbiased jury through *voir dire*. When potential jurors have read or heard prejudicial publicity, a trial judge inquires into the nature and extent of the exposure.

- Jurors need not be completely ignorant of the facts and issues. It is sufficient if the juror can lay aside his impression or opinion and render a verdict based on the evidence presented in court. *Irvin v. Dowd*, 366 U.S. 717 (1961).

- An inference of actual prejudice is shown by examining the totality of circumstances: the nature of the pretrial publicity, the community atmosphere reflected in the media at the time of trial, and whether the *voir dire* testimony revealed pervasive hostility within the community, with deference to the trial court in assessing that testimony. *Murphy v. Florida*, 421 U.S. 794 (1975); *Patton v. Yount*, 467 U.S. 1025 (1984).

3. Continuance

Another possible remedy for prejudicial pretrial publicity is for the trial court to grant a continuance of the case. Courts are inclined to take a wait-and-see attitude by denying the motion for a continuance while efforts are made to select a jury.

4. Jury Sequestration

As mentioned above, the trial judge has broad discretion to sequester the jury during trial and jury deliberations. Because the prospective jurors have already been exposed to pretrial publicity when the jury is selected, sequestration is not an effective remedy for claims of prejudicial *pretrial* publicity.

D. Gagging the Press

A prohibition on the media's publication of information is seldom, if ever, a permissible means for preventing prejudicial publicity. *Nebraska Press Association v. Stuart*, 427 U.S. 539 (1976).

- *Stuart* examined the nature and extent of pretrial news coverage, and how effectively a restraining order would prevent the threatened danger. In addition, the alternatives to prior restraint (change of venue, continuance, and jury admonitions) must be considered.

E. Public Access to Judicial Proceedings

Openness assures that established procedures are being followed and that any deviations become known. It also enhances both the fairness of the trial and the appearance of fairness that is essential to public confidence in the criminal justice system.

1. Sixth Amendment Right to Public Trial

The Sixth Amendment public trial right's purposes are to safeguard against any attempt to use the courts as instruments of persecution, and to inform the public about governmental actions against citizens. Trials themselves historically have been open to the press and public, and the Court has established a presumption in favor of access. *Waller v. Georgia*, 467 U.S. 39 (1984).

2. First Amendment Right of Access by Press and Public

A proceeding may be closed only if the trial judge makes specific findings that there is a substantial probability that the defendant's right to a fair trial will be prejudiced by publicity that closure would prevent, and reasonable alternatives to closure cannot adequately protect that right. *Richmond Newspapers, Inc. v. Virginia*, 448 U.S. 555 (1980).

- Courts emphasize the historical tradition of openness and the functional value of openness. For example, preliminary hearings are open to the public while grand jury proceedings are not. As to the value of openness, a court asks whether public access to the preliminary proceeding is similar to a trial and "plays a particularly significant positive role in the actual functioning of" the criminal justice process. *Press-Enterprise Co. v. Superior Court*, 464 U.S. 501 (1984).

- Under limited circumstances a portion of the trial may be closed when there is proof of an overriding interest that is likely to be prejudiced, as where a minor rape victim's testimony relates certain sensitive details. *Globe Newspaper Company v. Superior Court*, 457 U.S. 596 (1982).

- Trial courts must consider alternatives to closing courtrooms, even if no one identifies the nature of such alternatives. "Trial courts are obligated to take every reasonable measure to accommodate public attendance at criminal trials." *Presley v. Georgia*, 558 U.S. 209 (2010).

3. *Remedy for Violation of the Right to Public Trial*

The remedy depends on when the objection is raised. If an objection is made at trial and the issue is raised on direct appeal, the defendant generally is entitled to "automatic reversal" regardless of the error's actual "effect on the outcome."

If instead, the defendant raises the issue later in an ineffective assistance claim, the defendant must show either a reasonable probability of a different outcome or that the violation was so serious as to render the trial fundamentally unfair. In *Weaver v. Massachusetts*, 137 S.Ct. 809 (2017), the defendant was unable to prove either.

CHAPTER 17

Plea Bargaining

Key Terms

- *Alford* **plea:** a defendant wants to plead guilty but does not want to admit guilt, though she acknowledges that the record strongly indicates her guilt.

- **Conditional guilty plea:** avoids the necessity of a full trial for a defendant who wants to plead guilty but also obtain appellate review of a claim; the defendant reserves in writing the issue for appellate review.

- **Guilty but mentally ill plea or verdict:** a plea or verdict by which the defendant contends that she was mentally ill at the time of the crime.

- **Guilty plea:** an admission about committing the charges.

- **Intelligent plea:** the defendant has a sufficient amount of information about the charge to which he is pleading as well as the consequences of the plea.

- *Nolo contendere*: the defendant does not contest the charge, but the plea still constitutes a conviction.

- **Voluntary plea:** the defendant is mentally competent to plead, and the plea is not the result of improper force, threats or promises.

A. Why Plea Bargaining Is Important

Unlike what television dramas might lead you to believe, most criminal cases are *not* resolved by a jury trial. "Ninety-seven percent of federal convictions and ninety-four percent of state convictions are the result of guilty pleas." *Lafler v. Cooper*, 566 U.S. 156 (2012). Learning about the plea bargaining process is critical to an understanding about the disposition of criminal charges.

B. Types of Pleas

A guilty plea is a defendant's admission about committing the charge. It also is a waiver of all defects in any prior stage of the proceeding. A guilty plea constitutes a waiver of numerous constitutional rights, including the privilege against self-incrimination, the right to a trial by jury, the right to confront one's accusers, and the right to appeal the conviction.

- *Nolo contendere*: In many states, the accused may enter a plea of *nolo contendere* by which he is not contesting the charges. Generally, it is identical to a guilty plea except that, without supporting proof, it cannot be used as an admission of guilt in a subsequent civil or administrative proceeding. However, it is the equivalent of a criminal conviction for sentencing and recidivist charges.

- Guilty but mentally ill: The defendant can enter a plea of guilty but mentally ill if the court finds that the defendant was mentally ill at the time of the offense. Treatment is provided for the defendant until a treating professional determines that such treatment is no longer necessary or until expiration of the sentence, whichever occurs first.

- *Alford* plea: When the defendant acknowledges that the record strongly indicates guilt, an accused may voluntarily, knowingly, and intelligently consent to a prison sentence even though he is unwilling to admit participation in the crime. *North Carolina v. Alford,* 400 U.S. 25 (1970).

- Conditional guilty plea: A defendant avoids the necessity of a full trial but wants appellate review of a claim. The defendant reserves in writing the issue for appellate review, and the court and the prosecutor must consent to the plea.

C. Plea Negotiation

A defendant has no constitutional right to plea bargain, but the prosecutor may decide to negotiate with the defense attorney.

- Despite the threats of increased charges if a defendant refuses to plead guilty to the original charges, a guilty plea is likely to be found voluntary as part of the "give-and-take" of negotiations as long as the prosecutor has probable cause for any charges brought or threatened. *Bordenkircher v. Hayes,* 434 U.S. 357 (1978).

- Defense counsel is ineffective if she fails to properly inform the defendant of a beneficial plea agreement offered by the prosecution, or if she incorrectly advises the defendant on the state of the law or the consequences of a guilty plea. *Missouri v. Frye*, 566 U.S. 133 (2012); *Lafler v. Cooper*; *Padilla v. Kentucky*, 559 U.S. 356 (2010).

- A federal judge's participation in plea negotiations, in violation of Fed.R.Crim.P. 11(c)(1), is harmless error and does not require vacating a guilty plea, unless the record shows that the defendant would not have pleaded guilty in the absence of the error. *United States v. Davila*, 569 U.S. 597 (2013).

D. Types of Plea Agreements and Their Enforcement

1. Types of Plea Agreements

Fed.R.Crim.P. 11(c)(1)(A)-(C) describes common plea agreements.

- To recommend a lenient sentence to the judge or stay silent during sentencing.

- To reduce the charges or dismiss some charges against the defendant.

- To commit to a specific sentence or type of sentence, such as probation.

For the last two types of agreements, the judge must agree to the agreement; if the judge rejects the agreement, the agreement is void and the defendant may go to trial or the parties may negotiate a different agreement.

2. Enforcement of Plea Agreements

"[W]hen a plea rests in any significant degree on a promise or agreement of the prosecutor, so that it can be said to be part of the inducement or consideration, such promise must be fulfilled." *Santobello v. New York*, 404 U.S. 257 (1971).

- In *Santobello*, the successor of the prosecutor who made a promise about sentencing to the defendant was bound by that earlier promise.

- Generally, a plea agreement in a state prosecution is not binding on prosecutors in other jurisdictions or on officials in other parts of the same state if they are not parties to the agreement.

- If a defendant refuses to provide the testimony he promised against a codefendant in exchange for a reduction of charges, the guilty plea can be vacated even after sentencing, because the defendant has breached his agreement. *Ricketts v. Adamson*, 483 U.S. 1 (1987).

- The trial court has the discretion to decide the appropriate remedy for a broken plea agreement, *e.g.*, setting aside the guilty plea, or granting specific performance of the prosecutor's promise.

E. A Voluntary, Knowing, and Intelligent Plea

The issue of voluntariness includes whether the defendant is competent to plead guilty, as well as whether the plea is the result of force, threats or promises that are not part of a plea agreement.

- A defendant must be competent to plead guilty. The mental standard required to enter a guilty plea is the same as the standard to stand trial. Prior drug use or addiction will not always make a plea involuntary unless the defendant is under the influence of drugs at the time he enters the plea, *i.e.*, the intoxication must render the defendant incompetent which shows a lack of understanding about the plea. *Godinez v. Moran*, 509 U.S. 389 (1993).

- A plea also must be intelligently made, *i.e.*, the defendant must have a sufficient amount of information from defense counsel or the trial court about the elements of the charge to which he is pleading as well as the consequences of the plea. *Henderson v. Morgan*, 426 U.S. 637 (1976); *Bradshaw v. Stumpf*, 545 U.S. 175 (2005).

- The record must affirmatively show that the defendant both voluntarily waived the privilege against self-incrimination, the right to a trial by jury, the right to confront one's accusers, and understood those rights that he was waiving, as well as the range of penalties of the offenses to which he is pleading. *Boykin v. Alabama*, 395 U.S. 238 (1969).

- A judge does not have a constitutional duty to explain all consequences of a criminal conviction to a defendant before permitting him to plead guilty. Currently, the failure to inform a defendant about the risk of deportation is the only collateral consequence that a court constitutionally must disclose to a defendant before accepting a guilty plea. *Padilla v. Kentucky*, 559 U.S. 356 (2010).

F. Withdrawing a Guilty Plea

A defendant who has tendered a guilty plea may seek to withdraw that plea. Prior to acceptance of a plea, rules may permit withdrawal for any reason or no reason. *See, e.g.*, Fed.R.Crim.P. 11(d)(1).

- After acceptance of a plea agreement but before sentencing, a court may permit the defendant to withdraw the plea if the defendant presents "any fair and just reason." *See, e.g.*, Fed.R.Crim.P. 11(d)(2).

- After sentencing, most procedural rules do not provide for plea withdrawal, and withdrawal is rarely permitted absent a finding of a miscarriage of justice.

If a defendant's guilty plea relied on the incompetent legal or tactical advice of defense counsel, a trial court may permit the guilty plea to be withdrawn as a result of ineffective assistance of counsel. *Hill v. Lockhart*, 474 U.S. 52 (1985).

Jury Trials

Key Terms

- **Challenge for cause:** a prospective juror allegedly is unable to perform jury functions such as following jury instructions, or has a bias that compromises her ability to decide the case impartially.

- **Fair cross-section requirement:** the jury in a criminal case must be selected from the location where the crime occurred.

- **Jury trial right:** is constitutionally mandated for any offense that carries an *authorized* sentence of more than six months, regardless of the *actual* sentence imposed.

- **Peremptory challenge:** generally, challenge to a juror without having to offer any reason to the trial judge.

- ***Voir dire:*** the process by which the trial judge and the attorneys for the parties question prospective jurors.

A. Why Jury Trials Are Important

Lawyers who go to trial believe that jury selection is the most important part of litigation. Thus, awareness about the jury selection process, from the jury summons directed to a group of citizens to the *voir dire* questioning of prospective jurors, requires an understanding about a variety of issues.

B. Constitutional Right to Jury Trial

The Sixth Amendment provides that in all criminal prosecutions an "accused shall enjoy the right to a public trial, by an impartial jury of the State and district wherein the crime shall have been committed. . . ." Article III of the Constitution states that "[t]he trial of all crimes . . . shall be by jury; and such trial shall be held in the state where the said crimes shall have been committed. . . ."

- A jury decides: 1) questions of fact, and 2) how to apply the legal elements of the offense to those facts, drawing the ultimate conclusion of guilt or innocence. *United States v. Gaudin*, 515 U.S. 506 (1995).

- The right to a jury trial does not apply to juveniles convicted in juvenile court, because 1) a juvenile delinquency proceeding is neither civil nor criminal, and 2) accurate fact-finding is possible without a jury trial. *McKeiver v. Pennsylvania*, 403 U.S. 528 (1971).

- A jurisdiction may use a two-tier trial system in which no jury is provided for the first trial, but the defendant has a right to a jury trial *de novo* at the second trial. *Ludwig v. Massachusetts*, 427 U.S. 618 (1976).

- A defendant may waive the constitutional right to a jury trial in favor of a bench trial, but the prosecution and the court must concur in a defense waiver. *Singer v. United States*, 380 U.S. 24 (1965).

1. Authorized Sentence

A jury trial is constitutionally mandated for any offense that carries an *authorized* sentence of more than six months, regardless of the *actual* sentence imposed. *Baldwin v. New York*, 399 U.S. 66 (1970). The right to a jury trial for violations of multiple criminal statutes is determined on an offense-by-offense basis, rather than in the aggregate. *Lewis v. United States*, 518 U.S. 322 (1996).

For offenses with authorized sentences of six months or less, there is a presumption against a jury trial, rebuttable if the legislature considers the offense to be "serious" based upon the additional statutory penalties (*e.g.*, driver's license revocation for a long period) for that offense. *Blanton v. City of North Las Vegas*, 489 U.S. 538 (1989).

2. Contempt Proceedings

Because contempt proceedings have no legislatively authorized sentence, a jury must be afforded before an *actual* prison sentence for more than six months is imposed for a post-verdict finding of contempt. Direct contempts *during* trial are subject to immediate summary adjudication without a jury trial. *Codispoti v. Pennsylvania*, 418 U.S. 506 (1974).

3. Fines

A jury trial is also required when a court imposes *serious* fines for criminal contempt. Criminal contempt fines of $52 million for violation of a labor injunction are subject to the jury trial right.

International Union, United Mine Workers of Am. v. Bagwell, 512 U.S. 821 (1994).

C. *Apprendi v. New Jersey*

A sentence imposed by a judge where juries determine defendants' guilt or innocence and judges alone decide their punishment is constitutionally defective. *Apprendi v. New Jersey*, 530 U.S. 466 (2000). *Apprendi* applies to fact determinations that trigger or increase mandatory minimum sentences.

- Example: when an essential fact issue is whether the defendant brandished a weapon, a jury must decide that fact in order to increase the mandatory minimum sentence for the crime. *Alleyne v. United States*, 570 U.S. 99 (2013).

- Example: a statute is unconstitutional under *Alleyne* when a judge decides that a defendant released on community supervision must be returned to prison for a mandatory minimum sentence, using a preponderance of evidence standards; that process violates the defendant's right to have a jury find whether the facts trigger a mandatory minimum sentence, using a beyond a reasonable doubt standard. *United States v. Haymond*, 139 S.Ct. 2369 (2019).

- Example: a capital sentencing scheme that allows the trial judge rather than the jury to make critical findings of fact necessary to impose a death sentence is unconstitutional. *Hurst v. Florida*, 577 U.S. 92 (2016).

- The "relevant statutory maximum for *Apprendi* purposes is the maximum a judge may impose based

solely on the facts reflected in the jury verdict or
admitted by the defendant."

- Example: the defendant pled guilty to kidnapping, a
  crime which supported a maximum sentence of 53
  months. However, the sentence increased to 90
  months after the trial judge (in violation of
  Apprendi) found that the defendant had acted with
  "deliberate cruelty." *Blakely v. Washington*, 542
  U.S. 296 (2004); *United States v. Booker*, 543 U.S.
  220 (2005).

- *Apprendi* also applies to sentences of criminal fines.
  Juries must determine the facts that set a fine's
  maximum amount. *Southern Union Co. v. United
  States*, 567 U.S. 343 (2012).

D. Size and Unanimity Requirements

While the federal rule states that a federal jury should consist
of twelve jurors, the Supreme Court has upheld state rules requiring
fewer than twelve jurors. The Court used empirical data to establish
a constitutional minimum of six-person juries and to reject a jury of
only five persons. *Ballew v. Georgia*, 435 U.S. 223 (1978).

While federal court rules require a twelve-person jury verdict
to be unanimous, there is no federal constitutional requirement of
unanimity. *Richardson v. United States*, 526 U.S. 813 (1999).
However, a unanimous verdict is required of a jury consisting of six
members. *Burch v. Louisiana*, 441 U.S. 130 (1979).

- *Ramos v. Louisiana*, 140 S.Ct. 1390 (2020) requires
  unanimity for all state jury verdicts, overruling
  Johnson v. Louisiana, 406 U.S. 356 (1972).

- The defendant's Due Process rights are not violated
  when the trial court groups felony murder and

premeditated murder as alternative ways of committing the single crime of first-degree murder. *Schad v. Arizona*, 501 U.S. 624 (1991).

E. The Fair Cross-Section Requirement

The Sixth Amendment grants to criminal defendants the right to a "jury of the state and district wherein the crime shall have been committed." The trial jury must be selected from a larger jury panel that reflects a fair cross-section of the community where the crime occurred. A grand jury and the jury that *actually decides* the case do not have to reflect a cross-section of the community.

- For a *prima facie* violation of the Sixth Amendment fair cross-section requirement, the defendant does not have to be the same race, ethnicity, or gender as the excluded group. *Duren v. Missouri*, 439 U.S. 357 (1979); *Taylor v. Louisiana*, 419 U.S. 522 (1975).

- To prove a fair cross-section violation, the defendant must prove that the excluded group is a "distinctive" group playing a major role in the community. *Id.* Next, the group is not fairly and reasonably represented in the jury pool, as reflected in comparing the demographic percentages of the group in the jury pool and in the community. Finally, the underrepresentation is the result of "systematic exclusion" of the group from the jury selection process.

- "[G]roups defined solely in terms of shared attitudes" are not part of a distinctive group. *Lockhart v. McCree*, 476 U.S. 162 (1986).

- To rebut a *prima facie* showing of a fair cross-section violation, the prosecution must show that the disproportionate exclusion manifestly and primarily advances a significant government interest. *Id.*

- The defendant also may challenge the panel on Equal Protection grounds for discriminatory underrepresentation. The defendant *must* be from the same racial, ethnic, or gender group that allegedly is underrepresented. *Castaneda v. Partida,* 430 U.S. 482 (1977).

F. *Voir Dire* Questioning and Challenges for Cause

The purposes of *voir dire* examination are to 1) determine any possible basis for challenging jurors for cause and with peremptory challenges, and 2) learn about prejudices and attitudes in order to minimize their effect on the outcome of the case. *Mu'Min v. Virginia,* 500 U.S. 415 (1991).

1. *Questioning Potential Jurors*

Trial judges have broad discretion to decide the form of the *voir dire* questioning, as well as who should conduct the questioning to ask about juror biases, opinions and prejudices that could affect their ability to follow instructions to the jury and their consideration of the evidence. *Rosales-Lopez v. United States,* 451 U.S. 182 (1981).

- Juror impartiality does not require that jurors have no knowledge about a case. *Murphy v. Florida,* 421 U.S. 794 (1975).

- Questions about racial prejudice are necessary if special circumstances about the case create a substantial reason to believe that racial or ethnic prejudice might affect the jury's impartial

assessment of a case. *Ham v. South Carolina*, 409
U.S. 524 (1973).

- The possibility of bias is sufficiently real in an
  interracial killing to require questions about racial
  bias upon request, but not in an interracial armed
  robbery. *Ristaino v. Ross*, 424 U.S. 589 (1976).

2. *Grounds for Challenge for Cause*

The two general bases for a challenge for cause are an inability
to perform necessary jury functions, and a bias that could
compromise that juror's ability to decide the case impartially.

- A juror's inability to perform may result from a lack
  of physical or mental capacity or an inability to
  understand or follow legal principles.

- Bias may be actual or implicit, with the former
  requiring proof that the juror would be biased in the
  particular case and the latter shown by an
  assumption that the juror is so likely to be biased
  that the challenge is appropriate, *e.g.*, prospective
  jurors are employees of the governmental unit
  prosecuting the case. However, *Dennis v. United
  States*, 341 U.S. 494 (1951) held that federal
  employees are not challengeable for cause solely
  because of their employment.

- In capital cases, a juror may be challenged for cause
  because their opposition to the death penalty is so
  strong that it would prevent or substantially impair
  the performance of their duties as jurors.
  Wainwright v. Witt, 469 U.S. 412 (1985). Even a
  single misapplication of that standard invalidates a

death sentence. *Gray v. Mississippi*, 481 U.S. 648 (1987).

G. Peremptory Challenges

By rule in most jurisdictions, both parties can challenge a number of jurors without giving any reason whatsoever. Because peremptory challenges are not constitutionally required, a good faith but mistaken denial of a peremptory challenge does not alone violate the Constitution; states can decide whether the mistaken denial is reversible error. *Rivera v. Illinois*, 556 U.S. 148 (2009). If multiple defendants are being tried, each defendant usually is entitled to additional peremptory challenges.

1. The Batson Test

If opposing counsel believes that the other attorney has exercised the challenges based on race or gender discrimination, the issue must be raised immediately. *See Batson v. Kentucky*, 476 U.S. 79 (1986).

- The Equal Protection Clause prohibits intentional discrimination in jury selection on the basis of race and gender. *J.E.B. v. Alabama ex rel. T.B.*, 511 U.S. 127 (1994).

- Any defendant can object to the exercise of peremptory challenges, using third-party standing principles on behalf of the excluded juror. *Powers v. Ohio*, 499 U.S. 400 (1991).

- Any party can commit a violation. *Georgia v. McCollum*, 505 U.S. 42 (1992).

- Counsel must make *Batson* objections before the jury is sworn so that the trial judge can ensure that the jury is properly selected. *Ford v. Georgia*, 498 U.S. 411 (1991).

- *Batson* prescribed a three-part test.

a. *Prima Facie* Case

First, the complaining party must show "an inference that the [other party] used that practice to exclude veniremen from the petit jury" on account of their race or gender. It is then for the trial court, considering "all relevant circumstances," such as a pattern of exercising strikes and the nature of the prosecutor's questions and statements, to decide if the showing creates a *prima facie* case of discrimination.

b. Neutral Explanation

Second, if a *prima facie* case of discrimination is shown, the alleged offending party must offer a neutral explanation for having challenged the jurors, which requires more than a denial of a discriminatory motive.

- The neutral explanation does not have to rise to a level sufficient to satisfy a challenge for cause.

- If a prosecutor's "neutral explanation" is pretextual, there is an "inference of discriminatory intent" and an equal protection violation. *Snyder v. Louisiana*, 552 U.S. 472 (2008).

- Peremptory challenges were improperly used to strike ten of eleven qualified black venire panel members, because white jurors retained on the jury shared the same characteristic offered as the neutral explanation for striking the black jurors. *Miller-El v. Dretke*, 545 U.S. 231 (2005).

c. **Purposeful Discrimination**

Third, the court must determine whether the explanation is facially race-neutral and whether the opponent of the peremptory challenge has proven purposeful discrimination. *Id.* For example, the record indicates an inference of purposeful discrimination when it refutes the reasons the prosecution gave for striking black jurors. *Foster v. Chatman*, 578 U.S. 1023 (2016). The Court detailed its analysis of impermissible reasons for the exclusion of each juror and its rejection of the alleged race neutral reasons. The standard of appellate review of the trial court's ruling is "clearly erroneous." *Id.*

For example, *Flowers v. Mississippi*, 139 S.Ct. 2228 (2019), found clear error for Batson violations: 1) the prosecutor's history of striking black potential jurors; 2) using peremptory strikes against five of six black prospective jurors; 3) asking black prospective jurors an average of 29 questions each, while asking the eleven white jurors eventually seated an average of one question each; and 4) as in Miller-El, using a peremptory challenge to strike at least one black prospective juror who was similarly situated to white jurors who were accepted.

CHAPTER 19

Trial Rights

Key Terms

- **Burden of proof:** in criminal cases requires that the prosecution prove its case against the defendant beyond a reasonable doubt.

- **Compulsory process:** involves the defendant's right to offer the testimony of witnesses in her favor and compel their attendance at trial.

- **Confrontation rights:** enable a defendant the right to face adverse witnesses; the rights include the cross-examining adverse witnesses, and being present at any stage of the trial that would enable the defendant to effectively cross-examine adverse witnesses.

A. Why Trial Rights Are Important

The Supreme Court has issued constitutional decisions about significant issues that arise during trial, such as the burden of proof, the presumption of innocence, the defendant's right not to testify, the right not to have the prosecution comment on the exercise of that right, and jury instructions. Many of those issues become the grounds for appeal after the defendant is convicted.

1. Burden of Proof

Due Process "protects the accused against conviction except upon proof beyond a reasonable doubt of every fact necessary to constitute the crime with which he is charged." *In re Winship*, 397 U.S. 358 (1970).

The defendant may be required to prove affirmative defenses such as insanity, self-defense, and duress, by a preponderance of the evidence. *Patterson v. New York*, 432 U.S. 197 (1977).

Presumptions impermissibly shift the burden of proof. Instead of presumptions, a jury instruction may permit the jury to make "permissible inferences." For example, a jury instruction may state that the jury may infer that the defendant intended to kill from the fact that he aimed his weapon at the victim, and fired the shots that caused the victim's death. *Francis v. Franklin*, 471 U.S. 307 (1985).

2. Defendant's Right (Not) to Testify

The trial court cannot instruct the jury and the prosecution cannot comment about the defendant's failure to testify at trial. *Griffin v. California*, 380 U.S. 609 (1965). Such comments are a penalty for exercising the right to remain silent, and suggest evidence of guilt. However, at the defendant's request, the trial court can instruct the jury not to make adverse inferences from his decision. *Carter v. Kentucky*, 450 U.S. 288 (1981).

- The prosecutor's comment about a defendant's credibility is allowed. *Portuondo v. Agard*, 529 U.S. 61 (2000).

- Restrictions on the defendant's choice about when to testify during the defense's case-in-chief violates

Due Process. *Brooks v. Tennessee*, 406 U.S. 605 (1972).

3. *Jury Instructions on Lesser Included Offenses*

The right to a jury instruction on a lesser crime is constitutionally based, because depriving the jury of the option of conviction on a lesser offense increases the risk of conviction on the greater offense. *Beck v. Alabama*, 447 U.S. 625 (1980). But a lesser included offense instruction is appropriate only if there is evidence supporting a conviction for that offense.

B. Sixth Amendment Confrontation Rights

Besides the right to counsel and other trial rights, the Sixth Amendment also provides a defendant with the right to confront adverse witnesses, as well as compulsory process to offer the testimony of witnesses in her favor and compel their attendance at trial.

1. *Confrontation Rights at Trial*

The Sixth Amendment Confrontation Clause enables a defendant the right to cross-examine adverse witnesses, and to be present at any stage of the trial that would enable the defendant to effectively cross-examine adverse witnesses. *Maryland v. Craig*, 497 U.S. 836 (1990).

- Statutory or judicial limits on cross-examination are constitutional. *Delaware v. Van Arsdall*, 475 U.S. 673 (1986).

- In a joint trial, the admission of a codefendant's extrajudicial confession incriminating the defendant violates the defendant's right to confrontation when the codefendant does not testify at trial. *Bruton v. United States*, 391 U.S. 123 (1968). *See* Chapter 13.

2. Defendant's Right to Be Present

The right of a criminal defendant to be present arises from both the Confrontation and the Due Process Clauses. The Confrontation Clause assures a defendant the opportunity for effective cross-examination. Due Process provides a defendant with the right to be present in order to contribute to the fairness of the procedure. *Snyder v. Massachusetts*, 291 U.S. 97 (1934); *Kentucky v. Stincer*, 482 U.S. 730 (1987).

- The defendant waives the right to be present either after he voluntarily leaves the courtroom, *Taylor v. United States*, 414 U.S. 17 (1973), or after he engages in continuous disruption of the proceedings after warnings from the court. *Illinois v. Allen*, 397 U.S. 337 (1970).

- A criminal defendant has no right to be present when the defendant's presence would not contribute to a more reliable determination and the hearing raises no questions about substantive trial testimony. *United States v. Gagnon*, 470 U.S. 522 (1985).

3. Confrontation and Hearsay Evidence

The admission of hearsay evidence against a criminal defendant can implicate the Sixth Amendment because the defendant is not afforded the opportunity to confront the person making an out-of-court statement.

- Under the Sixth Amendment Confrontation Clause, a testimonial hearsay statement is admissible in evidence when the person who made the statement is unavailable after there was a prior opportunity for cross-examining that person. *Bullcoming v. New Mexico*, 564 U.S. 647 (2011).

- Conversely, where a witness is unavailable and there was *no* prior opportunity to cross-examine the witness, only *non-testimonial hearsay* falling within a firmly rooted hearsay exception can be admitted into evidence. The critical concern is the lack of opportunity to question and confront the person about their out-of-court statement. *Crawford v. Washington*, 541 U.S. 36 (2004).

- Examples of out-of-court "testimonial statements" include: 1) statements made to law enforcement officers, other government employees or officials, 2) statements made in courtrooms settings, such as prior testimony in a preliminary hearing, before a grand jury, at a prior trial, 3) police interrogation situations, 4) statements made by a victim at the crime scene to responding officers initially investigating the reported past criminal conduct, 5) statements contained in a forensic laboratory report created specifically to serve as evidence in a criminal proceeding, and 6) affidavits and depositions. The common thread among statements made in such environments is the more "official" or formal nature of such communications.

- By contrast, admissible non-testimonial statements include: 1) informal and conversational hearsay statements to family, friends, co-workers and neighbors, and 2) calls to 911 and similar statements to law enforcement with the primary purpose of enabling law enforcement to respond to an "ongoing emergency." *Davis v. Washington*, 547 U.S. 813 (2006).

- Assessment of whether an emergency threatening the police and the public is ongoing focuses on whether the threat to the first victim has been neutralized, the type of weapon employed, and the medical condition of the victim. The degree of informality of an encounter between a victim and police also bears on the purpose of the interrogation. For example, a shooting victim's out-of-court statements to police to assist them to meet an ongoing emergency were non-testimonial hearsay and were admissible at trial. *Michigan v. Bryant*, 562 U.S. 344 (2011).

4. *Compulsory Process*

A related Sixth Amendment right is the Compulsory Process Clause, which grants a defendant the right to offer the testimony of favorable witnesses and to compel their attendance at trial. A defendant must show that the testimony she seeks would be material, favorable to her, and not merely cumulative. *United States v. Valenzuela-Bernal*, 458 U.S. 858 (1982).

CHAPTER 20

Sentencing

Key Terms

- **Aggravating circumstance:** situation of victim's death that, by statute, makes a defendant eligible for the death penalty.

- **Determinate sentence:** a prison term for a fixed period without the possibility of early release.

- **Forfeiture:** loss of a defendant's property that is associated with commission of the offense.

- **Indeterminate sentence:** a prison term set within statutory limits, with the parole board having responsibility for deciding whether the defendant is eligible for early release.

- **Probation:** when a trial court suspends a criminal sentence and releases the defendant, under the supervision of a probation officer.

- **Proportionality:** whether the penalty for a crime exceeds what is a reasonable sentence for the defendant's conduct.

- **Restitution:** for crimes such as theft, restoration of property or its value to the victim.

A. Why Sentencing Is Important

Because courts resolve more than 90% of criminal cases by plea bargaining, knowing about sentencing standards and alternatives that may reduce a particular penalty is critical, *e.g.*, limitations on resentencing, alternative penalties, and certain notice rules.

B. Noncapital Sentencing Alternatives

1. Imprisonment

There are two types of prison sentences. An indeterminate sentence is set within statutory limits, with the parole board having responsibility for deciding whether the defendant is eligible for early release. A determinate sentence (also known as "flat time") is for a fixed period without the possibility of early release, but supervision often accompanies that release.

2. Fines and Costs

The punishment for a violation of the law may include a fine in addition to or, in some cases, instead of imprisonment. Fines cannot be imposed upon any person determined by the court to be statutorily indigent. While incarceration is still a possibility for an intentional refusal to pay, the court must explore alternative means of satisfaction of the fine. *Bearden v. Georgia*, 461 U.S. 660 (1983).

3. Restitution

A person convicted of certain types of crimes, *e.g.*, destruction of property, can be ordered to restore the property or its value to the victim. *See, e.g.*, 18 U.S.C. § 3663. An order of restitution may defer payment until the defendant is released.

4. Forfeiture of Property

A person convicted of certain types of crimes can be ordered to forfeit property used in connection with commission of the offense. Forfeitures, as payments in kind, are "fines" if they constitute punishment for an offense. *Austin v. United States*, 509 U.S. 602 (1993).

- Civil forfeiture actions are separate from the criminal charge, and proceed against the property itself, rather than against the owner. The government must prove by a preponderance of the evidence that the property was involved in a crime.

- Criminal forfeiture cases require that the government prove by a preponderance that the owner obtained the property around the time of the crime, and that it was unlikely the property came from any other source. The burden then switches to the defense to show this was not the case.

- Pretrial seizures of property are constitutional, as long as there is probable cause to believe both that the defendant has committed an offense that can lead to forfeiture and that the assets result from the allegedly criminal conduct. *United States v. Monsanto*, 491 U.S. 600 (1989).

5. Probation Eligibility and Revocation

Probation is granted when the sentencing court suspends a sentence of imprisonment and releases the defendant under the supervision of a probation officer.

- The right to counsel at a probation revocation hearing is case-by-case. *Gagnon v. Scarpelli*, 411

U.S. 778 (1973). The revocation hearing must be held with reasonable promptness.

- In most jurisdictions, the rules of evidence are inapplicable to a revocation hearing. *See Wolff v. McDonnell*, 418 U.S. 539 (1974). The defendant has trial type rights in presenting a defense. Due Process requires the court to make findings as a prerequisite to any unfavorable action. *Morrissey v. Brewer*, 408 U.S. 471 (1972).

C. Proportionality of Punishment

The Eighth Amendment, which forbids cruel and unusual punishments, contains a "narrow proportionality principle" that "applies to noncapital sentences."

- Example: a first-time offender was convicted of possessing 672 grams of cocaine and sentenced to life in prison without possibility of parole. A majority of the Court rejected the claim that the sentence was grossly disproportionate but it could not agree on the reason. *Harmelin v. Michigan*, 501 U.S. 957 (1991).

- Justice Kennedy concurred in *Harmelin*, identifying four principles of proportionality review—"the primacy of the legislature, the variety of legitimate penological schemes, the nature of our federal system, and the requirement that proportionality review be guided by objective factors—[that] inform the final one: The Eighth Amendment forbids only extreme sentences that are 'grossly disproportionate' to the crime."

- Using Justice Kennedy's *Harmelin* concurrence, the Court upheld the sentencing of a repeat felon to a prison term of 25 years to life. The state's interest in public safety and deterrence supported the recidivism principle, in the absence of a grossly disproportionate sentence. *Ewing v. California*, 538 U.S. 11 (2003).

- The Court has applied standards used in capital cases to a noncapital case. The Court prohibits sentencing juvenile defendants to life without parole for non-homicide offenses, *Miller v. Alabama*, 567 U.S. 460 (2012), and to mandatory life sentences, *Graham v. Florida*, 560 U.S. 48 (2010). A discretionary sentencing system is both constitutionally necessary and sufficient in LWOP cases for juveniles. *Jones v. Mississippi*, 141 S.Ct. 1307 (2021).

D. Capital Cases

1. When Death Penalty Is Inapplicable

- The Eighth Amendment permits the death penalty for any crime that results in the death of the victim, when the defendant committed the homicide intentionally or with indifference to human life. *Tison v. Arizona*, 481 U.S. 137 (1987).

- The Eighth Amendment prohibits capital punishment for a prisoner who is either insane or suffers from an intellectual disability at the time of the crime. *Atkins v. Virginia*, 536 U.S. 304 (2002).

- An intellectual disability diagnosis requires consideration of three core elements: (1) intellectual-functioning deficits (indicated by an IQ score "approximately two standard deviations below the mean"—*i.e.*, roughly 70—adjusted for "standard error of measurement"; (2) adaptive deficits ("inability to learn basic skills and adjust behavior to changing circumstances,"); and (3) "onset of these deficits while a minor." *Hall v. Florida*, 572 U.S. 701 (2014).

- Capital punishment also is prohibited for a person who was under the age of 18 at the time of the crime. *Roper v. Simmons*, 543 U.S. 551 (2005).

- While *Miller v. Alabama* requires consideration of a juvenile's youth, it does not require a separate finding of permanent incorrigibility before sentencing a juvenile to a sentence of life without prole.

2. *Prerequisites for Death Penalty*

A valid death sentence cannot be administered in an arbitrary and unpredictable fashion. Also, "the capital defendant generally must be allowed to introduce any relevant mitigating evidence," *California v. Brown*, 479 U.S. 538 (1987), but a jury instruction about mitigation does not have to define the burden of proof. *Kansas v. Carr*, 577 U.S. 108 (2016).

- The government must give defense counsel adequate notice that it will seek the death penalty. *Lankford v. Idaho*, 500 U.S. 110 (1991).

- The prosecution must prove at least one aggravating circumstance beyond a reasonable doubt to limit the application of the death penalty to the most serious homicides, *e.g.*, killing a police officer. *Romano v. Oklahoma*, 512 U.S. 1 (1994). If the jury does not find at least one aggravating circumstance, the judge cannot impose a sentence of death.

- The legislature decides the number and types of aggravating circumstances. In *Schiro v. Farley*, 510 U.S. 222 (1994), the Court approved the use of an intentional killing during the commission of rape as an aggravating factor during the sentencing proceeding.

- All evidence may be introduced in a capital sentencing hearing, even beyond factors in aggravation and mitigation, as long as it is relevant, reliable, and not prejudicial. *Zant v. Stephens*, 462 U.S. 862 (1983). Most states require that the aggravating circumstances outweigh the mitigating evidence.

- Persons may challenge the method of execution. *Baze v. Rees*, 553 U.S. 35 (2008) and *Glossip v. Gross*, 576 U.S. 863 (2015) govern any Eighth Amendment facial or as-applied challenges to methods of execution. A successful Eighth Amendment claim must show that the method creates a risk of severe pain and that the risk is substantial compared to known and available alternatives. For example, in *Baze v. Rees*, the Supreme Court upheld constitutionality of a lethal three-drug injection method. In *Bucklew v. Precythe*, 139 S.Ct. 1112 (2019), the Court rejected a challenge to a single-drug protocol.

E. Sentencing Considerations

The Court has rejected a Due Process challenge to a state sentencing procedure that permitted the sentencing judge to consider information about the offender's "past life, health, habits, conduct, and mental and moral propensities." *Williams v. New York*, 337 U.S. 241 (1949).

- The judge may consider a defendant's refusal to cooperate with law enforcement authorities. *Wasman v. United States*, 468 U.S. 559 (1984).

A presentence report prepared by a probation officer must include an analysis of the defendant's background and may include a victim impact statement under appropriate circumstances. *Payne v. Tennessee*, 501 U.S. 808 (1991). A defendant has the right to controvert the contents of any report.

CHAPTER 21

Appeals

Key Terms

- **Clear error:** standard of review defers to the lower court's findings of fact unless the findings are clearly erroneous.

- **Direct appeal:** as a matter of right is available to an intermediate appellate court for a convicted defendant.

- **Harmless error:** standard of review applies when the facts and circumstances indicate that an error did not affect the verdict.

- **Plain error:** applies when the defendant fails to object to a trial error, but the defendant shows harm to a substantial right that seriously affects the fairness or integrity of the proceedings.

- **Structural errors:** affect the framework within which the trial proceeds, as opposed to an error in the trial process itself. Such errors require automatic reversal, and are not subject to harmless error analysis.

A. Why Appeals Are Important

The defendant usually initiates the appellate process, seeking to overturn a finding of guilt made by a judge or a jury. In criminal cases, until there is a final judgment following a conviction or an acquittal, there can be no appeal, *i.e.*, an appellate court reviews only final judgments from a lower court. *See, e.g.*, 28 U.S.C. § 1291. There are two exceptions to the final judgment rule.

- The collateral order doctrine allows either party to appeal a decision that does not resolve guilt or innocence, but does resolve a collateral issue that relates to an important right that likely would be lost if appellate review awaited final judgment. *Abney v. United States*, 431 U.S. 651 (1977).

- Prosecutors may seek interlocutory review, which seeks to appeal a pre-jeopardy ruling about an issue that is regarded as especially significant.

B. Direct Appeals in State Courts

Most jurisdictions have created a two-tiered appellate structure in which the convicted defendant has a right of appeal to an intermediate appellate court, but any further appeal to a higher court, usually the state Supreme Court, is discretionary.

- The distinction between a right of appeal and discretionary review by an appellate court is important, because in felony cases, counsel must be provided to indigent persons exercising their *right* to appeal. *Douglas v. California*, 372 U.S. 353 (1963). Counsel need not be provided to indigent defendants seeking discretionary review. *Ross v. Moffitt*, 417 U.S. 600 (1974). *See* Chapter 8.

- The right to counsel on appeal stems from the Fourteenth Amendment. Although the Sixth Amendment guarantees the defendant's right to self-representation at trial, there is no such right at the appellate stage. *Martinez v. Court of Appeal*, 528 U.S. 152 (2000).

- The right to appellate review can be waived or forfeited. An appeals court may dismiss the appeal of a defendant who is a fugitive during the appellate process. Missed deadlines also may result in a waiver of the right of appeal. *Ortega-Rodriguez v. United States*, 507 U.S. 234 (1993).

C. Standards of Review in Criminal Cases

In criminal cases, there are three standards of review that are followed by appellate courts.

- *De novo* review occurs with questions of law, meaning that the appellate court does not defer to the trial court's decision. The appellate court reviews the issues as if no court in the case had looked at them.

- Clear error review is used for questions of fact, and defers to the lower court's findings of fact unless they are clearly erroneous.

- Abuse of discretion is the standard of review for issues that are consigned to the trial court's discretion. A court abuses its discretion when it acts beyond its decision-making options.

D. Trial *De Novo* After Conviction

In most appeals, a higher court is asked to check the trial record for errors that would require reversal of the conviction. Many misdemeanor cases, however, are tried in lower courts from which no record or transcript of the proceedings is available for review by a higher court. A defendant convicted in such a lower court is often granted an absolute right to a trial *de novo* in a superior or circuit court, sometimes called a court-of-record.

- The granting of a trial *de novo* is normally automatic upon the defendant's request. No error need be alleged from the first trial. A defendant who exercises his right to a trial *de novo* is not entitled to judicial review of the sufficiency of the evidence presented to the lower court. *Justices of Boston Municipal Court v. Lydon*, 466 U.S. 294 (1984).

- In an appeal based on a claim that the evidence was insufficient, a reviewing court examines the evidence in the light most favorable to the prosecution. That standard permits the jury to assert its role of evaluating the credibility of the evidence. *Jackson v. Virginia*, 443 U.S. 307 (1979).

E. Harmless Error and Plain Error

"The Constitution entitles a criminal defendant to a fair trial, not a perfect one." *Delaware v. Van Arsdall*, 475 U.S. 673 (1986).

- A trial error that is not of constitutional dimension (for example, the trial judge erred in admitting some minor item of evidence) is harmless when it plainly appears from the facts and circumstances of the case that the error did not affect the verdict. Reversal is required for a non-constitutional error only if it "had substantial and injurious effect or influence in determining the jury's verdict." *United States v. Lane*, 474 U.S. 438 (1986).

- Application of the harmless error doctrine to a constitutional error depends upon the nature of the error. A federal constitutional error must be harmless beyond a reasonable doubt. *Chapman v. California*, 386 U.S. 18 (1967).

- A structural error "affect[s] the framework within which the trial proceeds," and it defies harmless error analysis. Thus, when a structural error is objected to and then raised on direct review, the defendant is entitled to automatic reversal without any inquiry into harm.

1. *Case Law Examples of Structural Errors*

Type of Error	Case Relating to the Error
Defective reasonable doubt jury instruction	*Sullivan v. Louisiana*, 508 U.S. 275 (1993)
Discrimination in grand jury selection	*Vasquez v. Hillery*, 474 U.S. 254 (1986)
Denial of public trial	*Waller v. Georgia*, 467 U.S. 39 (1984)
Denial of self-representation at trial	*McKaskle v. Wiggins*, 465 U.S. 168 (1984)
Complete denial of counsel	*Gideon v. Wainwright*, 372 U.S. 335 (1963)
Biased trial judge	*Tumey v. Ohio*, 273 U.S. 510 (1927)
Trial by partial fact finder	*United States v. Gonzalez-Lopez*, 548 U.S. 140 (2006)

Non-disclosure of exculpatory evidence	*Kyles v. Whitley*, 514 U.S. 419 (1995)
Judicial recusal for conflict of interest	*Williams v. Pennsylvania*, 136 S.Ct. 1899 (2016)

2. Example of Non-Structural Error

A claim of ineffective assistance of counsel, stemming from counsel's brief absence from the courtroom during a witness's testimony about his client's co-defendants, is not a structural error requiring automatic reversal but instead is subject to harmless error review. *Woods v. Donald*, 575 U.S. 312 (2015).

3. Trial Errors and Harmless Error Analysis

On direct review, trial errors require reversal of the conviction unless the reviewing court finds such errors to be harmless "beyond a reasonable doubt." For example, *Apprendi* violations are subject to harmless error analysis when the trial court fails to submit a sentencing factor to the jury. *Washington v. Recuenco*, 548 U.S. 212 (2006). Such errors are treated differently if raised on collateral review.

- On collateral review, (*e.g.*, *habeas corpus* petitions) trial errors require reversal of the conviction only if the defendant proves "actual prejudice," *i.e.*, the error had a "substantial and injurious effect or influence in determining the jury's verdict." *Brecht v. Abrahamson*, 507 U.S. 619 (1993).

4. Plain Error

A more stringent standard of review is applied when the defendant failed to object to a trial error, but now is calling that "plain error" to the attention of the appellate court.

- Plain error analysis requires a "reasonable probability that the error affected the outcome of the trial," not just "any possibility no matter how unlikely." *United States v. Marcus*, 560 U.S. 258 (2010).

- *United States v. Olano*, 507 U.S. 725 (1993) established the elements for finding plain error: there was error, the error was plain, the defendant showed harm to a substantial right, and the error "serious affected the fairness, integrity or public reputation of judicial proceedings."

- An error is "plain" within the meaning of Fed.R.Crim.P. 52(b) so long as the error was plain at the time of appellate review. *Henderson v. United States*, 568 U.S. 266 (2013).

F. Appeals of Last Resort

A defendant who fails to obtain a reversal on direct appeal may make collateral attacks on the conviction, such as a petition for a writ of *habeas corpus*, discussed in Chapter 23.

As a supplement to judicial review, all jurisdictions grant a convicted defendant an opportunity to appeal to executive authority for a pardon or grant of clemency. For example, Article 2, Section 2, Clause 1 of the U.S. Constitution gives the President the power to "forgive the convicted person in part or entirely, to reduce a penalty in terms of a specified number of years, or to alter it with conditions which are in themselves constitutionally unobjectionable." *Schick v. Reed*, 419 U.S. 256 (1974).

CHAPTER 22

Double Jeopardy

Key Terms

- **Acquittal:** a termination of the proceedings in favor of the defendant, on the merits.

- **Dismissal:** a termination of the proceedings but not on the merits of the case.

- **Dual sovereignty:** permits multiple prosecutions for the same offense by courts of different sovereigns.

- **Manifest necessity:** justifiable grounds for granting a mistrial.

- **Mistrial:** a termination of the proceedings before a formal verdict is returned.

A. Why Double Jeopardy Is Important

A defendant has both federal and state constitutional protections against being placed in jeopardy twice for the same offense. The pertinent part of the Fifth Amendment states: "[N]or shall any person be subject for the same offense to be twice put in jeopardy of life or limb." Despite the "life or limb" language, double jeopardy protection extends to all crimes. Double jeopardy protection applies to the states through the Fourteenth Amendment. *Benton v. Maryland*, 395 U.S. 784 (1969).

The relationship between the "same offense" and double jeopardy was discussed in Chapter 13, about joinder. This chapter illustrates the myriad ways in which double jeopardy issues arise.

1. When Jeopardy Attaches

Double jeopardy bars a second prosecution only if jeopardy attached in the original proceeding. If a case is dismissed or terminated before trial, jeopardy has not attached and the defendant may have to respond to the same criminal charges in further proceedings.

- In a jury trial, jeopardy attaches when the jury is sworn. *Crist v. Bretz*, 437 U.S. 28 (1978).

- If a case is tried before a judge, jeopardy attaches when the first witness is sworn. *Serfass v. United States*, 420 U.S. 377 (1975).

- Jeopardy also attaches when the trial court sentences a defendant after accepting a guilty plea.

2. Dual Sovereign Doctrine

Federal and state governments or the governments of different states can prosecute a defendant for the same conduct without violating the Constitution. *Gamble v. United States*, 139 S.Ct. 1960 (2019). However, when governmental entities derive their authority from the *same* source, they are the same sovereign, and prosecution by both entities is prohibited.

- Successive prosecutions for the same offense based upon violations of state statute and local ordinance are prohibited by double jeopardy. *Waller v. Florida*, 397 U.S. 387 (1970).

- Similarly, while the federal government has delegated much power to Puerto Rico, the authority to govern Puerto Rico derives from the U.S. Constitution. Thus, Puerto Rico and the United States are not separate sovereigns. *Puerto Rico v. Sancho Valle*, 136 S.Ct. 1863 (2016).

B. Mistrials and the Possibility of a Retrial

When a judge terminates the proceedings prior to a formal verdict, she may exercise her discretion to declare a mistrial and end the case without a verdict.

- A mistrial is granted when an error in the trial cannot be cured by remedial action of the parties or the court. Case law in every state addresses which errors require a mistrial, and which errors are "curable" by instructions to the jury or continuances.

- Although a double jeopardy claim will not arise until subsequent charges are brought, that claim constitutes an attack on the propriety of the original mistrial declaration, *i.e.*, if there was no "manifest necessity" for the mistrial declaration that ended the first case, it violates double jeopardy to have a second trial.

- Defense consent to a mistrial ordinarily constitutes waiver of double jeopardy rights, *i.e.*, when the defendant requests or agrees to the mistrial, there is no barrier to further reprosecution. However, a defendant's mistrial motion does not waive double jeopardy rights if the prosecution or the trial court intentionally provoked him into seeking a mistrial. *Oregon v. Kennedy*, 456 U.S. 667 (1982).

C. Prosecution Appeals After Dismissal or Acquittal

The question for prosecutors following a dismissal or an acquittal is whether it can be appealed or retried. Prior to the attachment of jeopardy, whether a criminal proceeding was terminated because of a dismissal or acquittal has no double jeopardy significance. For example, when the defendant's pretrial motion to dismiss for insufficient evidence is granted, double jeopardy does not bar a government appeal, because jeopardy had not attached. *Serfass v. United States*, 420 U.S. 377 (1975).

Once jeopardy has attached, whether a trial ends in a dismissal or in an acquittal is important to resolving whether the government can appeal the adverse termination of the case and whether the defendant can be retried. A dismissal can be appealed, and generally an acquittal cannot.

- A dismissal is a termination of the proceedings but not on the merits of the case. When a court dismisses an indictment as legally defective, the prosecution may appeal the dismissal and have a retrial after a successful appeal.

- After the trial begins, when the trial court dismisses the charge for precharge delay before any factfinder has ruled on the defendant's culpability, *i.e.*, a midtrial dismissal, the prosecution can appeal the dismissal because it was not on the merits. *United States v. Scott*, 437 U.S. 82 (1978).

- An acquittal is a termination of the proceedings in favor of the defendant, on the merits. When an acquittal occurs after jeopardy has attached, it forever bars both the retrial of the defendant for the same offense, *Martinez v. Illinois*, 572 U.S. 833 (2014), and a prosecution appeal of the acquittal. An acquittal may be the result of a judge's ruling or a jury verdict.

- A unique exception to the general rule about acquittals: if the judgment of acquittal is granted after a jury's verdict of conviction, the acquittal is appealable by the government since the original verdict of guilt can be reinstated *without* another trial. *United States v. Wilson*, 420 U.S. 332 (1975).

D. Retrials After Defense Appeals and Implied Acquittals

- When a conviction is successfully appealed, the reason for the reversal determines whether another trial will occur.

- If reversal of the conviction was due to the insufficiency of the evidence against the defendant, a retrial is prohibited. *Burks v. United States*, 437 U.S. 1 (1978). The rule of insufficient evidence applies as well to motions for a new trial made in the trial court after a conviction.

- A new trial is allowed, however, if the trial judge believes that there was sufficient evidence but she would have decided the case differently than the jury did, based on the "great weight of the evidence." *Tibbs v. Florida*, 457 U.S. 31 (1982).

- If appellate reversal of the conviction is due to trial errors or to defects in the charging instrument, as opposed to insufficiency of evidence, the defendant can be retried. *Lockhart v. Nelson*, 488 U.S. 33 (1988).

- A defendant may be implicitly acquitted of a greater include offense. For example, when he is charged with first-degree robbery but is convicted of second-degree robbery, on retrial following a successful appeal he cannot be convicted of the robbery in the first degree, the greater included crime. The first verdict operated as an implied acquittal on the greater included offense, thereby precluding a retrial for that crime.

E. More Severe Punishment at a Later Trial

When a defendant successfully appeals his conviction, Due Process does not always preclude imposition of a more severe sentence if he is convicted on retrial.

- A court must base the increase upon a relevant event of which it was unaware at the time of the first trial's sentencing, such as a conviction for an offense committed before the original sentencing, or conduct occurring after the first trial. *North Carolina v. Pearce*, 395 U.S. 711 (1969).

The foregoing principle is inapplicable to capital cases. When a defendant is sentenced to life and succeeds in obtaining a new trial, he is no longer subject to the death penalty on any retrial. *Bullington v. Missouri*, 451 U.S. 430 (1981).

CHAPTER 23

Post-Conviction
Remedies

Key Terms

- **Cognizable claim:** relief granted for state court decisions that are "contrary to, or involved an unreasonable application of" federal law, clearly established by the Supreme Court.

- **Exhaustion of state remedies:** requires that a claim must be presented to the state court system before a federal court will consider it.

- *Habeas corpus*: a proceeding in which the petitioner challenges the legality of her conviction; separate from a direct appeal.

- **Procedural default:** occurs when a defendant failed to object to evidence or jury instructions.

- **Successive petitions:** a current claim already presented in a prior *habeas corpus* application for relief must be dismissed.

A. Why Post-Conviction Remedies Are Important

A defendant may file a collateral attack on the conviction, the most common form being a petition for a writ of *habeas corpus*. Most states have *habeas corpus*-like proceedings that closely follow federal *habeas corpus*, discussed in the remainder of this chapter. In fact, the filing of a state petition is usually a necessary component of the federal petition. 28 U.S.C. § 2254. A prisoner in federal custody challenges the legality of his sentence under 28 U.S.C. § 2255.

1. Habeas Corpus *Defined*

Habeas corpus, a Latin term meaning "you have the body," is a collateral attack because it is not a continuation of the criminal process, but instead is a separate *civil* suit brought to challenge the legality of the restraint under which a person is held. The petitioner has the burden to prove by a preponderance of evidence that his confinement is illegal. The respondent in a *habeas* action is the prisoner's custodian—the prison warden or other official.

2. *Summary Disposition of* Habeas Corpus *Petition*

Merely filing a *habeas corpus* petition does not insure that a federal court will review the merits of the petitioner's claim. If the *habeas corpus* petition is patently frivolous, or if the court can determine the merits of the allegations by reference to records of state or federal judicial proceedings, no evidentiary hearing is held.

B. Jurisdiction and Venue

A state prisoner may seek *habeas corpus* relief in the federal district in which she resides or in the district where the state sentencing court is located. 28 U.S.C. § 2241(d). By contrast, a federal prisoner may file a petition only in the federal sentencing court. 28 U.S.C. § 2255(a).

Unlike a trial where a defendant must be mentally competent to be tried or to plead guilty, a *habeas corpus* petitioner does not have to be competent to file a petition for relief. *Ryan v. Gonzales*, 568 U.S. 57 (2013).

C. Time Considerations

There is a rigid one-year limitation for filing a petition for *habeas corpus* relief. The one-year period can be suspended, or tolled. 28 U.S.C. § 2244(d)(1)(A)–(D). Tolling under 28 U.S.C. § 2244(d)(2) is triggered by judicial review of a state prisoner's request that the trial court use its discretion to reduce his sentence. *Wall v. Kholi*, 562 U.S. 545 (2011).

- The one-year limitation is also tolled while an application for state post-conviction review is pending, even if it contains procedurally-barred claims. *Artuz v. Bennett*, 531 U.S. 4 (2000).

- In *Holland v. Florida*, 560 U.S. 631 (2010), the Court held that the concept of equitable tolling may apply to the one year time limit for filing a writ of *habeas corpus*. Equitable tolling applies to a "serious instance of attorney misconduct." *See, e.g., Christeson v. Roper*, 574 U.S. 373 (2015) (attorney failed to file a timely petition).

- The filling deadline does not apply if there is compelling evidence of the petitioner's innocence. *McQuiggin v. Perkins*, 569 U.S. 383 (2013).

D. Custody

To apply for a writ of *habeas corpus*, a person must be "in custody pursuant to the judgment of a State court," per § 2254(a), when the petition is filed. The statute is liberally construed by the courts and includes significant restraints on personal liberty as well as physical incarceration. *Jones v. Cunningham*, 371 U.S. 236 (1963). However, when a state conviction serves as a predicate for a federal conviction, the petitioner is not "in custody pursuant to the judgment of a State court." *Alaska v. Wright*, 141 S.Ct. 1467 (2021).

Custody includes significant restraints on personal liberty as well as physical incarceration. The writ may not be used to attack a sentence that has been fully served, or to attack a conviction that merely imposed a fine or collateral civil disability not resulting in incarceration.

A petitioner serving consecutive sentences is considered "in custody" under *any* one of the sentences. A consecutive sentence that has not begun, is currently running, or already has expired may be challenged until all of the sentences have been served. *Peyton v. Rowe*, 391 U.S. 54 (1968).

If a petitioner is released from custody *after* filing a petition, a court may still hear the petition as long as she is subject to negative collateral consequences from the challenged conviction, *e.g.*, barred from jury duty, voting, or certain jobs requiring licenses. *Sibron v. New York*, 392 U.S. 40 (1968).

A person can attack a sentence already served if the petitioner is serving a new sentence that was enhanced on the basis of a prior conviction for which the sentence has been fully served. *See, e.g.*, *Maleng v. Cook*, 490 U.S. 488 (1989).

E. Successive Petitions

28 U.S.C. § 2244(b) establishes procedures for the disposition of second or successive petitions. Any claim that was presented in a prior application for relief must be dismissed.

A claim usually is construed as transactional, rather than based on a separate legal theory. For example, if a petitioner in a prior application sought relief from a trial court's refusal to suppress a confession on Fifth Amendment grounds, the "claim" regarding the admissibility of the confession has been heard; another petition challenging its admission based on a Sixth Amendment violation must be dismissed. 28 U.S.C. § 2244(b)(1). A claim that was not presented in a prior application generally must be dismissed. *See* 28 U.S.C. § 2244(b)(2).

Prior to filing, a second or successive petition also must pass through a "gatekeeping" system requiring a petitioner to seek authorization from a three-judge panel in the appropriate court of appeals before a district court may hear the petition. *Burton v. Stewart*, 549 U.S. 147 (2007). This certification decision is not appealable and is not subject to rehearing. 28 U.S.C. § 2244(b)(3).

F. Exhaustion of State Remedies

Before a federal court will review a constitutional claim in a *habeas corpus* proceeding that seeks review of a state conviction, the claim first must be fairly presented to the state court system by pursuing the claim through the entire state appellate process. 28 U.S.C. § 2254(b)(1)(A).

- In order to exhaust the state remedies, the petitioner must have pursued the claim *either* on direct appeal *or* through state post-conviction proceedings. The latter remedy is often used when the claim was not raised at trial or on appeal, or it involves matters not in the trial record.

- Exhaustion of remedies includes the presentation of claims to the state supreme court even though its review is discretionary. *O'Sullivan v. Boerckel*, 526 U.S. 838 (1999). The court need not address the claim to satisfy this requirement; it is adequate if the claim was *presented* to the state court.

In *Rose v. Lundy*, 455 U.S. 509 (1982), the Court held that a federal court must dismiss a petition with both unexhausted and exhausted claims.

- Following dismissal, the petitioner must return to state court to present the unexhausted claims or resubmit only the exhausted claims to the federal court. *See Rhines v. Weber*, 544 U.S. 269 (2005).

- If the petitioner fails to exhaust state remedies, the federal court generally may dismiss the petition until the petitioner has exhausted the available state remedies.

G. Evidentiary Hearings

Following the filing of a petition, the state's answer to the petition, and the record of the state court proceedings, the *habeas* court must determine whether an evidentiary hearing is required. If the petitioner failed to develop the factual basis of a claim in state court, the federal court usually cannot hold an evidentiary hearing. *See* 28 U.S.C. § 2254(e)(2).

- Federal fact-finding may occur only if the state court failed to decide a claim on the merits. *Cullen v. Pinholster*, 563 U.S. 170 (2011).

- In *Williams v. Taylor*, 529 U.S. 420 (2000), the Supreme Court held that the failure to develop a factual basis of a claim requires a "lack of diligence or some greater fault, attributable to the prisoner or to the prisoner's counsel."

If a federal district court grants a hearing on the *habeas* petition, both the petitioner and the government must be given the opportunity to present evidence.

Upon denial of the petition, the petitioner is remanded to custody. If the court grants the petition, the petitioner is discharged from custody, but the court may suspend execution of its order to allow the government to appeal or to institute a new trial within a specified period of time.

H. Violations of Federal Law Only Are Cognizable

Only federal issues are cognizable in federal *habeas* proceedings. The most common *habeas corpus* claims are ineffective assistance of counsel, incriminating statements obtained by illegal police interrogation, improper judicial or prosecutorial conduct, and insufficient evidence. 28 U.S.C. § 2254.

- *Stone v. Powell*, 428 U.S. 465 (1976) held that a state prisoner is not entitled to *habeas corpus* relief on the ground that evidence obtained in an unconstitutional search and seizure was introduced at trial, if there was an opportunity for full and fair litigation of the Fourth Amendment claim.

- The limitation on claims involving the Fourth Amendment does not apply to Sixth Amendment claims of ineffective counsel based on deficient representation in litigating a Fourth Amendment issue. *See Kimmelman v. Morrison*, 477 U.S. 365 (1986).

1. Legal Error: The State Decision Involved an Incorrect or Unreasonable Application of Federal Law

Habeas corpus relief will not be granted for any claim decided on the merits in state courts, unless the decision was "contrary to, or involved an unreasonable application of" federal law clearly established by the Supreme Court. 28 U.S.C. § 2254(d)(1). A state court's decision applying federal law must be *both* erroneous and unreasonable, based on the record before the state court that decided the claim. *Cullen v. Pinholster*, 563 U.S. 170 (2011). This legal standard is highly deferential to state court judgments.

- A state court denial of post-conviction relief without stating its reasons qualifies as a § 2254(d) "adjudication on the merits," deserving deference as a reasonable decision. *Harrington v. Richter*, 562 U.S. 86 (2011).

- A claim of ineffective assistance of counsel is "doubly deferential," *Cullen v. Pinholster*, because counsel is presumed to have rendered adequate assistance and exercised reasonable professional judgment. *Woods v. Etherton*, 136 S.Ct. 1149 (2016).

- "Contrary to" means that a state court either has arrived at a conclusion on a question of law opposite to that reached by the Supreme Court, or when confronted with materially indistinguishable facts from a Supreme Court precedent, arrived at an opposite result. *Williams v. Taylor*, 529 U.S. 362 (2000).

- An "unreasonable application" of established federal law means that a state court either identified the correct legal rule but unreasonably applied it to the facts of the case, or unreasonably extended the legal principle to a new context that should not apply. *Id.*

- Section 2254(d)(1) provides a remedy for unreasonable applications of Supreme Court precedent; state courts need not *extend* that precedent. *White v. Woodall*, 572 U.S. 415 (2014).

- Example where the standard was satisfied: a trial court's jury instructions prevented the jury from giving meaningful consideration and effect to relevant mitigating evidence during a capital trial's penalty phase. *Abdul-Kabir v. Quarterman*, 550 U.S. 233 (2007).

- Example where the standard was *not* satisfied: a state court applied precedent reasonably, by deciding there was effective assistance by counsel who advised the defendant about a plea offer before moving to suppress a confession. *Premo v. Moore*, 562 U.S. 115 (2011).

2. Factual Error: The State Decision Involved an Incorrect or Unreasonable Determination of Facts

When a state prisoner challenges the factual basis for a state court decision rejecting a claim, the federal court may overturn the state court's decision only if it was "based on an unreasonable determination of the facts in light of the evidence presented in the State court proceeding." § 2254(d)(2).

- The prisoner bears the burden of rebutting the state court's factual findings "by clear and convincing evidence." § 2254(e)(1).

- The state prisoner must "show that the state court's ruling on the claim . . . was so lacking in justification that there was an error . . . beyond any possibility for fairminded disagreement." *Harrington v. Richter*, 562 U.S. 86 (2011). *See Shinn v. Kayer*, 141 S.Ct. 517 (2020); *Mays v. Hines*, 141 S.Ct. 1145 (2021) ("fairminded jurists could not disagree with state court's determination").

- "A state court factual determination is not unreasonable merely because the federal *habeas* court would have reached a different conclusion in the first instance." *Wood v. Allen*, 558 U.S. 290 (2010).

- When a state court's failure to order specific performance of a plea agreement does not violate federal law, habeas corpus relief is unavailable. *Kernan v. Cuero*, 138 S.Ct. 4 (2017).

I. Procedural Defaults

In *Wainwright v. Sykes*, 433 U.S. 72 (1977), the failure to object to a confession barred federal *habeas* review in order to preserve the integrity of state procedures, and to promote federalism and comity. The most common form of procedural default is the defendant's failure to present a federal constitutional claim to the state trial court to preserve the issue for appellate review.

1. What a Petitioner Must Prove for Habeas Relief

When a defendant fails to comply with state contemporaneous objection rules, *habeas corpus* relief is available only when he can show either 1) cause for the procedural default and actual prejudice from a violation of federal law, or 2) the petitioner is actually innocent.

2. Cause for the Procedural Default

"Cause" exists when the prisoner can prove that some objective factor external to the defense prevented counsel from complying with the state's procedural rule. *Murray v. Carrier*, 477 U.S. 478 (1986). There are several ways to prove cause.

- The failure to object was due to constitutionally ineffective assistance of counsel at trial or on appeal, *e.g.*, missing the deadline for an appeal of the state court order denying post-conviction relief. *Maples v. Thomas*, 565 U.S. 266 (2012).

- Inadequate assistance of counsel in state post-conviction proceedings may excuse a procedural default of an ineffective assistance of *trial* counsel. *Trevino v. Thaler*, 569 U.S. 413 (2013); *Martinez v. Ryan*, 566 U.S. 1 (2012). By contrast, when a state prisoner fails in state post-conviction proceedings to challenge the effectiveness of his *direct appeal* lawyer, he may not raise that claim in a federal habeas petition—even if the failure was caused by ineffective assistance of his post-conviction counsel. *Davila v. Davis*, 137 S.Ct. 2058 (2017).

- Governmental interference constitutes cause by rendering procedural compliance impracticable. For example, governmental concealment of evidence that women and African-Americans were intentionally underrepresented on jury lists constituted cause for the defendant's failure to raise a timely challenge to the jury panel. *Amadeo v. Zant*, 486 U.S. 214 (1988).

3. *Prejudice to the Petitioner's Case*

Prejudice requires a showing that there is a "reasonable probability that the result of the trial would have been different." *Strickler v. Greene*, 527 U.S. 263 (1999). A reasonable probability is sufficient to "undermine confidence in the verdict."

- Prejudice is a stricter standard than the "plain error" doctrine applicable on direct review because a direct appeal is designed to afford a means for the prompt redress of miscarriages of justice. *See* Chapter 21.

4. *Actual Innocence to Overcome Procedural Default*

Despite a procedural default, a federal *habeas* court will consider a claim based on proof that the petitioner is actually and factually innocent. Innocence claims, however, must be based on actual innocence rather than mere legal insufficiency. *Herrera v. Collins*, 506 U.S. 390 (1993).

- For actual innocence, the petitioner must show that it is more likely than not that no reasonable juror would have convicted him. *Schlup v. Delo*, 513 U.S. 298 (1995). "Actual innocence" cases are "extraordinary." *Id.*

The actual innocence exception also applies to a defendant sentenced to death, claiming that an error in capital sentencing resulted in a death sentence when he was actually innocent of the death penalty, *i.e.*, no reasonable juror would find him eligible for the death penalty (though the conviction was upheld). *Sawyer v. Whitley*, 505 U.S. 333 (1992).

Table of Cases